Robert J. MacFadden, PhD
Brenda Moore, PhD
Marilyn Herie, PhD
Dick Schoech, PhD
Editors

Web-Based Education in the Human Services: Models, Methods, and Best Practices

Web-Based Education in the Human Services: Models, Methods, and Best Practices has been co-published simultaneously as *Journal of Technology in Human Services*, Volume 23, Numbers 1/2 and 3/4 2005.

Pre-publication
REVIEWS,
COMMENTARIES,
EVALUATIONS . . .

"MacFadden, Moore, Herie, and Schoech have produced an effective, comprehensive guide for human service programs seeking to infuse or convert their curriculum to web-based education (WBE). In contrast to literature that either champions or laments the proliferation of WBE, this book offers both a balanced perspective and valuable logical information on online learning and teaching."

Julie Birkenmaier, MSW
Associate Clinical Professor
Saint Louis University
School of Social Work

More Pre-publication
REVIEWS, COMMENTARIES, EVALUATIONS . . .

"AN ESSENTIAL RESOURCE FOR HUMAN SERVICE EDUCATORS who are implementing online learning in their programs. Drawing on international and interdisciplinary projects, this book provides a comprehensive synthesis of the use of Web-based education in human services. This important contribution to the literature incorporates key elements of effective online learning pedagogical theory, faculty and student perspectives, research related to a broad range of course content, and in-depth descriptions of digitized curricula and innovative projects."

Alan Knowles, PhD, MSW
Instructor, Social Work Program
Grant MacEwan College
Edmonton, Canada

"A valuable aid to the development of new research in this increasingly important field. . . . OF VALUE TO ALL WHO ARE INVOLVED IN THE DEVELOPMENT OR DELIVERY OF ONLINE LEARNING and also to researchers."

Stuart Toole, DSW, MBCS
Medici Fellow
University of Central England
Birmingham

The Haworth Press, Inc.

New York • London • Victoria (AU)
www.HaworthPress.com

Web-Based Education in the Human Services: Models, Methods, and Best Practices

Web-Based Education in the Human Services: Models, Methods, and Best Practices has been co-published simultaneously as *Journal of Technology in Human Services,* Volume 23, Numbers 1/2 and 3/4 2005.

Monographic Separates from the *Journal of Technology in Human Services*™

For additional information on these and other Haworth Press titles, including descriptions, tables of contents, reviews, and prices, use the QuickSearch catalog at http://www.HaworthPress.com.

The *Journal of Technology in Human Services*™, Volume 16 started in Spring 1999. Subscribers should note that Volume 1-Volume 15 were published under the title of *Computers in Human Services.**

Web-Based Education in the Human Services: Models, Methods, and Best Practices, edited by Robert J. MacFadden, PhD, Brenda Moore, PhD, Marilyn Herie, PhD, and Dick Schoech, PhD (Vol. 23, No. 1/2/3/4, 2005). *"This information-rich book reflects the vitality and diversity of WBE in human services and invites instructors to move beyond conversion of their courses to re-examine the educational process of their curriculum." (Julie Birkenmaier, Associate Clinical Professor, Saint Louis University School of Social Work.)*

Technology-Assisted Delivery of School Based Mental Health Services: Defining School Social Work for the 21st Century, edited by Bhavana A. Pahwa, MA, LMSW (Vol. 21, No. 1/2, 2003). *"A MUST for any school social worker trying to incorporate technology into practice. The on-line resource guide is extensive and the chapter on technology assisted program evaluation will help any school social worker." (Vaughn Morrison, MSEd, MSW, Executive Director, Illinois Association of School Social Workers)*

Human Services Technology: Innovations in Practice and Education, edited by Hy Resnick, PhD, and Phoebe Sade Anderson, MSW (Vol. 20, No. 1/2/3/4, 2002). *"This book provides you with a full manual in each of the specific spheres of the various human relation professions, as well as the technical specificity required within each sphere of practice. In reality, this book is an updated manual of contemporary practice with a full and clear review of competence requirements and the empirical research evaluation of each practice endeavor." (Henry W. Maier, PhD, DShc, Professor Emeritus, University of Washington)*

Using the Internet as a Research Tool for Social Work and Human Services, edited by Goutham M. Menon, PhD (Vol. 19, No. 2/3, 2002). *Explores ways to use the Internet in many aspects of social work research, including the development of online studies and psychological testing.*

New Advances in Technology for Social Work Education and Practice, edited by Julie Miller-Cribbs, PhD (Vol. 18, No. 3/4, 2001). *"A valuable tool for educators who want to introduce students of social work to the numerous applications of technology within the field. . . . Goes a long way toward helping social work become proactive in its approach to technology integration within the field." (Sharon D. Johnson, PhD, Assistant Professor, Department of Social Work, University of Missouri, St. Louis)*

Using Technology in Human Services Education: Going the Distance, edited by Goutham M. Menon, PhD, and Nancy K. Brown, PhD (Vol. 18, No. 1/2, 2001). *"A refreshingly realistic and balanced collection. . . . Highlights many innovative efforts in both education and practice. Will be extremely valuable in courses on technology in social work, or for courses examining emerging trends in social work practice." (Paul P. Freddolino, PhD, Professor and Coordinator of Distance Education, School of Social Work, Michigan State University, East Lansing)*

Human Services Online: A New Arena for Service Delivery, edited by Jerry Finn, PhD, and Gary Holden, DSW (Vol. 17, No. 1/2/3, 2000). *Focuses on the ways that human services are using the Internet for service delivery, social change, and resource development as more and more agencies can be found on the Internet.*

Computers and Information Technology in Social Work: Education, Training, and Practice, edited by Jo Ann R. Coe, PhD, and Goutham M. Menon, PhD (Vol. 16, No. 2/3, 1999). *Discusses the impact that recent technological advances have had on social work practice and education.*

Social workers and educators will discover ideas and projects that were presented at a week long conference presented at the University of South Carolina College of Social Work. This unique book covers a wide range of topics, such as different aspects of technology applied to assist those in helping professions, how computers can be used in child protective cases in order to practice more effectively, social services via videoconferencing, and much more.

Information Technologies: Teaching to Use–Using to Teach, edited by Frank B. Raymond III, DSW, Leon Ginsberg, PhD, and Debra Gohagan, MSW, ACSW, LISW* (Vol. 15, No. 2/3, 1998). *Explores examples of the use of technology to teach social work knowledge, values, and skills across the curriculum.*

The History and Function of the Target Cities Management Information Systems, edited by Matthew G. Hile, PhD* (Vol. 14, No. 3/4, 1998). *"Essential reading for anyone invested in improving the coordination and delivery of substance abuse services in large metropolitan areas." (Albert D. Farrell, PhD, Professor of Psychology, Virginia Commonwealth University, Richmond)*

Human Services in the Information Age, edited by Jackie Rafferty, MS, Jan Steyaert, and David Colombi* (Vol. 12, No. 1/2/3/4, 1996). *"Anyone interested in the current state of the development of human service information systems of all types needs to read this book." (Walter F. LaMendola, PhD, Consultant, Wheat Ridge, CO)*

Electronic Tools for Social Work Practice and Education, edited by Hy Resnick, PhD* (Vol. 11, No. 1/2/3/4, 1994). *"Opens a new world of opportunities for readers by introducing a variety of electronic tools available when working with various clients." (Ram A. Cnaan, PhD, Associate Professor, School of Social Work, University of Pennsylvania)*

Technology in People Services: Research, Theory, and Applications, edited by Marcos Leiderman, MSW, Charles Guzzetta, EdD, Leny Struminger, PhD, and Menachem Monnickendam, PhD, MSW* (Vol. 9, No. 1/2/3/4, 1993). *"Honest reporting and inquiry into the opportunities and limitations for administrators, managers, supervisors, clinicians, service providers, consumers, and clients. . . . A well-integrated and in-depth examination." (John P. Flynn, PhD, Associate Director for Instructional Computing, University Computing Services and Professor of Social Work, Western Michigan University)*

Computer Applications in Mental Health: Education and Evaluation, edited by Marvin J. Miller, MD* (Vol. 8, No. 3/4, 1992). *"Describes computer programs designed specifically for mental health clinicians and their work in both private practice and institutional treatment settings." (SciTech Book News)*

Computers for Social Change and Community Organizing, edited by John Downing, PhD, Robert Fasano, MSW, Patricia Friedland, MLS, Michael McCullough, AM, Terry Mizrahi, PhD, and Jeremy Shapiro, PhD* (Vol. 8, No. 1, 1991). *This landmark volume presents an original and–until now–unavailable perspective on the uses of computers for community- and social-change-based organizations.*

Computer Literacy in Human Services Education, edited by Richard L. Reinoehl and B. Jeanne Mueller* (Vol. 7, No. 1/2/3/4, 1990). *This volume provides a unique and notable contribution to the investigation and exemplification of computer literacy in human services education.*

Computer Literacy in Human Services, edited by Richard L. Reinoehl and Thomas Hanna* (Vol. 6, No. 1/2/3/4, 1990). *"Includes a diversity of articles on many of the most important practical and conceptual issues associated with the use of computer technology in the human services." (Adult Residential Care)*

The Impact of Information Technology on Social Work Practice, edited by Ram A. Cnaan, PhD, and Phyllida Parsloe, PhD* (Vol. 5, No. 1/2, 1989). *International experts confront the urgent need for social work practice to move into the computer age.*

A Casebook of Computer Applications in the Social and Human Services, edited by Walter LaMendola, PhD, Bryan Glastonbury, and Stuart Toole* (Vol. 4, No. 1/2/3/4, 1989). *"Makes for engaging and enlightening reading in the rapidly expanding field of information technology in the human services." (Wallace Gingerich, PhD, Associate Professor, School of Social Welfare, University of Wisconsin-Milwaukee)*

Web-Based Education in the Human Services: Models, Methods, and Best Practices

Robert J. MacFadden, PhD
Brenda Moore, PhD
Marilyn Herie, PhD
Dick Schoech, PhD
Editors

Web-Based Education in the Human Services: Models, Methods, and Best Practices has been co-published simultaneously as *Journal of Technology in Human Services,* Volume 23, Numbers 1/2 and 3/4 2005.

The Haworth Press, Inc.

New York • London • Victoria (AU)
www.HaworthPress.com

Web-Based Education in the Human Services: Models, Methods, and Best Practices has been co-published simultaneously as *Journal of Technology in Human Services*™, Volume 23, Numbers 1/2 and 3/4 2005.

The development, preparation, and publication of this work has been undertaken with great care. However, the publisher, employees, editors, and agents of The Haworth Press and all imprints of The Haworth Press, Inc., including The Haworth Medical Press® and Pharmaceutical Products Press®, are not responsible for any errors contained herein or for consequences that may ensue from use of materials or information contained in this work. Opinions expressed by the author(s) are not necessarily those of The Haworth Press, Inc. With regard to case studies, identities and circumstances of individuals discussed herein have been changed to protect confidentiality. Any resemblance to actual persons, living or dead, is entirely coincidental.

Cover design by Jennifer M. Gaska

Library of Congress Cataloging-in-Publication Data

Web-based education in the human services : models, methods, and best practices / Robert J. MacFadden . . . [et al.].
 p. cm.
 "Co-published simultaneously as Journal of technology in human services, volume 23, numbers 1/2 and 3/4 2005"
 Includes bibliographical references and index.
 ISBN-10: 0-7890-2629-5 (hard cover : alk. paper)
 ISBN-13: 978-0-7890-2629-3 (hard cover : alk. paper)
 ISBN-10: 0-7890-2630-9 (soft cover : alk. paper)
 ISBN-13: 978-0-7890-2630-9 (soft cover : alk. paper)
 1. Social work education–Technological innovations. 2. Human services education–Study and teaching (Higher). 3. Internet in education. 4. Distance education. I. MacFadden, Robert J.
 HV11.W43 2005
 361.3'078'54678–dc22   2005008244

Indexing, Abstracting & Website/Internet Coverage

This section provides you with a list of major indexing & abstracting services and other tools for bibliographic access. That is to say, each service began covering this periodical during the year noted in the right column. Most Websites which are listed below have indicated that they will either post, disseminate, compile, archive, cite or alert their own Website users with research-based content from this work. (This list is as current as the copyright date of this publication.)

Abstracting, Website/Indexing Coverage . . . . Year When Coverage Began

- *Applied Social Sciences Index & Abstracts (ASSIA)*
  (Online: ASSI via Data-Star) (CDRom: ASSIA Plus)
  <http://www.csa.com> **1993**

- *Behavioral Medicine Abstracts (Annals of Behavioral Medicine)* . . . **1996**

- *Business Source Corporate: coverage of nearly 3,350 quality*
  magazines and journals; designed to meet the diverse
  information needs of corporations; EBSCO Publishing
  <http://www.epnet.com/corporate/bsourcecorp.asp> **2003**

- *CareData: the database supporting social care management*
  and practice <http://www.elsc.org.uk/caredata/caredata.htm> . . . **1987**

- *CINAHL (Cumulative Index to Nursing & Allied Health*
  Literature), in print, EBSCO, and SilverPlatter, DataStar,
  and PaperChase. (Support materials include Subject Heading
  List, Database Search Guide, and instructional video).
  <http://www.cinahl.com> **1999**

- *Computer Abstracts* **1995**

- *Computer and Information Systems Abstracts*
  <http://www.csa.com> **2004**

- *Computer Science Index (CSI) (formerly Computer Literature*
  Index) (EBSCO) <http://www.epnet.com> **1993**

- *Computing Reviews <http://www.reviews.com>* **1992**

(continued)

(continued)

Special Bibliographic Notes related to special journal issues (separates) and indexing/abstracting:

- indexing/abstracting services in this list will also cover material in any "separate" that is co-published simultaneously with Haworth's special thematic journal issue or DocuSerial. Indexing/abstracting usually covers material at the article/chapter level.
- monographic co-editions are intended for either non-subscribers or libraries which intend to purchase a second copy for their circulating collections.
- monographic co-editions are reported to all jobbers/wholesalers/approval plans. The source journal is listed as the "series" to assist the prevention of duplicate purchasing in the same manner utilized for books-in-series.
- to facilitate user/access services all indexing/abstracting services are encouraged to utilize the co-indexing entry note indicated at the bottom of the first page of each article/chapter/contribution.
- this is intended to assist a library user of any reference tool (whether print, electronic, online, or CD-ROM) to locate the monographic version if the library has purchased this version but not a subscription to the source journal.
- individual articles/chapters in any Haworth publication are also available through the Haworth Document Delivery Service (HDDS).

Web-Based Education in the Human Services: Models, Methods, and Best Practices

CONTENTS

ABOUT THE EDITORS

Robert J. MacFadden, PhD, is Associate Professor at the Faculty of Social Work, University of Toronto with an extensive background in information technology (IT) in human services. He teaches at the graduate level on IT in social work practice and has researched and published extensively in this area. His current interest is on the role of emotions in learning and particularly web-based learning. He has published two recent articles in this area: MacFadden, R. J., Maiter, S., Dumbrill, G. (2002). High tech and high touch: The human face on online education. In H. Resnick and P. Anderson (Eds.). Innovations in technology and human services: Practice and education. NY: Haworth, and MacFadden, R .J., Herie, M., Maiter, S., Dumbrill, G. C. (in press). Achieving high touch in high tech: A constructivist, emotionally-oriented model of web-based instruction. *Journal of Teaching in Social Work.* He is on the Editorial Board of the *Journal of Technology in Human Services* and a member of the Executive Board of an international group dedicated to the ethical and effective use of IT in human services (HUSITA). Dr. MacFadden is the chief organizer for the association's next international conference (HUSITA8) in Toronto in the summer of 2007. He maintains a website at <*www.robertmacfadden.com*>.

Brenda Moore, PhD, received her BSW degree from Texas Christian University and her MSSW degree from the University of Texas at Arlington. She completed her PhD at the University of Texas at Arlington where her dissertation topic was on Web-based instruction in social work education. Her national research provided timely information which is included in this publication.

She has over ten years of professional experience in direct practice, administration and planning, consultation, and grant writing. She has been on the social work faculty at Texas A&M-Commerce since 1993, serving as the Field Coordinator until 2001 when she became the BSW Director. She has presented at several local, state and national conferences on topics including Web-based instruction in social work education and practice. She is a member of the following professional organizations: National Association of Social Workers, the Council of

Social Work Education, Influencing Social Policy (ISP), ACOSA (Association for Community Organization and Social Administration), and Baccalaureate Program Directors (BPD).

Dr. Moore is active in her local community. She serves on the board of several non-profit organizations. In addition to her research interests in technology in social work education, she also is engaged in community-based collaborative research that involves social work students in research activities on behalf of community-based groups.

Marilyn A. Herie, PhD, has been a therapist and project leader at the Centre for Addiction and Mental Health (CAMH) since 1992, and is currently an Advanced Practice Clinician in the Concurrent Disorders Unit. She is also Adjunct Professor at the Faculty of Social Work, University of Toronto, Social Work Coordinator of the Collaborative Program in Addiction Studies at the University of Toronto, and Sessional Instructor at Ryerson Polytechnic University. She is also a board member of HUSITA (Human Services in Technology Applications), an international group focused on sharing knowledge and tools in the field of human services. Dr. Herie's focus at CAMH has been on the development and dissemination of research-based practice protocols and continuing professional education. In addition, Dr. Herie is a clinical trainer and therapist specializing in the group and individual treatment of adults with alcohol/drug problems. She has co-authored books, book chapters, and articles in scholarly journals on brief treatment, alcohol dependence, relapse prevention, dissemination research, and online learning. Marilyn also teaches online courses on addictions treatment and cultural competence in the Faculty of Social Work, University of Toronto, and developed and facilitates online continuing professional education courses at CAMH. She received her doctorate in social work at the University of Toronto, where she conducted research on Web-based continuing education for therapists and health care practitioners.

Dick Schoech, PhD, is the Dulak Professor in Administrative and Community Practice at the University of Texas at Arlington (UTA) School of Social Work. He has previously worked as the Director of a five-county health planning council; as a regional planner in mental health, addictions, and disabilities; and in several other human service agencies. He received an interdisciplinary PhD from UTA in Administration from the Schools of Business, Social Work, and Urban Studies. He has written three books and numerous articles on human service technology. He is founder (1981) of the Computer Use in Social Services Network (CUSSN) and founding editor (1985) of the *Journal of Technology in Human Services*. He is currently the chair of HUSITA (Human Services Information Technology Applications), an international virtual association dedicated to promoting the ethical and effective use of IT to serve humanity better (www.husita.org). His research interests include networking, performance support systems, organizational learning, and high-technology culture. He has been the principal investigator on technology grants in child protective services, aging, HIV/AIDS, substance abuse, and developmental disabilities. His current research is designing a teen substance abuse prevention virtual community at <*www.SubstanceAbusePrevention.org*>.

Web-Based Education
in the Human Services:
Content and Connections

Robert J. MacFadden
Brenda Moore
Marilyn Herie
Dick Schoech

This volume provides a view of Web-based education (WBE) in human services at the beginning of the 21st Century. Previous texts have often mixed technologies such as Interactive Television (ITV) and two-way video and included examples where the web involvement was minimal. This collection deliberately focuses on web-based models, tools and techniques where the majority of the content is delivered online.

Any exploration of such an extensive phenomenon is necessarily selective. The editors, through the use of a book website at http://www.webedhumanserv.info/, provided interested authors with a description of the intended issue and a common template to address in their submissions. Authors were also asked to emphasize a particular feature or perspective that would highlight their courses. The editors wanted to profile fully online courses to ensure some comparability. This was essentially achieved, although a few course models reflect more of a web-enhanced offering. Additionally, some submissions that provided needed context for web-based courses were accepted to round out the

[Haworth co-indexing entry note]: "Web-Based Education in the Human Services: Content and Connections." MacFadden et al. Co-published simultaneously in *Journal of Technology in Human Services* (The Haworth Press, Inc.) Vol. 23, No. 1/2, 2005, pp. 1-9; and: *Web-Based Education in the Human Services: Models, Methods, and Best Practices* (eds: MacFadden et al.) The Haworth Press, Inc., 2005, pp. 1-9. Single or multiple copies of this article are available for a fee from The Haworth Document Delivery Service [1-800-HAWORTH, 9:00 a.m. - 5:00 p.m. (EST). E-mail address: docdelivery@haworthpress.com].

Available online at http://www.haworthpress.com/web/JTHS
Digital Object Identifier: 10.1300/J017v023n01_01

presentations. Some summary details of a few web-based course examples are provided in the appendix of this volume. All references to authors that follow refer to the authors and submissions within this publication.

The first section on the "Context of Web-Based Education" provides a literature review, theoretical perspectives, faculty perspectives on web-based courses, accessibility and the emotional dimension of web-based education. The second section on "International Collaboration" highlights two courses that focus on international collaboration and the final section on "Special Features and Examples of Web-Based Courses" presents a variety of web-based courses that emphasize particular features or perspectives.

THE CONTEXT OF WEB-BASED EDUCATION

Moore's literature review entitled, "Key Issues in Web-Based Education in the Human Services," provides a summary of current thinking in WBE along with reference to literature on best practices, comparative research on Face-to-Face (FTF) and online models, and theoretical perspectives in online education. The author foreshadows more recent consideration of special topics such as emotion in WBE, later identified by Jerry and Collins and featured by MacFadden within this volume. Moore makes the point that perhaps it is time that we move beyond our current preoccupation with comparing FTF with online education and develop the innovative and unique aspects of WBE.

Herie in her article entitled, "Theoretical Perspectives in Online Pedagogy," introduces a range of pedagogical theories relevant to WBE. She points out that the frequently weak pedagogical foundations of many online courses can reduce the quality and impact of these offerings. Although developers may use terms such as "constructivist" and "instructivist," they are not always well elucidated nor do they necessarily reflect what is actually included in the web-based courses (e.g., an instructivist assignment within a constructivist-labelled course). She presents content related to computer-mediated communication and theories of teaching and learning such as instructivist, critical, constructivist and adult learning. The discussion concludes with a statement that a strong theoretical foundation informs our responses to changing educational and learning environments and allows us to test and develop approaches that are effective.

Moore's second article entitled, "Faculty Perceptions of the Effectiveness of Web-Based Instruction in Social Work Education," provides a context for exploring the perceptions of Social Work faculty to FTF and WBE courses. Based on a recent nationwide study, the author notes that faculty perceive FTF instruction to be more effective in social work education. Additionally, faculty perceived WBE courses to be least effective in the areas of practice and most effective in the Human Behavior in the Social Environment, research and policy areas. Other authors such as Petracchi et al. make a similar point within this volume. Moore notes that these perceptions may run counter to the consistent research finding of "no significant difference" between FTF and WBE courses.

Steyaert, in his article "Web-Based Higher Education: The Inclusion/Exclusion Paradox" adds another perspective stemming from the value of inclusiveness rather than from theory. He cautions us that although WBE may make higher education more convenient for some learners, it can make education less accessible for those with functional impairments. He reviews how various software manufacturers have built in features to respond to certain special needs and explores several myths that may limit the responsiveness of educators and web developers. Steyaert challenges us as organizations and individuals to do whatever we can to build inclusiveness and accessibility into our web-based courses.

In "Souls on Ice: Incorporating Emotion in Web-Based Education," MacFadden highlights the neglected dimension of affect in developing and facilitating web-based courses. Through reviewing some of the history of emotions in learning and in online learning, he notes that emotion has been seen, by some educators, as secondary to cognition and an unnecessary and even counterproductive dimension. Yet recent brain research is revealing a complex process that integrates both emotions and cognition in helping us understand and learn. Indeed, emotions help to motivate learners and enable them to both focus and brainstorm when necessary. A constructivist, emotionally-oriented (CEO) model of web-based education is presented and the author concludes with some ideas on how we can build more affect into course development and delivery.

Prior to examining specific models of WBE, Collins and Jerry in their article entitled, "The Campus Alberta Applied Psychology Counselling Initiative: Web-Based Delivery of a Graduate Professional Training Program," present the details of an entire web-based graduate program that was developed for instructing counselors in counselling Psychology. The authors describe the objectives of the program, the pedagogical approaches, the structure, processes and resources involved. The important issue of ownership of the courses is discussed and lessons learned are shared. In a similar vein to Moore, the authors note that the online environment may actually offer an optimal learning approach for some students focusing on particular learning objectives. Like MacFadden, the authors intend on exploring the affective dimension in online learning in new iterations of the program.

The articles, to this point, provide more of a context for web-based education and courses. The following readings present specific examples of web-based courses, highlighting particular features or dimensions associated with each course.

INTERNATIONAL COLLABORATION

The next two articles describe the development and facilitation of courses from an international perspective. Wong and Schoech, in "A Tale of Three Cities: Teaching Online to Students in Shanghai from Hong Kong and Texas," discuss their experiences with a graduate level web-based course in Social Work Administration. This course was delivered to students in Shanghai, China and was co-taught by Dick Schoech from Texas, USA and Y. C. Wong from Hong Kong, China. The authors identify the considerable challenges faced with this collaborative offering. Practical issues such as language difficulties, cultural differences, unreliable technology, time differences and local relevance of the content are discussed. Employing a WebCam provided more direct contact and revealed some of the difficulties learners experienced in interpreting questions in English that was not readily apparent in chat and written material. Although the authors recommend such international collaboration, they caution that it is important to have a local partner to assist with the teaching and in applying the concepts to local realities.

Ford and Rotgans-Visser in their article, "Internationalizing Social Work Education Using Blackboard 6: INHOLLAND University, NL and James Madison University, USA," discuss a collaborative, online course experience between undergraduate social work students in the U.S. and the Netherlands. Based on a pre-existing FTF relationship between instructors, the authors constructed an online course to explore the issue of immigration in both countries. This Blackboard-based course emphasized asynchronous communication and compared the experience and attitudes within the two countries before and after September 11, 2001. While language was a significant challenge, the authors recommend this type of international collaboration to increase intercultural awareness and understanding and globalization of the curriculum.

SPECIAL FEATURES AND EXAMPLES
OF WEB-BASED COURSES

The articles in Part II present a variety of approaches to WBE with emphases on certain features or perspectives.

Rice-Green and Dumbrill, in "A Child Welfare Course for Aboriginal and Non-Aboriginal Students: Pedagogical and Technical Challenges," describe the development of an undergraduate online course to prepare social work students for child welfare work in aboriginal and non-aboriginal communities. This WebCT- based course incorporates a constructivist, anti-racist, radical, structural, feminist and First-Nations stance. The sequence of content is presented and the use of learning objects such as quizzes, PowerPoint and Real Audio presentations are highlighted. The authors see these learning objects as "way-points" rather than complete forms of knowledge. WBE can promote a consumer approach to education with discrete bits of knowledge and thereby marginalize more holistic, Aboriginal ways of knowing. The authors contend that their course model shows how learners can be presented with information and encouraged to develop their own understandings holistically.

Jerry and Collins in "Web-Based Education in the Human Services: Use of Web-Based Video Clips in Counselling Skills Training," provide an example of a course that is offered within the context of their complete online program described above. This course focuses on the development of counselling skills. The authors employ web-based video clips that feature client-counselor interactions and then provide an online grid for analyzing the interaction and for submitting the analysis to the instructors for evaluation. These video clips can be examined and reviewed in detail and they can be used as learning objects for other applications. The course is largely web-based with a three week FTF Institute. This ensures live experience and builds on the foundational content that is presented earlier online. The course occurs in the second semester, after a basic course on the theories of counselling. Relying on a "working alliance" concept, the course is both synchronous and asynchronous. A synchronous chat room experience enables role-playing and there are weekly discussion forums. The authors report that they have used almost every possible technical tool except for live video and audio. This article is rich in detail and a credible example of how a blended WBE model (i.e., online and some FTF) can be employed to instruct within a highly interpersonal domain.

Freddolino and Knaggs show how an online course can be developed through FTF and interactive television (ITV) formats in their article, "Building a Predominantly Web-Based Course from Face-to-Face and Interactive Video Pilots: Administrative Skills for Social Work Practice." Similar to Jerry and Collins who use video excerpts to teach counselling skills, Freddolino and Knaggs employ streamed videotaped lectures that focus on social work administration skills development. Using a homegrown course platform, a web-based course was constructed that incorporated the video lectures, discussion boards, online office hours in a chat room format, and an online synchronous chat assignment focused on sexual harassment. Considerable detail is provided about the staged development and the authors advise us that commencing a web-based course in an FTF format allows for pilot testing before being committed to digital form. Being able to test out the course within a distance ITV form prepares the instructor for the online format. This approach leads to the necessary refinements that characterize high quality courseware.

In "Field Clusters Online," Bushfield employs a web-based discussion group format to support social work students' field experiences. Although not an independent course, this experience is situated within the Practicum requirements and offers flexible support to students and field consultants. Offering largely asynchronous discussions, the content focuses on issues critical to the particular stage of the Practicum. One FTF session is held and there are some live chat opportunities. The time flexibility associated with this approach was valued by students with busy schedules who could largely determine where and when to participate. As noted in Barnett-Queen which follows, students' discussions within these online groups appeared to be richer and more focused than some traditional FTF discussions. Bushfield suggests that focusing on relevant topics and having the learners comment on other students' postings deepens the level of discourse. The asynchronous environment permits time for reflection and crafting reasoned responses to issues and other learners' remarks.

In an article that also focuses on web-based discussions, Barnett-Queen, Blair and Merrick emphasize how largely asynchronous discussion groups can promote reflection, debate, considered responses and open discussions. Their article, "Student Perspectives of Online Discussions: Strengths and Weaknesses," explores best practices for online discussions and provides details of their undergraduate, web-based course that incorporates text-based readings, lecture notes, online articles and a series of films. Initially the facilitators lead the online discussion, then student dyads become responsible for this. An online, flexible resource termed, "WebQuest" is employed and enables facilitators or students to set up a task for others to complete. Although the sample was small, a majority of students rated online discussions as promoting a better understanding of course content than traditional class discussions.

Biggerstaff, in "Social Work Ethics Online: Reflective Learning," presents another web-based course that provides content, but emphasizes online discussion. This is a graduate level course on social work ethics that is case-based and asynchronous. It emphasizes reflective learning, critical thinking and the examination of beliefs and actions. The author points out that reflective thinking may appear antithetical to WBE since most of the online development has occurred within areas such as social work history and research methods. This echoes the comments made by Moore earlier that social work faculty view areas such as research and policy as more appropriate for web-based courses. However, Biggerstaff notes that a number of developers have offered sensitive courses such as cultural diversity and societal oppression within an online environment. This course employs a "say-writing" approach where participants openly express themselves in text, take a stand, defend a point, and respond to the "say-writing" of other learners. The assumption is that learners may be more willing to do this online than FTF. As previous authors in this issue assert, learners in an asynchronous environment have time to reflect on their responses and to develop a reasoned response to the postings. Learners can't hide behind others' contributions and they need to have done some of the reading to participate. Examples of "say-writing" dialogue are presented. The authors caution that the involvement for facilitators in this approach is extensive and requires responses that encourage more critical reflection rather than providing "answers" to the comments. The course is depicted as "community-centered learning" which is especially appropriate for difficult ethical reasoning.

Weingardt and Villafranca describe a web-based course that attempts to address the gap between research and practice. In their article, "Translating Research into Practice: The Role of Web-Based Education," the authors use a "clinical practice guideline" (CPG) which was developed from research and informs nurses on how to screen patients with "alcohol withdrawal syndrome." This is a self-paced course that incorporates online reference tools and employs a blended strategy of instructivist and constructivist strategies. Built using Dreamweaver's Course Builder, the authors view this online application as a type of performance support courseware that greatly improves our ability to disseminate research and related practice-based implications through frameworks such as CPGs and other research-based tools.

MacKenzie and Bjornson highlight their web-based course designed to promote interdisciplinary awareness and practice within the context of social work, child and youth work and nursing. Their article, "Working Across the Disciplines/Shifting Perspectives: Student Experiences with an Online Course Focused on Interdisciplinary Practice with Children and Families," describes a web- based course that incorporates online discussion groups, case studies, interactive exercises, and role plays within the context of an experiential environment. Emphasizing WebCT's communication tools, the course involves 13 weeks and incorporates web links, detailed outline notes, and print-based readings. General and small group discussion areas were created. Assignments involve a reflecting journal, asynchronous role plays and a summary paper. The authors provide excerpts of student dialogue which describes their learning and the nature of their experiences in this online course.

Petracchi, Mallinger, Engel, Rishel and Washburn present a study that compares the relative efficacy of FTF and web-assisted sections of an undergraduate course in social work practice. Their article, "Evaluating the Efficacy of Traditional and Web-Assisted Instruction in an Undergraduate Social Work Practice Class," describes a study that uses a quasi-experimental design in evaluating performance on assignments. The web-assisted section experienced 50% of the lectures online and utilized an online discussion board for some of the course dialogue. The results indicated there was no significant difference between the FTF section and the web-assisted section on assignments, a mid-term exam and a videotaped exam project. Given the rigor of the study, the authors conclude that web-assisted delivery can be as effective as FTF course delivery in teaching beginning knowledge and skills in social work practice.

CONCLUSION

The content within this volume reflects the vitality and diversity of web-based courses being currently delivered within human services. There is some collective emphasis on discussion-based courses that are viewed as encouraging deep reflection and reasoned responses by learners. A constructivist pedagogical approach is shared by many authors which emphasizes the social aspect of learning. The contributions reflect topical areas that are not usually associated with web-based education such as practice and skills-based instruction. Several authors remind us of the extensive effort required in developing and facilitating web-based courses and the need to move beyond a preoccupation with how similar WBE is with FTF approaches.

The content within this collection reflects a course delivery medium coming of age. As Moore's survey points out, those with experience with web-based instruction are not yet convinced that web courses in certain areas, such as clinical practice, can be designed to be as effective as FTF courses. While many articles provide innovative ideas for delivering web-based content, Collins' and Jerry's contribution highlights the power of not viewing the design of each course separately, but the importance of designing a complete web-based curriculum. Several articles discuss the development of objects which are reusable throughout the curriculum. Overall, the articles point to the need to create virtual learning environments which incorporate a variety of techniques and strategies throughout many courses. These learning environments are much more robust and use concepts and tools beyond what packages, such as webCT, currently offer. However, virtual learning environments are often more limited by theoretical and conceptual thinking than by the limitation of web-based tools. Many of the successful uses of the web illustrated in the articles do not require sophisticated tools or programming, but creative design of interactive scenarios, emotional content, and feedback mechanisms. Finally, the volume points out the need for mentoring, monitoring, and support from readily available professionals, especially until the problems can be worked out of learning environments. While virtual learning environments move the "sage on the stage" to the "guide at the side," they do not restrict the instructor to a design only role which disappears once the course is developed. Especially in virtual learning environments educating human service students, the instructor's role continues to be the critical ingredient for success.

Key Issues in Web-Based Education in the Human Services: A Review of the Literature

Brenda Moore

SUMMARY. The literature on Web-based education reflects a paradigm shift as hundreds of colleges and universities are offering online courses. This paper provides an overview of the current literature on Web-based education, including frameworks for analysis. Key publications on Web-based education in social work and human services are presented. Attention is given to the theoretical perspectives relevant to Web-based education such as adult learning theories and the shift to a constructivist approach. This paper concludes with a discussion on related issues such as evaluation, leadership, emotional aspects of Web-based instruction, and teaching practice skills through Web-based technology. *[Article copies available for a fee from The Haworth Document Delivery Service: 1-800-HAWORTH. E-mail address: <docdelivery@haworthpress.com> Website: <http://www.HaworthPress.com> © 2005 by The Haworth Press, Inc. All rights reserved.]*

KEYWORDS. Web-based instruction, online learning, social work education, technology in higher education

---

Brenda Moore, PhD, LMSW-AP, is Assistant Professor and BSW Director, Department of Social Work, Texas A&M University-Commerce, P.O. Box 3011, Commerce, TX 75429.

[Haworth co-indexing entry note]: "Key Issues in Web-Based Education in the Human Services: A Review of the Literature." Moore, Brenda. Co-published simultaneously in *Journal of Technology in Human Services* (The Haworth Press, Inc.) Vol. 23, No. 1/2, 2005, pp. 11-28; and: *Web-Based Education in the Human Services: Models, Methods, and Best Practices* (eds: MacFadden et al.) The Haworth Press, Inc., 2005, pp. 11-28. Single or multiple copies of this article are available for a fee from The Haworth Document Delivery Service [1-800-HAWORTH, 9:00 a.m. - 5:00 p.m. (EST). E-mail address: docdelivery@haworthpress.com].

Available online at http://www.haworthpress.com/web/JTHS
© 2005 by The Haworth Press, Inc. All rights reserved.
Digital Object Identifier: 10.1300/J017v017n01_02

Higher education for human services is undergoing a transformation as "technology-assisted instruction has proliferated and changed the way teachers and students interact, as well as the manner in which educational entitities must now do business to meet the demands of a digitized society" (Beaudoin, 2003, p. 1). In fact, Twigg (2001) refers to this change as a paradigm shift, a change in the way we view our world and the assumptions that help us understand or predict behavior. Currently, hundreds of colleges and universities are offering online courses, altering centuries-old methods of traditional teaching and learning methods. The research literature is increasingly reflecting various aspects of this "paradigm shift."

This paper provides an overview of the current literature on Web-based education, including frameworks for analysis. Key publications on Web-based education in social work and human services will be presented. Attention will be given to the theoretical perspectives relevant to Web-based education such as adult learning theories and the shift to a constructivist approach. This paper concludes with a discussion on related issues such as evaluation, leadership, emotional aspects of Web-based instruction, and teaching practices skills through Web-based technology. While there are some subtle differences, the terms *distance learning, distance education, Web-based education, distributed learning, and online learning* will be used interchangeably throughout this paper (Twigg, 2001; Bates, 2003).

Web-based education is a complex phenomenon. Figure 1 provides a conceptual model for analyzing various interrelated aspects of Web-based education.

This model reflects the juxtaposition of information relevant to the application of Web-based education in higher education, social work and human services, theoretical perspectives, frameworks for Web-based instruction, and other related issues to Web-based education. As one reviews the literature, all of these aspects are important in understanding the transformation of our educational process.

WEB-BASED EDUCATION IN HIGHER EDUCATION

Changes occurring in work and educational environments have resulted in a demand for distance education as a "widely accepted means for higher education to provide broader access and achieve cost-efficiencies while maintaining quality programs" (Eastmond, 1998, p. 33).

FIGURE 1. Schematic Representation of Key Issues in Web-Based Education

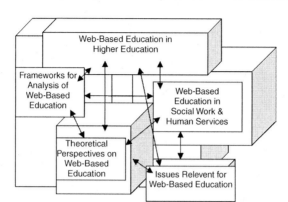

Web-based instruction reflects current efforts in the use of technology to enhance education.

The earliest generation of higher education, lasting for centuries and based on bricks and mortar, provided education in a specific place utilizing traditional methods of teaching. The following generation involved various forms of universities that used a range of distance delivery tools and technologies. The British Open University, founded in 1969, marked the beginning for degree-giving distance education universities with full degree programs, often referred to as "mega universities" (Holmberg, 1995; Moore, 1993, Bates, 2000; Green, 2003).

Moore (1993) describes the changes in the current generation of higher education as ". . . the development of the communications technologies of the 1990s–the electronic highways to our homes and workplaces–we are rapidly approaching technical readiness for the Virtual University" (p. 4). The rapid development of technology made it increasingly possible for learners to become independent from educational institutions in their acquisition of information and the Virtual University has become reality.

There is no denying the impact of technology on higher education. The role and availability of web-based and web-enhanced classes continues to expand. Moore (1999) compares the use of distance education to the retailing business, from the "Distance Education Superstore" such as the mega-universities with thousands of students purchasing classes online to the "Distance Education Boutique," where suppliers struggle to define their market, provide a specialized product and balance the costs and benefits of such endeavors. Related to market demands and driving economic factors, many higher education institutions have embraced online learning (Green, 2003). Eighty-one percent of all higher education institutions offer at least one fully online or blended course; complete online degree programs are offered at 34% of higher education institutions (Sloan-C Online Learning Survey Report, 2003).

FRAMEWORKS FOR ANALYSIS OF WEB-BASED EDUCATION

A number of studies have been published that provide frameworks for understanding Web-based education (American Distance Education Consortium, 2001; Chickering & Ehrmann, 1996; Li-Ling, 1997; Kearsley, 1998; Kahn, 2000, 2002, 2003). One model is based on a study from the State University of New York Learning Network (SUNY), an online instructional program developed for sixty-four colleges (with 3200 online courses with 50,000 students enrolled) that are a part of the SUNY system (Shea, 2003). This report integrates pedagogical research with principles of good practice in higher education and recent research on learning in asynchronous learning networks in higher education. This framework is based on modified guidelines from *How People Learn* (Bransford, Brown, Cocking, Donavan, & Pellegrino, 2000).

Another example of a comprehensive effort to analyze Web-based education is provided by Howell, Williams, and Lindsay (2003). Based on the study of more than 70 books, journal articles, reports, and web-sites published in the past three years, the authors identify thirty-two trends affecting distance education. These trends are organized into categories pertaining to students and enrollment, faculty, academics, technology, the economy, and distance learning.

A useful framework for effective Web-based education is the delineation of best practices for electronically offered programs proposed by the Western Cooperative for Educational Telecommunications (*www.wiche.edu*), an organization with substantial expertise in this area. These best practice principles, organized around the components of (1) institutional context and commitment; (2) curriculum and instruction; (3) faculty support; (4) student support; and evaluation and assessment, were developed by eight regional accrediting commissions. These standards reflect regional accreditation standards that are applicable to electronic learning environments.

Understanding the relationship of Web-based education as compared with traditional face-to-face education has been important as technology has evolved. Russell (1997) published a compendium of more than 355 research studies on "no significant difference" between face-to-face courses and technologically-based courses. While frequently cited as a rationale for support of online education, other research questions the "across the board" acceptance and application (Moore, 2003; Twigg, 2001; Shearer, 2002). What is now emerging in the literature is an effort to move beyond a comparison of "what used to be" with "what is" to understanding "what can be."

Perhaps the real question should be how and through what technology we use to accomplish our educational mission. "If we value human interactions and the aspects of social presence which exist in a class, then the real question is how and through what technology can we strive to achieve this for our students" (Shearer, 2002). Numerous efforts are underway to examine ways to improve the design and implementation of Web-based courses.

Twigg (2001) asserts that the majority of online courses are organized and offered in the same way as on-campus courses, resulting in "applying old solutions to new problems." The Center for Academic Transformation convened a symposium in 2000 of faculty and administrators to consider how to move online learning *beyond* being "as good" as traditional education. Their work is summarized in five areas: (1) Individualization of students (with an emphasis on the importance of students' learning styles); (2) Improving the quality of student learning (technology allows for customized courses like "pieces of a puzzle"); (3) Increasing access to higher education (the more virtual the delivery model, the more accessible); (4) Reducing costs of teaching and learning (restructuring how courses are developed and offered); and (5) Sustaining innovation (the need for a new kind of institutional research to "determine the most efficient and effective paths for different kinds of learners in particular curricula or courses") (Twigg, 2001).

WEB-BASED EDUCATION IN SOCIAL WORK

Distance education has developed more slowly in social work than in other degree programs (Blakely & Shoenherr, 1995). However, social work educators have begun to integrate technology as a part of the educational experience (McFall & Freddolino, 2000; Biner, Dean, & Mellinger, 1994; Ashery, 2001, Coe & Elliott, 1999, Schoech & Helton,

2001; Finn, 2002; Randolph & Krause, 2002; Frey, Faul, & Yankelov, 2003). Most traditional social work courses integrate computer technology to some extent, at least through e-mail or Web-based research resources. Some courses use Web-enhanced or Web-assisted instruction while some classes are offered totally online (Pollof & Pratt, 2001). The availability of electronic media is increasing and the costs associated with distance education using online and Web-based courses is decreasing, especially when compared with the spiraling costs of traditional on-campus programs (Schoech, 2000; Stocks & Freddolino, 2000).

Macy, Rooney, Hollister, and Freddolino (2001) summarize a number of studies on the use of technology in social work, listed in Table 1.

Other articles in the literature propose an organizing framework for considering various features of technology in social work education, including variables such as learner, instructor, presentation, course content, outcomes, and the instructional environment (Schoech, 2000). Forster and Washington (2000) suggest a model that includes accreditation standards compliance, resource requirements, curriculum adaptation, faculty development and program evaluation as a way to develop

TABLE 1. Overview of Distance Education Studies in Social Work

Studies comparing student learning from grades and/or performance on assignments in the following areas:	Hollister & McGee, 2000; Petracchi & Morgenbesser, 1995; Petracchi & Patchner, 2000
• Policy	Huff, 2000; Freddolino & Sutherland, 2000; Wong & Law, 1999
• Research	Petracchi & Patchner, 2000; Freddolino & Sutherland, 2000; Stocks & Freddolino, 2000; Wernet, Olliges, & Delieath, 2000; Dalton, 2002
• Statistics	Harrington, 1999; Henley & Dunlap, 1998; Wong & Law, 1998
• Human Behavior & the Social Environment (HBSE)	Barnett-Queen, 1998; Barnett-Queen & Zhu, 1999; Haslet, Lehmann, & McLaughlin, 1998; Freddolino & Sutherland, 2000
• Human Diversity & Social Justice	Huff, 2000; Johnson, 1999; Van Soest, Canon, & Grant, 2000
• Introduction to Social Welfare History	Faux & Black-Hughes, 2000; Hick, 1999
• Practice Methods	Coe & Elliott, 1999; Cumins, 1998; Hagan, 1998; Oullette, Sells, & Rittner, 1999; Sells & Ritner, 1998; Freddolino & Sutherland, 2000; Glezakos & Lee, 2002
• Field Instruction	Burke & Macy, 1998; McFall & Freddolino, 2000
• Substance Abuse	Hollister & McGee, 2000; Petracchi & Morgenbesser, 1995
• Child Welfare	Thyer, Polk, & Gaudin, 1997; Cauble & Thurston, 2000
• Values & Professional Identity	Cascio, 2001
• Mental Health	Knowles, 2001; Patterson & Yaffe, 1993
• Technology	Schoech, 2000
• Administration	Schoech & Helton, 2001

and manage distance education programs. Friedman, Ward, and Biagianti (1998) suggest adapting the classic educational theory proposed by Bloom's Taxonomy of Educational Objectives as a tool for integrating technology into the educational process.

Social work educators are encouraged to use electronic media to enhance both education and practice (Freddolino, 2002; Schoech, 2002; Sandell & Hayes, 2002). However, Kreuger and Stretch (2000a; 2000b) provide a more critical perspective on the use of technology in social work. The authors define "hypertechnology" as "an entire interconnected assemblage of various technologies operating worldwide which interact electronically. This includes personal and networked computers, the Internet and other webbed connections, telecommunications, satellite hookups, cellular communications, and synchronous and asynchronous capacities" (p. 103). They speculate that social work educators have been pressured to participate in the hypertechnology movement without fully considering the pedagogical implications. In a subsequent publication, they encourage an understanding of technology (or hypertechnology) as a tool to support the development of knowledge, skills, and values of the profession. They recommend better data to assess how students and practitioners "adapt to temporal and spatial distance, how they relate to the emerging physical and special aspects of learning or delivering services off site. . . . Gadgets and mechanical objects should not substitute for humanistic pedagogy" (Stretch & Kreuger, 2002, p. 13).

In spite of the opportunities afforded by technology, there is a limited number of social work faculty engaging in "cutting-edge" initiatives using the full range of Web-based tools available (Moore, 2003). Instead, the social work literature tends to reflect research on Web-enhanced or blended approaches (Frey, Faul, & Yankelov, 2003; Randolph & Kraus, 2002). Studies such as those offered in this publication provide much-needed insights for future social work and human service education.

THEORETICAL PERSPECTIVES
FOR WEB-BASED EDUCATION

There is a risk that educators will assume that if they are familiar with various technology tools, they will be effective. Educators are encouraged to consider what teaching strategies can be enhanced by technology rather than looking at what strategies can be used to enhance the available technology (Erhmann, 1995; Friedman, Ward, & Biagianti, 1998). A particular technology may be either well or poorly suited to support a particular teaching-learning method. The analogy used is that many tools can be used to turn a screw, but some can do the job better than others. "Better to turn a screw with a screwdriver than a hammer–a dime might do the trick, but a screwdriver is usually better!" (Chickering & Ehrmann, 1996, p. 1).

Technology has influenced the way educators view the process of education. The challenge for distant educators is that current pedagogy or adult learning theories are based on print, audio, and video distance delivery systems. Distance educators cannot consider distance delivery systems, including the Internet, in isolation from other modes of delivery. When distance separates the teacher from the learners, and technology mediates the learning experience, the assumption that learners must become more independent and autonomous follows (Wagner & McCombs, 1995). Web-based education provides a unique opportunity to shift from teacher or education-centered to learner-centeredness.

Theoretical shifts in adult learning perspectives have occurred concurrently with technological advances, changing from behavioral to cognitive to constructivist learning perspectives (Herrington & Standen, 2000; Dalgarno, 2001). Constructivists believe that the world is constructed in the mind and personal constructions define personal realities (Jonassen, Davidson, Collins, Campbell, & Haag, 1995). The constructivist view of learning is not listening and then mirroring, but rather participating and interacting with the environment in order to create personal meaning. Constructivists emphasize the design of the learning environment rather than instructional sequences. Emphasis is placed on the context of learning rather than the content (Jonassen, 1994, Jonassen, Davidson, Collins, Campbell, & Haag, 1995).

Constructivist environments involve learners in knowledge construction through collaboration that allows for learning through interaction with other learners and reflection upon what has been learned through the process. A constructivist learning environment is facilitated by the use of technology and distance education. The paradox is that many distance education programs are using traditional, objectivist approaches when constructivism can more effectively support the benefits of new technologies (Jonassen, Davidson, Collins, Campbell, & Haag, 1995, Twigg, 2001; Blocher, Echols, Sujo de Montes, Willis, & Tucker, 2003; Shutkin, 2004).

The Internet allows for the development of knowledge-building communities in which participants can share information, reflect on the knowledge they construct, and learn from the processes they used (Huang, 2002). New technologies have contributed to a movement away from traditional instructional methods, both in the classroom and at a distance, towards an approach that minimizes the role and focus on the teacher as the main source of knowledge (Jonassen, 1994). In a traditional classroom, the teacher contributes up to 80% of the verbal exchange; in online classes, the instructor contributes only 10-15% of the messages (Jonassen, Davidson, Collins, Campbell, & Haag, 1995).

A constructivist view of the learner taking responsibility for constructing meaning can help maintain focus on the benefits available through technology. Such theoretical perspectives are contributing to an evolving Web-based pedagogy. Online courses have characteristics that are unique to the technology being used and therefore, allows for consideration of new pedagogical models (Institute for Higher Education Policy, 2000).

ISSUES RELATED TO WEB-BASED EDUCATION

Evaluation of Web-Based Education

There are many ancillary issues related to Web-based education. Researchers and scholars of distance education programs are striving to develop effective means to evaluate the new technologies (Achtemeier, Morris, & Finnegan, 2003; Phipps & Merisotis, 1999; Reeves & Reeves, 1996; Reeves, 2000; Berge & Meyers, 2000; Brown, 1997; Roblyer & Knerzek, 2003). Evaluation efforts have broadened beyond course evaluation to looking at how to improve implementation methods, monitor technology's impact on societal goals, and report on current technology uses that help shape desired directions (Roblyer & Knerzek, 2003). Ideally, evaluation efforts are moving beyond simple comparisons with more traditional classroom teaching to consideration of cutting-edge technology in determining "what can be" rather than "what has been" (Twigg, 2001).

Leadership in Web-Based Education

Educators and administrators are beginning to consider the role and impact of leadership in Web-based education. "Thus, as the boundaries and distinctions between traditional and so-called non-traditional education are blurring, there is a need for leaders to be able to function effectively in both contexts" (Beaudoin, 2003). Some of the venues that new leaders may find themselves in distance education include collaborative partnerships, such as alliance building with for-profit companies, meta-university configurations, expansive global markets, more free-standing virtual entities, and more exclusively online delivery systems rather than mixed-media approaches (Beaudoin, 2003). These not-so-future changes require creative leadership of both "groundbreakers" and "pace setters" (Twigg, 2001).

Bates (2000) differentiates between "single-mode" universities, such as the British Open University, and "dual-mode" institutions that offer regular programs on campus as well as distance education. These dual-mode institutions, which historically have been the old land-grant universities in the United States, are facing challenges as a result of "changing markets, developments in technology, reduced government spending, privatization of higher education, globalization, and increased competition" (Bates, 2000). As a result, there is a need for "trans-formative leadership" to help organizations reshape traditional ap-proaches to education. This new style of leadership moves beyond Hershey and Blanchard's (1977) situational leadership to a call for edu-cational leaders who are capable of helping stakeholders (administra-tors, faculty and students) accept the benefits of teaching and learning in new ways (Beaudoin, 2003).

Emotional Aspects of Web-Based Education

One of the least researched areas intrinsic to Web-based education is the emotional aspects of online teaching and learning. While traditional education literature is replete with research which structures, catego-rizes, and describes human interaction in the classroom (Baumgartner, 2001; Brookfield, 1995a & 1995b; Bruner, 2002; Caffarella & Caffarella, 1986; Donaldson & Graham, 1999; Galbraith, 1994; Kasworm & Marienau, 1997; Knowles, 1980; Mezirow, 1978; Merriam, 2001), research is needed to understand the role of emotions in Web-based education.

Despite the importance of emotions in daily life, the focus for years in instructional design and technology was the learner's cognitive and motivational processes, with little or no attention to human emotions (Astleitner & Leutner, 2000; Reigeluth, 1997). MacFadden, Herie, Maiter, and Dumbrill (in press) describe a model, based on a con-structivistic approach, which emphasizes the emotional dimensions in online learning. This model was developed in response to research on teaching cultural competence through Web-based instruction (MacFadden, Maiter, & Dumbrill, 2002). As more educators critically evaluate their Web-based courses, the aspect of emotionality should not be ignored.

Another framework to ensure that Web-based instructional strategies are emotionally sound is called a "FEASP" approach. This model includes attention to elements associated with: fear reduction, envy reduction, anger reduction, sympathy increase, and pleasure increase (Astleitner & Leutner, 2000). While many studies consider student attitudes and perceptions to their Web-based learning experiences (Clawson, Deen & Oxley, 2002; Coulter, Konold, & Feldman, 2000; Ferdig & Roehler, 2003/2004), the experiences and emotions of the Web-based *teaching experience* of instructors should not be ignored (Smith, Ferguson, & Caris, 2002; MacFadden, Herie, Maiter, & Dumbrill, in press).

Teaching Practice Skills Through Web-Based Technology

The number of counselors and clinicians offering services over the Internet is growing significantly (Wilson, Jencius, & Duncan, 1997; Abney & Maddux, 2004; Clinical Social Work Federation, 2001; Freeny, 2001; Ainsworth, 2001). Providing mental health and therapeutic services online has raised many questions and issues, but most research in this area has been exploratory or descriptive (Helton, 2003; Ainsworth, 2001). It seems evident that professional helpers would (or should) have training or education on providing Web-based services, but Suler (2000) indicates that online therapy is very different than face-to-face approaches. The Clinical Case Study Group of the International Society for Mental Health Online recommends that professionals who are using Internet-based applications should have specific training to provide services online (Fenichel et al., 2002).

Finn (2002) suggests that social work students may not be taught about e-therapy in practice classes; therefore, their beliefs about the effectiveness of this modality of treatment may be negatively influenced. Moore (2003) found that practice courses were reported as using Web-based instruction more frequently than other curriculum areas (such as policy, HBSE, or research) but that faculty perceived Web-based instruction in teaching practice classes to be less effective than face-to-face instruction. This contradiction reflects the challenges facing human services professionals and educators as to the best way to prepare practitioners to use technology effectively.

CONCLUSION

Distance education technologies are viable media for teaching social work content and they allow educators to prepare students for the increasing use of technology in practice. Some components of social work programs may be more appropriate for traditional approaches. There may be some groups of students for who distance education technologies may be the best, or only, viable alternative. Distant education technologies need to be viewed as tools that can help social work educators, students, practitioners, and clients in accessing resources, delivering services, networking efficiently, teaching, and learning (Freddolino, 2002).

REFERENCES

Abney, P. C., & Maddux, C. D. (2004). Counseling and technology: Some thoughts about the controversy. *Technology in Human Services, 22,* 3, 1-24.

Achtemeier, S. D., Morris., L. V., & Finnegan, C. L. (2003). Considerations for developing evaluations of online courses. *Journal of Asynchronous Learning Networks, 7* (1). Available [online] at http://www.sloan-c.org/publications/jaln/v7n1/v7n1_achtemeier.asp.

Ainsworth, M. (2002). E-therapy: History and survey. *ABCs of Internet Therapy.* Available [online] at http://www.metamonia.org/imh/history/htm.

American Distance Education Consortium (2001). Homepage. Available [online] at http://www.adec.edu.

Ashery, R. S. (2001). The utilization of technology in graduate schools of social work. *Journal of Technology in Human Services, 18* (1/2), 5-18.

Astleitner, H., & Leutner, D. (2000). Designing instructional technology from an emotional perspective. *Journal of Research on Computing in Education, 32* (4), 497-510.

Barnett-Queen, T. (1998, August). HBSE on the Web: Demonstration of an interactive HBSE distance education course utilizing the WWW as the primary delivery method. Paper presented at the conference on Informational Technologies for Social Work Education and Practice. Charleston, SC.

Barnett-Queen, T., & Zhu, E. (1999). Distance education: Analysis of learning preferences in two sections of an undergraduate HBSE-like human growth and development course: Face-to-face and web-based distance learning [CD Rom]. *Third Annual Technology Conference for Social Work Education and Practice. Conference Proceedings.* Columbus: University of South Carolina College of Social Work.

Bates, A. W. (2000). Distance education in dual mode higher education institutions: Challenges and changes. *University of British Columbia Distance Education and Technology, Continuing Studies.* Available [online] at http://bates/cstudies.ubc.ca/papers/challengesandchanges.html.

Baumgartner, L. M. (2001). An update on transformations learning. *New Directions for Adult and Continuing Education, 89,* 15-23.

Beaudoin, M. F. (2003). Distance education leadership for the new century. *Online Journal of Distance Learning Administration, 6*(2). Available [online] at http://www.westga/edu/~distance/ojdla/summer62/beaudoin62.html

Berge, Z., & Meyers, B. (2000). Evaluating computer-mediated communication courses in Higher Education. *Journal of Education Computing Research, 23* (4), 431-450.

Biner, P. M., Dean, R. S., & Mellinger, A. E. (1994). Factors underlying distance learner satisfaction with televised college-level courses. *American Journal of Distance Education (8)* 1, 60-71.

Blakely, T., & Schoenherr, P. (1995). Telecommunication technologies in social work distance education. *Journal of Continuing Social Work Education, 6* (3) 8-12.

Blocher, J. M., Echols, J., Sujo de Montes, L., Willis, E., & Tucker, G. (2003). Shifting from instruction to construction: A personal meaningful experience. *Action Teaching Education, 24* (4), 74-78.

Bransford, J., Brown, A., Cocking, R., Donovan, M., & Pellegrino, H. (2000). *How people learn*. Washington, DC: National Academy Press.

Brookfield, S. (1995). Adult learning: An overview. In A. Tuinjman (Ed.), *International Encyclopedia of Education*. Oxford: Pergamon Press.

Brookfield, S. D. (1995). *Becoming a critically reflective teacher*. San Francisco: Jossey-Bass.

Brown, A. (1997). Designing for learning: What are the essential features of an effective online course? *Australian Journal of Educational Technology, 13* (2), 115-126.

Bruner, J. (2002). Constructivist theory. *TIP Theories*. Available [online] at http://tip.psychology.org.bruner.html.

Burke, K., & Macy, J. A. (1998, August). Opportunities and challenges in distance education. Paper presented at the conference on Informational Technologies for Social Work Education and Practice. Charleston, SC.

Caffarella, R. S., & Caffarella, E. P. (1986). Self-directedness and learning contracts in adult education. *Adult Education Quarterly, 36* (4), 226-234.

Cascio, T. (2001). Everyone has a shining side: Computer-mediated mentoring in social work education. *Journal of Social Work Education, 27*(2), 283-294. Available [online] through Academic Search Premier.

Cauble, A. E., & Thurston, L. P. (2000). Effects of interactive multimedia training on knowledge, attitudes and self-efficacy of social work students. *Research in Social Work Practice, 10* (4), 428-438.

Chickering, A. W., & Ehrmann, S. C. (1996). Implementing the seven principles: Technology as lever. AAHE Bulletin, Oct 1996. Available [online] at http://www.aahe.org/technology/ehrmann.htm.

Clawson, R. A., Deen, R. E., & Oxley, Z. M. (2002). Online discussions across three universities: Student participation and pedagogy. *PS, Political Science & Politics, 35* (4), 713-718.

Clinical Social Work Federation (2001). CSWF position paper on Internet text-based therapy. Available [online] at http://www.cswf.org/therapy/html.

Coe, J. R., & Elliott, D. (1999). An evaluation of teaching direct practice courses in a distance education program for rural settings. *Journal of Social Work Education, 35* (3), 353-365.

Coulter, B., Konold, C., & Feldman, A. (2000). Promoting reflective discussions: Making the most of online resources in your classroom. *Learning and Leading with Technology, 28* (2).

Cummins, L. K. (1998, August). Social work skills demonstrated: Beginning direct practice. Paper presented at the conference on Informational Technologies for Social Work Education and Practice. Charleston, SC.

Dalgarno, B. (2001). Interpretations of constructivism and consequences for computer-assisted learning. *British Journal of Educational Technology, 32* (2), 183-194.

Dalton, B. (2002). Distance education: A multidimensional evaluation. Paper presented at Annual Program Meeting, Council on Social Work Education, Nashville, TN. February 24, 2002.

Donaldson, J. F., & Graham, S. (1999). A model of college outcomes for adults. *Adult Education Quarterly, 50* (1), 24-40.

Eastmond, D.V. (1998). Adult learners and Internet-based distance education. *New Directions for Adult & Continuing Education, 78* (summer), 33-41.

Ehrmann, S. C. (1995). Asking the right question: What does research tell us about technology & higher learning? *Change, 27* (2), 20-27. Available [online] at http://www.learner.org/index/html.

Faux, T. L., & Black-Hughes, C. (2000). A comparison of using the Internet versus lectures to teach social work history. *Research on Social Work Practice, 10* (4), 454-467.

Fenichel, M., Suler, J., Barak, A., Zelvin, E., Jones, G., Munro, E. et al. (2002). Myths and realities of online clinical work. In J. Suler (Ed.), *Psychology of cyberspace*, pp. 1-14. Available [online] at http://www.rider.edu/~suler/psycyber/myths.htm.

Ferdig, R. E., & Roehler, L. R. (2003/2004). Student uptake in electronic discussions: Examining online discourse in literacy preservice classrooms. *Journal of Research on Technology in Education, 36* (2), 119-136.

Finn, J. (2002). MSW student perceptions of the efficacy and ethics of Internet-based therapy. *Journal of Social Work Education, 38* (3), 403-419.

Forster, M., & Washington, E. (2000). A model for developing and managing distance education programs using interactive video technology. *Journal of Social Work Education, 36* (1), 147-158.

Freddolino, P. (2002). Thinking "outside the box" in social work distance education: Not just for distance anymore. *Electronic Journal of Social Work, 1* (1), February 15, 2002.

Freddolino, P. P., & Sutherland, C. A. (2001). Assessing the comparability of classroom environments in graduate social work education delivered via interactive instructional television. *Journal of Social Work Education, 36* (1), 115-129.

Freeny, M. (2001). Better than being there. *Psychotherapy Networker, 25*(3), 31-39, 70.

Frey, A., Faul, A., & Yankelov, P. (2003). Student perceptions of Web-assisted teaching strategies. *Journal of Social Work Education, 39* (3), 443-457.

Friedman, B. D., Ward, D., & Biagianti, A. (1998). Using technology to forge new alliances in social work education. *New Technology in the Human Services, 11* (2), 13-18.

Galbraith, M. W. (1994). Connecting instructional principles to self-esteem. *Adult Learning, 5* (3), 24-31.

Glezakos, A., & Lee, C. D. (2002). Differences in competencies and course preferences between on-campus and distance education students. Available [online] at http://www2.uta.edu/cussn/husita/proposals/glezakos.htm.

Green, K. G. (2003). Digital tweed. *Syllabus, 16* (10), 14.

Hagan, C. B. (1998, August). *Distance education: Teaching practice methods using ITV.* Paper presented at the conference on Informational Technologies for Social Work Education and Practice. Charleston, SC.

Harrington, D. (1999). Teaching statistics: A comparison of traditional classroom and programmed instruction/distance education learning approaches. *Journal of Social Work Education, 35* (3), 343-350.

Haslet, D., Lehmann, B., & McLaughlin, C. (1998, August). Easing onto the information superhighway: Affordable classroom applications from rural America. Paper presented at the conference on Informational Technologies for Social Work Education and Practice. Charleston, SC.

Helton, D. (2003). Online therapeutic social service provision (Therap-pc): A state of the art review. *Journal of Technology in Human Services, 21*(4), 17-36.

Henley, H. C., & Dunlap, K. M. (1998, August). *Traditional and distance learning: Can they be compatible?* Paper presented at the conference on Information Technologies for Social Work Education and Practice. Charleston, SC.

Herrington, J., & Standen, P. (2000). Moving from an instructivist to a constructivist multimedia learning environment. *Journal of Educational Multimedia and Hypermedia, 9* (3), 195-205.

Hershey, & Blanchard, K. (1977). *Management of organizational behavior.* Englewood Cliffs, NJ: Prentice Hall.

Hick, S. (1999). Learning to care on the Internet: Evaluating an online introductory social work course. *New Technology in the Human Services, 11* (4), 1-8.

Hollister, C. D., & McGee, G. (2000). Delivering substance abuse and child welfare content through interactive television. *Research on Social Work Practice, 10* (4), 417-427.

Holmberg, B. (1995). The evolution of the character and practice of distance education. *Open Learning, 10* (2), 47-52.

Howell, S. L., Williams, P. B., & Lindsay, N. K. (2003). Thirty-two trends affecting distance education: An informed foundation for strategic planning. *Online Journal of Distance Learning Administration, 6* (3). Available [online] at http://www.westga. edu/~distance/ojdla/fall63/howell63.htm.

Huang, H. (2002). Toward constructivism for adult learners in online learning environments. *British Journal of Educational Technology, 33*(1), 27-37. Available [online] through Wilson Select Plus.

Huff, M. (2000). A comparison study of live instruction versus interactive television for teaching MSW students critical thinking skills. *Research on Social Work Practice, 10* (3), 400-416.

Institute for Higher Education Policy (2000). Quality on the line: Benchmarks for success in Internet-based distance education. Available [online] at http://www.ihep.com/publications.php.

Jonassen, D. H. (1994). Thinking technology. *Educational Technology, 34*(4), 34-37.

Jonassen, D., Davidson, M., Collins, M., Campbell, J., & Haag, B. B. (1995). Constructivism and computer mediated communication in distance education. *American Journal of Distance Education, 9* (2), 7-26.

Kasworm, C. E., & Marienau, C. A. (1997). Principles for assessment of adult learning. *New Directions for Adult and Continuing Education, 75,* 5-16. Available [online] through Wilson Select Plus.

Kearsley, G. (1998). Educational technology: A critique. *Educational Technology, March/April,* 47-51.

Khan, B. (2000). A framework for web-based learning. *TechTrends, 44* (3), 51.

Khan, B. (2002). Discussions of e-learning dimensions. *Educational Technology,* January-February, 59-60. Available [online] at http://bookstoread.com/framework/.

Khan, B. (2003). A framework for open, flexible and distributed e-learning. *eLearn magazine*. Available [online] at http://elearnmag.org/subpage/sub_page.cfm? section=3&list_item=12&page=1.

Knowles, A. J. (2001). Implementing web-based learning: Evaluation results from a mental health course. *Journal of Technology in Human Services, 18* (3/4), 171-187.

Knowles, M. S. (1980). *The modern practice of adult education: From pedagogy to andragogy.* (2nd ed.). Chicago, IL: Follett Publishing Company.

Kreuger, L. W., & Stretch, J. J. (2000). How hypertechnology in social work education bites back. *Journal of Social Work Education, 36* (1), 103-114.

Kreuger, L. W., & Stretch, J. J. (2000). What is the role of hypertechnology in social work today? *Social Work, 45*(5), 457-463. Available [online] through Academic Search Premier.

Li-Ling, C. (1997) Distance delivery systems in terms of pedagogical considerations: A reevaluation. *Educational Technology, 37* (4), 34-38.

McFall, J. P., & Freddolino, P. P. (2000). The impact of distance education programs on community agencies. *Research on Social Work Practice, 10* (4), 438-456. Available [online] through Academic Search Premier.

McFall, J. P., & Freddolino, P. P. (2000). Quality and comparability in distance field education: Lessons learned from comparing three program sites. *Journal of Social Work Education, 36* (2), 293-307.

MacFadden, R., Dumbrill, G.C., & Malter, S. (2000). High tech and high touch: The human face of online education. *Journal of Technology in Human Services, 20* (3/4), 283-300.

MacFadden, R. J., Herie, M., Maiter, S., & Dumbrill, G. C. (in press). Achieving high touch in high tech: A constructivist, emotionally-oriented model of web-based instruction. In Beaulaurier, R., and Haffey, M. (Eds.), *Technology and Social Work Education.* NY: The Haworth Press, Inc.

Macy, J. A., Rooney, R. H., Hollister, C. D., & Freddolino, P. P. (2001). Evaluation of distance education: Programs in social work. In J. Miller-Cribbs (Ed.), *New Advances in Technology for Social Work Education* (pp. 63-85). NY: The Haworth Press, Inc.

Merriam, S. B. (2001). Andragogy and self-directed learning: Pillars of adult learning theory. *The New Update on Adult Learning Theory, 89* (Spring), 3-13.

Mezirow, J. (1978). Perspective transformation. *Adult Education, 28* (2), 100-110.

Moore, B. (2003). Faculty perceptions of the effectiveness of Web-based instruction in social work education: An exploratory study. Unpublished doctoral dissertation, University of Texas at Arlington. Arlington, Texas.

Moore, M. G. (1993). Free trade in higher education. *The American Journal of Distance Education, 7* (3), 1-7.

Moore, M. G. (1999). Institutional restructuring: Is distance education like retailing?! *The American Journal of Distance Education, 13* (1), 1-7.

Ouellette, P., Sells, S., & Rittner, B. (1999). Combining teleconferencing with Web-based instruction to teach an advanced social work practice course for working with difficult children, adolescents and families: A journey in collaborative teaching and learning. [CD Rom]. *Third Annual Technology Conference for Social Work Educa-*

tion and Practice. Conference Proceedings. Columbus: University of South Carolina College of Social Work.

Patterson, D. A., & Yaffe, J. (1993). Using computer-assisted instruction to teach Axis II of the DSM III-R to social work students. *Research on Social Work Practice, 3* (3), 343-353.

Petracchi, H. E., & Morgenbesser, M. (1995). The use of video and one-way broadcast technology to deliver continuing social work education: A comparative assessment of student learning. *Journal of Continuing Education, 6* (3), 18-22.

Petracchi, H. E., & Patchner, M. A. (2000). Social work students and their learning environment: A comparison of interactive television, face-to-face instruction, and the traditional classroom. *Journal of Social Work Education, 36* (2), 335-346.

Phipps, R., & Merisotis, J. (1999). *What's the difference? A review of contemporary research on effectiveness of distance learning in higher education.* Washington, DC: The Institute for Education Policy.

Polloff, R. M., & Pratt, K. (2001). *Lessons from the cyberspace classroom. The realities of online teaching.* San Francisco: Jossey-Bass.

Randolf, K. A., & Krause, D. J. (2002). Mutual aid in the classroom: An instructional technology application. *Journal of Social Work Education, 38* (2), 259-271.

Reeves, T., & Reeves, P. M. (1996). Effective dimensions of interactive learning on the World Wide Web. *Web-based Instruction.* B. H. Khan (Ed.). Englewood Cliffs, NJ: Educational Technology Publications, 59-66.

Reeves, T. (2000). Evaluating what really matters in computer-based education. Available [online] at http://www.educationau.edu.au/archives/cp/reeves.htm.

Reigeluth, C. M. (1997). Instructional theory, practitioner needs, and new directions: Some reflections. *Educational Technology, 37*, 42-47.

Roblyer, M. D., & Knezek, G. A. (2003). New millennium research for educational technology: A call for a national research agenda. *Journal of Research on Technology in Education, 36* (1), 60-71.

Russell, T. L. (1997). The "no significant difference phenomenon." Available [online] at http://nt.media.hku.ht/no_diff/phenom1.html.

Sandell, K. S., & Hayes, S. (2002). The Web's impact on social work education: Opportunities, challenges, and future directions. *Journal of Social Work Education, 38* (1), 85-99.

Schoech, D. (2000). Teaching over the Internet: Results of one doctoral course. *Research on Social Work Practice, 10* (4), 467-486.

Schoech, D., & Helton, D. (2001). Qualitative and quantitative analysis of a course taught via classroom and Internet chatroom. *Qualitative Social Work, 1* (1), 111-124.

Sells, S. P., & Rittner, B. (1998, August). Teaching across Georgia: A dual campus course. Paper presented at the conference on Informational Technologies for Social Work Education and Practice. Charleston, SC.

Shea, P. J., Picket, A. M., & Pelz, W. E. (2003). A follow-up investigation of "teaching presence" in the SUNY Learning Network. *Journal of Asynchronous Learning Networks, 7* (2), 61-80.

Shearer, R. (2002). No significant difference and distance education. *Distance-Educator.com Daily News.* Available [online] at http://www.distance-educator.com/dnews/modules.php?

Shutkin, D. (2004). Thinking of the other: Constructivist discourse and cultural difference in the field of educational technology. *Journal of Educational Thought, 28* (1).

Sloan-C Online Learning Survey Report (2003). Online learning is as good as being
there. Available [online] at http://www.sloan-c.org/resources/survey.asp.

Smith, G.G., Ferguson, D., & Caris, M. (2002). Teaching over the Web versus in the
classroom: Differences in the instructor experience. *International Journal of Instructional Media, 29* (1), 61-67.

Stocks, J., & Freddolino, P. (2000). Enhancing computer-mediated teaching through
interactivity: The second iteration of a World Wide Web-based graduate social
work course. *Research on Social Work Practice, 10* (4), 505-519.

Suler, J. (2000). Psychotherapy in cyberspace: A 5-dimension model of online and
computer-mediated psychotherapy. *Cyberpsychology and Behavior, 3,* 151-160.

Thyer, B. A., Polk, G., & Gaudin, J. G. (1997). Distance learning in social work education: A preliminary evaluation. *Journal of Social Work Education, 33* (2), 363-367.

Twigg, C. (2001). Innovations in online learning: Moving beyond no significant difference. Center for Academic Transformation. Available [online] at www.center.
rpi.edu/PewSym/mono4.html.

Wagner, E. D., & McCombs, B.L. (1995). Learner-centered psychological principles
in practice: Designs for distance education. *Educational Technology, 35* (6), 32-35.

Wernet, S. P., Olliges, R. H., & Delicath, T. A. (2000). Postcourse evaluations of Web
CT (Web Course Tools) classes by social work students. *Research on Social Work
Practice, 10* (4), 487-504.

Western Cooperative for Educational Telecommunications (2003). Best practices for
electronically offered degree and certificate programs. Available [online] at www.
wiche.edu.

Wilson, F. R., Jencius, M., & Duncan, D. (1997). Introduction to the Internet: Opportunities and dilemmas. *Counseling and Human Development, 29*(6), 1-16.

Wong, Y. C., & Law, C. K. (1999). Learning social work online: A WebCT course on
policy issues among Chinese students. *New Technology in the Human Services, 11*
(4), 18-24.

Theoretical Perspectives in Online Pedagogy

Marilyn Herie

SUMMARY. Sound pedagogy supported by strong theoretical foundations is of key importance in online learning. Yet because this literature is
largely situated in the field of education, it is not always well articulated in
human services education. This article provides an overview of major theoretical approaches in the education field and links these with both online
learning and human services education, with an emphasis on bridging the
gap between theory and practice. *[Article copies available for a fee from The
Haworth Document Delivery Service: 1-800-HAWORTH. E-mail address:
<docdelivery@haworthpress.com> Website: <http://www.HaworthPress.com>
© 2005 by The Haworth Press, Inc. All rights reserved.]*

KEYWORDS. Education theory, pedagogy, constructivist theory, critical pedagogy, instructivist theory

Why include an article specific to pedagogical theory in this compendium, when the emphasis in this collection is on *practical* applications
for online teaching and learning? Lavooy and Newlin (2003) note that
critics of online learning have argued that student interaction and overall quality of education suffer in this medium, and "[t]he implications of
web-based courses without sound pedagogy can be as bleak as critics

Marilyn Herie, PhD, RSW, is affiliated with the Centre for Addiction and Mental
Health, and the University of Toronto.

[Haworth co-indexing entry note]: "Theoretical Perspectives in Online Pedagogy." Herie, Marilyn.
Co-published simultaneously in *Journal of Technology in Human Services* (The Haworth Press, Inc.) Vol. 23,
No. 1/2, 2005, pp. 29-52; and: *Web-Based Education in the Human Services: Models, Methods, and Best
Practices* (eds: MacFadden et al.) The Haworth Press, Inc., 2005, pp. 29-52. Single or multiple copies of this
article are available for a fee from The Haworth Document Delivery Service [1-800-HAWORTH, 9:00 a.m. -
5:00 p.m. (EST). E-mail address: docdelivery@haworthpress.com].

Available online at http://www.haworthpress.com/web/JTHS
© 2005 by The Haworth Press, Inc. All rights reserved.
Digital Object Identifier: 10.1300/J017v023n01_03

make it sound" (p. 6). Just as in classroom-based courses, online applications need to be informed by strong theoretical foundations in order to ensure educational excellence. Further, there is a general consensus among human service educators that linking theory with practice is essential. However, linking can be a challenge for professionals whose research and practice domains lie outside of the education field. Thus, although terms like "constructivist pedagogy" and "problem-based learning" are often cited as theoretical foundations of chosen applications, these are not always well-elucidated. Given the emphasis in this volume on cutting-edge developments in online pedagogy in the human services, this article aims to outline the major theoretical domains in the education field and to link these with current directions in online teaching and learning.

Theoretical perspectives in education and learning range from the broad and overarching, encompassing different educational contexts and applications to the very specific, such as theories aimed at adult learners, or those focused on particular modes of education, such as distance learning. Given that a discussion of education and learning theory and its relationship to online pedagogy could fill several volumes, the challenge is to present major trends in theoretical development while containing the scope of this review to theories that are most relevant to online human service education. Thus, some detail has been sacrificed in order to present a broad overview of major theories, with specific attention given to how these link to online learning approaches and applications.

This review will summarize the theoretical and research literature in two general areas, drawing from a variety of disciplines: (1) theoretical concepts related to computer-mediated communication (CMC); and (2) theories of teaching and learning (instructivist, critical, constructivist and adult learning approaches). These theories provide an analytical framework that incorporates both individual learners and groups of learners. In addition, these theoretical perspectives have been selected on the basis of their relevance to Web-based learning in human services education (Coulshed, 1993; Dean, 1993; Rossiter, 1993; Weick, 1993; Graham, 1997; Visser, 2000). Figure 1 summarizes the theoretical frameworks and the disciplines in which they have been developed, illustrating the overlap in these areas of inquiry. Computer-mediated communication and theories of teaching and learning complement and inform one-another. This article begins with a discussion of the major theories in education relevant to online pedagogy and follows with a discussion of how these theories relate to practical applications in an online context.

FIGURE 1. Theoretical Frameworks in Online Pedagogy

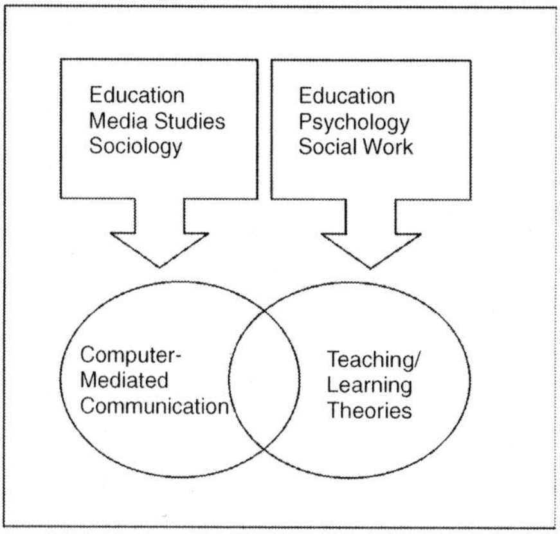

THEORETICAL FRAMEWORKS

A number of theoretical models related to CMC and teaching/learning theories will be considered in this section. The discussion of CMC (group and individual levels of analysis) can inform research on patterns of participation in online classrooms. This illuminates the ways in which computer-based interaction differs from spoken communication, as well as some of the unique challenges it presents for learners. In addition, theories of teaching and learning, drawing from these different paradigms, provide a basis for understanding the learning processes in online and face-to-face educational contexts at the individual level. Taken together, this analysis "sets the stage" for the research findings and practice examples that follow.

Computer-Mediated Communication

There has been considerable theorizing in the areas of virtual reality, artificial intelligence, virtual communities, and the nature of the "body" in cyberspace, where the Internet has been conceptualized as a unique and distinct cultural form. This literature on computer-mediated communication can inform the analysis of online learning in human services, since it suggests that Internet-based education is not merely another educational "channel." Rather, the Internet has been conceptualized as a medium that shares many of the properties of a physical place. This section will briefly explore the conceptual dimensions of "cyberspace," and the particular features and impact of computer-mediated communication (CMC) on human services education. Much of the seminal theorizing on CMC applications, which is still relevant to our understanding of online communication, was done during the 1990s in the fields of education, media studies, semiotics and sociology.

Romiszowski and Mason (1997) identify three main characteristics of CMC. First, CMC communication is able to support complex interactional processes between individuals and groups that combine the permanence of written communication with the speed and (to some extent) the dynamism of spoken telecommunication. Second, CMC can readily support multi-way communication, where all participants of a group can respond to the messages of all other participants. Finally, CMC can have both synchronous and asynchronous characteristics. These characteristics mark CMC as fundamentally different from other communications technologies, which are generally either one-way (text, television) or two-way (telephone), and are either asynchronous (text) or synchronous (telephone), but not both.

Semiotics and literary theory contribute to our understanding of CMC by looking at the relationships between *author, text* and *reader*. Traditionally, the author of a textual narrative (such as a book or article) is regarded as having the authority of understanding the meaning of that text. An alternative perspective in literary theory views the text itself as the "authority," where the task becomes one of interpretation or translation by the reader of what the text really means. This is in direct contrast to the positivist view of media (or text) as neutral. McLuhan's famous statement that "the medium is the message" directly addresses the non-neutrality of technology (McLuhan & Zingrone, 1995, p. 8). Thus, media affect us physically (e.g., sitting in front of a television, talking on a telephone, or working at a computer), and influence the interpretation of the messages they transmit. This suggests that text on a computer screen will be viewed in a qualitatively different way than text in print–the computer mediates and alters how the text is experienced or understood.

Despite the inorganic virtuality of computer networks, individuals seem compelled to try to inject a sort of "real world" quality to them. For example, the expression of the Internet as an "Information Highway," and Microsoft's "where do you want to go today?" advertising campaign reinforce the metaphor of the Internet as a transportation device (Jones, 1997). In addition, Jones suggests that the Internet can be regarded as *content* (storage and retrieval of information) and *context* (a virtual "place"), sharing many of the characteristics of real places. Computers in education have sought to capitalize on these characteristics of transportation, communication and storage by combining the learning activities of independent research with collaborative discussion and problem-solving. Computer-mediated communication via the Internet can take a number of forms, including electronic mail (e-mail, a one-to-one interaction), network discussion groups (handled by listservs, which distribute asynchronous unstructured messages to users via e-mail), electronic chat (many-to-many synchronous messaging), and computer conferencing (many-to-many asynchronous messaging, typically structured by topic area, known as discussion "threading").

CMC research and theory has traditionally related to text-based, computer-mediated communication. As computer bandwidth limitations cease to be an issue, the conceptualization of CMC will expand to include audio and video chat and conferencing. However, these applications have not yet found their way into widespread use in educational applications. With respect to communication, Fernback (1997) suggests that cyberspace is becoming increasingly like physical space, with its own dimensionality, continuity, curvature, density and limits. In this view, virtual reality is socially constructed and re-constructed, and can serve as a repository for cultural memory:

> [Cyberspace] is popular culture, it is narratives created by its inhabitants that remind us who we are, it is life as lived and reproduced in pixels and virtual texts. It is sacred and profane, it is workspace and leisure space, it is a battleground and a nirvana, it is real and it is virtual, it is ontological and phenomenological. Cyberspace is an arena of power; CMC users act every day on the assumption that the tyranny of geography can be overcome within cyberspace. It is smaller, more intimate, and almost more imaginable that "the public," which, Peters (1995) noted, can no longer fit into a stadium (or be conceived of as such). (Fernback, 1997, p. 37)

The notion of cyberspace as "place" is echoed in Eastmond's (1995) conceptualization of adult distance learners using computer conferencing as both "alone but together" and "together yet apart." On the one hand, computer conferencing in education promotes a sense of connectedness and solidarity among learners, but at the same time can be experienced as isolating and disjointed. Just as in other teaching/learning modalities, online learning is not a panacea. Some individuals, particularly those with prior online experience, thrive in this environment, while others miss the face-to-face interactions of the classroom (Eastmond, 1995).

Although the application of the metaphor of community to virtual environments has been contested in the literature, there is general acceptance that the symbolic and relational elements of the term make it an appropriate descriptor (Fernback, 1997). Watson (1997) notes that because communities first existed in shared physical space, it may be conceptually difficult for many to extend the term to electronic networks. However, as communications media make geographic borders more permeable, and as people's sense of community is less and less determined by physical proximity, it may make sense to rethink the notion of community "as a product not of shared space, but of shared *relationships* among people" (Watson, 1997, p. 120, emphasis in original). In other words, community can be said to occur in any context regardless of physical proximity, since it is based on relational as opposed to spatial dimensions. Given that individuals tend to learn best in settings where a sense of community exists, CMC systems in education should attempt to foster online "virtual" learning communities (Cook, 1995; Maor, 2003; Leiononen, Jarvela & Lipponen, 2003; Linder & Rochon, 2003). In conjunction with the sense of being part of a learning community, students' learning is also influenced by a variety of other factors. The theoretical models of teaching and learning discussed next illustrate how epistemology intersects with the learning context in influencing students' learning.

THEORIES OF TEACHING AND LEARNING

Theories of teaching and learning constitute an enormous body of literature, primarily situated within the fields of education and psychology. A complete review of this work is beyond the scope of this article. Instead, this section will review three major paradigms: positivist and post-positivist (instructivist) paradigms, critical pedagogy, and constructivism.

POSITIVIST AND POST-POSITIVIST PARADIGMS

The positivist teaching/learning paradigm is based on the assumption that an objective, value-free reality exists and can be understood. According to this framework, reality is governed by natural, immutable laws, and understanding these laws is a precondition to understanding reality. The post-positivist perspective differs from the positivist in the assertion that no one can completely understand reality, since no one can ever completely comprehend its underlying laws. From an educational standpoint, however, both paradigms focus on knowledge acquisition by students, imparted primarily by the teacher. In addiction, these perspectives understand learning as an internal psychological process (as opposed to an interactional process of person and social context/environment) (Illeris, 2003). Major teaching methods in these paradigms include assigned readings and lectures and student evaluations that emphasize objective testing and assessment. This "transmission model" of education suggests that:

> Teaching is the giving of accurate information, within a structured environment, sequentially over time, leading to a reward for performance; while learning is the correct performance of task, based on cumulative practice, until such time as the information, skills or behaviours imparted by the teacher have been mastered and can be reproduced. (Rumble, 2001, p. 35)

Graham (1997) points out that post-positivist teachers may also incorporate group discussion and subjective assignments (such as essay questions), but these are generally combined with more structured approaches (such as lectures, quizzes and examinations). In both positivist and post-positivist classrooms, the course structure, readings, assignments, and grading are decided by the instructor in advance.

Just as social work research has long been mired in paradigm debates over appropriate research and practice methodologies (see Reamer, 1993 for an excellent summary of this debate), the field of education has seen a similar discourse pitting instructivist versus constructivist approaches (Rumble, 2001; Illeris, 2003). The constructivist perspective argues, in essence, that knowledge is a socially mediated process (where knowledge represents the integration of social construction and internal acquisition and elaboration), as opposed to an individual, cognitive event (Illeris, 2003). Duffy and Cunningham (1997) articulate how the debate is often polarized as "instructivist (or positivist) approaches equal bad teaching," and "constructivist approaches equal good teaching":

> Unfortunately much of the discussion is at the level of slogan and cliché, even bromide. "Students should construct their own knowledge" is being reverentially chanted throughout the halls of many a school/college/department of education these days, and any ap-

proach that is other than constructivist is characterized as promoting passive, rote sterile learning. (p. 170)

In practice, an instructivist approach is often appropriate, and can be used effectively. Edelson (1997) asserts that computer-assisted instruction (a form of individual, computer-based learning that tends to be instructivist in orientation) will always exist for self-directed, independent learners with "on-demand educational needs." In addition, some forms of knowledge need to be expressed uniformly. As Winn and Snyder (1997) put it, "Idiosyncratic understanding of brain surgery or how to fly a plane could lead to disaster!" (p. 131). In addition, Ehrmann (1996) notes that there is considerable variance among instructional methods that fall within the positivist or post-positivist paradigms.

CRITICAL PEDAGOGY

Unlike–and in many ways, as a reaction to–the instructivist approach to teaching, critical pedagogy (also sometimes called emancipatory education) critiques how power operates through the educational process (Foley, 2001). According to critical theorists, institutions of education replicate the forms of dominance and oppression that occur throughout a society. Thus, issues of gender, culture, race, ethnicity, class, age, sexual orientation and disability are reflected and indivisible from curricula, forms and methods of instruction, and classroom interactions. Rossiter (1993) summarizes critical pedagogy as spotlighting the cultural politics inherent in practices that organize knowledge and meaning:

> Critical pedagogy seeks to understand education's role in producing and maintaining relations of domination through the power of knowledge to define what is normative. The project of critical pedagogy is to liberate potential through reflection and action on the complex relations between politics and pedagogy. (p. 77)

The notion that educational institutions are not neutral, but instead support the interests of society's dominant groups ("ruling classes") has its roots in Marxist theory. This perspective challenges systems of education to rethink the roles of instructors and students, and the importance of honouring students' experience and perspectives.

Critical pedagogy directly addresses how traditional forms of education do not adequately address the learning needs of an increasingly diverse student body. For example, bell hooks (1994) notes that most educators (and most students) are poorly prepared to confront diversity in the classroom. She stresses the importance of accepting alternative ways of knowing, or new epistemologies, in a multicultural setting. hooks points out that this can be a challenge for students as well as teachers: students have been conditioned to forms of authority and the presentation of knowledge as neutral, so that attempts to acknowledge the socio-political ideologies underpinning systems of knowledge may be met with resistance. Similarly, Rossiter (1993) argues that the social work curriculum does not always interrogate its own participation in social regulation, even as it speaks about client self-determination and social action. Both writers lament the frequency with which educators operating within the critical pedagogy perspective are marginalized within their disciplines as "radical." As Foley (2001) puts it, "How do we talk about radical adult education in these times, which seem to work only against it?" (p. 71). Field (2001) notes that contemporary perspectives on adult and lifelong learning have resulted in an emphasis on individual solutions to systemic occupational injustices by focusing on individual solutions, thus "fragment[ing] the excluded" (p. 13).

One of the shortcomings of the critical perspective is its tendency to polarize itself in opposition to more mainstream teaching/learning paradigms. In its struggle to articulate the very real problems in educational institutions, there is a tendency to discount attempts by "mainstream" educators and administrators to introduce more student-centred practices. In addition, universities have not solely served to reinforce and replicate cultural hegemony–they have long been the site of social activism and the critique of dominant ideologies. Nonetheless, a significant value of critical pedagogy lies in its challenge to educators to turn their critical gaze toward themselves and their teaching practices. This willingness to explore alternative teaching/learning models has been especially evident in the online learning literature. Perhaps because the medium itself is relatively new or because of its potential to supplement (or supplant) both distance learning and classroom-based approaches, much has been written about equal access to information by students from disadvantaged backgrounds, the balance of power in the classroom, and how to support diverse student voices (Eastmond, 1995). Finally, in general, the rise of constructivism in education, discussed in the next section, is partly the result of the critiques offered by the critical pedagogy perspective.

CONSTRUCTIVIST PARADIGM

Constructivist pedagogy refers to a shift in orientation from teacher-centred to student-centred learning (Murphy, Cathcart et al., 1997). This approach engages students' experiences and underlying beliefs, and emphasizes skills associated with lifelong learning, so that individuals learn how to access the knowledge they need to solve real-life problems (McAlpine, 2000). Current research on learning processes and curriculum design has made constructivism the pedagogical strategy of choice for educators due to its perceived advantages over other instructional models (Organization for Economic Cooperation and Development, OECD, 1996; Oliver, 1999; Smith, 2001). As Oliver (1999) points out, "Theoretically, the strengths of constructivism lie in its emphasis on learning as a process of personal understanding and meaning-making which is active and interpretive. In this domain, learning is viewed as "the construction of meaning rather than the memorization of facts" (p. 242).

There has been considerable research support for the notion that a transmission-model instruction does not generally lead to integrated, long-term learning (Hung, 2002). Indeed, the futility of communicating knowledge that does not address learners' underlying belief systems was devastatingly illustrated in the documentary film *A Private Universe* (Schneps, 1987, cited in Ehrmann, 1996). This film documented the responses of 22 graduating seniors, alumni and faculty from Harvard University, the questions: "Why is it warmer in summer than in the winter?" and "Why does the moon seem to have a different shape each night?" Only two respondents answered the questions correctly, in spite of all graduates having been taught about these phenomena repeatedly while in school. The documentary then shifts to a group of ninth graders who are asked the same questions immediately before and after being taught the material that year. They also answered the questions incorrectly just as the Harvard graduates did. The videotaped instruction of the ninth graders shows an animated teacher who uses models and asks questions, but who never attempts to understand students' pre-existing beliefs or theories which remained essentially untouched by instruction. Other video studies show graduating seniors from Harvard and the Massachusetts Institute of Technology who claim that air weighs nothing and who do not understand what an electric circuit is, along with other research that shows that adults have strong misconceptions about the laws of chance and probability (Organization for Economic Cooperation and Development, 1996). In addition, past research on business school graduates has shown that students taught through traditional (instructivist) modes were perceived to lack the analytical, communication and interpersonal skills that were required to provide effective leadership in the "real world" (McAlpine, 2000). These examples illustrate how individuals' "common sense" continues to prevail over material that is repeatedly taught throughout primary, secondary, and post-secondary school. The individuals may achieve excellent grades, yet not understand nor apply the material they have been taught.

In response to the dilemma of how to promote deep and meaningful learning, all levels of education have been experiencing a "paradigm shift" in instructional orientation. Constructivism has become a widely used umbrella term for a range of theoretical perspectives on learning in the educational research, theory and policy literature (Duffy & Cunningham, 1997). Although constructivist practices in the classroom may share many of the features characteristic of critical pedagogy (such as an emphasis on balanced power in the classroom and the subjective construction of knowledge), this approach is less overtly political, and has its roots more firmly planted in an educational "movement" that has characterized the field of education in the 1990s. The constructivist perspective is based on the key grounding assumptions that "(1) learning is an active process of constructing rather than acquiring knowledge; and (2) instruction is a process of supporting that construction rather than communicating knowledge" (Duffy & Cunningham, 1997, p. 171). In their comprehensive review of constructivist theory and research, Duffy and Cunningham identify four general viewpoints of what constitutes constructivism in education. These include:

1. *Reciprocal teaching*, where the teacher acts as a coach or manager. In this model, learners are assumed to bring valuable knowledge and experience to the learning context, and build knowledge through peer-to-peer interaction, as well as student-teacher and student-content interaction. The instructor's role is primarily facilitative of a collaborative learning process among students.
2. *Problem-based learning* (PBL), which has as its focus student "ownership" of the learning activity. PBL poses real-life, authentic problems, where students discover and develop knowledge and skills through the group process of conceptualizing the salient issues, identifying relevant knowledge domains, and applying new knowledge to resolve the problem. This approach is meant to support students in developing critical thinking, reflection, collaboration and knowledge acquisition.

3. Curriculum development based on *student query*, which acknowledges that students learn more by formulating questions than by answering them. In this model, students are asked to critically engage with course material by posing questions that further group reflection and debate.
4. The *cultural embeddedness* of learning, using the methods and framework of cultural anthropology. In this more explicitly postmodern approach, learning is understood as context-dependent, and different ways of knowing are acknowledged and valued.

Social constructivists also add the importance of peer-to-peer communication and collaboration in the construction of knowledge, where "[l]earning is a process of social negotiation or collaborative sense making, mentoring, and joint knowledge construction" (Wu, 2003, p. 2).

Casting education and learning as processes (as opposed to outcomes) has direct practice implications. In this view, the emphasis is on the learner as an active creator or discoverer of context-relevant skills and information. Constructivist principles have been heavily influenced by the work of John Dewey, who argued against memorization and recitation in favor of learning situated in real-life contexts. Other philosophers such as Jean Jaques Rousseau (1979) and Alfred North Whitehead (1985) also influenced constructivist thought with their assertions that meaningful learning and intellectual development takes place in the learner's interaction with the environment. In addition, the constructivist standpoint draws heavily on the work of Piaget (1977) in that all knowledge is regarded as subjectively constructed. In this view, the learner *creates* meaning from interaction with media and texts, as well as previous experiences and outside influences (such as family and peers) (Krendl, Ware et al., 1997).

Post-modern and poststructural theories, described as less an ideology than a "condition," have also influenced constructivism. Post-modernism is a response to the faith in science and technology and progress characteristic of late modernity (Yeaman, 1997; Yeaman et al., 1997). The condition of postmodernity rejects the modernist notions of infinite progression towards betterment, and replaces them with (a) a belief in plurality or multiple "realities," (b) a critical questioning of the benefits of technology, and (c) a questioning of the inevitability of progress, including how progress itself is defined and measured. Yeaman and colleagues (1997) note that the modernist (or post-positivist) educational model has been one of *define-develop-evaluate*, and that "much of the history of instructional development has been a series of attempts to 'fine-tune' this model" (p. 256). They argue that an alternative to viewing education as the transmission of knowledge is to regard it as the *making of meaning*.

These philosophical roots have led to practice models that emphasize both learner engagement (with other learners) and active construction of knowledge. Shneiderman (1999) argues that instructional models such as discovery learning and problem-based learning represent the next step in education:

> We all remember the empty faces of students seated in rows, intermittently taking notes, and trying to retain disjointed facts. This old lecture style seems as antiquated as a 19th century clockwork mechanism; familiar and charming, but erratic and no longer adequate. . . . The post-TV era will be different. Computing and communications technologies offer opportunities for engagement with other people and the power tools to construct remarkable artifacts and experiences. (p. 1)

Although Shneiderman's somewhat tongue-in-cheek review of education and media is fairly reductionist and simplistic, he does capture the general trend towards concern with more active learning by students. Within the constructivist paradigm, problem-based learning (PBL) in particular has emerged as an instructional strategy of choice (Duffy & Cunningham, 1997; Hmelo, Gotterer et al., 1997; Shneiderman, 1999; Hung, 2002). These authors suggest that new technologies such as on-line learning are the "power tools" which will facilitate the adoption of alternative teaching/learning practices.

However, online tools and applications are insufficient to create truly constructivist learning communities, even where instructors have been explicitly constructivist in their design of collaborative tasks and problem-based scenarios. Research on learners' critical engagement with online, collaborative learning tasks has shown a discrepancy between the instructor's intentions of student behaviour, and students' actual behaviour (Linder & Rochon, 2003; Leinon et al., 2003). This research reinforces the notion that it may be important to engage students in a "meta-narrative" about the nature of learning in order to prepare them for a constructivist "classroom."

PBL begins with a focus on real-life problems presented in authentic, relevant contexts, where students are guided towards acquiring knowledge and skills (Hung, 2002). Duffy and Cunningham (1997) view PBL as superior to such other "problem-focused" instructional models as case-based learning and goal-based learning. The latter two focus on a case description or goal-oriented decision situated in the past, while PBL demands action learning on a "real time" problem or issue. They note that PBL emerged in medical education in the 1970s and has since gained popularity across other professional disciplines and fields, including education, business, psychology and social work.

The primary grounding assumption of PBL is that "we do not learn in a content domain simply to acquire information but rather to bring that information to bear on our daily lives" (Duffy & Cunningham, 1997, p. 190). Furthermore, instructors can use problems in a number of different ways, including as a reference point to focus the learner's attention, as an assessment of learning, to illustrate a particular point, as a vehicle for developing critical thinking skills, or as a stimulus for authentic activity in the learning context (Hmelo, Gotterer et al., 1997). One of the key elements in PBL is its introduction of learner-generated experiences of surprise, conflict or novelty in the educational process (Marshall et al., 1999). Because learners "discover" knowledge in the process of solving real-life problems, its relevance and limitations are directly experienced.

Although PBL approaches appear promising, their application in human service has a number of potential problems. Fenwick and Parsons (1998) argue that PBL in the helping professions positions the professional as the "custodian of the truth. The professional's normalizing gaze divines, adjudicates and classifies the world's problems, then deploys its disciplinary knowledge to systematically reform and regulate these problems" (p. 57). In this view, PBL biases student practitioners to frame problems and arrive at solutions, thus reinforcing their role as the authority or expert. This critique is especially relevant to social work education, which emphasizes an ecological understanding of the client's situation and perspective. Fenwick and Parsons suggest the situative perspective as an alternative to PBL. This view stresses that each learner is influenced by his or her social, cultural and historical factors intersecting with the network of people, objects and meanings in any particular case. Thus, understanding is itself perceived as situational; they note that a more suitable professional response to life's difficulties is not to solve, but to seek to understand. The authors point to professional responses of compassion, consolation and solidarity as preferable to the "professional rush to transform the flux and pain of life into solve-able problems" (p. 62). Therefore, it may be important to re-frame "problems" as "situations" requiring the collaborative understanding of both professionals and clients. The key issue is who has the authority to define a situation as a problem? In many cases, "problems" are the result of structural inequities, systemic oppression or marginalization, and casting these as individual problems can obscure alternative interpretations or understanding.

Grabinger (1996, cited in Molenda, Russell & Smaldino, 1998) has coined the acronym REAL (Rich Environments for Active Learning) to summarize the desired outcome of PBL/constructivist models. This model emphasizes the importance of situating learning within the context in which the learning will be applied. Currently, however, REALs in academic settings tend to occur as local experiments, in spite of growing consensus that "constructivist learning environments" are an ideal (Molenda, Russell et al., 1998). Nevertheless, Molenda and colleagues point out that "the upward slope of this trend is still low but could accelerate as educational institutions are held more accountable for the transferability of student learning to the world of work" (p. 9). This is especially likely in professional disciplines such as social work, nursing, medicine, and business, with their emphases on practice skills. Indeed, many faculties of medicine and business administration have been completely restructured around the PBL model.

Also based on a real-world orientation, *adult education/learning* constitutes a fairly specialized field of inquiry within the disciplines of education and psychology. Adult learning is defined in contrast to theoretical and practice research with students in the primary and secondary grades. This field overlaps with, and is informed by both critical and constructivist teaching/learning theory and research, but has as its focus adult higher education. Charters (1982) defines adult education as,

> . . . the identification, selection, provision, arrangement, and evaluation of learning activities for persons with certain characteristics. They must be physically mature and consciously learning in order to achieve their selected goals. They must be learning as part of their life pattern, on a part-time basis or learning on a full-time basis for only short periods of time. They are also learning in order to assume fuller responsibilities as a citizen, worker, family person, and social being living in and with concern for the physical environment. (p. 2)

Although this definition is somewhat restrictive, it is useful in its implication of the three major features underlying adult education/learning: (1) learners bring rich and important life experiences to the learning context; (2) learners are generally motivated and capable of self-directing their learning; and (3) the learning itself is goal directed towards real-life applications. Coulshed (1993) notes that up until the 1970s, the adult education field was primarily concerned with improving instructional techniques and models, and the focus was primarily on the instructor.

Educational "reformers" such as Paolo Freire (1972) questioned the authority of the teacher and argued that such a role robs students of self-respect and makes critical learning impossible. Carl Rogers was also instrumental in his emphasis on the democratization of education (Foley, 2001). This shift in perspective led to the emergence of the andragogical model to describe the unique qualities that adults bring to learning situations (Knowles, 1984). Andragogy can be defined as a process in which educators work collaboratively with students to transform their meaning schemes (that is, their beliefs, feelings, interpretations and decisions) through reflection (Mezirow, 1991). The model assumes that learners are self-directing, that adults bring a greater volume and different quality of experience from younger learners, that adults are motivated to learn by a need for information or knowledge related to some aspect of their lives, that their perspectives on learning are life-centred, problem-centred or task-centred, and that their motivation is primarily internal (Knowles, 1984; Cranton, 1994). The concept of transformative learning goes beyond an addition to existing knowledge, representing a fundamental shift "in which the learner actually creates a new self" (Gasker & Cascio, 1998, p. 161). The principle of self-directed learning has been most associated with andragogy, and characterizes the major aim of adult education (Eastmond, 1995).

DISCUSSION:
TOWARD AN INTEGRATED THEORETICAL FRAMEWORK

Graham (1997) identifies four teaching/learning paradigms, each tied to a particular epistemological stance. These paradigms, positivist, postpositivist, critical and constructivist, imply different educational approaches and outcomes, as well as different ontological and epistemological world views. Coulshed (1993) draws on adult education theory and research, noting that "andragogical" concepts represent "a paradigm shift from looking at teaching to looking at the whole nature of learning" (Coulshed, 1993, p. 5). This theory of learning proposes a circular or cyclical (as opposed to linear) representation of knowledge acquisition, involving processes of concrete experience, reflective observation, abstract conceptualization and active experimentation.

Traditionally, human services education has meant "face-to-face contact with students in 'closed-system' classrooms" (Jennings, Siegel et al., 1995, p. 3). However, clinically-focused distance education programs are growing in response to professional education and development needs by professionals who cannot attend classroom-based programs (Blakely, 1992; Jennings, Siegel et al., 1995; Jennings & Dirksen, 1997). Online learning is unique in that it can span both these learning contexts: computer-based courses have been delivered as social work distance education offerings (Bemister & Kamp, 1998; Ouellette, 1998; MacFadden, Dumbrill et al., 2000; Schoech, 2000), and have been integrated into classroom-based social work courses to enrich learning and communication/networking (Latting, 1994; Patterson & Yaffe, 1994; Lancaster, Stokes et al., 1998).

Implementing online learning in human services education implies a need to reassess and possibly alter existing pedagogy. In considering the implications of applying a critical/constructivist approach in the social work classroom, Coulshed (1993) notes that integrating this model demands a commitment from both faculty and students:

> Feedback from students usually indicates that "chalk and talk" teaching has grave limitations. It does not create the conditions for self-directedness, fails to use learners as a resource for each other, tends to be formal and authority-oriented, is balanced toward content, and reduces learning-by-doing. And yet, in the past, some students' earlier experiences of power relations in education had left them anxious, leading to dependency and of relying on "being fed" information. Thus, to remove these obstructions to adult learning, it has had to be discussed at some lengths with each intake of students in a prolonged induction/transition phase, how the staff view the nature of teaching and learning. (p. 8)

One of the problems, however, with Coulshed's account of implementing an adult learning model in social work education is that it polarizes adult learning/constructivist methods as "good," and traditional post-positivist (or instructivist) methods as "bad." For example, it is false to claim that "chalk and talk" teaching does not use students as resources for each other. Many lecture-style courses include student tutorials or study groups for precisely this function. Didactic instruction may be accompanied by activity-based assignments in order to promote "learning by doing." On the other hand, constructivist methods may be subtly oriented toward pre-determined content if the instructor sets problem-based or case-based scenarios with a prior "right" answer in mind.

Thus, it may be more helpful to conceptualize constructivist theory as leading to a clear set of principles or guidelines, but recognizing that other frameworks still have a contribution to make.

Reeves and Reeves (1997) position Web-Based Instruction along a number of pedagogical or learning dimensions, illustrating that this medium can accommodate a mix of instructivist (or positivist/post-positivist) and constructivist philosophies. They note that the type of subject matter, learner goals and learning context may suggest different pedagogical (andragogical) techniques and orientations. This "informed eclecticism" in applying educational theory to practice is consistent with Schön's (1991) concept of the 'reflective practitioner' in social work, where practice wisdom is used in an eclectic combination with research and theory. Reeves and Reeves (1997) argue that it is not the technology that makes online learning unique, but the pedagogical dimensions that it can be designed to deliver. Thus, online learning can be regarded as more a channel than a container of learning tools.

Figure 2 demonstrates the reciprocal relationships between human services education, WBI and teaching learning theories, where each influences, and is influenced, by the other. The dotted arrows represent the influence of CMC on the relationships between social work education, teaching/learning theories and online learning. Given that technology is not neutral, it is important to acknowledge the mediating effect that online communication and contexts would be expected to have on these relationships.

FIGURE 2. Integrated Theoretical Framework for WBI in Human Services Education

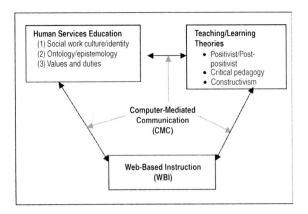

LINKING THEORY WITH PRACTICE

This review of major teaching and learning theories is intended to assist human services educators to reflect on how their online courses are informed by particular frameworks and orientations. Further, it is important to explicitly link these theoretical underpinnings with online teaching strategies and applications. Table 1 summarizes key theoretical principles of instructivist, critical and constructivist perspectives, and how these can be applied in an online learning context. In addition, the advantages and disadvantages related to the application of these principles are noted.

One of the difficulties in distilling the principles and strategies of these different forms of teaching and learning is that it fails to take into consideration how students respond to individual instructors, and not just pedagogical strategies. For example, in order for critical and constructivist aims to be realized, it is essential to develop a learning community characterized by psychological safety, learner engagement and self-motivation. Indeed, is it possible to create a truly critical or constructivist classroom in an educational system that is structured around instructivist principles? When grades become the primary vehicle for student advancement, it is difficult to foster a learning environment predicated on collaboration, support and shared power. In practice, many instructors employ a blend of strategies, even as they may approach teaching from a particular theoretical stance. As constructivist approaches become more widely-accepted and institutionalized, and as new technologies in online learning become available and accessible, online pedagogy will continue to change and evolve.

CONCLUSION

This article summarizes major and current pedagogical theory, with an emphasis on its relationship to online teaching and learning. Only through a clear understanding of theoretical frameworks in education is it possible to critically analyze the approaches taken in online learning applications and assess their pedagogical value. In addition, the fields of education, technology and human services are continuing to change and evolve. The importance of theory in responding to these changes is articulated by Illeris (2003), who points out:

TABLE 1. Implications of Theoretical Perspectives for Online Learning

Theoretical Framework	Key Principles	Online Learning Tools and Techniques	Advantages	Disadvantages/Challenges
Positivist/Post-positivist (Instructivist)	• Pre-determined instructional content/outcomes • Knowledge communicated by the teacher • Teacher as expert • Emphasis on content over process	• Learning objects/modularized content • Quizzes and tests • Individual assignments • Assigned readings • Rubrics (sets of guidelines facilitating objective assessment)	• Clarity re: content to be covered • Clearly defined roles and responsibilities of instructor/students • Easier to assign grades and other "objective" assessment measures	• Fails to engage in underlying belief systems • Rote learning emphasized over deeper learning • Gap between educational content and real-world applications • May encourage learner passivity (versus critical engagement) • May be responsible for the drop-out problem in online education
Critical	• Lack of precise learning aims • Democratic (power is shared between teacher/students) • Goal is to help learners act collectively against oppressive structures • Emphasis on process over content and the development of alternative ways of knowing/understanding	• Peer mentoring • Synchronous and asynchronous group discussion • Problem-based learning • Community development and social action	• Demands critique and reflection on the part of students • Links learning with real-world issues and problems • Fosters critical thinking • Moves towards empowerment/social change	• This form of education can be challenging to incorporate into academic structures that emphasize external assessment (e.g., grading) • Can engender feelings of discomfort in learners • Demands a radical departure from traditional forms of teaching
Constructivist	• Knowledge is socially constructed • Learning is a collaborative process versus a discrete cognitive event • Instructor as guide versus expert • Emphasis on real-world applications of knowledge	• Peer mentoring • Synchronous and asynchronous discussion groups • Guidelines re: participation • Problem-based learning • Online simulations/role plays • Student self-assessment	• Relevance of knowledge to real-world settings • Engages underlying belief systems • Promotes "deep" learning, critical thought and reflection	• Challenging for instructors and students to depart from traditional forms of teaching • May be difficult to create truly authentic learning problems in an online context • Not all students willing to engage at this level.

48

. . . adequate theories can help us to understand what happens to learning when conditions change. The changes of late modernity are fundamentally changing the conditions of learning, and if politicians, administrators and educators are to cope adequately with this, as educational researchers we must be able to develop adequate theories matching the problems experienced at all levels. (p. 404)

Theory, research, and practice are inextricably linked. A strong theoretical foundation can inform our responses to changing educational and learning environments, guide the development of new pedagogical approaches, and increase our understanding of students' learning needs and preferences. The shift from instructivist modes of teaching to a constructivist conceptualization has been of major importance in the education field, and is increasingly seen in online learning applications. Our task as educators and researchers is to continue to test and build on theoretical developments in ways that inform increasing pedagogical excellence in online teaching and learning.

REFERENCES

Bemister, C. and Kamp, R. (1998). *Testing the waters in distance education: You don't have to get your hair wet.* 2nd Annual Information Technologies for Social Work Education and Practice Conference, Charleston, SC, University of South Carolina.

Blakely, T. J. (1992). A model for distance education delivery. *Journal of Social Work Education,* 28(2): 214-221.

Charters, A. N. (1982). Counselors in adult and continuing education. Conference on Guidance and Counselling Services and the Selection of Appropriate and Efficient Information Supports and Resources for Adult Education, Zimbabwe, Africa, UNESCO/EDRS.

Cook, D. L. (1995). Community and computer-generated distance learning environments. *New Directions for Adult and Continuing Education,* 67: 33-39.

Coulshed, V. (1993). Adult learning: Implications for teaching in social work education. *British Journal of Social Work,* 23: 1-13.

Dean, R. G. (1993). Constructivism: An approach to clinical practice. *Smith College Studies in Social Work,* 63(2): 126-146.

Duffy, T. M. and Cunningham, D. J. (1997). Constructivism: Implications for the design and delivery of instruction. in Jonassen, D. H. (Ed.), *Handbook of Research for Educational Communications and Technology.* New York: Simon & Schuster Macmillan: 170-198.

Eastmond, D. V. (1995). *Alone but together: Adult distance study through computer conferencing.* Cresskill, NJ: Hampton Press, Inc.

Edelson, P. J. (1997). *Technology and the adult classroom of the future: New possibilities for teachers and learners.* Twenty-second International Conference on Improving University Teaching and Learning, Rio de Janeiro, Brazil, U.S. Department of Education, Educational Resources Information Centre (ERIC).

Ehrmann, S. C. (1996). *Asking the right question: What does research tell us about technology and higher learning?* Annenberg/CPB Projects/Learner Online. http://www.learner.org/edtech/rscheval/rightquestion.html, accessed July 27, 2004.

Fenwick, T. and Parsons, J. (1998). Boldly solving the world: A critical analysis of problem-based learning as a method of professional education. *Studies in the Education of Adults*, 30(1): 53-66.

Fernback, J. (1997). The individual within the collective: Virtual ideology and the realization of collective principles. *Virtual culture: Identity and communication in cybersociety.* S. G. Jones. London: Sage Publications: 36-54.

Field, J. (2001). Lifelong education. *International Journal of Lifelong Education*, 20(1/2): 3-15.

Foley, G. (2001). Radical adult education and learning. *International Journal of Lifelong Education*, 20(1/2): 71-88.

Freire, P. (1972). *Pedagogy of the oppressed.* Harmondsworth, Penguin.

Gasker, J. A. and Cascio, T. (1998). Computer-mediated interaction: A tool for facilitating the educational helping relationship. Second Annual Information Technologies for Social Work Education and Practice Conference, Charleston, SC: University of South Carolina.

Graham, M. A. (1997). Empowering social work faculty: Alternative paradigms for teaching and learning. *Journal of Teaching in Social Work*, 15(1/2): 33-49.

Hmelo, C. E., Gotterer, G. S., and Bransford, J.D. (1997). A theory-driven approach to assessing the cognitive effects of PBL. *Instructional Science*, 25: 387-408.

hooks, b. (1994). *Teaching to Transgress: Education as the Practice of Freedom.* New York: Routledge.

Hung, D. (2002). Situated cognition and problem-based learning: Implications for learning and instruction with technology. *Journal of Interactive Learning Research*, 13(4): 393-415.

Illeris, K. (2003). Towards a contemporary and comprehensive theory of learning. *International Journal of Lifelong Education*, 22(4): 396-406.

Jennings, J., Siegel, E., and Conklin, J.J. (1995). Social work education and distance learning: Applications for continuing education. *Journal of Continuing Social Work Education*, 6(3): 3-7.

Jennings, M. M. and Dirksen, D. J. (1997). Facilitating change: A process for adoption of Web-based instruction, in Khan, B. H. (Ed.), *Web-Based Instruction.* Englewood Cliffs, NJ: Educational Technology Publications: 111-116.

Jones, S. G. (1997). The Internet and its social landscape. *Virtual Culture: Identity and Communication in Cybersociety.* S. G. Jones. London: Sage Publications: 7-35.

Knowles, M. S. (1984). *Andragogy in Action.* San Francisco, Jossey-Bass.

Krendl, K. A., Ware, W. H., Reid, K. A., and Warren, R. (1997). Learning by any other name: Communication research traditions in learning and media, in Jonassen, D. H. (Ed.), *Handbook of Research for Educational Communications and Technology.* Toronto: Prentice Hall.

Lancaster, K., J., Stokes, J., and Summary, L. (1998). *The use of WebBoard conferencing in social work education.* Second Annual Information Technologies for Social Work Education and Practice Conference, Charleston, SC, University of South Carolina.

Latting, J. K. (1994). Diffusion of computer-mediated communication in a graduate social work class: Lessons from "The Class from Hell." *Computers in Human Services,* 10(3): 21-45.

Lavooy, M. J. and Newlin, M.H. (2003). Computer-mediated communication: Online instruction and interactivity. *Journal of Interactive Learning Research,* 14(2): 157-166.

Leinonen, P., Jarvela, S., and Lipponen, L. (2003). Individual students' interpretations of their contribution to the computer-mediated discussions. *Journal of Interactive Learning Research,* 14(1): 99-123.

Linder, U. and Rochon, R. (2003). Using chat to support collaborative learning: Quality assurance strategies to promote success. *Education Media International,* 40(1/2): 75-89.

MacFadden, R. J., Dumbrill, G. C., and Maiter, S. (2000). Web-based education in a graduate faculty of social work: Crossing the new frontier. *New Technology in the Human Services,* 13(1/2): 27-38.

Maor, D. (2003). The teacher's role in developing interaction and reflection in an online learning community. *Education Media International,* 40(1/2): 127-137.

Marshall, J. N., Brett, P.J., Stewart, M.A., and Truls, O. (1999). *Using e-mail based continuing medical education for family physicians–Can it work?* http://www.Med-Ed-Online.org/t000009.htm. Accessed July 27, 2004.

McAlpine, I. (2000). Collaborative learning online. *Distance Education,* 21(1): 66-80.

McLuhan, E. and Zingrone, F. (1995). *Essential McLuhan.* Concord, Ontario: Anansi.

Molenda, M., J., Russell, D., and Smaldino, S. (1998). Trends in media and technology in education and training. *Educational Media and Technology Yearbook.* R. M. Branch and M. A. Fitzgerald. Englewood, CO: Libraries Unlimited, Inc.

Murphy, K. L., Cathcart, S., and Kodali, S. (1997). Integrating distance education technologies in a graduate course. *TechTrends, Association for Educational Communications and Technology,* 42(1): 24-28.

Oliver, R. (1999). Exploring strategies for online teaching and learning. *Distance Education* 20(2): 254.

Organization for Economic Cooperation and Development, OECD (1996). *Adult Learning in a New Technological Era.* Paris: OECD.

Ouellette, P. M. (1998). Moving toward computer-supported instruction in social work practice: The "Virtual Classroom." 2nd Annual Information Technologies for Social Work Education and Practice Conference, Charleston, SC, University of South Carolina.

Patterson, D. A. and Yaffe, J. (1994). Hypermedia computer-based education in social work education. *Journal of Social Work Education,* 30(2): 267-277.

Piaget, J. (1977). *The Development of Thought: Equilibration of Cognitive Structures.* New York: Viking.

Reamer, F. G. (1993). *The Philosophical Foundations of Social Work.* New York: Columbia University Press.

Reeves, T. C. and Reeves, P. M. (1997). Effective dimensions of interactive learning on the World Wide Web, in Khan, B.J. (Ed.) *Web-Based Instruction*. Englewood Cliffs, NJ: Educational Technology Publications: 59-66.

Romiszowski, A. J. and Mason, R. (1997). Computer-mediated communication, in Jonassen, D. H. (Ed.) *Handbook of Research for Educational Communications and Technology*. New York: Simon & Schuster Macmillan: 438-456.

Rossiter, A. (1996). Finding meaning for social work in transitional times: Reflections on change, in Gould, N. and Taylor, I. (Eds.), *Reflective learning for social work*. Brookfield, VT: Ashgate Publishing Company.

Rossiter, A. B. (1993). Teaching from a critical perspective: Towards empowerment in social work education. *Canadian Social Work Review*, 10(1): 76-89.

Rousseau, J. J. (1979). *Emile: Or, On Education*. New York: Basic Books.

Rumble, G. (2001). Re-inventing distance education, 1971-2001. *International Journal of Lifelong Education*, 20(1/2): 31-43.

Schoech, D. (2000). Teaching over the Internet: Results of one doctoral course. *Research on Social Work Practice*, 10(4): 467-486.

Schon, D. (1991). *The Reflective Practitioner*. Vermont: Aldershot, Gower.

Shneiderman, B. (1999). *Engagement and construction: Education strategies for the post-TV era, University of Maryland.* http://citeseer.nj.nec.com/shneiderman92engagement.html. Accessed July 27, 2004.

Smith, E. S. (2001). Writing Web-based distance education courses for adult learners. *American Journal of Distance Education*, 15(2): 53-65.

Visser, J. A. (2000). Faculty work in developing and teaching Web-based distance courses: A case study of time and effort. *American Journal of Distance Education, 14(3): 21-32.*

Watson, N. (1997). Why we argue about virtual community: A case study of the Phish. net fan community. *Virtual Culture: Identity and Communication in Cybersociety.* S. G. Jones. London: Sage Publications: 102-132.

Weick, A. (1993). Reconstructing social work education. *Journal of Teaching in Social Work*, 8(1/2): 11-30.

Whitehead, A.N. (1985). *The Aims of Education and Other Essays.* New York: Free Press.

Winn, W. and Snyder, D. (1997). Cognitive perspectives in psychology in Jonassen, D. H. *Handbook of Research for Educational Communications and Technology*. New York: Simon & Schuster Macmillan: 112-142.

Wu, A. (2003) Supporting electronic discourse: Principles of design from a social constructivist perspective. *Journal of Interactive Learning Research*, 14 (2): 167-185.

Yeaman, A. R. J. (1997). The Discourse on Technology in Branch, R. M. and Minor, B. B. (Eds.), *Educational Media and Technology Yearbook*. ERIC Clearinghouse on Information & Technology 22: 46-57.

Yeaman, A. et al. (1997). Postmodern and poststructural theory in Jonassen, D. H. (Ed.), *Handbook of Research for Educational Communications and Technology*. New York: Simon & Schuster Macmillan: 253-269.

Faculty Perceptions of the Effectiveness of Web-Based Instruction in Social Work Education: A National Study

Brenda Moore

SUMMARY. This paper presents the findings of a national study that examined the perceptions of faculty with Web-based teaching experience concerning the effectiveness of Web-based instruction as compared to face-to-face instruction in social work education. The findings suggest that faculty perceived face-to-face instruction to be more effective than Web-based instruction in all curriculum areas. However, the extent of perceived effectiveness of Web-based instruction varied by curriculum area. Also, online teaching in areas such as practice was viewed as least effective, suggesting that the traditional "no significant difference" conclusions between face-to-face and online teaching need to be examined more closely. *[Article copies available for a fee from The Haworth Document Delivery Service: 1-800-HAWORTH. E-mail address: <docdelivery@haworthpress.com> Website: <http://www.HaworthPress.com> © 2005 by The Haworth Press, Inc. All rights reserved.]*

KEYWORDS. Perceptions, Web-based instruction, online learning, social work education

Brenda Moore, PhD, LMSW-AP, is Assistant Professor and BSW Director, Department of Social Work, Texas A&M University-Commerce, P.O. Box 3011, Commerce, TX 75429.

[Haworth co-indexing entry note]: "Faculty Perceptions of the Effectiveness of Web-Based Instruction in Social Work Education: A National Study." Moore, Brenda. Co-published simultaneously in *Journal of Technology in Human Services* (The Haworth Press, Inc.) Vol. 23, No. 1/2, 2005, pp. 53-66; and: *Web-Based Education in the Human Services: Models, Methods, and Best Practices* (eds: MacFadden et al.) The Haworth Press, Inc., 2005, pp. 53-66. Single or multiple copies of this article are available for a fee from The Haworth Document Delivery Service [1-800-HAWORTH, 9:00 a.m. - 5:00 p.m. (EST). E-mail address: docdelivery@haworthpress.com].

Available online at http://www.haworthpress.com/web/JTHS
© 2005 by The Haworth Press, Inc. All rights reserved.
Digital Object Identifier: 10.1300/J017v023n01_04

Technology is impacting social work education in significant ways. Technology has progressed rapidly, and research is focused on understanding the pedagogical questions raised by web-based education (Luchini, 1998). Technology is being used extensively in classroom instruction; even more revolutionary is instruction that relies totally on technology as the means of transmission and interaction. Regardless of the type of technology or the extent to which it is used, Brand (1995) cautioned that technologies must "serve, not pervert, the best traditions and successes of American higher education" (p. 39). What are the implications of education changing from traditional methods, featuring students and instructors together in classrooms, to Internet technologies that link students and instructors who may never meet face to face? How do faculty perceive the utility of Web-based instruction as compared with face-to-face instruction and do these perceptions vary across different areas in the social work curriculum?

The use of the Web is an inevitable part of higher education and an integral part of the 21st century. The purpose of this study was to explore how faculty with experience in Web-based instruction perceived the effectiveness (defined as meeting course objectives) of Web-based instruction across the social work curriculum.

LITERATURE REVIEW

Distance Education in Social Work Instruction

Changes occurring in work and educational environments have resulted in a demand for distance education as a "widely accepted means for higher education to provide broader access and achieve cost-efficiencies while maintaining quality programs" (Eastmond, 1998, p. 33). Web-based instruction reflects current efforts in the use of technology to enhance education. The challenge for distance educators is moving from the use of traditional, low-tech delivery technologies (such as print, telephone, television, and mail) to using a variety of new software technologies such as 3-D virtual reality, animation, and streaming audio and visual technology (Fleishman, 1996).

Wilson (1999) described three chronological phases for distance education in social work over the past twenty years: distance education, distributed classroom model, and computer-based education. This most recent phase of development, computer-based education, reflects the use of computers, the Internet, and the Web to transmit coursework. A key element in this type of distance education delivery system is the change from a synchronous (real time) interaction to asynchronous interaction. In asynchronous interaction, the classroom is wholly or partly replaced by individualized interactions or independent work (Wilson, 1999).

Recently, social work educators have begun using a variety of electronic media to provide instruction (Ashery, 2001; Blakely & Schoenherr, 1995; Coe & Elliott, 1999; Forster & Washington, 2000; Stocks & Freddolino, 2000; Schoech & Helton, 2001; Faux & Black-Hughes, 2000). While there is limited information regarding the extent of exclusively Web-based instruction (Schoech, 2000; Sharkey, 2000), many Web tools are used routinely in social work education (Giffords, 1998). There have been national conferences that covered technology and social work education since 1997 at the University of South Carolina. There has also been a proliferation of social work websites and resources linking technology and social work (Vernon, 2001). Proceedings of these conferences and reviews of relevant web sites have been published in the *Journal of Technology in Human Services*.

The Web has changed how social workers teach and learn (Vernon, 2001; Rafferty, 1998). Social work education needs to teach skills for using new technologies, provide information about the impact and influence of technology on social work practice, and actively use technology as a tool to teach social work (Rafferty, 1998). Sharkey (2000) issued the challenge that social work educators need to be models of lifelong learning and be open to new ideas, skills, and opportunities presented by technological changes, including Web-based instruction. However, the historical development of computer-based education emphasized a dichotomy between social work faculty, professionals, and students who embrace new technologies and those who are emphatically resistant to it (Marson, 1997; Hick, 1999).

Social Work Curriculum and Content Areas

The purposes of social work education are to "prepare competent and effective professionals, to develop social work knowledge, and to provide leadership in the development of service delivery systems. . . . Social work education enables students to integrate the knowledge, values, and skills of the social work profession for competent practice" (CSWE, 2002, p. 6). All social work programs must provide "foundation content" that is the basis for developing the knowledge, values, and skills of the profession. CSWE requires all social work programs to have objectives and courses reflecting the following content areas: values and ethics, diversity, populations-at-risk, social and economic justice, human behavior and the social environment, social welfare policy and services, social work practice (with individuals, families, groups, organizations, and communities), research, and field education. The Education and Policy Accreditation Standards of CSWE further defines the specific content for each area that should be reflected in the curriculum. While there are a number of existing studies on the use of technology in specific social work courses, research is needed to understand the use of technology across the curriculum and whether technology is more suited to the content in some content areas.

Research and Evaluation of Distance Education and Web-Based Instruction in Social Work

Research and publications on various aspects of distance education, technology, and social work education have proliferated in the past few years. In a survey completed by 239 accredited U.S. schools of social work in 1995-96, approximately 16% reported using distance learning primarily in the forms for satellite transmission, television, and compressed video (Siegel, Jennings, Conklin, & Napoletano-Flynn, 1998). The courses that were most frequently taught at a distance were HBSE, policy, research, and methods. The authors concluded that the content areas selected for distance education were consistent with the profession's emphasis on students' relationships and interpersonal skills (Siegel, Jennings, Conklin, & Napoletano-Flynn, 1998). A number of studies also indicated that equivalent outcomes existed when distance education courses were compared with face-to-face courses in terms of student satisfaction, interactions, and performance (Macy, Rooney, Hollister, & Freddolino, 2001; McFall & Freddolino, 2000; Biner, Dean & Mellinger, 1994).

The use and types of technologies presented in these studies vary greatly, measuring different independent and dependent variables (Macy et al., 2001). Findings from studies on earlier forms of distance learning cannot necessarily be generalized to courses that are provided through Web-based instruction. The implications for the teacher, the learner, and the presentation of content may be quite different in an asynchronous environment. Some of these studies raise additional issues that merit further consideration, such as what elements of Web-based instruction facilitate different aspects of social work education.

Macy et al. (2001) posed questions as to whether each type of technology is equally effective for teaching different content areas. What characteristics of teaching style and pedagogy are associated with success in different formats of instruction? What characteristics of teaching style are associated with success across different technologies? These issues require additional research in order to more fully understand the implications of Web-based instruction in social work education.

METHOD

This study surveyed the opinions of those with experience in web-based teaching. Specifically, it explored the perceived effectiveness of Web-based instruction in social work education in order to determine if there were any differences when comparing Web-based instruction and face-to-face instruction across various CSWE-defined curriculum areas.

Participants

There are approximately 6,600 full-time faculty teaching in accredited social work programs (Lennon, 2002). However, there is no data available on the number of faculty who are experienced in Web-based instruction. An e-mail letter was sent to 538 deans and directors of CSWE-accredited social work programs across the United States who had e-mail addresses or websites published in the CSWE 2002 directory of accredited programs, asking for names of faculty who had experience using Web-based instruction in social work. The same request was published on the BPD (Baccalaureate Program Directors) listserv.

Using a snowball sampling method, faculty were identified by social work deans and program directors. In addition, authors of published articles and presenters at national conferences on Web-based education were included. The 174 faculty who were identified as having expertise in Web-based instructions were invited to participate in the study and provided with the survey website. Of these, 81 faculty agreed to participate.

Of the 81 respondents, 59 completed all sections of the survey and the remaining 22 respondents only partially completed the survey. Three of the 59 respondents were omitted from the study sample because none of their reported courses used more than 50% Web-based instruction, resulting in 56 responses for analysis. For the purposes of this study, Web-based instruction was defined as 50% of the course content offered via the Web. Because there is a small number of social work faculty who are teaching social work classes completely online, this definition of Web-based instruction helped to maximize the number of respondents from this relatively small pool of experts.

In terms of rank and tenure, 29% of the sample indicated they were professors, 30% were associate professors, 30% were assistant professors, and the remaining 11% were adjuncts, part-time instructors, or other. The study sample included 27 tenured faculty (48%), 22 untenured faculty (39%), and 7 (13%) respondents who indicated they were non-tenure track.

The range of full-time teaching experience of the sample faculty was from 3 years to 32 years. Twenty-one percent of the sample had less than 5 years of full-time teaching experience, 30% had 6-10 years of experience, 17% had 11-20 years experience, and 32% had more than 20 years of full-time teaching experience.

Instrumentation

An online survey was developed as the instrument to collect data. The survey used a Likert scale to measure the perceived effectiveness of Web-based instruction and face-to-face instruction in teaching about values and ethics, diversity, populations-at-risk, and social and economic justice, based on 14 CSWE accreditation standards. A score of "1" indicated "not at all effective" and a score of "5" indicated "completely effective." The survey also asked respondents to indicate their perceptions of effectiveness for both Web-based instruction and face-to-face instruction in meeting the 35 CSWE standards related to the five core curriculum areas (HBSE, policy, practice, research and field) using the same 5-point rating scale.

RESULTS

Respondents were asked to provide information about the Web-based courses they had taught. The study sample (N = 56) indicated they had taught from one to ten different courses using Web-based instruction, reflecting a total of 139 different courses taught. (The information on courses taught more than once are addressed in Table 2). Table 1 provides a breakdown on the number of different courses taught.

In addition to reporting on the number of different courses they had taught, faculty were asked to list and provide information on each

TABLE 1. Number of *Different* Courses Taught by Sample (n = 50) Using Web-Based Instruction

Number of different WBI courses taught	Number of responses to this question	Total number of different Web-based courses (Col 1 × Col 2)
Total	50 (100.0%)	139
1	14 (28.0%)	14
2	11 (22.0%)	22
3	12 (24.0%)	36
4	6 (12.0%)	24
5	4 (8.0%)	20
6	1 (2.0%)	6
7	1 (2.0%)	7
10	1 (2.0%)	10

course they had taught. They listed the course title, the level of instruction (BSW, MSW or PhD), how many times they had taught this course, what percentage of the course was taught using Web-based tools rather than face-to-face instruction, and which CSWE curriculum content the course most reflected. Respondents were allowed to enter information for up to seven courses.

The total number of Web-based courses reflected in subsequent areas of data analysis was based on responses to each Web-based course listed. In other words, a respondent may have indicated teaching two different Web-based courses (Table 1), but they may have taught each of those two courses several times (Table 2). When the listed courses were multiplied by the number of times taught, a total of 336 online courses were taught by the sample.

Respondents were asked to identify the level of instruction (BSW, MSW or PhD) for each of the listed courses. The preponderance (56%) of Web-based courses described in this study was taught at the BSW level, less than half (40%) were MSW courses, and only a few were taught at the PhD level.

Another aspect of the course description was what percentage of the course was taught using Web-based tools. While the survey attempted to be explicit in defining Web-based instruction as "more than 50% of the class taught using Web-based tools rather than face-to-face instruction," some of the responses included information on courses that were taught using less than 50% Web-based instruction. Courses that were not taught using at least 50% Web-based instruction were excluded from data analysis.

TABLE 2. Number of Times Web-Based Courses Were Taught (N = 56)

Number of Times Taught	Number of Responses	Percent
Missing	1	0.0
Taught one time	54	37.3
Taught two times	34	23.5
Taught three times	22	15.2
Taught four times	11	7.6
Taught five times	7	4.8
Taught six times	8	5.5
Taught seven times	0	0.0
Taught eight times	6	4.1
Taught nine times	0	0.0
Taught ten times	1	< 1.0
Taught twelve times	1	< 1.0
Taught eighteen times*	1	< 1.0
Total	146* responses	100.0

* Respondent was contacted to ensure this number was accurate. This figure was based on teaching two or three sections of a Web-based course each semester for several years.

Table 3 illustrates information on the number of courses taught using Web-based instruction for each CSWE curriculum areas. Respondents were asked to identify which curriculum area was most relevant for that course: HBSE, policy, practice, research, field, or elective.

The most frequently reported curriculum areas using Web-based instruction were practice and electives, both reported as applicable for 36 courses. However, when considering courses that are offered multiple times, the number of courses taught presented a different picture. There were 75 elective courses and 75 HBSE courses taught using Web-based instruction. Next, research and practice courses were taught 60 and 58 times, respectively. Policy courses and field seminar were reported and taught the least frequently.

Paired (dependent) t-tests were run on the 49 statements from the CSWE standards which were identified with the nine CSWE curriculum areas. The paired t-tests compared the means scores for perceived effectiveness of Web-based instruction with the means scores of perceived effectiveness of face-to-face instruction using a 5-point Likert scale ("1" = not at all effective and "5" = completely effective). Table 4 depicts the overall findings from the paired t-test analysis.

TABLE 3. CSWE Curriculum Areas

CSWE Content Areas	Number of Responses	CSWE Content Areas	Number of Courses Taught
1. Practice	36	1. Electives	75
2. Electives	36	2. HBSE	75
3. HBSE	24	3. Research	60
4. Research	24	4. Practice	58
5. Policy	17	5. Policy	42
6. Field	9	6. Field	26
Total	146	Total	336

TABLE 4. Comparison of Means Scores of Web-Based Instruction (WBI) to Face-to-Face (F2F) Instruction (N = 56)

Construct	WBI Mean	F2F Mean	Mean Difference	t	df	Sig** (2-tailed)
Teaching Values & Ethics	3.607	4.167	−0.559	−4.950	55	.000*
Teaching about Diversity	3.589	4.103	−0.513	−4.287	55	.000*
Teaching about At-Risk Populations	3.917	4.196	−0.279	−2.937	55	.005*
Teaching Social & Economic Justice	3.889	4.219	−0.330	−3.209	55	.002*
Teaching HBSE	3.993	4.189	−0.196	−2.918	55	.005*
Teaching Policy	4.014	4.162	−0.148	−1.751	55	.086
Teaching Practice	3.534	4.244	−0.710	−6.327	55	.000*
Teaching Research	3.848	4.113	−0.265	−2.606	55	.012*
Teaching Field	3.442	4.205	−0.763	−5.198	55	.000*

**significant at $p < .05$, t-test for paired dependent samples (2-tailed)

As indicated in Table 4, the differences in the mean scores for face-to-face instruction as compared to Web-based instruction were higher in all nine curriculum areas and significantly different in all areas except for Policy.

Another area of consideration is the ranking of content areas according to the mean scores of perceived effectiveness for both methods of instruction. Table 5 presents data on the rankings for content areas using the responses on the 5-point Likert scale ("1" = not at all effective and "5" = completely effective).

TABLE 5. Rank Order of Content Area Means (N = 56)

WBI Content Area	WBI Means	F2F Content Area	F2F Means
1. Policy	4.0139	1. Practice	4.2435
2. HBSE	3.9929	2. Social & Econ Justice	4.2188
3. At-Risk Populations	3.9167	3. Field	4.2054
4. Social & Econ Justice	3.8884	4. At-Risk Populations	4.1964
5. Research	3.8482	5. HBSE	4.1893
6. Values & Ethics	3.6071	6. Values & Ethics	4.1667
7. Diversity	3.5893	7. Policy	4.1627
8. Practice	3.5341	8. Research	4.1131
9. Field	3.4420	9. Diversity	4.1027

Table 5 indicates that Policy received the highest mean scores for the perceived effectiveness of Web-based instruction. Practice and Field received the lowest scores for the effectiveness of Web-based instruction. Overall, all scores for both methods of instruction were fairly high, indicating ratings from moderately effective to completely effective.

Faculty in this study were asked to respond to all areas of the curriculum, even curriculum areas in which they did not have experience using Web-based instruction. In order to strengthen the research model, additional analysis was conducted to determine the mean scores on perceived effectiveness for each of the five distinct curriculum areas based on the responses of faculty who had experience using Web-based instruction in those areas. The mean scores for perceived effectiveness of Web-based and face-to-face instruction for HBSE were computed for faculty who indicated they had taught HBSE using Web-based instruction. Responses from faculty who had not had experience teaching HBSE were excluded. Table 6 illustrates the comparison of the mean scores for the five curriculum areas based on responses from faculty with experience using Web-based instruction in that area.

Table 6 indicates that faculty who were surveyed about the curriculum areas in which they had taught perceived face-to-face instruction to more effective than Web-based instruction for all curriculum areas when responding to the 5-point Likert scale ("1" = not at all effective and "5" = completely effective). The effect size was statistically significant in all areas except for the responses to policy (both for faculty who had taught policy online and for faculty who had not taught policy) and for responses from faculty with experiences teaching research online.

TABLE 6. Comparison of PES for WBI and F2F Instruction by Curriculum Area
(N = 56)

Curriculum Area	n	WBI Mean	WBI SD	F2F Mean	F2F SD	ES	P*
HBSE (Overall Sample)	14	4.128	.625	4.243	.533	.21	.03*
	56	3.993	.761	4.189	.593	.29	.00*
Policy (Overall Sample)	12	3.935	.711	4.139	.737	.28	.32
	56	4.014	.664	4.162	.622	.23	.08
Practice Overall Sample	20	3.763	.587	4.109	.635	.49	.02*
	56	3.534	.787	4.244	.592	1.01	.00*
Research Overall Sample	12	4.069	.894	4.180	.660	.14	.15
	56	3.848	.764	4.113	.660	.37	.01*
Field Overall Sample	8	3.562	1.050	4.187	.651	.72	.00*
	56	3.442	1.074	4.205	.686	.85	.00*

* alpha < .05

Overall, all scores for both methods of instruction were fairly high, indicating ratings from moderately effective to completely effective.

DISCUSSION AND IMPLICATIONS FOR SOCIAL WORK EDUCATION

The purpose of this study was to examine the perceived effectiveness of Web-based instruction in social work education for various curriculum areas. The literature on specific courses suggests there is no significant difference between Web-based and face-to-face instruction (Russell, 1998; Twigg, 2001). However, when examining the similarities and differences across the social work curriculum, those involved in web-based teaching suggest there are indeed differences between the perceived effectiveness of Web-based and face-to-face instruction.

Web-based instruction is not perceived by the experts in this sample to be as effective as face-to-face instruction in all of the nine CSWE curriculum areas, a difference that is statistically significant in all areas except policy. Based on the findings, it appears that courses that are more "content based" (such as policy, research, and HBSE) are more appropriate for Web-based instruction.

While practice courses in this study are reported as using Web-based instruction the most frequently, these courses are perceived to be among the least effectively taught using Web-based instruction and the most effectively taught using face-to-face instruction. Conversely, policy courses are rated as most effectively taught using Web-based instruction, but are taught among the least frequently. This suggests that perhaps educators are choosing the least appropriate courses (practice) for Web-based instruction. Because the findings from this study clearly contradict the assumptions of "no significant differences" between web-based and face-to-face instruction of previous studies (Russell, 1997; Twigg, 2001), additional study is needed.

Future research should include measures for "perceived effectiveness" related to students' perceptions and performance in addition to the measure of achieving course objectives used in this study. Research efforts should continue on other elements of Web-based instruction across the social work curriculum, including further exploration of elective courses and the effectiveness of using Web-based instruction for different types of elective courses.

This study examined the similarities and differences of web-based and face-to-face instruction across the social work curriculum. The use of Web-based instruction in social work has the potential to increase student access, add new dimensions to the educational process, and build new skills in technology. However, the most important issue is learning how to use Web-based instruction in ways that enhance the professional preparation of future social workers.

As new courses are being put online and new social work programs are being offered entirely through Web-based instruction, educators and researchers need to continue to explore ways to increase the effectiveness of the teaching approaches and use of Web-based tools in teaching social work, especially with practice courses. Experts surveyed for this study suggest that Web-based instruction may not be equivalent to face-to-face instruction in accomplishing these efforts, especially if the efforts involve direct practice with clients. Social work educators and administrators have professional and ethical obligations to carefully consider effective ways to educate future social workers. As our understanding of the potential of Web-based technology grows and changes, as well as our underlying theoretical approaches (such as constructivism) that affect our use of the technology, findings from studies such as this one should continue to be evaluated and explored in new ways.

Goldstein (2001) posed the question "How does one learn to become a social worker?" (p. 3). He continued to describe essential purposes of the learning process as "socialization, knowledge building, and growth enhancement, the foundations on which the progression of 'becoming' a professional rest" (p. 25). As social work educators pursue their efforts to assist students to become professionally socialized, develop the requisite social work knowledge and skills for practice, and experience personal and professional growth, careful consideration needs to be given to the ways in which Web-based instruction can facilitate or hinder these efforts.

REFERENCES

Ashery, R. S. (2001). The utilization of technology in graduate schools of social work. *Journal of Technology in Human Services, 18*(1/2), 5-18.

Biner, P. M., Dean, R. S., & Mellinger, A. E. (1994). Factors underlying distance learner satisfaction with televised college-level courses. *American Journal of Distance Education (8)*1, 60-71.

Blakely, T., & Schoenherr, P. (1995). Telecommunication technologies in social work distance education. *Journal of Continuing Social Work Education, 6* (3) 8-12.

Brand, M. (1995). *The wise use of technology. Educational Record, 76*(4), 39-45.

Coe, J. R., & Elliott, D. (1999). An evaluation of teaching direct practice courses in a distance education program for rural settings. *Journal of Social Work Education, 35*(3), 353-365.

Council on Social Work Education (2000). *Guidelines for using distance education in social work programs.* Division of standards and accreditation. Available online: www.cswe.org.

Council on Social Work Education (2002). *Educational Policy and Accreditation Standards.* Washington, DC: Author. Available online: www.cswe.org.

Eastmond, D.V. (1998). Adult learners and Internet-based distance education. *New Directions for Adult & Continuing Education, 78* (summer), 33-41.

Faux, T. L., & Black-Hughes, C. (2000). A comparison of using the Internet versus lectures to teach social work history. *Research on Social Work Practice, 10*(4), 454-467.

Fleishman, J. (1996). The web: New venue for adult education. *Adult Learning, 8*(1), 17-18.

Forster, M., & Washington, E. (2000). A model for developing and managing distance education programs using interactive video technology. *Journal of Social Work Education, 36*(1), 147-158.

Giffords, E. D. (1998). Social work and the Internet: An introduction. *Social Work, 43*(3), 243-252.

Goldstein, H. (2001). *Experiential Learning: A foundation for social work education and practice.* Alexandria, VA: Council on Social Work Education.

Hick, S. (1999). Learning to care on the Internet: Evaluating an online introductory social work course. *New Technology in the Human Services, 11*(4), 1-8.

Lennon, T. M. (2002). *Statistics on Social Work Education in the United States: 2000.* Alexandria, VA: Council on Social Work Education.

Luchini, K. (1998). Problems and potentials in Web-based instruction, with particular focus on distance learning. *Educational Technology & Society, 1*(1). Available online: http://ifets.lece.org/periodical/vol_1_98/informal_summary_katy_luchini.html.

Macy, J. A., Rooney, R. H., Hollister, C. D., & Freddolino, P. P. (2001). Evaluation of distance education: Programs in social work. In J. Miller-Cribbs (Ed.), *New Advances in Technology for Social Work Education* (pp. 63-85). Boston: The Haworth Press, Inc.

Marson, S. M. (1997). A selective history of Internet technology and social work. *Computers in Human Services, 14*(2), 35-49.

McFall, J. P., & Freddolino, P. P. (2000b). Quality and comparability in distance field education: Lessons learned from comparing three program sites. *Journal of Social Work Education, 36*(2), 293-307.

Rafferty, J. (1998). Social work and information and communication technologies: The tortoise and the hare? *New Technology in the Human Services, 11*(2), 10-12.

Russell, T. L. (1997). *The "no significant difference" phenomenon* [On-line]. Available: http://tenb.mta.ca/phenom.

Schoech, D. (2000). Teaching over the Internet: Results of one doctoral course. *Research on Social Work Practice, 10*(4), 467-486.

Schoech, D., & Helton, D. (2001). Qualitative and quantitative analysis of a course taught via classroom and Internet chatroom. *Qualitative Social Work, 1*(1), 111-124.

Sharkey, P. (2000). Running hard to stand still: Communication and information technology within social work training. *Social Work Education, 19*(5), 513-521. [online: Academic Search Premier]

Siegel, E., Jennings, J. G., Conklin, J., & Napoletano-Flynn, S. A. (1998). Distance learning in social work education: Results and implications of a national survey. *Journal of Social Work Education, 34*(1), 71-80.

Stocks, J., & Freddolino, P. (2000). Enhancing computer-mediated teaching through interactivity: The second interation of a World Wide Web-based graduate social work course. *Research on Social Work Practice, 10*(4), 505-519.

Twigg, C. (2001). Innovations in online learning: Moving beyond no significant difference. *Center for Academic Transformation* [On-line]. Available: www.center.rpi.edu/PewSym/mono4.html.

Vernon, R. F. (2001). Back to the future. *Journal of Social Work Education, 37*(3), 571-573. [online: Wilson Plus Select].

Wilson, S. (1999). Distance education and accreditation. *Journal of Social Work Education, 35*(3), 326-330.

Web-Based Higher Education:
The Inclusion/Exclusion Paradox

Jan Steyaert

SUMMARY. Increasingly, education is delivered through computers and the internet. This article highlights that while such development is beneficial for some students with functional impairments, it might be excluding others if insufficient attention is paid to accessibility. Both the electronic learning environment (Blackboard, WebCT and the like) as well as the content author need to design for accessibility. *[Article copies available for a fee from The Haworth Document Delivery Service: 1-800-HAWORTH. E-mail address: <docdelivery@haworthpress.com> Website: <http://www.HaworthPress.com> © 2005 by The Haworth Press, Inc. All rights reserved.]*

KEYWORDS. Accessibility, e-learning, electronic learning environments

INTRODUCTION

The digital divide is a concept that is irrelevant to most students in higher education. In most countries, higher education implies being in

Jan Steyaert, PhD, is Professor of 'Social infrastructure and technology' at the Fontys University of Professional Education in Eindhoven (the Netherlands) and research fellow at the University of Bath, UK.

[Haworth co-indexing entry note]: "Web-Based Higher Education: The Inclusion/Exclusion Paradox." Steyaert, Jan. Co-published simultaneously in *Journal of Technology in Human Services* (The Haworth Press, Inc.) Vol. 23, No. 1/2, 2005, pp. 67-78; and: *Web-Based Education in the Human Services: Models, Methods, and Best Practices* (eds: MacFadden et al.) The Haworth Press, Inc., 2005, pp. 67-78. Single or multiple copies of this article are available for a fee from The Haworth Document Delivery Service [1-800-HAWORTH, 9:00 a.m. - 5:00 p.m. (EST). E-mail address: docdelivery@haworthpress.com].

Available online at http://www.haworthpress.com/web/JTHS
Digital Object Identifier: 10.1300/J017v023n01_05

the lead of the rat race for socio-economic positions. Consequently, higher education students are one of those groups with the highest access to new technology.

There is at least one specific group of higher education students for whom the digital divide is unfortunately very real, and might even be expanding. Students with functional impairments often find higher education environments very disabling. Although the development towards web-based higher education is a great opportunity for these students and can imply a significant gain in inclusion, the reality is often gloomy with web-based higher education failing to transpose the basic accessibility notions from the physical to the digital environment. As a result, the current development towards web-based higher education includes the threat of increased exclusion.

This article will expand on this apparent paradox that the technology that provides a great platform for inclusion, in reality appears to be excluding. A five step analysis and some mythology will describe what this paradox is and how to overcome it.

FROM DISABILITY TO IMPAIRMENTS

The first step in the analysis of the inclusion/exclusion paradox takes us back 25 years when a subtle change occurred in the language used to refer to handicaps. Rather than talk about handicaps, we started talking about impairments. Someone restricted to a wheelchair was no longer a handicapped person, but somebody with a mobility impairment. A blind person became somebody with a vision impairments. Some made it their mission to promote the use of politically correct jargon in this area while others joked we should no longer talk about a Lilliputian or dwarf, but about somebody with a vertical growth impairment.

The words we use are however but a reflection of our thinking. Beneath the war of words, a fundamental transition took place from a medical to a social perspective on disability. Traditionally, much of the health and social policy on disability was based on a *medical model* that viewed disability as a "personal" problem, directly caused by disease, trauma or health conditions, and one which required medical care provided in the form of individual treatment by professionals. The *social model* of disability, on the other hand, sees the issue mainly as a "societal" problem. Disablement is not an attribute of a person, but created by the environment in which persons with impairments live and act.

When I am driving a car and wish to locate a specific station on the car radio, I am temporarily vision impaired (at least, if you want to keep driving and not crash into something) and unable to read all the labels on the radio buttons. When I wish to enjoy a sunny afternoon in the city and take my young (grand) child in its stroller for a walk, I am temporarily mobility impaired and struggling with the high entries to buses. Dyslexia is no big problem, until some professor insists I do a written exam and excludes the option of a verbal assessment.

This change in perspective is well documented in many publications (Oliver, 1990, 1996, 1991). Its formal start date can be pinned down to the publication in 1980 of the World Health Organization's *ICIDH-1980* classification on impairment, disability and handicap. These terms are central constructs to the classification and used in a precisely defined way. An *impairment* is any loss or abnormality of a psychological, physiological or anatomical structure or function. A *disability* is any restriction or lack of ability, resulting from an impairment, to perform an activity in a manner considered normal for people. A *handicap* is a disadvantage, resulting from an impairment or disability, that limits the fulfillment of individual goals.

DESIGN FOR EXCLUSION, OR NOT

The consequences of this change of perspective from a medical to a social model include a shift of management of the situation from the individual to society. Or rather, a supplement, as medical treatment of impairments of course maintains its importance. Disability requires social action and is the collective responsibility of society to make the environmental modifications necessary for the full participation of people with impairments. The way products and services are designed makes them, often by non-decision, exclusive or inclusive (Norman, 1988).

This is most recognized in the domain of the built environment. Fortunately, it has become commonplace to build or renovate every public building so that they include features for people with impairments. Such public buildings encompass theatres, town halls, museums and also, buildings for higher education. To move between levels, stairs are supplemented with elevators and ramps to accommodate not only users of wheelchairs, but also parents pushing prams or people carrying heavy luggage. Another feature increasingly common are induction loops in lecture halls or at ticket services of, e.g., train stations. These induction loops are essentially loops of insulated wire that are placed in rooms which directly transmit sound to hearing aids. The sound is either taken directly from the radio, television or other medium, or indirectly through a microphone. Their presence is indicated by the universal symbol for hearing impairments with a T-symbol added (see Figure 1). These are just the most obvious examples of how to make a built environment more accessible to people with varying capabilities and impairments. There are numerous guidelines from which architects and city planners and similar professionals can benefit to design for inclusion and several good overviews are available (Preiser & Ostroff, 2001).

An area related to this built environment is public transport. Not only is accessibility a feature of railway and subway stations, also the access to train carriages or bus coaches can be a significant threshold for mobility impaired people. This situation can be addressed by constructing carriages and coaches with floors that level the entry platform at the stations, and by providing areas in the carriages and coaches without seats that but allow for wheelchairs and strollers.

An area very different but no less central to daily life is packaging. As people get older, they lose strength in their hands and have increasing problems with opening jars and packaging. Again, the impairment of weak hand power does not need to become a disability when the packaging is designed in such a way as to require minimal hand power. For instance, bottle caps require significantly less power to open upon first time use when they are not round but eight-square. Why should industry not adopt such an accessibility feature as standard and design for inclusion rather than exclusion? Surely the cost element between producing a round or eight-square cap to bottles is non-existent or minimal.

Design for inclusion does not always relate to tangible products but also includes attitudes and gestures. Hearing impaired people often en-

FIGURE 1. Universal symbol for hearing impairments with a T-symbol added.

counter a disability when people talk to them without facing them, or while covering their mouth with their hand. Try to monitor for a couple of days during your meetings how often this happens, and you'll be surprised. Although a small detail of life, for hearing impaired persons it implies they cannot support their hearing with facial expressions and rudimentary lip reading.

The notion that design of products and services can be exclusive as well as inclusive and should be the latter has been encapsulated in the concepts of "design-for-all" and "universal design." While the latter is more commonplace in North America, the first has been adopted by the European Commission. However, there are no substantial differences between these two concepts, or alternatives like inclusive design or "barrier free design" used by, e.g., OECD (Organization for Economic Co-operation and Development). All these labels refer to designing products and services in such a way that usage is independent of impairments.

NEW MEDIA DESIGNED TO EXCLUDE

What goes for the built environment, public transport and packaging also goes for new media. Products and services can be designed to include or to exclude. Just consider the following situation that occurred some months ago after a long meeting. Because the meeting took more time than scheduled, one of the participants asked if he could use my mobile phone. So I gave him my phone, with the instruction to punch the number and then the green button. Blank stare. Green button ?? This man happened to be colour blind, an impairment not easily observed but neither rare. Although 8% of men are colour blind and can't tell the difference between green and red, that is exactly the colour that the overwhelming majority of mobile phones use to distinguish between the buttons to place or cancel, to accept or disregard a call. Some phones use redundancy of signals, and supplement the colour coding with the words "yes" and "no" as, e.g., on the latest Sony Ericsson phones. This is basically the same principle used in European traffic lights for pedestrians. That is red and green colours, top light is stop and bottom light is walk, supplemented by an icon of a walking or waiting person and sometimes by tinkering sounds. Redundancy of signals is good practice in terms of accessibility and make your message hard to miss.

Although the difference between red and green buttons on a mobile phone may sound trivial because you can easily learn how to use it without having to rely on the colour coding, it becomes more cumbersome if you use the same colours to offer different menu options in a computer program. Microsoft's Word uses green and red coding to distinguish between spelling and grammar mistakes. And there is the story of Amazon.com that had a button "click here to confirm your order" in a colour that made it indistinguishable to its background for those 8% of male colour blind citizens (Follansbee, 2001).

But accessibility of new media isn't limited to colour blindness. Hardware and software can accommodate for other impairments and be inclusive, or disregard their specific user requirements and be inclusive. Illustrative examples of new media that are or were excluding by design are the mobile phones that were incompatible with hearing aids and thus disabling hearing impaired persons. Another example concerns video recorders (OK, maybe not so "new" media) that do not record the captioning of programmes thus disabling the hearing impaired persons.

Fortunately, not all is gloomy. Recent versions of software have seen a substantial increase in accessibility. For instance, Windows XP now embodies several accessibility features such as coping with the use of the mouse by left and right handed persons, high contrast on the screen, sticky keys that are useful when one is unable to hold down, e.g., shift and another key at the same time. Several other features are also included. Web browsers allow for increased or decreased font size. Other major software providers have included accessibility features in their products (Adobe, 2004; Corel, 2004; Macromedia, 2004; Microsoft, 2004). Unfortunately, many higher education institutes have computer management turning off use of these features to improve efficiency of computer maintenance, but thus excluding students and staff with impairments.

Much gain in accessibility of new media is the result of legislation in the U.S., such as the Telecommunication Act and the Americans with Disability Act, but most specifically to section 508 of the Rehabilitation Act (Wall & Sarver, 2003) (see also http://www.section508.gov). This section requires Federal agencies to make their electronic and information technology accessible to people with impairments and has inspired legislative action at the state level and international. European legislation is slowly mirroring this American legislation and encouraging public authorities to include design for all requirements when awarding public contracts. This is done both through European legislation as well as member states legislation, for instance Germany or Ireland.

Not only can hardware and software producers design for inclusion or exclusion, but content providers become increasingly important in influencing the accessibility of the information society. Fortunately, the

World Wide Web consortium (W3C) is continuously hosting a global "Web Accessibility Initiative" that produces guidelines and information on how to make web sites accessible. The initiative includes a set of basic guidelines such as (1) to always provide an alternative text to a graphics on your web page, (2) do not only include the image of your company logo, but also the alternative text 'logo of company XYZ,' (3) always indicate the language(s) used on the webpage, and similar guidelines. Most of these guidelines also apply to content produced in Word and Acrobat documents. In Word, right-click on an image, select "format picture" and use the tab "Web" to include alternative text. Some of these guidelines are encapsulated in the most common website authoring software, but they are not "enforced" by these authoring environments. Content provider still need to be aware of the accessibility issues involved in designing a web site. One only needs to google for the keywords "accessibility" and the name of the authoring software one uses, such as FrontPage or Dreamweaver, to find out how to design for inclusion. Needless to say, these accessibility features in software environments can be improved upon, but more significant gains in accessibility can be attained by using those features already available. This not only implies the software industry, but also the content authors need to have accessibility in mind while designing their courseware.

WEB-BASED HIGHER EDUCATION DESIGNED TO EXCLUDE

The fourth step in our analysis of the inclusion/exclusion paradox is a logical consequence of the previous step. What goes for generic new media products, also goes for web-based higher education and the specific applications involved in it. Similar to generic software, environments to develop and deliver web-based higher education have incorporated features to facilitate the production of accessible courseware. These include the well-known products Blackboard and WebCT. You can google on the keywords "accessibility" and the name of your favorite working environment to learn more about these features.

Blackboard as well as WebCT include accessibility features by providing alternative texts to all system images and allowing content authors to include alternative text to all imported images. Framesets can be titled and tables are optimized for use by screen readers. The companies also makes manuals available on how to author content for learning environments while meeting accessibility requirements. From version 6 of Blackboard onwards, the virtual classroom has been redesigned to make it more accessible, although the speed of communication in chatrooms will always be problematic for any student with low typing abilities. The timing for assessments needs to be set on an individual basis to allow for extra time for students with functional impairments, where appropriate.

In general, new editions of educational software have increased accessibility features. From that perspective, it is useful to upgrade to new versions whenever these are released. This progress also implies one should be careful with web information on accessibility and this software, and carefully check which version is being discussed. However, upgrading to new versions should not be a replacement for content authors doing their share of work to include accessibility in electronic higher education.

Within web-based higher education, it is necessary to remember that accessibility is not limited to the actual delivery of the course contents, but also relevant to, e.g., information about and registration to, these courses and student assessments. As such, one also needs to include accessibility features in computer-based assessment environments like Question Mark (Wiles, 2002). Also access to digital libraries, such as Ingenta and Sciencedirect, needs to be an issue. Again, since these services are also geared towards American higher education, they are thus subject to the previously mentioned U.S. legislation and do attempt to provide accessible applications.

CONTENT PROVIDERS EXCLUDE

Having accessibility features in web authoring environments for generic purposes or specifically for educational content is only a necessary and not a sufficient condition to making web-based higher education inclusive rather than exclusive.

A March 2004 survey of UK web sites found that 79% of the tested web sites failed basic compliance testing on accessibility. Government sites fared better, but still 40% failed accessibility standards set by UK legislation (Web Accessibility Study 2004). A Dutch accessibility monitor that surveyed web sites during November 2003 to January 2004 found that 95% of them did not meet the first level of accessibility as specified by the Web Accessibility Initiative. More amazing than these high percentages was the observation that all failed to meet accessibility criteria due to small and easy to correct omissions, such as alternative text to graphics or indication of language used.

Similar older surveys show comparable results. Where these surveys sampled generic web sites, another survey that sampled general, not course delivery, web sites of institutes of higher education in the Netherlands found equally high levels of exclusion. No equivalent surveys for web-based higher education are available. However, there is no reason to assume these higher education web applications are more accessible.

This draws our 5-step analyses of the inclusion/exclusion paradox of web-based higher education to an end. The key conclusion is that but a small change is required to guarantee that web-based higher education proves to be a gain in inclusion rather than a new ground for exclusion for students with impairments. Content providers are the key stakeholders that can tip the balance by the way they use, or not use, the accessibility features provided by authoring environments, ranging from Microsoft Word to Blackboard and Question Mark.

There are some myths around accessibility and web-based content that prevent content providers to implement the relatively easy changes required to make web-based higher education inclusive.

MYTH 1

The most persistent myth states that including accessibility in web sites decreases their attractiveness to users. The fear of many content providers is that following the accessibility guidelines forces them to reduce the use of graphics and design elements. This is a myth because accessibility in no way calls for a reduction of design features. Rather, it calls for allowing as much flexibility as possible to the users so they can change, e.g., colour, font, screen layout, etc., according to their needs. It also calls for the provision of alternative designs for users with impairments such as text supplementing a graphic, captioning supplementing sound in digital video, a text description supplementing a flash animation. It is common though not good practice to invest in a non-graphic, text-only version of a web site. In practice, such text-only web sites are a severely limited edition of the graphic-rich version, and remain non-updated. Furthermore, many of the guidelines on accessibility are similar to guidelines for generic web usability and consequently should be included in the main web site.

Having said this, one also needs to recognize that web sites of several organizations working in the area of impairments have a sober design and thus reinforce this myth of incompatibility between accessibility and attractiveness. I call upon these organizations to upgrade the design level of their web sites while maintaining accessibility to actively debunk this myth.

MYTH 2

A next myth relates to the planning of including accessibility in web design or design of web-based higher education. Many content providers plan their work so that their end product is 80 or 90 percent finished before accessibility features are added. The myth is that one can design inclusion/exclusion neutral and make the necessary changes in the final stages just before the formal launch. Unfortunately, accessibility is not a layer of coat that needs to be applied at the end of a building project, but rather the iron that strengthens the concrete. As everybody knows, that iron needs to be there before the concrete, and cannot be inserted afterwards. Still, with accessibility and web-based content, that is exactly what many try to do, and they find it hard or impossible to accomplish.

MYTH 3

A final myth involves the lack of information. When talking to content providers about accessibility, many recognize the need for inclusive web sites but refer to a lack of detailed information on how to accomplish this. In the era that google replaced the Encyclopedia Britannica as the ultimate source of knowledge, it is hard to envisage somebody maintaining this myth. For those who need more than their favorite search machine, two references should suffice. The Web Accessibility Initiative is the best portal to start finding information about accessibility for generic web applications, while TechDis (UK, see http://www.techdis.ac.uk) and the National Center on Accessible Information Technology in Education (USA, see http://www.washington.edu/accessit) are good places for information on higher education applications.

CONCLUSION: WHAT TO DO

Finally, and by way of conclusion, here's a limited shortlist of what any person or institute involved with higher education should do to contribute to tipping the balance towards an inclusive web-based higher education.

The first step is to include accessibility features in all computerized higher education content. If such content is produced in-house, this can be achieved by ensuring that all authoring software comes with updated accessibility modules which can almost always be downloaded for free from the provider's web site. The next task is ensuring that content producers are aware of why and how to make use of these modules. In the case that content is produced in a home-made virtual learning environment, the institute can consider enforcing accessibility guidelines, such as, not accepting a graphic without a meaningful alternative text. If the web publication of content is purchased rather than home-made, accessibility needs to be included in the purchasing requirements. Many providers will reply by referring to the myths mentioned above, but fortunately an increasing number of web designers are aware of the importance of inclusive web design and the similarity between accessibility guidelines and those for web usability.

Second, once accessible web-based higher education is available or in the making, one should validate and monitor. The basic attitude behind validation should not be to sanction, but to detect areas of improvement. For validation, one can rely on freely available validation applications such as Bobby (see http://bobby.watchfire.com) or Vischeck (for colour blindness, see www.vischeck.com) or TABLIN (for tables, see www.w3. org/WAI/Resources/Tablin). However, such validation services can never fully be relied upon and can result in inappropriate trust in having provided accessible web sites (Witt & McDermott, 2004). For instance, they check for the presence of alternative text to graphics, but do not assess whether such alternative text is meaningful. One could fool all validation services by including "a picture" as alternative text to all graphics, but still have an inaccessible web site. Higher education organizations should supplement such validation by validation made by students or staff with impairments. Once certain levels of accessibility are achieved, one can also communicate this by including an accessibility label on the homepage.

REFERENCES

Adobe. (2004). *Adobe accessibility.* Retrieved 22nd May 2004, from the World Wide Web: http://access.adobe.com/.

Blackboard. (2004). *Blackboard accessibility.* Retrieved 22nd May 2004, from the World Wide Web: www.blackboard.com/products/access.

Corel. (2004). *Corel accessibility*. Retrieved 22nd May 2004, from the World Wide Web: www.corel.com/accessibility.

Follansbee, T. (2001). Colorblindness and usability. *WebWord*, http://www.WebWord.com/moving/colorblindness.html.

Macromedia. (2004). *Macromedia accessibility*. Retrieved 22nd May 2004, from the World Wide Web: www.macromedia.com/macromedia/accessibility/.

Microsoft. (2004). *Microsoft accessibility*. Retrieved 22nd May 2004, from the World Wide Web: www.microsoft.com/enable.

Norman, D. (1988). *The design of everyday things*. London: MIT Press.

Oliver, M. (1990). *The politics of disablement*. London: MacMillan.

Oliver, M. (1996). *Understanding disability, from theory to practice*. London: Macmillan.

Oliver, M. (Ed.). (1991). *Social work, disabled people and disabling environments* (English ed.). London: Jessica Kingsley.

Preiser, W., & Ostroff, E. (Eds.). (2001). *Universal design handbook*. New York: McGraw Hill.

Wall, P., & Sarver, L. (2003). Disabled student access in an era of technology. *The internet and higher education, 6*, 277-284.

WebCT. (2004). *WebCT accessibility*. Retrieved 22nd May 2004, from the World Wide Web: http://www.webct.com/products/viewpage?name=products_accessibility.

Wiles, K. (2002). Accessibility and computer-based assessment: A whole new set of issues? In L. Phipps & A. Sutherland & J. Seale (Eds.), *Access all areas: Disability, technology and learning* (pp. 61-65 and available from www.techdis.ac.uk). Bristol: Joint Information Systems Committee.

Witt, N., & McDermott, A. (2004). Web site accessibility: What logo will we use today? *British Journal of Educational Technology, 35*(1), 45-56.

Souls on Ice:
Incorporating Emotion
in Web-Based Education

Robert J. MacFadden

SUMMARY. Emotions have been neglected in education and online education, in favor of a heavy emphasis on cognition and rationality. This article explores the significance of emotion in learning and how recent research is identifying some pathways and dynamics in the way emotions impact on learning and on web-based learning. Online learners have not been considered as "emotional beings" and web-based education has not addressed this dimension in any significant way. A constructivist, emotionally-oriented (CEO) model of web-based education is introduced which emphasizes safety, challenge, and new thinking, and offers several strategies to enhance the emotional experience of learners. *[Article copies available for a fee from The Haworth Document Delivery Service: 1-800-HAWORTH. E-mail address: <docdelivery@haworthpress.com> Website: <http://www.HaworthPress.com> © 2005 by The Haworth Press, Inc. All rights reserved.]*

Robert J. MacFadden, PhD, is Associate Professor, Faculty of Social Work, University of Toronto, Canada (www.robertmacfadden.com). He teaches courses on research, clinical practice and information technology in social work. His current work involves exploring the role of emotions in web-based and education. Dr. MacFadden is on the Executive Board of HUSITA (Human Services Information Technology Applications), an international association of professionals dedicated to promoting the ethical and effective use of IT to better serve humanity (www.husita.org).

[Haworth co-indexing entry note]: "Souls on Ice: Incorporating Emotion in Web-Based Education." MacFadden, Robert J. Co-published simultaneously in *Journal of Technology in Human Services* (The Haworth Press, Inc.) Vol. 23, No. 1/2, 2005, pp. 79-98; and: *Web-Based Education in the Human Services: Models, Methods, and Best Practices* (eds: MacFadden et al.) The Haworth Press, Inc., 2005, pp. 79-98. Single or multiple copies of this article are available for a fee from The Haworth Document Delivery Service [1-800-HAWORTH, 9:00 a.m. - 5:00 p.m. (EST). E-mail address: docdelivery@haworthpress.com].

Digital Object Identifier: 10.1300/J017v023n01_06

KEYWORDS. Online education, web-based education, learning, emotions, affect, feelings

Education has existed in some form since the beginnings of human history. In relative terms, web-based education (WBE) has just appeared and blends learning with technology in unique ways. Much research and writing in this area emphasizes the similarities between WBE and traditional methods. Accreditation frameworks declare that the experience of students in online education must be equivalent to face-to-face instruction (FTF). Yet we know that WBE is a significantly different approach to learning that is mediated by technology and that the experiences will differ. One difference is in the way emotions are conceived and communicated in a web-based environment. Currin (2003) quotes Thissen as remarking that ". . . nearly all of the [e-learning] environments I know metacommunicate dreariness and boredom, and they only address the cognitive part of learning." Computer-mediated communication has been depicted as less friendly, impersonal, less emotional and more serious, businesslike with a task orientation (Rice & Love, 1987). Campbell-Gibson (2000) depicts teaching and learning online as the "ultimate disorienting dilemma" where the markers of everyday life (e.g., color of skin, gender, accents) no longer exist in familiar forms. Yet online communication is not without an emotional dimension (e.g., hyper-emotional "flaming" or criticizing harshly online) and may be an "emotionally different" medium which needs to be understood and considered in constructing web-based courses.

This chapter explores emotions and learning in general, then considers emotions in online education. A constructivist, emotionally oriented (CEO) model of web-based education is presented, followed by a discussion of the emotional landscape of online courses, ideas about enriching online communication and a summary.

EMOTIONS AND LEARNING

Emotion is an exceedingly complex phenomenon and Plutchik (2001) reports that there have been more than 90 definitions of "emotion" proposed in the 20th century. O'Regan (2003) notes that emotions can be viewed as some combination of physiological, psychological and psychomotor components. Some theorists (e.g., Damasio, 1994) have proposed "primary emotions" (e.g., happiness, sadness, anger, fear and disgust) and "secondary emotions" such as euphoria, ecstacy, melancholy, wistfulness and these are considered derivations of primary ones. Some more recent brain research (e.g., Damasio, 1994) has distinguished between feelings as being a mental image of the state of the person's body and emotion as being the reaction to a stimulus and the associated behavior such as facial changes. For the purpose of this discussion, the terms emotions and feelings will be used interchangeably.

The primary role of emotion in learning has largely been ignored in favour of an emphasis on cognition and rationality (Astleitner & Leutner, 2000). Indeed, emotion has been viewed as the polar opposite to cognition (O'Regan, 2003) and the direct expression of emotion has historically not been seen as appropriate in education (Coles, 1999; Sylwester, 1994). The history of emotions in instructional design (Astleitner, 2000) reveals a progression from emotions first being seen as intangible factors which are disruptive of cognitive objectives. Emotions were then viewed as being consequences of the learning process. Later, emotions were seen as attitudes towards or against something. More recently emotions have been associated with a type of intelligence or emotional intelligence (EQ) (Goleman, 1997). Mayer (1999) refers to this as the ability to reason with emotion in four areas: to perceive emotion, to integrate it in thought, to understand it and to manage it. Cherniss (2000, Conclusion section, para. 2) notes that ". . . there now is a considerable body of research suggesting that a person's ability to perceive, identify, and manage emotion provides the basis for the kinds of social and emotional competencies that are important for success in almost any job." With the EQ emphasis, emotions have become the content of instruction itself–teaching about emotions. Another current approach has been characterized as "emotionally sound instruction" and highlights the importance of incorporating emotions in learning and the need to increase positive and decrease negative emotions during instruction (Taylor, 1994; O'Regan, 2003).

Increasingly, emotions are being viewed as mediating all learning. Brain studies have revealed that learning involves not only the left-brain, or fact oriented side, but the whole brain, including the amygdale, the limbic system and the cortex. Emotions cannot be separated from logical, rote learning. For example, everyone is familiar with the way emotions influence memory of events such as the experiment that stages an emotional event in the classroom and then asks details of the event.

Jensen (1998) points out that emotions drive attention, meaning and memory and are critical to patterning in the brain. Stock (1996, p. 6) notes that ". . . every sensory input we receive is processed through our emotional center first . . . before it is sent on and processed in our rational mind. . . ." Others describe the centrality of emotion as ". . . mak[ing] possible all creative thought" (Greenspan, 1997), ". . . a sort of biological thermostat [which] activates attention . . . which then activates a rich set of problem-solving and response systems and . . . In fact, of driv[ing] everything" (Brandt, 2000). Sylwester (1994) states that emotion ". . . drives attention, which in turn drives memory" and Vail (2002) terms emotions, the "On/Off Switch for Learning."

University students' emotions measured early in the semester predicted cumulative grades and final course exam scores at the end of semester (Pekrun, Molfenter, Titz, & Perry, 2000). Academic self-efficacy, academic control of achievement and subjective values of learning and achievement related significantly to students' academic emotions (Pekrun Goetz & Titz, 2002).

Norman (2002) notes that understanding emotion is important for the science of design and that emotions directly impact on cognition. Positive affect enhances creative, breadth-first thinking whereas negative affect encourages depth-first processing and minimizes distractions. Norman observes that ". . . neurochemicals change the parameters of thought, adjusting such things as whether reason is primarily depth first (focused, not easily distracted) or breadth first (creative, out of the box thinking but easily distractible)." Positive affect broadens the thought process and leads to creative thinking with a side effect of easy distractibility. As an example, discovering new information easily on the Web can be exciting for some and this excitement might lead some learners away from the main topic through exploring interesting tangents. Negative affect, such as anxiety, focuses the mind to a point leading to better concentration. As Norman notes, "Anxiety and fear squirt neural transmitters into the brain that narrow the thought process. In general this is good to focus upon a specific threat or problem." Positive emotions can assist us in difficult tasks whereas negative emotions can make it harder to do even simple tasks. As an example, a person may be able to walk across a plank placed on the ground without much thought, but suspend the plank fifty feet in the air and the anxiety generated may seriously affect the person's ability to think and perform this otherwise simple task. A person may be able to successfully complete a quiz online, but add a visible countdown timer that leads to increased anxiety and the person's memory and other thinking processes can become impaired. Emotions then can alter our performance on cognitive tasks.

EMOTIONS IN ONLINE EDUCATION

Like mainstream education, emotions are rarely considered in developing online education. Great emphasis is given to the logic and structure of the content, the pedagogical philosophy, the range and extent of the information available to the learner and other logical, rational parameters. While factors which can relate to emotions, such as the visual appeal of the site, the ease of navigation and the degree of interactivity, are usually addressed, they are not often considered in terms of the emotional impact on the learner.

Yet the literature strongly suggests that web-based education can generate considerable negative emotions such as anger, frustration, confusion, boredom and isolation to name only a few. Thissen (2000) notes that too often web-based environments lose people in hyperspace, promote problems in locating information, contain long navigation paths, confuse users with too many choices, violate basic ergonomic rules related to screen color, text layouts, and unintuitive user interfaces. He urges attention to learners as emotional beings which means being stimulated and motivated, having their curiosity excited and encouraged, good feedback and confirmation, a sense of achievement at intervals. Learners should have an opportunity to express emotions, to communicate them clearly to others and to themselves.

Redden (2003) indicates that negative emotions can be generated by dead links, tangled navigation, dropped connections, full pages of narratives, nonstop animation and large downloads, as examples. She believes that instructors and developers need to pay attention to emotions in the cyber classroom and make the experience interesting. Instructors need to respond to learners positively and with humor when appropriate, personalizing communications, using emotions, and providing encouragement to explore their own meanings with the materials. Instructors are encouraged to purposely express their own emotions, and to name them in different ways including describing body language ("my eyes grew wide"). She notes that when educators talk about content being authentic and meaningful they are really referring to this as an emotionally-mediated process. Chat groups have developed a completely new online language of emotions with terms such as LOL (laughing out loud) and HHOJ (ha, ha, only joking). There are many web sites that feature this topic and that provide lists of emotionally-related acronyms and emoticons (e.g., http://www.angelfire.com/wa/jerbo/chat.html#acro, http://www.ker95.com/chat101/html/abbreviations.html, http://help.expedient.com/mailnews/emoticons.shtml).

Assessing emotions in online learning can be difficult without the usual range of emotional cues generated in face-to-face communications. MacFadden, Maiter, and Dumbrill (2002) describe the problem experienced by facilitators who were unable to gauge the level of emotional engagement of the class on an issue within an online context. Rather than continue to challenge the learners, the facilitators decided not to risk student alienation so they discontinued the discussion. They noted that if this had been a FTF class, they likely would have continued to "push" the issue.

Redden (2003) points out that many of the most well-accepted recommendations to facilitators in web-based education are directed at addressing emotional issues. Facilitators are encouraged to respond quickly to learners' problems because these problems usually involve emotions such as: confusion, frustration, anger and disappointment. An early response leads to the learner feeling validated, appreciated and grateful and reduces the levels of negative emotions. Facilitators should regularly inform students of their progress because students worry about their abilities, may feel insecure and may not participate or "lurk" within the online classroom. Feedback about performance given in a helpful manner can motivate, engage and lead to higher levels of participation in the course.

Facilitators are encouraged to be active and to personalize their communications with learners. Web-based courses where the facilitators are largely absent can lead to loss of momentum in the learning, a lack of engagement in the process and result in learners feeling unimportant and angry over lost learning opportunities. Class situations where the learner and his or her contributions are not acknowledged can lead to learner feelings of disengagement, meaninglessness and frustration. Using the learner's name regularly, along with acknowledging the specific contributions made, can increase the learner's sense of engagement and reinforce good work.

While these negative feelings can occur within a FTF classroom situation, web-based education has more limited information available, a lack of usual reference points, and delayed communication that can considerably amplify the effect of these experiences.

THE CEO MODEL:
A CONSTRUCTIVISTIC, EMOTIONALLY-ORIENTED MODEL
OF WEB-BASED INSTRUCTION

A new model that incorporates a focus on emotions was developed by the author and his colleagues and has been described elsewhere

(MacFadden, Herie, Maiter & Dumbrill, in press). This CEO model was developed for the type of web-based education that involves social interaction through various means including discussion groups, shared assignments and joint activities. The model is grounded in a constructivistic approach and also emphasizes the emotional dimensions in online learning. Learners are encouraged to formulate and reformulate their ideas, to order, reorder, test and justify their ideas, all within an emotional context of safety and trust (Gold, 2001).

Constructivism is based on the idea that people construct their own meanings and that learning is both an active process and a social activity. Caine and Caine (1991) identify several principles associated with learning, constructivism and brain research. Four of these principles are:

- The brain is a parallel processor and processes thoughts, emotions and cultural knowledge simultaneously and teaching should incorporate a range of learning strategies;
- Learning involves the entire physiology and instructors shouldn't just involve the intellect;
- Searching for meaning happens through patterning and emotions are critical to patterning;
- Challenge improves learning while threats inhibit it. A challenge can become a threat when the learner believes that the challenge threatens some important factor such as self-image or grades and the learner believes he or she may not be successful in meeting this challenge.

These authors note that,

> . . . content that is emotionally sterile is made more difficult to understand. . . . To teach someone any subject adequately, the subject must be embedded in all the elements that give it meaning. People must have a way to relate to the subject in terms of what is personally important, and this means acknowledging both the emotional impact and their deeply held needs and drives. Our emotions are integral to learning. When we ignore the emotional components of any subject we teach, we actually deprive students of meaningfulness. (Caine and Caine, 1991, p. 58)

Rather than simply encouraging positive emotions and discouraging negative emotions, this model recognizes that sometimes learning involves negative emotions. Piaget (Bybee & Sund, 1982) believes that learners change their perspectives when they are brought to a place of some discomfort, when their existing ideas no longer explain new information. The disequilibrium that is engendered can result in new understandings and new paradigms in thinking for learners.

The CEO model has been updated from the earlier version (Mac-Fadden, R. J., Herie, M., Maiter, S., Dumbrill, G. C., in press) and incorporates four learning stages which reflect the constructivist paradigm, enhanced by a focus on emotions (see Table 1).

STAGE 1: SAFETY

The first stage of the CEO model involves creating a safe learning environment is critical for learners to be able to think freely, to express opinions, and to challenge themselves and others. All learners and facilitators are asked to deliberately make the course a place where everyone feels safe to risk themselves through expressing ideas. Rules of netiquette (i.e., socially proper behavior on the Net) are posted, discussed and monitored, and group discussions are reviewed by facilitators to ensure a safe and supportive environment. Group members are encouraged to

TABLE 1. A Model for Online Education Focusing on Emotions and Paradigmatic Change

Stage	Purpose	Activity	Potential Feelings of Learners
1. Safety	To create a safe learning environment that facilitates risk taking and examining one's ways of thinking	Construct rules to foster free communication and ensure safety. Monitoring of communication to ensure compliance and safety	Safety, support & acceptance
2. Challenge	To provide the opportunity for participants to critically examine their knowledge and world views	Introduce exercises and processes that allow participants to step outside their existing ways of thinking	Disequilibrium, confusion, anxiety, frustration in a context of safety support & acceptance
3. New Thinking	To create opportunities for engaging with new knowledge and gaining new ways of viewing the world	Introduce alternative knowledge and ways of viewing the world	"Ah ha!" moments leading to a new way of thinking, excitement
4. Consolidation	To create opportunities for the new ideas to be integrated and understood	Provide learning situations that involve the use of this new knowledge to encourage further understanding	New equilibrium brings feeling of deepened understanding and satisfaction until ideas challenged again and disequilibrium re-occurs

use any of the various channels to contact facilitators (i.e., course e-mail, private e-mail, phone) early if they have any concerns in this area. Safety is always a fundamental and primary concern and this is communicated throughout the course.

STAGE 2: CHALLENGE

The second stage of the CEO model involves challenge. A constructivist approach offers a deepening of the educational experience through challenging participants' thinking (Gold, 2001). In a web-based course on enhancing cultural competency that used the CEO model, participants were asked to describe their own cultures by finding and sharing a website that reflected their own culture with other learners. This assignment usually provoked considerable annoyance and frustration because many found this to be impossible since culture and individual identity are so complex and personal that it is unlikely a single website could capture this. Learners were asked to explore their feelings and experience about this and to reflect on how clients might feel about professionals who attempt to understand their cultures based on a single source. With these emotions "switched-on" (i.e., active), learners were asked to think about what this means for professionals who depend on a cultural literacy approach which relies largely on written content about cultures (e.g., reading books on a particular culture, listening to music from that culture and other similar methods). Many learners who depended solely on the cultural literacy approach experienced some dissonance and understood both cognitively and experientially the limitations of catalogued definitions of culture. Additionally, strengths of existing models of understanding culture are reviewed to acknowledge parts that might still inform the learners' practice. In the example above, some learners did not experience dissonance since their experience confirmed what they already knew.

STAGE 3: NEW THINKING

This third stage involves the development of new ideas and thinking. Some dissonance and disequilibrium are helpful in learning since it motivates and encourages new ways of thinking. When information is introduced that promotes this dissonance new models are explored to provide alternatives. As an example, a social worker with experience in working with people from China may firmly believe that there is a strong cultural mandate to respect and look after the elderly. When confronted with a particular case that shows a Chinese family's clear lack of concern about the grandparents, this information makes her uncomfortable because it creates a dissonance with her existing knowledge. This dissonance or disequilibrium may challenge the social worker to explore various reasons for the inadequacy of her knowledge and eventually refine her understanding to incorporate this new reality. Her original thinking may not have included regional differences, socio-economic status and generational differences within Chinese families. The social worker may generate new knowledge based on the challenges to her existing perceptions from this one case. She may decide that her ideas about the "Chinese family" are too narrow and stereotypical. She may conclude that she needs to consider each situation uniquely, as an opportunity to understand how each family views the relationship between itself and its elders.

STAGE 4: CONSOLIDATION

This is the fourth stage that refers to the time after the learner has constructed new knowledge. Opportunities are provided for the learner to integrate and reinforce this new understanding. The learner is encouraged to "try out" this new knowledge through problem-based practice activities so that it can be better understood and integrated into the learner's understanding. The learner may reap the rewards of these new insights in seeing things in new ways and in generating feelings of competency. Through this experience, the learner's feelings may involve satisfaction, comfort and excitement at seeing things in new ways. However, it may not be long before this new knowledge becomes challenged and requires critical examination, which would lead to a cycling back to stage two within the CEO model. This constructivist model reflects the belief that each learner does not passively "receive" knowledge, but rather the learner constructs it. This process of knowledge construction continues constantly as ideas are created, evaluated, refined, discarded and utilized. The CEO model creates a situation for this learning to occur within a web-based environment and uses an understanding of emotion to enhance this learning.

In the CEO model which is focused on the discussion and social interaction approaches to web-based education, there is recognition that the early stages (e.g., first two weeks) of a course should be devoted to assisting the learner to become comfortable and engaged with the online environment. While this may be commonplace in many models, it is particularly emphasized with the CEO approach. This includes meeting other learners, and test driving the website, understanding the structure and knowing where things are. Social engagement is critical since so much of learning is socially oriented, and co-learners can be an important source of support and confirmation. Some web-based courses give bonus grades to fellow students who assist others with problems (Wong & Schoech, 2005). Friendly biography sections where learners can travel to and remind themselves about the background of co-learners and facilitators can be helpful to build connections and ongoing support.

In this early stage, the CEO model focuses the learning objectives on understanding and using the technology to develop a sense of competency. This is accomplished by having the learners sign-on, navigate through the course area, read various formats of posted files such as PowerPoint, Adobe (pdf) and sound files (e.g., wav). Success at this time is crucial and fosters an early sense of competency. There is increased monitoring by facilitators during these early stages to detect and respond to difficulties. Assignments are aimed at building technical expertise and experiencing early success, posting the bio information to foster connections and overviewing the content of the course. Course assignments become progressively more challenging as the learner feels increasingly comfortable with the technology, the content and the co-learners. While some of this is common to many web-based courses, the CEO model recognizes the crucial role of the emotional experience of learners and develops structure and processes that enhance the learning experience.

AN EMOTIONAL LANDSCAPE

Is it possible to think about the emotional landscape of an online course, the emotional contours, and common affective experiences in order to encourage the best possible experience for a learner? As an example, a common emotional experience might be heightened excitement and anxiety at the beginning of the e-course when learners are challenged with understanding the course and its expectations, and with also being able to use the technology competently so the course can be completed successfully. Mastering the demands of the technology within a limited time period can be particularly stimulating and anxiety-provoking, and clearly different from a usual FTF course experience.

During the e-course there would likely be emotional hills and valleys particularly associated with ongoing assignments, presentations and engagement with co-learners and facilitators. The ending phase of the course might be associated with raised excitement, high activity, some anxiety, frustration, some sense of accomplishment, relief, and possibly some sadness at ending relationships. While many events within a course could substantially alter these patterns, the emotional contours of a course experience are important to consider. As an example, a facilitator who is largely inactive within the first part of a course, may cause students to become confused, angry, distrustful and disengaged from the course and the instructor may have to find ways to help learners become more connected, active, trustful and learning if the course is going to be a successful experience.

Although the emphasis may be on encouraging positive emotions, there might be more conscious use of emotions such as anxiety to heighten and sustain motivation. For instance, having three assignments rather than one might promote more ongoing attention and focus on the work and provide more feedback to learners. Again, balance is critical since too many assignments might elevate anxiety to a point where the learner disengages or is not able to think analytically or creatively.

The dynamics of a game, for instance, where one is striving so vigorously and so completely to accomplish something that has reward value, may be instructive. A game may invoke empathy, challenge problem-solving skills, create a sense of risk and offer a chance to be successful and become a "winner" or risk becoming a "loser." There is a strong emotional component in games that serves to heighten motivation, increase performance and foster tenacity and persistence. Could specific components of a game be incorporated more into e-learning to utilize the power of emotions?

Online learning has been criticized by some because of a high drop-out rate (Currin, 2003). Would paying more attention to the emotional experience of the learners reduce early drop-out and increase the quality of the experience overall? Facilitators need to be vigilant to how learners are adapting to this learning environment. With fewer cues from the learners, online facilitators may not be understanding the nature of learners' experience and misinterpreting actions. One qualitative study (Hara & Kling, 2001) found that much early learner communication within a web-based course was negative and reflected considerable learner discontent. When this discontent lessened, the facilitator assumed the early problems had been rectified. Further analysis indicated that many learners had given up expressing concerns and essentially decided to put up with the problems until the course was over. Even after the course was completed, the facilitator was not aware of the level of discontent within the course. Would this have been any different within a FTF course?

There may be other points within an online course where certain kinds of emotions predominate that might benefit from some differential response. The final assignment period, for instance, typically engenders considerable anxiety among learners in an FTF context. How does this get expressed within an online course? Again, while some anxiety may be functional to motivate and encourage thinking and production, how much is too much and to what extent do specific online environments promote more, less or the same amount of anxiety? Should online facilitators respond differently than FTF instructors?

One of the paradoxes in online research is that it is not unusual for learners to report more contacts and satisfaction with an instructor than in comparable FTF classes and instructors. Facilitators are frequently more available during more of the course and responses can be fairly quick. Assignments can be completed late in the schedule and transmitted immediately–no running into the university to be there by five in the afternoon. Clearly there are other factors within an online course that may increase the anxiety around assignment time.

Norman (2002) recommends blending cognitive and emotional elements together in order for e-learning to foster:

- strong motivation, because the problem is one that a learner cares about;
- positive encouragement where efforts to explore are rewarded;
- social commitment which is achieved through working in groups and a positive learner-instructor relationship;
- and some level of stress, through assignments, to increase learner focus and activity.

ENRICHING COMMUNICATION

While communication via computer may be more limited than FTF interaction, online communication can be enriched. Many of the examples in Table 2 below are already in use and/or are being currently developed within different contexts. Several of these tools can be integrated within WBE and combined to form a new style of communication called "emotionally enhanced communication" or EEC. These ways of communicat-

TABLE 2. EEC Strategies to Incorporate Emotions

Punctuation	Exclamation Marks	No way!!! *Conviction, amazement, disbelief*
	Question Marks	You said what??? *Puzzlement, disbelief*
	Capitalization	We CAN'T do that. NO WAY. *Anger, shouting*
	Ellipses	Can't say.... Not sure ... *Uncertainty, thinking*
	Spacing	He just appeared. Out of nowhere. *Pausing, incredulity*
	Underlining	This has to be done today. *Urgency, emphasis*
	Special Characters	<<<Remember>>> *Urgency, attention*
	Bracketing	I need you to do this [feeling guilty just asking]
Font	Style	**You're so funny! (comic sans)** *Humor*
	Color	This is making me burn. *Anger, upset*
	Size	**Believe it.** It must be so. *Importance, attention*
Acronyms		BC *Be cool* EG *Evil grin* FCOL *for crying out loud*
Emoticons	Text-Based	:) *smiling* ;) *winking* :(*sad*
	Graphical	☺ *smiling* ☹ *sad*
Grammar	Metaphor	"I just finished reading your last therap-e-mail, Angie, and my smile is a mile wide" (Collie, Mitchell & Murphy, 2000, p. 226). Descriptive immediacy & metaphor

Note: The comments in italics after each example reflect only some of the possible meanings. Similar to face-to-face non-verbal communication, there is some ambiguity inherent what each expression means.

ing have been derived from several sources, including Glazer (2002) and Murphy and Mitchell (1998), and Collie, Mitchell, and Murphy (2000).

The last two examples come from the development of a form of on-line therapy or e-therapy called "therap-e-mail" (Murphy & Mitchell, 1998). In developing a helping relationship it is critical to communicate feelings such as respect and concern. The authors use many of the above tools to communicate and create these feelings which provides a foundation for the help that flows through their e-mail relationships.

Reflecting on these EEC strategies, one student informed the author that she would only use some of these strategies and actively avoid others (e.g., emoticons). As in FTF communications, the way we actually express emotion online may reflect our own personalities and other factors such as gender. As an example, some people may find using capitalization a RUDE way to communicate. A study by Witmer and Katzman (1997) found that women tended to use graphic accents (e.g., emoticons) more than men in communicating over computers.

In exploring what makes learning effective, Hiltz and Turoff (2002) identify the need for facilitators to establish *swift trust* with learners within the first week or two of a web-based course. Swift trust, a concept developed by Myerson Weick, and Kramer (1996), relates to groups who work around a clear purpose, and have a common task within a finite time period. Swift trust involves a willingness to suspend doubt about others to work on the group's task and a positive expectation that the activity will be beneficial. To build swift trust, Hiltz and Turoff recommend that facilitators provide: early encouragement of learners through explicit statements of commitment, excitement, and optimism; clear contributions that each learner can make; help with any technical or task uncertainties; modeling and encouraging responses to each others' contributions. They also recommend developing collaborative learning opportunities and generating active participation with appropriate types of software. Zheng Veinofft, Bos, Olson, and Olson (2002), also found that in online textual environments, participants who engage in a range of getting-acquainted exercises have higher levels of trust than those who do nothing. Examples of this might be having learners post bios, share personal stories and share personal web sites.

In an article in this issue, Paul Jerry describes a new online program in Applied Psychology that has adopted a "working alliance" approach to web-based education. A working alliance involves three components: agreement on goals, tasks and the development of trust. Goleman (1997) views *trust* as one of the love family of emotions. A major philosophy of this program in Applied Psychology is that the core features of the working alliance are applicable to any successful relationship whether it is programmatic, clinical or educational (Jerry & Collins, 2005). From this perspective, the feeling of trust generated within the context of web-based learning is essential in building a successful learning experience.

CONCLUSION

This article has explored emotions and learning within an online context. The content highlights the importance of ensuring that developers and facilitators have an awareness of the emotional dimension and emotional landscape of an online course and that they build this knowledge into how the course is structured, facilitated and experienced by the learners. Some instructors have the emotional intelligence and awareness to do this without conceiving of it from an emotionally sound perspective. From the ideas raised within this article, the following suggestions are offered:

1. Address both the cognitive and affective dimensions of the learner. Deliberately structure assignments so that they engage the affect of the learner-instead of talking about the concept of social work values, definitions, dilemmas, create a scenario where learners find themselves in the middle of an important ethical quandary within a case situation and they have to work it out. Instead of discussing the components of a social assistance system, engage them in a "game" which finds them on the street and looking for food and a job.

2. Design the online course so that the structure and content are clear, navigation is easy, links are active and downloads can be completed quickly. Avoid complicated file types that may require specialized software or hardware on the learner's end. Being unable to readily participate in the course requirements can marginalize a learner and lead to frustration and disengagement. Pilot test the course with volunteers to ensure that the technology is functional and easy to follow so that it becomes secondary to the learning experience within the course.

3. Develop assignments in a strategic order, starting out with less demanding ones while students are working through the technology, course structure, and getting to know other learners and then increase the challenge, complexity and engaging nature of the assignments. Where possible, involve learners with others in critiquing ideas and constructing new knowledge.

4. Facilitators should maintain a detailed awareness of what is happening with individuals and the class regarding the emotional experience and emotional landscape of the course. Explore the reasons for drop-out and monitor the class communications for changes in volume and affective content. Respond to problems early. As an example, students who appear frustrated, confused or disconnected, should receive a phone call early to try and short-cut difficulties and to increase the positive experience of the learning. Use an excellent technology help system (24/7) so learners can get technical problems solved quickly anytime and not have to "fume" over the problems for a week and then find themselves frustratingly behind the class.

5. Facilitators should try to optimize motivation and maintain reasonable levels of anxiety in students. Instructors need to ensure some level of safety within the class so that learners are willing to risk with new ideas and challenge others in a way that is supportive.

6. Build "swift trust" and acknowledge learners and their contributions by name. For example, feedback such as, "I really appreciated Bob's last comment about this issue–I had never looked at the problem in this way and it makes me think differently about it now." When learners share an opinion or idea there should be some response or acknowledgement of the contribution, however big or small. It can be disheartening for a learner who posts a message to be completely ignored by the participants and facilitator. This can happen easily within an asynchronous environment where the timing and order of communication may not be clear.

7. Incorporate some emotional emphasis directly within the communication. As an example, facilitators can use forms of emotionally enhanced communication (EEC) that they are comfortable with, modeling this for learners.

8. Enhance the positive affect and experience of the learners. For example, use humor whenever possible, being careful to avoid misunderstandings that can occur within this online medium. Provide ongoing feedback about performance through assignments and facilitators' comments. Encourage reactions and comments from others that are appropriate from a Netiquette perspective. Celebrate achievements, individually and collectively.

Emotions are a critical part of learning and need to be considered and addressed in all forms of education. Web-based education specifically presents some unique challenges related to the more limited and different communication opportunities and its reliance on technology-mediated processes. These limitations will always be changing as new technologies enable innovative ways to communicate and instruct. Neurobiologist Joseph LeDoux remarked that cognitive science only focuses on thinking, reasoning, and intellect. He indicates, "It leaves emotions out. And minds without emotions are not really minds at all. They are souls on ice–cold, lifeless creatures devoid of any desires, fear, sorrow, pains and pleasure" (LeDoux, 1996, p. 25). While brain research is unlocking some fascinating and fundamental relationships between emotions and learning, more investigation is needed to identify ways that a focus on emotions can inform and strengthen the web-based learning experience. There is a need to recover the humanity that lies at the basis of this important new learning process. Many of the recommendations for accomplishing this, that are identified within this article, are based on experience and will need to be addressed as hypotheses in future research.

REFERENCES

Astleitner, H. (2000). Designing emotionally sound instruction: The FEASP approach. *Instructional Science, 28*, 169-198.

Astleitner, H., & Leutner, D. (2000). Designing instructional technology from an emotional perspective. *Journal of Research on Computing in Education, 32* (4), 497-510.

Brandt, R. (2000). On teaching brains to think: A conversation with Robert Sylwester. *Educational Leadership*, April.

Bybee, R.W., & Sund, R.B. (1982). *Piaget for educators* (2nd ed). Columbus, OH: Charles Merrill.

Caine, R.N., & Caine, G. (1991). *Making connections: Teaching and the human brain.* Alexandria, VA: Association for Supervision and Curriculum Development.

Campbell-Gibson. (2000). The ultimate disorienting dilemma: The online learning community. In T. Evans, & D. Nation (Eds.), *Changing university teaching: Reflections on creating educational technologies.* London: Kogan Page.

Cherniss, C. (2000). Emotional intelligence: What it is and why it matters. Retrieved October 3, 2004 from Rutgers University, Consortium for Research on Emotional Intelligence in Organization Web site: http://www.eiconsortium.org/research/what_is_emotional_intelligence.htm.

Coles, G. (1999). Literacy, emotions and the brain. Retrieved May 24, 2004 from http://www.readingonline.org/critical/coles.html.

Collie, K. R., Mitchell, D., & Murphy, L. (2000). Skills for online counseling: Maximum impact at minimum bandwidth. In J. W. Bloom & G.R. Walz (Eds.), *Cybercounseling and cyberlearning: Strategies and resources for the millennium.* Alexandria, VA: American Counseling Association.

Currin, L. (2003). Feelin' groovy. *Elearn Magazine*. Retrieved from http://www.elearnmag.org/subpage/sub_page.cfm?article_pk=10221&page_number_nb=1&title=FEATURE%20STORY on May 2nd, 2004.

Damasio, A. (1994). *Descarte's error: Emotion, reason and the human brain.* London: Papermac.

Glazer, C. (2002). Play nice with others: The communication of emotion in an online environment. Retrieved from http://www.scholarlypursuits.com/dec_comm.pdf on May 2, 2004.

Gold, S. (2001). A Constructivist approach to online training for online teachers. *JALN* 5(1), June. Retrieved May 23, 2004 from the World Wide Web: http://www.sloan-c.org/publications/jaln/v5n1/v5n1_gold.asp.

Goleman, D. (1997). *Emotional intelligence.* NY: Bantam.

Greenspan, S. (1997). *The growth of the mind and the endangered origins of intelligence.* Reading, MA: Addison-Wesley.

Hara, N., & Kling, R. (2001). Student distress in web-based distance education. *Educause Quarterly*, Number 3, 68-69.

Hiltz, S., & Turoff, M. (2002). What makes learning effective? *Communications of the ACM*, Vol. 45, No. 4, 56-59.

Jensen, E. (1998). *Teaching with the brain in mind.* Alexandria, VA: Association for Supervision and Curriculum Development.

Jerry, P., & Collins, S. (2005). Web-based education in the human services: Use of web-based video clips in counselling skills training. In R. MacFadden, B. Moore, D. Schoech, & M. Herie (Eds.), *Web-based education in human services: Models, methods and best practices.* NY: The Haworth Press, Inc.

LeDoux, J. (1996). *The emotional brain: The mysterious underpinnings of emotional life.* New York: Simon & Schuster.

MacFadden, R. J., Herie, M., Maiter, S., & Dumbrill, G. C. (in press). Achieving high touch in high tech: A constructivist, emotionally-oriented model of web-based instruction. In Beaulaurier, R., and Haffey, M. (Eds.), *Technology and Social Work Education.* NY: The Haworth Press, Inc.

MacFadden, R.J., Maiter, S., & Dumbrill, G. (2002). High tech and high touch: The human face on online education. In H. Resnick and P. Anderson (Eds.), *Innovations in technology and human services: Practice and education.* NY: The Haworth Press, Inc.

Mayer, J. D. (1999). Emotional intelligence: Popular or scientific psychology? *APA Monitor Online*, Volume 30, Number 8. Retrieved October 3, 2004 from http://www.apa.org/monitor/sep99/sp.html.

Murphy, L., & Mitchell, D. (1998). When writing helps to heal: E-mail as therapy. *British Journal of Guidance and Counselling*, 26, 21-31.

Myerson, D., Weick, K.E., & Kramer, R. (1996). Swift trust and temporary systems. In R. Kramer and T.R. Tyler (Eds.), *Trust in organizations.* Sage: Thousand Oaks, CA, pp. 166-195.

Norman, D. A. (2002). Emotion and design: Attractive things work better. *Interactions Magazine*, ix (4), 36-42. Retrieved May 24, 2004 from http://www.jnd.org/dn.mss/Emotion-and-design.html.

O'Regan, K. (2003). Emotion and e-learning. *Journal of Asynchronous Learning Networks.* Volume 7, Issue 3, September, 78-92.

Pekrun, R., Molfenter, S., Titz, W., & Perry, R. (2000). Emotion, learning and achievement in university students: Longitudinal studies. Paper presented at the annual meeting of the American Educational Research Association, New Orleans, LA, April.

Pekrun, R., Goetz, T., & Titz, W. (2002). Academic emotions in students' self-regulated learning and achievement: A program of qualitative and quantitative research. *Educational Psychologist*, 37(2), 91-105.

Plutchik, R. (2001). The nature of emotions. *American Scientist*, Vol. 89, Issue 4, July/August.

Redden, C. (2003). Emotions in the cyber classroom. *Educator's Voice.* Retrieved May 24, 2004 from http://www.ecollege.com/news/EdVoice_arch_0611.learn.

Rice, R., & Love, G. (1987). Electronic emotion. *Communication Research*, Vol.14, No.1, pp. 85-108.

Stock, B. (1996). Getting to the heart of performance. *Performance Improvement*, Vol. 35, No.8. Retrieved May 24, 2004 from http://www.byronstock.com/pdfs/heart.pdf.

Sylwester, R. (1994). How emotions affect learning. *Educational Leadership*, Vol. 52, Number 2, pp. 60-65.

Thissen, F. (2000). *The medium and the message. Interface design for online learning environments and cooperative learning in virtual worlds.* Retrieved, May 24, 2004 from http://www.frank-thissen.de/mediumandmessage.pdf.

Vail, P. (2002). *Emotion: The on/off switch for learning.* Retrieved May 23, 2004 from http://www.schwablearning.org/pdfs/expert_vail.pdf.

Witmer, D., & Katzman, S. (1997). On-line smiles: Does gender make a difference in the use of graphic accents? *Journal of Computer Mediated Communication*, Vol.2, No.4. Retrieved May 23, 2004 from http://www.ascusc.org/jcmc/vol2/issue4/witmer1.html.

Wong, Y.C., & Schoech, D. (2005). *A tale of three cities: Teaching online to students in Shanghai from Hong Kong and Texas.* In R. MacFadden et al., Web-based education in human services: Models, methods, and best practices. NY: The Haworth Press, Inc.

Zheng, J., Veinofft, E., Bos, N., Olson, J. S., & Olson, G. M. (2002). *Trust without touch: Jumpstarting long-distance trust with social activities.* In Proceedings of Conference on Human Factors in Computing Systems. ACM Press: Minneapolis, MN, 131-146.

The Campus Alberta Applied Psychology Counselling Initiative: Web-Based Delivery of a Graduate Professional Training Program

Sandra Collins
Paul Jerry

SUMMARY. The Campus Alberta Applied Psychology: Counselling Initiative is a collaboration between three universities in western Canada to offer a predominantly Web-based Master of Counselling program. This paper describes the basic structure of the program, the Web-based delivery system, communication tools employed, and the philosophical, pedagogical, programmatic, and administrative principles and concepts foundation to the development and implementation. Development of

Sandra Collins, PhD, is Associate Professor and Director, Centre for Graduate Education in Applied Psychology, Athabasca University. Her major academic and research interests are in counsellor education, program planning and evaluation, multicultural counselling, online and distance learning.

Paul Jerry, PhD, is Assistant Professor, Centre for Graduate Education in Applied Psychology, Athabasca University. His research interests focus on single case research design, counsellor education, distance and online learning, and assessment.

Address correspondence to authors: Centre for Graduate Education in Applied Psychology, Athabasca University, 1 University Drive, Athabasca, Alberta T9S 3A3 Canada.

[Haworth co-indexing entry note]: "The Campus Alberta Applied Psychology Counselling Initiative: Web-Based Delivery of a Graduate Professional Training Program." Collins, Sandra, and Paul Jerry. Co-published simultaneously in *Journal of Technology in Human Services* (The Haworth Press, Inc.) Vol. 23, No. 1/2, 2005, pp. 99-119; and: *Web-Based Education in the Human Services: Models, Methods, and Best Practices* (eds: MacFadden et al.) The Haworth Press, Inc., 2005, pp. 99-119. Single or multiple copies of this article are available for a fee from The Haworth Document Delivery Service [1-800-HAWORTH, 9:00 a.m. - 5:00 p.m. (EST). E-mail address: docdelivery@haworthpress.com].

Digital Object Identifier: 10.1300/J017v023n01_07

curricular content and learning processes have been driven by explicit examination of learner needs, a program-level competency matrix reflective of professional practice standards in the discipline of psychology, and deliberate and continuous formative evaluation and learner engagement in the process. *[Article copies available for a fee from The Haworth Document Delivery Service: 1-800-HAWORTH. E-mail address: <docdelivery@haworthpress.com> Website: <http://www.HaworthPress.com> © 2005 by The Haworth Press, Inc. All rights reserved.]*

KEYWORDS. Online learning, distance delivery, program development, counsellor education

THE CAMPUS ALBERTA APPLIED PSYCHOLOGY: COUNSELLING INITIATIVE

The Campus Alberta Applied Psychology: Counselling Initiative (CAAP) is an inter-university collaboration in western Canada that provides a predominantly Web-based alternative for individuals seeking graduate level training in counselling psychology. This initiative is unique in a number of ways: (1) It is the first distance and web-based applied psychology graduate program in Canada; (2) It is a joint venture between three of the major universities in Alberta; and (3) It is designed specifically to meet the needs of students who are already in the work force or are coping with multiple demands on their time and resources. This paper describes the philosophical, pedagogical, programmatic, and administrative principles and concepts that have formed the foundation for developing and implementing this initiative.

Unique Features

One of the most significant features of this initiative is the collaborative and purposeful development process that forms the foundation for its current structure and content. Following the typical steps in program planning and evaluation models (Burton & Merrill, 1991; Sylvia, Sylvia, & Gunn, 1997), we have carefully built into each step in the process stakeholder input and feedback. The CAAP initiative emerged from a 1998 meeting of university, government, and private sector individuals from across Alberta who had identified gaps in the provision of quality educational services and expressed an interest in collaborating to address those gaps. A comprehensive market analysis was conducted, with the overwhelming majority of the 800 respondents calling for on-line distance programming. Potential students wanted to be able to continue working and complete the program on their own timelines. They had personal, family, and job-related responsibilities to balance with their desire to continue their professional training. Many were in positions where they were already providing some form of counselling services and wished to increase their knowledge and skills, as well as their employability and autonomy.

What was clear from the results of the market analysis was that it would be difficult for any one university or academic department to fully respond to the needs expressed, particularly through traditional means of program delivery. The resulting collaboration between three Alberta universities draws on the strengths and resources of each in the delivery of curricula, student services, library and other supports for learning, and administrative functions. Faculty and administrative staff are housed at three universities, in four different cities. All administrative functions are distributed across the partner institutions and are accessible through a central website, which acts as a portal for seamless delivery of services to students, instructors, and other program staff. Students graduate with a parchment bearing the crests of all three universities. This is the first joint degree program in Alberta, and, the first in this discipline, in Canada.

OVERVIEW OF THE PROGRAM

Design and Duration

The CAAP initiative offers several graduate programs. The focus in this paper will be on the Master of Counselling program. This program is designed to be equivalent to the on-campus course-based Master of Education in Counselling programs at Alberta universities, with a 12 course (36-credit) requirement, plus a final exit project that is seen as the equivalent of 6 credits. While many on-campus programs have one practicum, this program has two practica that add up to an equivalent number of hours to the traditional programs (approximately 260 hours). It is anticipated that the number of practicum hours will be raised over the next few years to meet Canadian and American accreditation criteria for counselling programs.

Unlike most masters programs in Canada, this program was designed with a three-year completion timeframe specifically to accommodate the needs of students working full-time. Students normally take four half courses (12 credits) per year. A typical course runs 13-weeks and is scheduled on the traditional semester basis, although our courses run year round with a heavier load in the spring-summer semester. The academic year begins in the winter term (January). Four courses have mandatory face-to-face components, the rest are offered entirely online. Two of the four face-to-face courses are offered with a mix of 5 weeks of online study and 3-week residential Summer Institute. The other two courses are practica that add two intensive weekend schools to the 13-weeks of online study and concurrent field placement. Figure 1 outlines the course structure and modes of delivery for the Master of Counselling program.

Contact hours are less easily defined in a virtual environment and students typically invest much more time in our online courses than in face-to-face equivalents. However, minimal participation in the online activities is considered equivalent to 3 hours per week, 39 hours per semester, not including advance readings and other preparation. Students entering the program are advised to plan for a 15-hour per week minimum investment in each 3-credit course.

Costs

Currently, base program cost for the three-years is $10, 287 US. Students pay fees at a fixed rate over three years. Individual courses are available to non-program students at $727 US. The program operates on a cost-recovery basis, with approximately $447,260/year of funding from the Ministry of Learning in Alberta. Fee increases of 5% per year are anticipated over the next three years until we reach our peak enrollments, at 120 new admissions per year. At our projected steady state, there will be 8-9 full-time faculty and 4-5 administrative staff, serving over 300 students. Instructional and supervisory tasks are supported by a cadre of part-time instructional associates and adjunct faculty. The cost per course registration is currently estimated at $1,305 (total program expenditures/number of course registrations). These costs include all course materials, stipends for practicum and research project supervisors, administrative overhead, and so on. The cost recovery nature of the program makes it possible for us to respond to the market demands rather than to artificial caps on student enrollments that are the typical admission drivers in Canadian graduate programs.

FIGURE 1. CAAP program design and delivery.

Phase I: Counselling Foundations

Year	Semester	Courses	Mode of Delivery
I	Winter	601: Theories of Counselling and Client Change	Online
	Spring-Summer	603: Professional Ethics 605: Developing a Working Alliance	Online + 3-week Summer Institute
	Fall	617: Methods of Inquiry	Online
II	Winter	607: Equity and Diversity Issues in Counselling	Online

Phase II: Counselling Specialization

Year	Semester	Courses	Mode of Delivery
II	Spring-Summer	613: Assessment 615: Intervening to Facilitate Client Change	4 modules online or optional summer institute
	Fall	611: General Counselling Practicum	Online + Field placement + 2 weekend schools
III	Winter	Specialization Option I	Online
	Spring-Summer	Specialization Option II Specialization Option III	Online
	Fall	619: Specialized Practicum	Online + Field placement + 2 weekend schools

Status and Recognition

The program is fully accredited through the institution accreditation processes that apply to all Canadian universities. CAAP courses are recognized at other universities across Canada as equivalent to a traditional on-campus course. A transfer guide listing equivalent courses in the on-campus graduate programs in Alberta has been developed. Students in the on-campus programs are permitted to take CAAP courses and vice-versa, creating a broader range of options for all students, regardless of their home institution or program. The courses have been designed specifically to meet the academic credential requirements for students who wish to pursue two different professional paths: licensure as a psychologist through provincial regulatory bodies (specific under-graduate coursework is also required) or registration as a Canadian Certified Counsellor through the Canadian Counselling Association.

While we do not yet have graduates from the program, representatives from many of the major professional associations and employers in Alberta continue to be actively involved as members of the Advisory Board for the program and all indications are that our graduates will be well received in the field. Students who have taken other graduate programs but are missing particular courses for licensing have been referred to this program to obtain those additional requirements.

CAAP PROGRAM CONTENT

Building Content from a Foundation in Professional Practice Competencies

On the surface, the program content reflects typical masters level training in applied psychology professional programs in Canada (see Figure 1). Courses include clinical training and non-clinical/theoretical learning. Where this program is quite unique is in the competency-based model employed for all curriculum development. As with many human services disciplines, there is a growing consensus in psychology in Canada and the United States about the core competencies for professional practice (Canadian Counselling Association, 2003; Canadian Psychological Association, 1991; Council for Accreditation of Counseling and Related Educational Programs, 2001; Weaver, 2002). In fact, Canada has now established a Mutual Recognition Agreement to permit mobility of psychologists across provinces based on agreed upon core competencies (Regulatory Bodies for Professional Psychologists in Canada, 2001). However, few attempts have been made to systematically apply these competencies to the development of curricula in professional training programs. More often, course titles are used as the basis for assuring that the content reflects professional practice demands. The actual content of any given course varies from semester to semester based on the interests and quality of the instructor. In addition, there is little explicit relationship between the course content and the overall learning objectives of the program (Roque, Elia, da Motta, & de Campos, 2003).

The advantage of a web-based platform for curriculum delivery is that there is a much greater opportunity for standardization of content across sections of a course and for purposeful integration of content based on an overall conceptual framework for the program. The conceptual framework was drafted using the competencies outlined in the current literature and refined through a process of successive consultations with key stakeholders (Jerry, Collins, Hiebert, & Strong, 2002). The resultant competency matrix is organized by the functions that graduates of the program might perform. The competencies are grouped into seven clusters or domains: Basic Human Functioning, Professional Behaviour, Interpersonal Relationships, Assessment, Intervention, Teaching and Group Process, and Applied Research. Within each competency domain, *specific functions* are performed. Further, *specific competencies* are required to successfully complete each function. The *specific competencies* can then be thought of in terms of the traditional categories of: *knowledge, skills, and attitudes*. Figure 2 illustrates the relationship between domains, functions, and competencies for one particular function in the interpersonal relationships domain.

Web-Based Facilitation of Purposeful Course Design

These outcome competencies for the overall program are then mapped onto specific courses to ensure that each student who successfully completes the core curriculum of the program will exit with a defined competency set. A comprehensive competency matrix for the program allows students to link competency development and curriculum throughout the program. The learning objectives, interactive web-based learning objects and activities, and online discussion forum topics for each course, as well as the online course evaluations, reflect this overall competency foundation. The web-based nature of the program facilitates this standardization of curriculum.

Course assignments are also mapped onto Bloom's taxonomy of educational objectives (Bloom, 1956; Krathwohl, Masia, & Bloom, 1965) to reflect the knowledge, affective, and skills domains targeted in the overall competency framework and to provide clear criteria for grading in each area. Since this is an applied practice program, emphasis is placed in all courses on the application of knowledge to practice. The focus on development of professionally-relevant attitudes and beliefs, in particular, is often ignored in university programs but is clearly relevant to human services disciplines (Johnson & Campbell, 2002). By continual linking of course objectives to professional practice competencies and the inclusion of experiential and reflective activities, students are challenged to address personal biases and attitudinal barriers.

FIGURE 2. The relationship between domains, functions, and competencies.

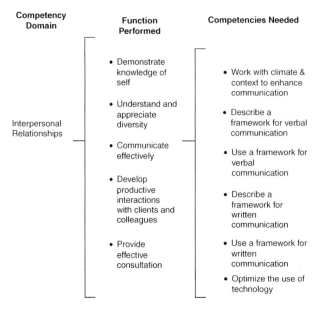

Web-Based Facilitation of the Infusion Model for Graduate Curriculum

The web-based delivery platform and the overall conceptual framework for the program enable us to address another common criticism of graduate training–the focus on individual courses in particular content areas versus infusion of critical professional issues across a number of courses. Take, for example, the current emphasis in the professional literature on integration of cultural awareness into professional practice (Achenbach & Arthur, 2002; Murdock, Alcorn, Heesacker, & Stoltenberg, 1998; Sue, Arredondo, & McDavis, 1992). While we offer a course specifically designed to address these issues, the course materials are organized as distinct electronic learning objects and the course readings are located in a digital reading room. The materials are then cross-referenced and integrated into other courses. The emphasis on competences rather than courses in curriculum design also encourages course authors to infuse various components of the core competencies across multiple courses, resulting in a much richer and more integrated learning experience for students.

Another example of the integration of core competencies at the curricular and programmatic levels is the use of the working alliance as a core construct for conceptualizing the counselling process and as a philosophical foundation for faculty and administrative functioning and student-faculty interactions. This concept is explored in more detail in the Collins and Jerry (2005) article in this volume. An effective working alliance is defined as a collaboration between counsellor and client(s) [faculty and students, supervisor and staff, etc.] designed to facilitate change that involves three key components (Bordin, 1979; Horvath & Symonds, 1991; Gelso & Carter, 1994):

1. Agreement on the goals to be accomplished through the relationship;
2. Agreement on the tasks to be fulfilled by each partner in the relationship; and
3. A relationship characterized by mutual trust and respect that provides a solid foundation for facilitating the identified goals and tasks.

This construct has provided an operational principle for managing the inter-university collaboration, for involving students in the development and on-going refinement of the program, and for building an effective academic and managerial team. The learners in this system are taught from the outset that this philosophical stance brings with it an expectation of responsiveness, mutual respect, and collaboration at all levels.

THE CAAP LEARNERS

There are approximately 220 students currently in the program, each taking 3-4 courses per year. CAAP students represent a broad cross-section of individuals seeking to upgrade their academic credentials. The approximate age range is 28 to 60 years, with most in mid-career, seeking further academic training in order to advance in their careers. Demographically, the majority of students are female (83%) and there is a slightly higher number of urban (60%) versus rural residents. However, reaching approximately 88 rural residents in our first three years of the program reflects our goal of increasing access to graduate training. For many of these students, this was the only cost-effective and accessible means of furthering their education. At present, the majority of learners are located in Canada, although the most recent intake (our third cohort) includes a number of international students.

STRUCTURING A WEB-BASED GRADUATE PROGRAM FOR OPTIMAL SUCCESS

Creating a One-Stop Web-Interface for the CAAP Community

One of the greatest challenges we faced in the development of this program was integrating staff, administrative structures, services, and resources from three geographical dispersed universities into a seamless delivery system for students. Students in this program have the advantage of an increased range of supports for learning and wider scope of faculty expertise. Major administrative functions are negotiated and distributed among the partners–library, technical support, financial services, registry, etc. From the perspective of the student, however, the systems are integrated into a comprehensive package.

All services, resources, faculty, and courses are accessed through a central website at www.abcounsellored.net. Access to the various levels of the comprehensive web system is driven by username. Students who log in are taken directly to the Student Home Page which acts as a portal through which they access all program information, library services at all three institutions, digital reading rooms, registry and financial services, student services, online tutorials for web-based learning, research skills, etc., program announcements, job and conference postings, and open discussion forums in various program related topic areas. On this page, the students will also find links to all courses they are currently registered in and to the student information system. From the perspective of the learner, there is one system of program delivery, although the virtual paths lead to systems and services at three different physical locations and institutions. Faculty and instructional staff, administrators, and other user groups who log into the CAAP system are taken to similar home pages, tailored to that particular group.

Learner-Driven Rather than Platform-Driven Course Design

The web portal has been custom designed by a small technical team and continues to be expanded and refined over time. It has been designed in such a way that the actual courseware system we are using to provide interactive tools at the program and course levels can be changed as new options arise. Currently, we are drawing on an open-source platform called Bazaar (http://klaatu.pc.athabascau.ca/cgi-bin/b7/main.pl?rid=1) developed at Athabasca University. The advantage of this system is that it allows us to customize the platform to suit our individual needs. We have designed our program and course delivery pages independent of the courseware, based on our vision for effective web-based instructional design. Students have also had an active role in providing continual feedback on the design to ensure optimal user-friendliness.

One of the challenges that we have faced in developing courses is combining subject matter expertise with instructional design skills for the online environment. We have solved this dilemma by providing a standardized process for course development, with templates for the structure of syllabi, lessons, assignments, and course evaluations. We have also matched each course developer with a core faculty member for mentoring. A systematic review by a team of academics from the partner institution ensures quality in both content and curriculum design. Finally, the course development coordinator for the program reviews each course to ensure that the study process takes optimal advantage of the interactive tools and potential online learning processes and revises the final materials accordingly.

Each course has a similar look and feel so that students don't spend unnecessary time learning how to access information: overview, learning objectives, key terms and concepts, digital and print-based readings, step-by-step study process, online discussion questions, and additional resources. The types of interactive communication tools used vary across courses. A single link provides students with the list of relevant web tools for the course: discussion forums, assignment drop box, white board, student presentations forum, group sign-up, and/or chat rooms. The types of tools used are driven by the learning objectives and content of course. Depending on the course, we also integrate in various customized audio and video functions. A digital reading room of faculty-selected resources is created for each course and remains accessible and searchable by all students. Readers may view the CAAP links, along with those of other Athabasca University programs, at http://library.athabascau.ca/drr/index2.html.

DESIGNING WEB-BASED CURRICULUM

CAAP Course Design

CAAP courses all run in a paced format with one lesson per week. While it may be argued that this imposes restrictions on learner self-pacing, from a programmatic perspective we see this as essential in ensuring that students engage in the level of critical and analytical discussion of the concepts that one would expect in graduate education (Fahy, Crawford, & Ally 2001; Garrison, Anderson, & Archer, 2000). Pedagogically, we are committed to a constructivist notion of knowledge development (Jerry, Collins, & Demish, 2003; Garrison et al., 2000; Kanuka & Anderson, 1998), which sees learning as generated through social interaction. Research points to the importance of an active pattern of the construction of knowledge through a series of phases including sharing/comparing of information; discovery and exploration of dissonance or inconsistency among the ideas; testing of the proposed syntheses of the evolving knowledge; negotiation of meaning and/or co-construction of knowledge that culminates with an active phrasing of agreement statements; and applications of the newly constructed meaning (Gunawardena, Lowe, & Anderson, 1997). Our commitment to creating a learner-driven system is balanced by our higher-level commitment to ensuring an optimal graduate learning experience.

Feedback from instructors who teach both online and face-to-face indicates that the depth of critical thinking and active learning in the online forums exceeds what they observe in traditional classroom settings. Similar observations were made by an external evaluator who conducted a program review in March 2003 (Schultz, 2003). Following are some of the advantages we note of paced, asynchronous discussions:

- Specific criteria can be developed to ensure the quality of each learner's posts. In CAAP courses, 20% of the student's grade is attached to specific measures of both quantity and quality of posts. Figure 3 illustrates the standard criteria we have developed for assigning grades to this portion of the course activities.
- The web-based interface has an equalizing effect among students who might otherwise tend to remain silent or to monopolize the conversations. Clear guidelines about the minimum and maximum words for the required posts force students to think through carefully the statements they would like to make.
- Each discussion forum remains open for a one-week period (typically Wednesday to Tuesday to allow working students to post over the weekend). Both students and faculty report processing the course content continuously throughout the week in a way that does not happen when they attend a 3-hour class on-campus. There is also increased opportunity to integrate learning into applied practice throughout the week and report back to the discussion forum or to re-think a position and post new learning later in the week.

Combining Individual and Group Learning Activities

The curriculum for each weekly lesson is divided into activities that involve both individual and group modes of learning. Students engage with required reading materials, information-gathering activities, experiential or self-reflective learning activities, learning objects that may involve audio and video clips, and applied practice assignments. In addition to the online discussion forum that forms a mandatory process in all CAAP web-based courses, students may participate in other large or small group activities: collaborative tasks through chat rooms or email, participation in smaller group discussions, group assignments, and so forth. All courses are limited in size to 20 students to ensure an optimal environment for large group interactions.

Combining Online and Face-to-Face Formats for Skill-Based Courses

One of the challenges in developing a web-based program for graduate education in an applied practice discipline is how to ensure that students receive the same quality of professional skill development that they would in a traditional classroom environment. While we anticipate that technology will continue to enhance the quality of skill training at a distance, we have opted to use a mixed modal delivery process for our counselling skill-based courses, either drawing on weekend seminars or summer institutes (see Figure 1). Collins and Jerry (2005) in this volume describe one such counselling skills course. The actual number of face-to-face contact hours for summer institute courses is 39, which means that the 15 hour equivalent online portion of the course is actually an addition to the number of hours in a typically equivalent on-campus course. Similarly the weekend schools for the practica allow for approximately 24 hours of face-to-face contact in addition to the 39 hour equivalent of online discussions.

Use of Modular Format in Some CAAP Courses

There are two senses in which we apply modularization. First, individual learning activities in each lesson are set apart as distinct learning objects, stored in individual files. As discussed earlier, this allows for integration or interconnection of material across courses. In addition, several courses have been specifically designed in modular format to allow students to tailor the curriculum to their individual learning needs.

FIGURE 3. Assessment criteria for grading participation in online discussion forums.

Evaluation Component	Grading Criteria	Weight
Extent of Participation	• **Three postings** to the questions or issues raised in the weekly forum. When more than three questions are provided, you are welcome to engage in the discussions of all questions. You are required to respond to at least three. • **Two responses** (minimum) per week in response to the postings of other students. Responses to questions or issues posted in the forums must be no longer than 100-200 words. You should look at your participation in the discussion forums as roughly equivalent to the three hours you would traditionally spend in an on-campus graduate seminar. Your reading, preparation, and assignment time takes place in addition to those three hours. You are permitted to miss posting to the discussion forum for one week during the semester without impacting your grade.	10 marks
Quality of Comments	• Core constructs accurately identified and described • Material from previous units integrated to formulate ideas and generate dialogue • Personal perceptions, attitudes, values reflected in the contributions • Self-awareness, sensitivity to others, openness to personal growth demonstrated • New and related perceptions of an issue raised • Ability to synthesize, personalize, and apply learning to personal development demonstrated • Relevant readings and research cited to support points The quality of your comments is evaluated on the basis of criteria similar to those used in evaluating written assignments. Comments should demonstrate that you have read the background material and have given thought to the issues raised. You should also demonstrate your active engagement in the process of self-reflection. At least one of your postings each week should incorporate specific reference to the core readings or additional resources that you have accessed to prepare for the discussion. Marks are awarded for a pattern of responses:	10 marks

The Assessment and Intervention courses both contain an initial conceptual framework, consisting of five online lessons. The remainder of the course is comprised of either 10-hour face-to-face workshops or 3-week online modules on a variety of topics. Students customize their learning experience based on their career interests. Students may also opt to take additional modules at a minimal cost.

Professionals in the community are also invited to participate in these modular offerings as a professional development activity. They register through a separate online registration system and receive a certificate of completion. They may take as many modules as they like, provided there is sufficient space available. Since this is a new initiative, we have not yet sought continuing education credit recognition for these modules, but that will be a next step in the process. Over time, our intention is to develop further this branch of our educational offerings as a means of enhancing the professional practice of counselling and psychology in Canada.

Synchronous and Asynchronous Activities

All CAAP courses make use of both synchronous and asynchronous activities, with decisions based on the educational/pedagogical value of the interactive process for a particular learning objective. The counselling skills course, for example, makes use of a logged chat room to allow students to develop an "instantly transcribed" counselling session for skills analysis (see Collins and Jerry [2005] in this volume).

PREPARING FACULTY TO FUNCTION EFFECTIVELY IN A WEB-BASED ENVIRONMENT

Critical to the success of any web-based course delivery process is the skill level of the course instructors. There are a number of means that have been used in this program to enhance the skills of instructors in web course development and facilitation. Central to these has been the development of a comprehensive instructor orientation that covers such issues as: use of the online learning tools, how to effectively manage the online discussion, expectations for grading of student assignment (including standardized templates for providing feedback), and how to access additional supports. In addition, each course has an assigned course coordinator from among the core faculty at one of the three participating universities who provides supervision to the course instructors, both individually and through group processes (online discussion forums or conference calls).

LEARNER-CENTRED PEDAGOGY

We also conceive of this program as primarily learner-centred in the sense that there is a significant onus on each student to participate actively to gain the greatest benefit from the learning process. The quality of course materials, learning activities, or interactive communication tools is only as effective as the engagement of the learner with these processes (Jerry, Demish, & Collins, 2003). The philosophical and pedagogical stance of the program focuses on developing a working alliance with students and facilitating a co-construction of both learning process and learning outcomes. This is only possible, however, through active engagement of students in all levels of program development. For web-based distance learning programs, this active engagement is even more challenging, particularly as the size of the program increases. There are a number of means that we have discovered for accomplishing this goal:

1. Foster the development of an active Graduate Students Association and offer them opportunities for significant involvement in program activities. At this point, the GSA is refining its own home page within our centralized web system.
2. Provide frequent opportunities for formal and informal feedback on program, technological, and course levels. We conduct evaluations of all course content, instruction, Summer Institute activities, and technological processes (online applications, web-based content design, communication tools). We also maintain open discussion forums where students can post issues of concern, questions, or ideas for program improvement.
3. Provide an orientation to both online learning and graduate education. In our case, this involves a mandatory 5-week online module prior to the start of the program.
4. Engage students in mentoring each other. During the online orientation new students are connected to a senior student as mentor (20 students/mentor). These mentors continue to track students through their first course in the program to respond to questions about graduate school expectations, web-based learning tools, academic writing, and so on.

SUCCESSES AND CHALLENGES

Preliminary Evaluation Data

In large part, our success will be determined by the professional recognition and career advancement of our graduates. However, there are some preliminary indicators of success. Seventy-three percent of the 1st cohort and 88% of the 2nd cohort remain in program. These attrition rates are comparable to on-campus programs; however, we have observed that the withdrawals happen very early on in the distance program, either during the online orientation or the first course. Informal evaluation suggests that a mismatch between the student and the Web-based learning platform is a significant factor. Students have entered the program without attending to the minimum standards for computer hardware and software and ended up withdrawing and, on occasion, re-applying after they had upgraded their computer systems. Similarly, some students have entered the student orientation without basic computer skills or without a real sense of what it is like to work in this virtual environment and have decided that a more traditional classroom approach was more suited to their needs. A second major factor is the misperception that distance education requires less work or sets lower standards than traditional university education when, in fact, the time commitment on students' part is often greater.

One of the goals of the program was to increase access to quality graduate training in applied psychology. The rates of admission to the program were 59% in 2002 and 63% in 2003, considerably higher than those of the on-campus programs. In addition, the actual overall numbers admitted to the *Campus Alberta* program in the last two years were five times that of the on-campus programs. This is now the largest graduate counselling program in Alberta.

Based on evaluation data from the first two program years, the following observations were made:

- There was a strong correlation between the student ratings of the quality of the instructor and their ratings of both course content and the delivery process. This correlation carried over into the ratings of the individual online communication tools and multimedia learning objects, suggesting that the efficacy of instructional content and learning processes is mediated by the quality of instructor input into that process.
- In spite of this variation across instructors, the learning tools that received the highest ratings in most courses were the discussion forums and library services, followed by the internal email system and the student presentations forum. The chat rooms were used less and received lower ratings, as were the optional online task planner and the whiteboard.
- Students expressed some intermittent frustration with the developmental nature of the online delivery platform, but still rated the delivery process and the tools as follows (on a scale ranging from 0 = very poor to 4 = excellent):

- Course delivery process (for combined online and summer institute courses) = 3.13
- Course delivery process (for completely online courses) = 3.32
- Communication tools and resources (for combined online and summer institute courses) = 3.04
- Communication tools and resources (for completely online courses) = 3.24

It is interesting to note that the data from the completely online courses yielded higher levels of satisfaction. Modifications to individual courses have been made based on the feedback received and a new version of the courseware platform that incorporates feedback from students and instructional staff was recently implemented.

Over the next few years, we intend to conduct some formal cross-platform evaluations to compare both learning outcomes and ratings of student satisfaction between equivalent on-campus and online courses. At this point, our primarily means of comparison has come from faculty who teach in both programs and consistently report being amazed at the comparative quality of the online discussions. Comparisons of student grade distributions between equivalent courses have not yielded any significant patterns at this point, but this is an additional source of data that we will continue to track.

Lessons Learned and Pitfalls to Avoid

As program developers, stepping out into new territory on two fronts, online delivery of applied professional practice in psychology and joint inter-university delivery of graduate training, we have certainly learned a few lessons along the way. Primary among them is the tendency to underestimate the time and energy involved in developing online learning processes. Faculty were stretched beyond their comfort zones into areas of curriculum design not normally required of them. We strongly recommend a year and a half lead time for development of a graduate course in this format. Secondly, we underestimated the complexity of coming to agreement across three universities about all aspects of policy, procedures, and administrative functioning. Nonetheless, we have broken down barriers, paved pathways to new models of program development and delivery, and have arrived at an end product that provides significant advantages to students over traditional training programs. The following recommendations emerge from our collective experience:

- Success is maximized through a philosophy of collaboration and active engagement of stakeholders at all levels (employers, professional associations, faculty, administrators, and students). This often means breaking down barriers and territorial attitudes.
- Plan for things to take longer than you anticipate and invest the time upfront to establish templates, models, and conceptual frameworks before beginning to develop curricular content. Thinking on both a macro and micro level is essential for seamlessness and internal congruity at course and program levels.
- Focus on training faculty and instructors in online curriculum development and learning. The transition from traditional classroom environments is not seamless and requires development of new skills, adoption of new philosophies of education and service delivery, and willingness to embrace a more inter-dependent and collaborative model of working with each other and with students.
- Provide resources and training for students about how to function in an online environment. Our application process is completely online so that students begin learning to function in that environment from the time they apply. The orientation then takes place prior to the first class so that a student is not struggling to master the technology and adjusting to graduate course demands simultaneously.

Looking Forward

The CAAP experience has transformed the thinking of those involved from an initial pursuit of equivalency to on-campus programming to a belief that the online environment may actually offer an optimal approach to learning success for some students targeting certain learning objectives. Over the next few years, evaluation plans focus on comparing outcomes between equivalent on-campus and online courses, tracking the success of program graduates, and exploring particular aspects of the online learning experience (e.g., affect as a specific learning objective, community building, constructivist learning processes). We look forward to the continued growth of this initiative and our own learning through this process.

REFERENCES

Achenbach, K., & Arthur, N. (2002). Experiential learning: Bridging theory to practice in multicultural counselling. *Guidance & Counselling, 17,* 39-45.
Bloom, B.S. (Ed.) (1956). *Taxonomy of educational objectives: The classification of educational goals: Handbook I, cognitive domain.* Toronto: Longmans, Green.

Bordin, E. S.(1979). The generalizability of the psychoanalytic concept of the working alliance. *Psychotherapy: Theory, Research, & Practice, 16*(3), 252-260.

Burton, J.K., & Merrill, P.F. (1991). Needs assessment: Goals, needs, and priorities. In L.J. Briggs, K.L. Gustafson, & M.H. Tillman (Eds.), *Instructional design: Principles and applications* (pp. 21-45). Englewood Cliffs, N.J.: Educational Technology Publications.

Canadian Counselling Association (2003). *Accreditation Procedures and Standards for Counsellor Education Programs at the Master's Level.* Ottawa, Ontario: Author. Retrieved February 25, 2004 from http://www.ccacc.ca/CACEP.htm.

Canadian Psychological Association. (1991). *Accreditation manual.* Ottawa, Ontario: Author.

Council for Accreditation of Counseling and Related Educational Programs (CACREP). (2001). *The 2001 Standards.* Available at: http://www.counseling.org/cacrep/2001standards700.htm.

Fahy, P., Crawford, G., & Ally, M. (2001). Patterns of interaction in a computer conference transcript. *International Review of Research in Open and Distance Learning, 2*(1), 1-24.

Garrison, D. R., Anderson, T., & Archer, W. (2000). Critical inquiry in a text-based environment: Computer conferencing in higher education. *The Internet and Higher Education, 2*(2-3), 1-19.

Geslo, C. J., & Carter, J. A. (1994). Components of the psychotherapy relationship: Their interaction and unfolding during treatment. *Journal of Counselling & Development, 41*(3), 296-306.

Gunawardena, C. N., Lowe, C. A., & Anderson, T. (1997). Analysis of a global online debate and the development of an interaction analysis model for examining a social construction of knowledge in computer conferencing. *Journal of Educational Computing Research, 17*(4), 397-431.

Horvath, A. O., & Symonds, B. D. (1991). Relation between working alliance and outcome in psychotherapy: A meta-analysis. *Journal of Counselling Psychology, 38*(2), 139-149.

Jerry, P., Collins, S., Hiebert, B., & Strong, T. (2002). Changing the face of graduate education. *Consultation Proceedings: Eighth Annual Building Tomorrow Today: Alberta Regional Consultation for Career Development.*

Jerry, P., Collins, S., & Demish, H. (2003). Defining the challenges: The juxtaposition of technology and humanity in distributed learning environments. *Proceedings of the 20th Annual Conference of the Canadian Association for Distance Education.*

Jerry, P., Demish, H., & Collins, S. (2003). Managing affect and attitude in distance education. *Proceedings of the 9th Annual North American Web-based Learning Conference,* 41-49.

Johnson, W.B., & Campbell, C.D. (2002). Character and fitness requirements for professional psychologists: Are there any? *Professional Psychology, Research & Practice, 33*(1), 46-53.

Kanuka, H., & Anderson, T. (1998). Online social interchange, discord, and knowledge construction. *Journal of Distance Education, 13*(1), 57-74.

Krathwohl, D.R., Masia, B. B., & Bloom, B. S. (1965). *Affective domain: The classification of educational goals* (Taxonomy of educational objectives.) Longman Schools Division: Pearson Education Co.

Murdock, N. L., Alcorn, J., Heesacker, M., & Stoltenberg, C. (1998). Model training program in counseling psychology. *Counseling Psychologist, 26*, 658-672.

Regulatory Bodies for Professional Psychologists in Canada. (2001). *Mutual Recognition Agreement of the Regulatory Bodies for Professional Psychologists in Canada.* Retrieved February 25, 2004 from http://www.cpa.ca/MRA.pdf.

Roque, G. O. B., Elia, M. D. F., da Motta, C. L. R., & de Campos, G. H. B. (2003). The concept of competencies and its use in the evaluation of learning in distance courses in the web. In A. M. Vilas, J. A. Gonzalez, & J. M. Gonzalez (Eds.), *Advances in Technology-Based Education: Towards a Knowledge-Based Society, Proceedings of the Second International Conference on Multimedia and ICTs in Education, Volume II*, 1080-1084.

Schulz, W. (2003). *Campus Alberta Applied Psychology: Counselling Initiative: External Evaluation.* Unpublished manuscript.

Sue, D. W., Arredondo, P., & McDavis, R. J. (1992). Multicultural counseling competencies and standards: A call to the profession. *Journal of Counseling & Development, 70*, 477-483.

Sylvia, R. D., Sylvia, K. M., & Gunn, E. M. (1997). Program planning and evaluation for the public manager (2nd ed.). Long Grove, IL: Waveland Press.

Weaver, K. A. (2002). The value of national standards. *American Psychologist, 57* (6-7), 450-451.

A Tale of Three Cities:
Teaching Online to Students in Shanghai
from Hong Kong and Texas

Yu Cheung Wong
Dick Schoech

SUMMARY. The University of Hong Kong collaborated with the Fudan University in Shanghai to offer a Master of Social Service Management (MSSM) part-time degree for students in Shanghai. While most courses of the program were taught by instructors sent from Hong Kong and other overseas countries on weekends and holidays, the "Information and Communication Technology in Social Service Organizations"

Yu Cheung Wong, PhD, is a lecturer, Department of Social Work and Social Administration, University of Hong Kong. He teaches social policy, community work, and human services technology. His current research involves working with a rehabilitation organization to develop technology-based training materials for students with learning disabilities. He is the director of the part-time BSW program in his department (http://bswpt.sw.hku.hk).

Dick Schoech, PhD, is the Dulak Professor, University of Texas, Arlington School of Social Work. He teaches courses on administration, community practice, and human services technology. His current research involves working with teens to develop www.SubstanceAbusesPrevention.org and using OLAP (Online Analytical Processing) technology to help staff visualize child protective services data. He is chair of HUSITA (Human Services Information Technology Applications), an international association of professionals dedicated to promoting the ethical and effective use of IT to serve humanity (www.husita.org).

[Haworth co-indexing entry note]: "A Tale of Three Cities: Teaching Online to Students in Shanghai from Hong Kong and Texas." Wong, Yu Cheung, and Dick Schoech. Co-published simultaneously in *Journal of Technology in Human Services* (The Haworth Press, Inc.) Vol. 23, No. 1/2, 2005, pp. 121-145; and: *Web-Based Education in the Human Services: Models, Methods, and Best Practices* (eds: MacFadden et al.) The Haworth Press, Inc., 2005, pp. 121-145. Single or multiple copies of this article are available for a fee from The Haworth Document Delivery Service [1-800-HAWORTH, 9:00 a.m. - 5:00 p.m. (EST). E-mail address: docdelivery@haworthpress.com].

121

course was offered online and supplemented by several face-to-face sessions. Instructors in Texas and Hong Kong collaborated and offered the course to the students in Shanghai. Teaching and learning online was a completely new experience for the students. Technical, social, cultural, and linguistic issues arose throughout the four months during which the course was offered. This paper shares the teaching experience and reflection of the instructors as well as the learning outcome and evaluation of the students. *[Article copies available for a fee from The Haworth Document Delivery Service: 1-800-HAWORTH. E-mail address: <docdelivery@haworthpress.com> Website: <http://www.HaworthPress.com> © 2005 by The Haworth Press, Inc. All rights reserved.]*

KEYWORDS. Online education, chatroom teaching, cross-cultural teaching online, multinational teaching

Online education has opened new teaching and learning possibilities that enable instructors and students to overcome geographic and time constraints typical to traditional classroom teaching. It also enhances collaboration among higher education institutions to offer programs and courses so that students do not have to travel long distances to pursue their studies. One form of collaboration is for a higher education institution in a developed country/region to work with its counterpart in a developing country/region to offer programs that award students a degree from the institution in the developed side. Such programs provide opportunities for students to earn a degree outside their country/region without spending the money and time necessary to stay away from home.

This paper documents and evaluates the experience of one such course, namely, "Information and Communication Technology for Human Services Organizations." The course was offered to students in Shanghai, China studying in a collaborative program between Hong Kong and Shanghai. This paper focuses particularly on the social, cultural, linguistic, and learning issues experienced while offering the course.

Starting from 2001, Fudan University of Shanghai (Department of Sociology) and University of Hong Kong (Department of Social Work & Social Administration) launched the MSSM (Master of Social Service Management) and MSW (Master of Social Work) collaboration programs. Both programs offered three-year part-time degrees to Chinese students, most of whom worked and resided in Shanghai. Both degrees were awarded by HKU.

The Master of Social Service Management (MSSM) program trained experts in social service management in Mainland China. The program provided competencies in planning and resource management, research, policy analysis and decision-making, staff management, and leadership. It targeted mid-management and directorate level staff of social service organizations as well as those who are prepared to take up administrative positions of increasing responsibility. The designers of the collaborative program considered the Information and Communication Technology course content crucial to developing students with knowledge and critical perspectives in applying technology to meet the information need of social service organizations to improve management and service delivery. This paper presents the experience of teaching the course within an overall evaluative framework which includes learners, instructors, presentation, content, outcomes, and instructional environment. Data were collected via techniques such as structured questionnaires, chatroom discussion records, and classroom evaluation meeting.

LITERATURE REVIEW AND BACKGROUND

Web-based teaching has gained wide applications. Its effectiveness in teaching social work courses has been demonstrated (Ligon, Markward, & Yegidis, 1999; Stocks & Freddolino, 1998; Stocks & Freddolino, 2000; Wernet, Olliges, & Delicath, 2000; Schoech & Helton, 2002; Macy, Rooney, Hollister, & Freddolino, 2001; Massimo, 2003). So far, most of the experiences documented are within the developed countries where networked computers are easily available and students are proficient in using them.

Although developing countries are limited in IT infrastructure, they have much to benefit from using the Internet to improve teaching and learning and in fact, much effort has been put in promoting the use of IT in education (Carr-Chellman & Zhang, 2000; Mutula, 2002). The Internet also provides unprecedented opportunities for instructors and students in both developed and developing world to collaborate in their research, teaching, and learning (Jones, 2001; Roach, 2001; Winner & Shields, 2002; Wong, Shen, & McGeorge, 2002). One such arrangement is to offer web-based courses to students in another country without having the instructors and students travel long distances to meet in traditional classrooms. However, similar to teaching in traditional classrooms in an overseas country, addressing social, cultural, linguistic issues, and in the case of web-based teaching, technological problems, will form part of the teaching and learning experience (Bar-On, 2001; Tunney, 2002).

Students studying in this master program aspire towards being managers in social services organizations (mainly governmental); though very few of them have training in social work during their undergraduate studies. In fact, social work education has become very popular in China in recent years (CASWE, 2002), though professional practice is still very limited. The first formal social work training program approved by the Chinese Minister of Education started in 1999. By 2002, 124 approved social work programs at the undergraduate level had been established all over China (Qin, 2003).

Chinese learners, being influenced by Confucian Heritage Culture (CHC), place great importance on education. They emphasize memorizing and replicating course content for better understanding a subject, respect for adults and authority, harmony, and induce a peculiar emphasis on face saving (Bond, 1991; Watkins & Biggs, 2001; Chan, 1999). Such cultural characteristics have an effect on students' perceptions and behaviours in web-based teaching that uses bulletin board discussion as a major learning activity. Classroom students, for example, exhibit passivity in expressing opinions and uncertainty about their learning without a teacher's assurance, and avoiding conflicts with classmates (Wong & Law, 1999; Wong, 2003).

Internet accessibility, especially via a broadband connection, is still not available to most in Shanghai. Accessibility problems exist even though Shanghai is among the most developed cities in China with a per capita GDP of 4909 US dollars in 2002, which is around 5 times that of the country's overall figure (World Bank, 2003). While the number of Internet accounts has grown on average nearly 60% for the past three years in China (China Internet Network Information Center, 2003), the Shanghai penetration rate of one million Internet users (as of Sept., 2002) is not particularly high for a city with 17.0 million. The figure is still lower for the country as a whole with only 68 million Internet users in a country of 1300 million people. A survey in Shanghai indicates that of the households with Internet access, 61.7% have dial-up modem and 38.3% have broadband access (Chu, 2002). These facts and issues affected the learning process and outcome the instructors had to address throughout the course.

BACKGROUND AND CULTURAL CONTEXT

Two instructors, one based in Texas and one in Hong Kong, taught the course via an Internet chatroom with a supporting web site. Course materials were developed by the instructor in Texas. Chat was considered an acceptable medium for several reasons. The Texas instructor had positive experiences teaching various courses in a chatroom over the past several years (Schoech, 2000; Schoech & Helton, 2002). Chat is synchronous, and thus allowed for immediate discussion and solution of any student questions or problems that might surface. For example, since the class was held on weekends, chat allowed immediate discussion and resolution of the many scheduling issues that arose due to holiday celebrations, work demands, and personal schedules. It was also hoped that relying on synchronous techniques like chat rather than on asynchronous techniques like e-mail and discussion forums would reduce the high dropout rate often associated with online courses. Another consideration was language. English proficiency, based on the HKU entrance requirement, was expected of students. The program required English as the teaching medium. Online courses remove some of the problems that some students have with speaking and understanding spoken English.

The course was compulsory for students in the collaborative program. The overall goal of the course was to enable students to view human services as a data/information/knowledge based profession and to investigate the computer and telecommunication tools available to work with the data/information/knowledge necessary to support human service practice. The first third of the course was a review of generic IT and human service IT applications. The second two-thirds focused on developing IT applications. IT development was seen as following the generic social work change process. The two major assignments were assessing the IT needs and capacities of a human services problem/situation and developing solution options. Thus, the theories underlying the course were change theories like Rogers (1962), diffusion of innovation theory.

The course adopted mixed pedagogical strategies which include self-study (web-based materials and textbook), classroom sessions, chatroom sessions, student presentations, and assessment portfolios, etc., in teaching and assessment. Since this was the first time that the course was offered to students in Shanghai, before and during the course the instructors had to address social, cultural, and linguistic issues such as characteristics of the Chinese learner, relevance of course materials to local context, and linguistic problems.

The course was designed so that underlying generic content and processes could be supplemented by local knowledge and culture. Examples of generic content and processes include the use of English since it is the universal language of IT, links to web sites since most are in English and many Chinese web sites also can be viewed in English, the IT development process which is similar worldwide, and Roger's change theories which are supported by research in numerous cultures. Local knowledge and culture were included since the human service problems the students assessed and the solutions designed were based in local traditions, values, and culture. For students addressing an organizational problem, such as communications between decentralized offices in modern Shanghai, cultural issues were not dissimilar to those faced in any large modern city. However, the assessment and solution design papers of students addressing social problems in rural China or problems of the elderly and poor had to take into account the limitations of IT as well as the cultural issues of those experiencing the problem and stakeholders considered part of the solution. Naturally, the digital divide was a topic of discussion throughout the course.

Developing and implementing an actual IT application were beyond the scope of the course, but often after the course ended, students continued work to design and implement the application designed in class.

COURSE DETAILS

Course Arrangement

The course adopted mixed pedagogical strategies which stressed self-study, interactions, and student sharing of their learning outcome. The course assessment took the form of portfolios which included class participation and other individual assignments. No examination was required. The assignments were (1) preparation of personal webpage to compensate for the impersonality of online learning, (2) reviewing several computer applications, (3) writing a systems analysis paper about a social or organizational problem or situation, and (4) writing and presenting a paper focusing on the IT options available to address the systems analysis.

A class supporting web site was developed which contained detailed information about the course, such as course objectives, assignments, course related materials, and assessment. The course was divided into 13 sessions (roughly one session per week). Ten class sessions were conducted via a text-based Internet chatroom by the instructor from Texas. Each class session had a main theme of discussion which was associated with certain chapter(s) in the course textbook written by the instructor in Texas. PowerPoint files were prepared for each class and were posted onto the course web site before class started. Students were expected to read the textbook chapters and review the PowerPoint slides before joining the class sessions. The instructor in Hong Kong went to Shanghai to conduct the first session, which briefed the students about the course arrangement and prepared them for the technical aspects of the course such as navigating the course web site, preparing a personal homepage, and connecting to the Internet chatroom. In addition, a teacher in Fudan University helped out with logistics such as arranging classrooms, distributing textbooks, setting up and maintaining video-conferencing facilities, etc.

During the 10 class chat sessions, students joined the Internet chatroom from places convenient to them. Instead of lecturing in the chatroom, students were encouraged to discuss the text and reading materials by asking questions and seeking clarifications. The instructor also asked questions relating to the topic of the chatroom session. During several chatroom sessions, debates were arranged where small groups of students would debate on controversial issues such as "Access to IT for many of social work's constituents (the poor, people with disabilities) is a major problem that social workers must address." The contents of the chatroom sessions were saved and posted on the course web site. Two guest speakers were invited to join the chatroom for about half an hour on topics specific to two sessions. The instructors also asked students to visit web sites during chat sessions and come back to discuss what they have learned about the topic under discussion from reviewing those web sites.

The Hong Kong instructor planned to conduct the final two classroom sessions of the course in Shanghai. In these sessions, students used PowerPoint to present their solution design papers and answered questions from the instructors and other students. However, due to the HK instructor being unable to securely travel in China for fear of contracting SARS, the presentation was postponed twice. Presentations were finally made online through a video-conferencing program. Students e-mailed their PowerPoint presentations, which were uploaded to the course web site for all to review prior to their presentation. It should be noted that at a time when SARS closed all primary and secondary schools as well as most university classes in Hong Kong, this course was one of the few that continued as scheduled.

Evaluative Framework and Data Collection

The evaluation focused on the learner, instructor, delivery, content, outcomes, and instructional environment (Schoech, 2000). Each of these variables will be discussed in the findings/experiences section. Information about the students' background was collected from the program administrators. A 23-item questionnaire collected student demographics and their "Attitude towards technology-based learning" during session one, although some questionnaires were returned via e-mail afterwards. The captured text of the chat sessions were analyzed for students' involvement and the nature of their messages. At the completion of the course (but before grades were given), a face-to-face evaluation meeting was conducted in Shanghai by the instructor from Hong Kong while the instructor in Texas took part via video-conferencing. The students were asked to complete another set of questionnaires via e-mail regarding their opinion about the course content (12 items), course delivery tools and techniques (7 items), learning environment (17 items), overall experience and learning (4 items), and basic IT knowledge and attitudes (23 items). The score of each item ranged from no (1) to yes (5). The post test included the "Attitude towards technology-based learning" instrument completed at the beginning of the course. The data were analyzed with SPSS 11.5.

FINDINGS AND EXPERIENCES

Instructional Environment

Findings about the instructional environment concern administrative support, organizational planning, technology infrastructure, library and other supports, and structures that make a course run smoothly and easy to deliver. Being a collaborative program, both Hong Kong and Shanghai administrative systems impacted course delivery.

Several unexpected issues had to be addressed. First, due to complicated bureaucratic reasons, the collaborative program administrators were unable to complete negotiations with the Fudan University for students to use its library facilities. In addition, up until the completion of the course, the students were unable to use the digital library resources in HKU. Furthermore, the price of the textbook, which was USD $50, was too expensive for most Shanghai students who typically earn around CNY 3000 (USD $362) a month. Fortunately, the publishing company donated 15 copies of the textbook to the students to share among themselves. The course web site, textbook, and the Internet served as major sources of learning materials for the students.

Second, the facility booking system in Fudan University was problematic. During the initial face-to-face course briefing in Shanghai, the classroom that had been booked for the class was occupied for university examination without prior notice. The instructor had to approach the departmental staff to arrange another classroom immediately. The session was conducted an hour late inside a meeting room in the sociology department.

Third, with the absence of a computer laboratory at Fudan University for the program, some students had to attend the chatroom session in a Netbar, which charged about CNY 5 per hour. The Netbar refused to allow two students to use their facilities because they did not bring along their personal identity card in accord with government's regulation. An additional limitation was that students could not download and install software on the Netbar computer, thus MS Word had to be used to prepare students' web pages.

Current events also impacted the course, e.g., the Iraq war and SARS. The Iraq war was discussed periodically because it was on everyone's mind and impacted the discussion of government's information and communication policies. Similarly, discussions of SARS focused on government information policies as well as students fears of its severity and impact. Other events, such as the spread of the HTML.Redlof.A virus among students' computers due to the sharing of files, unexpectedly became part of the web-based learning environment. These events, which were shared by everyone in the class regardless of their location, illustrate just how closely our world is linked.

Content and Presentation

Findings on content include discipline of the course, learning objectives, type of material, and metadisciplinary skills used. Findings on presentation concern the time and spacing of materials, the modalities and technologies used to deliver content, attention or entertainment characteristics of presentation, and the environment in which the presentation was made.

Course content. The contents of the course consisted of subject-specific knowledge and those from other disciplines. For example, system and management theories and knowledge from computing science were employed to help students understand the process of developing IT applications in human services organizations. Given the growing development of social services under the auspices of the civil affairs bureau in Shanghai and the eagerness of the city to keep pace with international trends, the course content addressed their concerns. However, one issue that kept emerging during the class chat sessions and students final presentations was that IT and Internet connectivity was still far from affordable for individuals living in less well-off cities and the countryside. While IT might greatly empower the less-educated and poor to improve their livelihood, lack of access forced many IT based solutions to social problems to be based in large government organizations that had the necessary IT infrastructure. Lack of access forced many IT solution papers in rural and poor areas to include schools and community centers where citizens might find internet connected computers.

Relevance of course content to local context. This was probably the first such course ever offered to students in China. Locally published or translated materials about the subject were not available. In fact, since the degree was to be offered by the collaborating institution in Hong Kong, the awarding institution required that 90% of the courses had to be taught by instructors from Hong Kong. The collaborative program structure did not make it easy for the instructors to develop locally relevant course content and make extensive use of local materials and knowledge. In the other courses of the program, instructors from Hong Kong or overseas would typically travel to Shanghai on two weekends and teach intensively for four days to cover the entire course content. In this course, the 10 weeks of chatroom discussion enabled students and instructors to have more lengthy and in-depth discussions of course materials especially about locally relevant issues. For example, the issue of the digital divide in China is much different from that of the United States and Hong Kong. In addition, students could focus most of the assignments, such as application review and course paper, on local issues. However, both the instructors and students felt a gap often existed between the course content and the specific issues pertinent to the local situations.

Chatroom. A free commercial chat program (AOL, IM, Chat) was used because it was widely available and easy to set up and use. It provided color coding of text for each user and transcripts could be saved and posted for future reference. Students sometimes had a problem remaining in chat due to unstable connections. Instructors with stable connections infrequently had connectivity problems, e.g., only during a thunderstorm with much lightening. A less flexible Java based backup HKU chatroom was set up, but not used.

Because Texas and Shanghai/Hong Kong have a time difference of 14 hours, it was not easy to find a time slot convenient to both parties. The best time was in the morning in Shanghai on weekends (e.g., Saturday from 9:00a.m.-11:00a.m. in Shanghai and Friday 7:00p.m.-9:00p.m. in Texas). Since the students had classes on some weekends, some online chatroom sessions had to be arranged on weekdays during their lunch hours (11:30a.m.-1:30p.m.). Weekday classes caused difficulties because some students could not concentrate on chat because their boss and colleagues were around in their office. Some, who did not have Internet access in their office and attended chat using a nearby Netbar or Internet Café, had to leave chat early to return to their office work.

To keep the chat active and from being off-topic, instructors needed to be very resourceful and ask a lot of stimulating questions. Chat requires fast typing speed, since long sentences might result in idle time and easy distractions. Short sentences and frequent postings of short phrases better kept the students' attention. One way to improve the flow of information in chat is for presenters to have their ideas typed out before the session and then paste them in during chat discussion. This technique applied to guest speakers as well as the formal debates that were held in chat on IT issues. However, chat viewers can quickly experience information overload. This is especially true where various cultures and languages are involved. The debates illustrated this situation, as the teams that quickly pasted in a lot of persuasive content often failed to convince their classmates to change their position. Information overload can also exist in a traditional classroom; however, an instructor can often see the signs of information overload on the students' faces. A chatroom has one advantage in that chat transcripts are easily captured and post for future use by those experiencing information overload.

Using a supporting web site. The class web site and text operated as a lecture for each session. The class web site also allowed tracking of assignments, links to homepages, posting of debate, etc. It contained forms so that students could submit some of their assignments online (such as application reviews and proposed study topics). It also provided information about individual students' progress as compared to their classmates. When instructors wanted to add course materials, make announcements about the course or modify assignments, it could be done easily. In fact, when several papers were submitted that did not seem to address the requirement of the assignment, forms were developed on the web site that allowed students to enter key pieces of information and obtain a basic draft of the paper which they could enhance. In summary, the web site helped overcome some of the language and cultural problems associated with this course by being a place where important information was written and consistently communicated. Students having difficulties reading, understanding, or posting in the chatroom could peruse the web site at their own speed and find most information on the course, including the chat transcripts.

Online PowerPoint presentation. During student presentations, the presenter sat in front of a WebCam equipped computer in an office of the civil affairs bureau where one of the students worked. Their presentation was transmitted through the web-based video-conferencing software for the instructors and classmates not present in the WebCam room. Each presentation was in English and lasted for about 10-20 minutes. Questions (from instructors and students) were asked through voice or text chat. Students answered questions in voice.

The WebCam presentation provided the first time for the Texas instructor to see and hear the students and observe them interpreting questions. The meaning of questions asked by the instructors was often discussed by several in the class before the presenter answered. This experience emphasized the difficulties some students had with English, something that was not readily apparent from chat and written papers. An interesting observation is that while video and audio add important cultural and contextual cues, they seem to add little formal content. That is, online video personalized but probably decreased the informational content disseminated during the presentation time. PowerPoint slides and text more effectively and efficiently communicated the content of the presentations.

Learners

Findings on learners concern demographics, personality, general abilities, motivation, prior knowledge, learning history and styles, past scholastic achievement, performance skills, and the learner's reaction to the course and presenter.

Student background. The students were in the second year of the program. According to the student records provided by the program administrators, nearly two-thirds (63.7%) of the students were male and 36% had a degree in a human service related subject (e.g., social work, soci-

ology). At the beginning of the course (end of 2002), the average age of
the class was 27.7.

Thirty-two students completed their first year. However, some of
them decided not to continue with their studies in the second year and
some deferred their studies for a year or more. When the course ended,
only 22 of the 32 students remained in the class. Since the course, like
all the other courses of the program, was compulsory, the drop out rate
of the course was in fact the drop out rate of the program as a whole. Because many factors influence dropout, for example, course placement
within the overall program, course difficulty, etc., we were unable to
calculate whether this online course was a larger factor in overall program dropout than other courses. Discussion with students during the
course debriefing sessions indicated that one student dropped out of the
program because s/he could not catch up with this particular course. The
rest dropped out with other reasons not relating to this course, for example, encountering financial difficulties, pursuing overseas studies, increasing demand from work, and overall program not meeting their
needs, etc.

Fifteen students completed the questionnaire at the beginning of the
course. According to the information they provided, the students on average, had a history of 69.2 months in using a computer and 49.6 months
using the Internet. They had also undergone an average of 78.4 hours of
formal computer training and were familiar with 5.4 pieces of computer
software. All had a computer at work, and only one did not have an
Internet connection at work. On average, they had to travel slightly over
2 hours (round trip) to the campus.

Student involvement. Only fifteen students, about 60% of the class,
attended the first evaluation session. It was conducted in Mandarin. The
low turn-out at the beginning of the course worried the instructors.
However, the students said this attendance was normal for courses.

The involvement of the students in the chatroom varied (Table 1).
The average number of students in each chatroom session was 14.8; the
attendance rate was 67.3%. The average number of messages posted by
each student in a chatroom session was 33. Usually, postings were short
sentences. For analysis purposes, the number of postings for each session were categorized into low (less than 20), medium (20-40) and high
(greater than 40). Six students (27.3%) fell into the low category with an
average pf only 8.1 messages. Seven students (31.8%) fell into the high
category with an average of 64.4 messages in each participating session.
The "low" involving students attended only 4 (out of ten) chat sessions
on average, while the "high" attended 8.9 sessions.

Message content was analyzed to try to distinguish quantity from quality.

Table 2 presents the nature of students' messages in one of the chatroom sessions by three different students, with "low," "medium," and "high" level of involvement respectively. The "high" involved student posted 62 messages during the session, but only 10 messages expressed an opinion related to the topic. Most of his messages (37%) were expressing simple statements of agreeing or disagreeing with others (for example, "yes," "agree," or "right") or greetings/making fun with others (34%). Several times during the semester, the chat transcript was sorted by student name and the number of entries tallied. This information was then sent to all students with an encouraging message about participation.

Communication issues. Information about student' computer skills, Internet access, and availability of computer equipment was collected via a structured questionnaire at the beginning of the course to identify

TABLE 1. Involvement of Students in Class Chat Sessions

Level of participation in chatroom	No. of students	% of students	Average no. of chatroom sessions attended (out of 10)	Average no. of messages in each chatroom session
Low (0-20 messages)	6	27.3	4.0	8.1
Medium (20-39 messages)	9	40.9	6.9	25.1
High (40+ messages)	7	31.8	8.9	64.4
Overall/Total	22	100	6.7	33.0

TABLE 2. Nature, Number, and Percent of Students' Messages in One of the Chat Sessions

	Level of participation					
	Low		Medium		High	
Nature of messages	#	%	#	%	#	%
Ask question	0	0%	0	0%	1	2%
Course matters	0	0%	0	0%	5	8%
Encounter technical problem	1	14%	3	20%	2	3%
Express simple agree/disagree	3	43%	4	27%	23	37%
Express opinion	1	14%	6	40%	10	16%
Greetings/Make fun	2	29%	2	13%	21	34%
Total No. of messages posted	7	100%	15	100%	62	100%
Total No. of words posted	29		122		366	

students' needs and capacities. The result indicated that most students had no problem with access and computer proficiency. They were technically ready for the present mode of course delivery.

Using English as a teaching medium is an issue for many students in China. On admission to this collaborative program, students were to have a score of 550 on the TOEFL (Test of English as a Foreign Language). However, even though many students could not meet this criterion, they were allowed to enroll into the program but were required to meet this standard upon graduation. It appeared that not many students had read the textbook before the session. Some had told the instructor that they could only read a few pages in an hour due to spending a lot of time looking up words in a dictionary. Final student presentations emphasized that English proficiency varied. Some students fluently spoke English. Others spoke in a way that indicated they had problems with English. The initial assumption of the program that after a whole year of teaching and learning in English, the students' English proficiency should have greatly improved did not hold for all. Possibly conducting one half of the first session in English might have allowed the instructors to understand this difficulty better.

Since social work is relatively new in China, many social work concepts, particularly non-management concepts like generalist direct practice, were very difficult for students to understand. Having students go to an English web site during chat sessions to illustrate a concept was not very useful because it took students too much time to get an overview of a site. If a web site is in a student's native language, students can quickly skim the site and return to discuss major concepts. The Shanghai students indicated that they needed to go back to the sites after class and study them before they could comment and discuss related concepts.

Instructors

Findings related to the instructor concern teaching style, subject-matter knowledge, and extent of training and experience in distance and F2F education. The instructor in Texas has many years of teaching, researching, and developing IT applications in human services organizations and had attended conference and visited human service IT applications in Hong Kong and Shanghai. The instructor from Hong Kong has many years of experience supervising Hong Kong social work students taking their field work placements in Mainland China (Wong & Leung, 2001). In 2002, he stayed in Shanghai for three months to supervise the MSW students from Shanghai studying in the collaboration program for their first field work placement.

Apart from the issue of content discussed above, the instructors encountered many cultural and linguistic issues that had to be addressed during the course. Apparently, some students were constrained by their English proficiency and computer access. Their progress in reading the textbook and completing assignment was slow. Without knowing whether this slow performance was consistent with Shanghai educational standards, the instructors continually encouraged students' involvement, reading, and completing the assignments. For example, the quantity and quality of participation presented in Tables 1 and 2 point out the difficulty of placing student performance in the local context. The instructors tried to show appreciation to students who demonstrated understanding of the textbook materials during chat. They also tried giving extra credits to students who were reported by their peers to have helped others resolve technical problems, for example, in preparing homepages and Power-Point files. Five students were awarded this type of extra credit. The instructors had also sent e-mail to the class recognizing the contribution of those students. During the chat sessions, the instructor in Texas led the class discussions and the instructor from Hong Kong would send messages to the late comers or those who seemed disconnected from the chat discussion about their participation in the discussion and briefed them about the focus of chat sessions. Thus, the instant messaging capacity of the AOL chat program proved beneficial to the instructors. We do not know the extent of students instant messaging with each other either in Chinese or English during the class chat session. The instructors also developed forms on the class web site to guide the students to complete their assignments and posted sample papers of written assignments in previous Texas classes as a reference.

Also, the instructors, and especially the Texas instructor, had difficulty understanding the social service delivery system in China. Students often made comments in slogans and platitudes which probably had complex meanings in Shanghai. The instructors might not have understood these subtleties, yet all the students did. Clarification for the instructors alone was not always worth the time it took for the students to explain complex meaning behind the slogans. Some examples of these slogans were: "Till good is better and better is best," "Data to summarize the factors through the figures."

Finally, grading was very difficult given that the instructors had limited knowledge of the typical standards required for students' grades. Students typically are not a good source for information on grading standards, yet other standards were not available since this was a new course.

Learning Outcome

Findings on student outcomes concern final course grades, questionnaires results, and a face-to-face student debriefing session. Of the 22 students, 6 received an "A" grade, ten received a "B" and 2 received a "C." Four failed the course. Of the six students who either received a "C" grade or failed the course, four of them were "low" in their chatroom involvement. Of those who received an "A" grade, all but one had "high" involvement in the chat sessions. Significant correlation was found between the marks and the average number of messages posted by the students in the class chat sessions they attended; ($r = .45$, $p = .019$) and between the marks and the number of class chat session attended ($r = .462$, $p = .030$).

Most students' papers initially focused on management information systems to solve the problem/situation analyzed. As student papers evolved, it was interesting to see applications moved from a top down bureaucratic approach to one involving a more decentralized Internet base systems with more citizen and stakeholder involvement. This evolution in thinking is typical when traditional IT solutions that are based in internal organizational networks are expanded to take advantage of the distributive capacities of the Internet.

Fifteen students completed the set of questionnaires on "Attitude towards technology based learning" at the beginning of the course. The scores were compared with the 17 questionnaires completed at the end of the course (Table 3). These scores indicated that students had a very positive attitude towards IT applications and use of technology in education at course beginning. Given this positive initial attitude, the comparisons between the two sets of scores were not significant, except for one item. Students significantly increased their agreement with the item "Certain social work content should not be taught over the Internet, but reserved for the classroom." This suggests that after taking one online course, students were more able to distinguish the advantages of classroom vs. online teaching. It would be interesting to see whether a similar finding would occur in a different type of online course, for example, an asynchronous course delivered via WebCT.

Due to the small sample size, the effect size was included to help understand the differences between pre and post test scores. The traditional interpretation of effect sizes suggests that $d = .20$ is a small effect, d = .50 is a medium effect and d = .80 is a large effect (Cohen, 1988). While no item exhibited a large effect, four showed medium effects. Upon course completion, students felt Internet based courses were more personal (.50), were more self paced (.60), had more assessable instructors (.58), and that certain social work content should not be taught using the Internet (.67). These findings are consistent with previous findings (Schoech & Helton, 2002) and show students' opinions changing to a more realistic view of online learning.

Table 3 also presents post test only items that had a high mean score (over 4.5) and those that had a low one (under 3.8) from the set of questionnaires completed by students at the end of the course. The overall satisfaction of the course was very high. Among the items related to "Overall experience and learning," no item had a mean less than 3.8. Specifically, the mean scores for "I would recommend this course to my colleagues," "Overall, I am satisfied with the learning that occurred in this course," and "Overall, I am satisfied with how this course was delivered" were all above 4.6. One reason for the very high marks might be that those less satisfied dropped out of the course and thus did not complete the post test.

In terms of the course content, two items scored high. They were "I am satisfied with the web site and other resources provided by this course" and "I am satisfied with building your personal web page assignment." Both were 4.59. The lowest item was "I am satisfied with non-text readings assigned."

Regarding the "course delivery tools and techniques," the students gave high scores indicating their satisfaction in using the Internet chat and e-mail. They also gave high score on "My instructor was more available in this course than in other courses." The need for face-to-face communication in this course did not score high (3.47). In addition, students also gave low scores to two items that measured whether they knew and worked better with other students in this course. They also did not find it easier to work in this course than most other courses (3.53).

About 15 students attended the face-to-face course evaluation session that was conducted in Shanghai by the HK instructor. The TX instructor was connected via web video-conferencing software. Both instructors asked questions and students answered. Some answers were made in Chinese and were translated into English. Most of the opinion was similar to those presented above. However, one issue that stood out was about the workload. Some felt that the workload was heavier as compared to other courses of the program which typically asked the students to attend classes (four whole days) and complete a term paper and/or prepare for an examination.

TABLE 3. Attitude Towards Technology Based Learning and Course Evaluation Where 1 = No and 5 = Yes

Items	Post Test (Mean)	Pre Test (Mean)	Effect Size (Pooled SD)	Paired T-test (Sig.)
Attitude Towards Technology Based Learning				
I have a positive attitude towards the use of technology for learning	4.71	4.73	−0.06	0.34
I have a positive attitude toward the use of the Internet for learning	4.76	4.60	0.28	0.72
Internet-based courses have more technical difficulties than classroom-based courses	3.29	3.33	−0.03	0.88
Internet-based courses are more personal than classroom-based courses	3.94	3.47	0.50	0.43
Internet-based courses are more flexible in regards to my time than classroom-based courses	4.00	4.13	−0.15	0.62
Internet-based courses are easier than classroom-based courses	2.82	2.60	0.22	0.43
Internet-based courses allow students to learn at their own pace more than classroom-based courses	4.06	3.53	0.60	0.17
Internet-based learning environments are better for learning than classroom-based environments	3.29	3.27	0.02	0.84
Internet-based teaching techniques encouraged students to learn more than classroom-based teaching techniques	3.94	4.27	−0.38	0.59
Students in Internet-based courses learn more than students in classroom-based courses	3.71	3.53	0.20	0.49
Students in Internet-based courses feel more comfortable asking questions than students in classroom-based courses	4.00	4.13	−0.13	0.48
Students in Internet-based courses ask more questions than students in classroom-based courses	4.00	3.93	0.08	0.72
Students in Internet-based courses know their instructors better than students in classroom-based courses of the same size	3.35	3.07	0.29	0.30
Students in Internet-based courses know other students better than students in classroom-based courses of the same size	2.65	2.67	−0.02	0.74
Students in Internet-based courses communicate with each other more than students in classroom-based courses of the same size	3.06	2.87	0.17	1.00
Students in Internet-based courses have fewer problems getting help than students in classroom-based courses	2.82	2.93	−0.10	1.00
Students in Internet-based courses learn social work values and ethic better than students in classroom-based courses	3.00	3.07	−0.07	1.00
Students in Internet-based courses will be more satisfied than students in classroom-based courses	3.59	3.53	0.06	0.59
Working on student projects in Internet-based courses is easier than working on student projects in classroom-based courses	3.41	3.33	0.07	0.49
Class discussion in Internet-based courses is of better quality than class discussion in classroom-based courses	3.59	3.33	0.30	0.43
Instructor in Internet-based courses are more available than instructors in classroom-based courses	4.06	3.53	0.58	0.22

TABLE 3 (continued)

Items	Post Test (Mean)	Pre Test (Mean)	Effect Size (Pooled SD)	Paired T-test (Sig.)
Attitude Towards Technology Based Learning				
Certain social work content should not be taught over the Internet, but reserved for the classroom	4.41	3.87	0.67	0.04*
Students in an online course are more responsible for their learning than in a traditional course	3.47	3.67	−0.22	0.71
Course Evaluation–Course Content				
I am satisfied with the Web site and other resources provided by this course	4.59			
I am satisfied with building your personal Web page assignment	4.59			
I am satisfied with non-text readings assigned	3.76			
Course Evaluation–Course delivery tools and techniques				
I liked the use of Internet chat	4.71			
I liked the use of email	4.65			
My instructor was more available in this course than in other courses	4.59			
I know the students in this course better than those in most courses	3.59			
I had fewer problems getting help in this course than in other courses	3.59			
Working with other students in this course was easier than working with students in most courses	3.53			
I often felt the need for face-to-face communication in this course	3.47			
I liked breaking away to Internet sites during class discussion	3.29			
Course Evaluation–Overall Experience and Learning				
I would recommend this course to my colleagues	4.71			
Overall, I am satisfied with the learning that occurred in this course	4.71			
Overall, I am satisfied with how this course was delivered	4.65			
Course Evaluation–Basic IT Knowledge and Attitude				
I know how to use information technology to support and manage my work	4.65			
I know how to use information technology to further my personal education and learning	4.65			
I am prepared for the technology that I will encounter in my future professional work	4.59			
I know the basics of computer networking	4.53			
Most IT applications fail due to a lack of planning	3.71			
Most IT applications fail due to failures to select the right software	3.59			
Most IT applications fail due to failures to select the right hardware	3.12			

*Difference is significant at the 0.05 level (2-tailed)

DISCUSSION AND SUGGESTIONS

The findings on this course were encouraging. They suggest that web-based teaching by non-resident instructors using chat was readily accepted by students in China. Findings also suggested that the course was challenging for the students and instructors as both had to address social, cultural, and linguistic issues throughout the course. This section discusses the findings with emphasis on the cultural, personalization, and linguistic issues and makes suggestions with regard to these issues.

Cultural and Institutional Issues

Very limited local research, teaching materials, and teaching personnel were available for this course. To enhance the course, it would probably be useful to appoint an instructor or teaching assistant from the local institution to work with the instructors in course development and delivery. The local partner could help sorting out issues relating to students' ability, their prior knowledge in the subject, availability of local resources, and standards/practices for attendance and grading. It would be even better if groundwork on the subject areas of the course could be conducted by local researchers in the hosting country. This information would promote interest and knowledge in building up locally relevant teaching materials and personnel.

In this course, the involvement of the students in bringing in local resources was useful. In fact, in recent years, many IT applications have been developed for the human service sector in China. However, students' knowledge of and about local IT applications were limited. The application reviews as well as the assignments did bring in useful information. We recommend that more systematic and cumulative effort be put in researching the local situation and bringing in locally relevant applications, examples, and materials.

In the chatroom sessions, the involvement of the students was mixed. The ability of the instructor from Texas to ask stimulating questions attracted attention and positive responses from the students. Despite the fact that many gave simple statements of agreeing/disagreeing with others, a more active student would still post an average of 10 statements and a moderate student an average of 6 statements in expressing their opinions. This is impressive among Chinese students. The students were particularly cooperative in answering instructors' questions that were short and stimulating. This might reflect the characteristics of the Chinese students discussed in the literature review. Unfortunately, over a quarter (27.6%) of the students were low in the number of statements they posted in a session and in their overall attendance rate. Although all but one student indicated that they had workplace access to the Internet, some students might have had difficulty getting online during work hours. Special attention and arrangement have to be made to quickly identify and provide additional support to students with technological and access problems.

We would recommend also that more feedback mechanisms be introduced to channel students' opinion about the course to the instructors. Probably, a mid-semester feedback form and discussion should have been used. This could be done via the class bulletin board, which was available but underutilized in this course. Another mechanism might be to bring up for wider class discussion some of the observations that students expressed in private messages with the instructors exchanged during chat sessions. These individual concerns might reflect broader issues that teachers need to address.

Personalization and Building Learning Community

Teaching completely via Internet chat with no face-to-face contact with students does not give the instructor a personal perspective of students (Schoech, 2000). The initial face-to-face sessions and the home-page assignment allow the class to overcome the lacks of visual and auditory cues. If handled properly, a chatroom class can be as personal as a F2F class (review Table 3, Item 4). Other techniques can be employed. Involving the Texas instructor in a WebCam introduction to the students would have provided a visual image of the student during their text chat conversations throughout the semester.

In this course as well as others, some students have a better understanding of the topic and delivery methods. In a F2F class, students often help each other during breaks and other informal activities. This networking needs to be encouraged in chatroom classes. Posting information to the class listserv is one helping mechanism, although students in this class rarely communicated via the class listserv. We encouraged students' mutual helping behavior by giving extra marks for those who helped others. The five students who received help reported to the instructors about who had offered help to them. We recommend that extra credit be used to encourage the helping of others throughout the course and that the instructors request information on the type of help students received before awarding extra credit.

Linguistic Issue

The findings and our experiences indicate that some students have more constraints in using English as a learning medium especially in reading course materials, quickly understanding English content, and completing class assignments. This suggests that either a more stringent requirement of English proficiency is needed or better assessment and strategies to accommodate the language limitation need to be developed. Strategies to compensate for language problems could be expanded to include sharing of learning from the readings each week using a class bulletin board/forum or answering short questions prepared by the instructors before each chat session. These assignments could constitute part of the assessment portfolios in order to recognize the efforts students have put into their learning. The online form, which was designed to help students generate a draft document that they could expand and edit when writing their paper, could be introduced earlier and expanded to other major assignments. Instructors could give the students feedback based on the ideas submitted in the forms to help guide them before the final writing begins.

Teaching strategies to overcome varied reading and comprehension skills and Internet connection speeds have to be adjusted to each situation. For example, the visiting of English web sites during chat to illustrate concepts was not appropriate in this course due to language comprehension. The visiting of Chinese web sites was difficult for the Texas instructor to understand. Although video-conferencing brings visual images and stronger personal impression, it can transmit less informational content in a course with many linguistic and technical constraints. Having a record of class activities available is helpful to address linguistic problems. Students found reading the chat transcription useful to them because they could pick up what was missed during the chat sessions. Also, the posting of previous sample papers was useful for students to understand what was expected from the written assignment.

CONCLUSION

Web-based teaching can enhance international collaboration in offering programs and courses for students around the world. China has been very active in forging such collaboration in recent years. The outcome and experience in this course was positive but instructors had to address content relevance, cultural, technical, and linguistic issues throughout the course. Internet chat offers an effective teaching medium in international programs with linguistic issues because it does not require lengthy responses from students and allows them to review the class contents easily. As with most distant education programs, having a local partner to assist in teaching and conducting local research helps explain and apply concepts locally and enhances student interest. Based on this positive experience, this course is being enhanced with the suggestions offered in this paper and delivered again in 2004.

REFERENCES

Bar-On, A. (2001). When assumptions on fieldwork education fail to hold: The experience of Botswana. *Social Work Education, 20*(1), 123-136.

Bond, M. H. (1991). *Beyond the Chinese Face: Insights from Psychology.* Hong Kong: Oxford University Press.

Carr-Chellman, A. A., & Zhang, K. (2000). China's future with distance education: Rhetoric and realities. *Information, Communication, & Society, 3*(3), 303-312.

CASWE. (2002, July 2002). *China Association for Social Work Education CASWE.* Retrieved December 5, 2003, 2003, from http://www.iassw.soton.ac.uk/en/News Items/ReportFromChinaAssociationForSocialWorkEducationJuly2002.pdf.

Chan, S. (1999). The Chinese learner–A question of style. *Education & Training, 41*(6/7), 294-304.

China Internet Network Information Center. (2003). *Semiannual survey report on the development of China's Internet.* Retrieved November 25, 2003, from http://www. cnnic.net.cn/e-index.shtml.

Chu, L. (2002, September 10). A million user getting online. *Jeifang Daily* (in Chinese).

Cohen, J. (1988). *Statistical power analysis for the behavioral sciences (2nd ed.),* Hillsdale, NJ: Lawrence Erlbaum.

Jones, R. (2001). Lessons learned in a European-Latin American collaboration for developing postgraduate education in public health. *European Journal of Public Health, 11*(2), 227-230.

Ligon, J., Markward, M. J., & Yegidis, B. L. (1999). Comparing student evaluations of distance learning and standard classroom courses in graduate social work education. *Journal of Teaching in Social Work, 19*(1/2), 21-29.

Macy, J. A., Rooney, R. H., Hollister, C. D., & Freddolino, P. P. (2001). Evaluation of distance education programs in social work. *Journal of Technology in Human Services, 18*(3/4), 63-84.

Massimo, V. (2003). Integrating the WebCT discussion feature into social work courses: An assessment focused on pedagogy and practicality. *Journal of Technology in Human Services, 22*(1), 49-65.

Mutula, S. M. (2002). E-learning initiative at the University of Botswana: Challenges and opportunities. *Campus-Wide Information Systems, 19*(3), 99-109.

Qin, X. F. (2003). Minister of education–Approved lists of higher education institutes in setting up undergraduate social work programs (on record). *China Social Work Education Communication* (in Chinese), *17*, 4.

Roach, R. (2001). 'Metacourse' explores new opportunities for U.S.-African collaboration. *Black Issues in Higher Education, 18*(10), 28.

Rogers, E. M. (1962). *Diffusion of innovations.* NY: The Free Press.

Schoech, D. (2000). Teaching over the Internet: Results of one doctoral course. *Research on Social Work Practice, 10*(4), 467-486.

Schoech, D., & Helton, D. (2002). Qualitative and quantitative analysis of a course taught via classroom and Internet chatroom. *Qualitative Social Work, 1*(1), 111-124.

Stocks, J. T., & Freddolino, P. P. (1998). Evaluation of a World Wide Web-based graduate social work research methods course. *Computers in Human Services, 15*(2/3), 51-69.

Stocks, J. T., & Freddolino, P. P. (2000). Enhancing computer-mediated teaching through interactivity: The second iteration of a World Wide Web-based graduate social work course. *Research on Social Work Practice, 10*(4), 505-518.

Tunney, K. (2002). Learning to teach abroad: Reflections on the role of the visiting social work educator. *International Social Work, 45*(4), 435-446.

Watkins, D., & Biggs, J. B. (2001). *Teaching the Chinese learner: Psychological and pedagogical perspectives.* Hong Kong: Comparative Education Research Centre University of Hong Kong.

Wernet, S. P., Olliges, R. H., & Delicath, T. A. (2000). Postcourse evaluations of WebCT (Web Course Tools) classes by social work students. *Research on Social Work Practice, 10*(4), 487-504.

Winner, T., & Shields, T. (2002). Breaking the island chains: A case study exploring the intricate powers of language shared on the World Wide Web. *Computers and Composition, 19*, 273-283.

Wong, K. W., Shen, Q. P., & McGeorge, D. (2002). Development of a higher educational programme in China: The Hong Kong experience. *Journal of Further & Higher Education, 26*(1), 81-89.

Wong, Y. C., & Law, C. K. (1999). Learning social work online: A WebCT course on policy issues among Chinese students. *New Technology in Human Services, 11*(14), 18-24.

Wong, Y.C., & Leung, J.C.B. (2001) Community work in Guangzhou–Five years of HKU field work experience (in Chinese). In HKCSS (Ed.), *Community Development Service* (pp. 116-131). Hong Kong: Hong Kong Council of Social Services.

Wong, Y. C. (2003) *Constructivist online learning environment for social work education: An evaluation of students' learning process and outcome.* Unpublished PhD thesis, University of Hong Kong, HK.

World Bank. (2003, July 2003). *World development indicators database.* Retrieved November 25, 2003, from http://www.worldbank.org/data/databytopic/GNIPC.pdf.

Internationalizing Social Work Education Using Blackboard 6: INHOLLAND University, NL and James Madison University, USA

Karen A. Ford

Rina J. Rotgans-Visser

SUMMARY. Creating, delivering, and evaluating a pilot course in two countries and at two universities via Blackboard 6 presents pedagogical, cultural, and technological challenges as well as many rewards. The developmental process and negotiations required by both universities to bring the course to fruition are explored, including faculty workload, interactivity requirements connected to the course and credit assignment. The concepts of community building and cultural awareness are explored from faculty and students perspectives. Evaluation by the students and next steps from the developers' perspectives are important components supporting the efficacy of this approach. *[Article copies available for a fee from The Haworth Document Delivery Service: 1-800-HAWORTH. E-mail address: <docdelivery@haworthpress.com> Website: <http://www.HaworthPress.com> © 2005 by The Haworth Press, Inc. All rights reserved.]*

Karen A. Ford, DSW, is Associate Professor, Department of Social Work, James Madison University, MSC 4303, Harrisonburg, VA 22807.

Rina J. Rotgans-Visser, MA, is International Coordinator, Social Work, Rotterdam/Den Haag, INHOLLAND University, Theresiastraat 8, 2593 AN Den Haag, NL.

[Haworth co-indexing entry note]: "Internationalizing Social Work Education Using Blackboard 6: INHOLLAND University, NL and James Madison University, USA." Ford, Karen A. and Rina J. Rotgans-Visser. Co-published simultaneously in *Journal of Technology in Human Services* (The Haworth Press, Inc.) Vol. 23, No. 1/2, 2005, pp. 147-165; and: *Web-Based Education in the Human Services: Models, Methods, and Best Practices* (eds: MacFadden et al.) The Haworth Press, Inc., 2005, pp. 147-165. Single or multiple copies of this article are available for a fee from The Haworth Document Delivery Service [1-800-HAWORTH, 9:00 a.m. - 5:00 p.m. (EST). E-mail address: docdelivery@haworthpress.com].

Available online at http://www.haworthpress.com/web/JTHS
Digital Object Identifier: 10.1300/J017v023n01_09

KEYWORDS. International social work, technology, distance education, blackboard, community building

Social work education tends to be culturally bounded. This is not intrinsically negative since the vast majority of students will practice in their country of origin requiring grounding in national and culturally specific policies and practice methods. However, internationalizing social work education helps students move beyond their typically ethnocentric perspective, providing a means to enlarge the idea of what constitutes social welfare in theory and in practice. At this juncture, professional social work education, regardless of level, cannot afford to dismiss the importance of internationalizing the curriculum.

Globalization involves economic and political considerations. Globalization impacts our students' worlds through entertainment, music, and technology. While globalization is a reality in the larger world, the concept may not always be intentionally present each day in the classroom. A long-standing and important value in social work practice and education has been the sensitivity to and knowledge about cultural differences. The professional literature in the United States discusses these topics under the themes of cross-cultural, multicultural and international social work (Holmes & Mathews, 1993). In the Netherlands, discussions of these topics are found under the themes of "diversiteit," "multiculutrele samenleving," "interculturele communicatie" and "integratie" (NRC, 2000).

The importance of these topics in practice and education provide a natural segue for interest and involvement in international activities (Boyle & Cervantes, 2000). Global interdependence resulting in the movements of populations has changed U. S. and Dutch domestic social work practice demanding new skills and knowledge. These movements of populations insert an international perspective in social work practice as we work with immigrants, refugees, and migrants. Noting that work with immigrants, refugees, and migrants is a current and pressing issue in both the Netherlands and United States, the broad area of immigration was chosen as the topic for a pilot Blackboard based course. The focus of this work is the examination of the creation, simultaneous delivery and initial review of a Blackboard based course developed by social work educators in undergraduate programs in the Netherlands and the United States. The institutions are INHOLLAND University, Rotterdam, and James Madison University, Harrisonburg, Virginia. This work also presents the pedagogical, cultural and technological challenges faced by the two distance educators during the process of creating and delivering this course.

INTERNATIONALIZING SOCIAL WORK EDUCATION

Internationalizing social work education can take several forms, typically conceived of as study abroad opportunities, exchanges as well as creation and integration of international content into new and existing courses (Ford & Ericson, 2003; Boyle & Cervantes, 2000; Link, 1999). Graduate social work programs in the U.S. have long emphasized the importance of incorporating international issues into the curriculum through coursework, exchanges and more recently with the help of technology, field placements (Anders, 1975; Boehm, 1980; Healy, 1986 & 1988; Hokenstad, 1984; Saunders, 1977; and Boyle & Cervantes, 2000).

"Since global issues are inherent in BSW programs, we should draw more explicit attention and conscious expansion to international perspectives" within the classroom and the field experience (Link, 1999, p. 13). Becoming more global in baccalaureate social work education means, among other things, "expanding choices for students to travel and meet social workers in a variety of environments and bring their learning home" (p. 13). As a result, students and faculty alike have increased their contacts with counterparts from other regions of the world despite economic and political considerations (Desruisseaux, 2000).

"Typically, international activities of most American colleges and universities have operated with very modest budgets" (Boyle & Cervantes, 2000, p. 11). This is the case at James Madison University. The current travel based course is, of necessity, self supporting through the fees and tuition paid by students to cover actual costs. At INHOLLAND students also pay a significant portion of the fees for the travel course.

It is not possible for all students to finance an overseas experience, so it is incumbent that social work educators address internationalization in other ways. Given the curricular standards for diversity and international content promulgated by Council on Social Work Education for U.S. programs, it is doubly important that multiple delivery methods are explored and evaluated.

Internationalizing education is a value in Dutch higher education. The Netherlands Organization for International Cooperation in Higher Education (Nuffic), a nonprofit organization, supports activities and partnerships designed to internationalize Dutch higher education. Programs and grants include sending Dutch students out of country as well as sponsoring students and scholars from partner counties. Various support schemes are provided for educators as well (Nuffic, 2004). Additional backing for internationalization is found in the European Community Socrates program.

The European Community is a dynamic force in expanding the mobility and exchange of students and professors. The European Community encourages transnational cooperation between institutions through the Socrates/Erasmus program. The Socrates/Erasmus program focuses on Higher Education and defines diversity as a source of enrichment. The European Community stresses the multicultural character of Europe and the need to counter social exclusion making multiple delivery methods critical in the Netherlands too (European Communities, 2002).

Educational by-products of globalization are the Internet and globally available commercial course platforms. The Internet enables students and faculty worldwide to connect, communicate and collaborate irrespective of geographic location or time zone. The scholarly literature identifies a range of technology based teaching tools and methods. The key terms found are distance education, Internet based courses, computer mediated communication, computer supported collaborative learning and online courses. Internet based or facilitated courses using course platforms can be a cost effective way to expand international contact with social work students and practitioners in a variety of environments. Students can easily integrate learning with faculty mediation at their home institution.

Social work practitioners and educators have recognized the currency of computer-assisted technology in the delivery of their services. *Research on Social Work Practice* (10(4), 2000) devoted the entire volume to technologies being used in social work education. The *Journal of Community Practice* (7(1), 2000) highlighted assignments and exercises using technology to teach community organization skills.

Specifically related to web-based international collaboration, Johnson (1999) discusses an e-mail partnership project that was part of an international social work course. Students discussed social issues through a professional pen-pal relationship (p. 380). Warf, Vincent, and Purcell (1999) present a web-based project in the discipline of geography involving students in three English-speaking countries. These authors report many of the same issues and conclusions found in this work.

THE AMERICAN/DUTCH EXPERIENCE

Developing the Partnership

Building on a shared and evolving relationship over six years of baccalaureate student/ faculty study exchanges, INHOLLAND University and James Madison University (JMU) social work program's together developed a jointly and simultaneously delivered Blackboard based course entitled Immigration: Dutch and U.S. Views. Conversations about the development of a web-based pilot course took place over two years stimulated by the knowledge of complementary technological and economic resources in the distance education arena.

The primary faculty members involved in the exchange program have developed both a strong professional and personal relationship. This relationship formed basis for the development of the joint course. Creating a mutual level of trust is critical for successful development of an international distance course. Johnson (1999) and Warf et al. (1999) also indicate that interpersonal trust among the participating faculty is a precursor to a successful experience. Course development began with face-to-face meetings in each country continuing with on-line and telephone communication during the actual development of the course. While there is a formal agreement between both universities, the agreement itself is not sufficient to carry forward ongoing development of educational programming. The primary faculty members maintain relationships with key players at their respective institutions providing faces and products of the partnership. The faculty members are also in a position to translate various aspects of the partnership to their international offices in relation to the stated goals and themes of each partner.

Both the Netherlands and the United States have well-developed social work education programs at the baccalaureate level and extensive social work service systems. The similarity of the educational and service delivery components in each country provides a foundation and commonality for beginning the discussion and comparison of immigration issues.

One of INHOLLAND University's policy goals for the 2003-2006 period is "Borderless Education" (INHOLLAND Instellingsplan 2003-2006). A goal at JMU is to further develop international offerings that enhance the global awareness of the student (James Madison University Mission, 2002). The jointly developed and delivered Blackboard course complements the internationalization efforts of each university leading to support as the course continues to evolve.

CREATING THE COURSE

Immigration as a topic is well suited for a cross-cultural comparative survey course although priorities, politics, opinions, and available resources differ in each country. The globalization of welfare concepts and practices is a reality as both nations struggle with diminishing resources and stresses on service delivery systems. Both countries are post-industrial representative democracies providing another level of comparison for the issue.

Immigration suggests the infusion of others and differences into a culture. These unfamiliar variations are sometimes seen as strangers or threats in our communities. Social work values push us to recognize differences and similarities and to work toward building bridges of understanding through communication with our clients. Discussing immigration issues with students internationally transports them into an unfamiliar space pushing the students to move into dialogue without complete knowledge of the other culture, the subject, the language, and perhaps the technology. The intentional creation of this situation produces an environment where the unfamiliar must necessarily become a resource rather than a threat (Bateson, 1994). Linking the concepts that intersect in social work values, internationalizing education and current immigration issues provides both students and faculty with an environment rich in pedagogical opportunities and practice skills.

Selecting the course topic proved to be the least complicated step in creating the course. The amount of time it takes to create an online course cannot be underestimated. This fact is liberally supported in the literature and should not be dismissed (Smith & Rose, 2003; Yoder, 2003; Lorenzetti, 2003). The most time consuming factor was negotiating primary workload responsibilities followed closely by the actual work of creating and posting the course on Blackboard. The back and forth communication between the developers was slightly more complicated even in this age on instant communication given the time differences. Additionally, the authors dealt with the factors of complementing two curricula, administrative procedures, and language nuances.

Course development began with conversations on how to improve our current study exchanges focusing on our desire to foster international peer learning over longer periods of time and involving larger numbers of students. Central to the instructors' concept was the idea of providing a context where extensive class discussions could take place leading to the formation of an online community. Interpersonal communication is communication between two people, physically face to face or between two people on line. Although the students in this case were separated by significant physical distance, Shedletsky and Aitken (2004) argue in their text that immediacy and community can be developed through computer mediated communication (CMC). As noted earlier this pilot course offering was designed to complement the existing physical exchange program and further embed the connection between the two universities. Creating this course creates another venue for ongoing connections and collaboration, a community.

A foundational pedagogical approach in the Netherlands is group-centered learning using projects. Building on this practice, the two faculty members developed the course with students setting the tone and direction through the project directed responses (v. Ryssen, 2001).

Beginning with the focus on curriculum impact and not technology is key to garnering administrative support as well as creating viable pedagogical tool. This strategy allowed faculty in consultation instructional technology professionals to choose a technological platform that met the curriculum goals. Based on the course goals, the Blackboard platform was selected.

Both institutions regularly use Blackboard in the delivery of courses insuring a level of familiarity with students and faculty alike. Additional complementary factors for students and faculty alike include easy access to institutional computer labs, institutional e-mail systems and access to technological support. Given the preceding, an a priori assumption was the students' comfort, familiarity, and skill communicating online. Finally, and perhaps most importantly, there is a corresponding level of cultural support at the institutional and disciplinary levels related to the acceptance, use and positive impact of web-based learning at both universities making the move to an international course seamless (Collis, 1999).

Curricular discussions began with the creation of the course objective that follows: This course is designed to allow students to explore immigration from a personal, historical and current context within two cultures using a social work perspective. A key word in the sentence is explore. The specific learning objectives follow:

1. identify and discuss the basic components of immigration policy and services in the U.S. and the Netherlands,
2. identify, define, sand discuss the attitudes, values, and motivations that are the foundations of modern immigration policy and services in the U.S. and the Netherlands,
3. identify and discuss social, political, and economic issues as they impact on the development of immigration policy and services in the U.S. and the Netherlands,
4. identify, define, and discuss current issues and future alternatives in immigration policy and services in the U.S. and the Netherlands,
5. demonstrate a professional level of written and oral communication

A hoped for outcome was that students would work from both personal impressions and interpretations of the historical and current materials provided. Student responses and outcomes as well as course evaluation are discussed later in this paper.

Particular attention was given to the development of the joint syllabus in the presentation of the learning objectives as well as assignments and performance expectations insuring they were clearly stated and easily identified on the course platform. Login information was recapped and instructor contact information was also clearly posted on the course platform. Providing a welcoming statement, a paragraph on the cutting edge nature of the course and a photo of the instructors together also facilitated the creation of an inviting on line community (Collis, 1999; Smith & Rose, 2003; Yoder, 2003).

Each instructor developed the readings for their cohort. Several websites relating to immigration from each country's government were posted for all students to access. There was some information in English on the Dutch websites with most of the information in Dutch providing the U.S. students with an idea of the situation faced by non-English readers trying access information in the United States regarding immigration policies. Additionally each instructor's information to their respective students was visible to all students again reinforcing the language divide especially for the U.S. students.

"Social theories of learning posit that meaning is constructed from appropriating dialogue of others and forming dialogue in response, so that communication is shaped by prior knowledge as well as the knowledge of others" (Wu, 2003, p. 169). Recognizing this, the instructors worked to create a climate and context for students to get to know each other online. Cognizant that electronic communication is bereft of non-verbal cues, creating a rich qualitative base for students to draw on is imperative. The first two discussion threads were designed to help create this qualitative base. Students were first asked to complete an exercise calculated to elicit a variety of responses regarding messages, manifest and latent, they received growing up in their family and social group. The concept of how other groups were perceived was also a point of reaction. Students were asked to respond/react to at least two other student postings. The second discussion thread requested students to reflect on their national identity by asking them to discuss what makes one Dutch or American and asking that they again respond to at least two other postings.

Following the postings designed to promote a sense of connectedness among the class participants the course moved into the more specific immigration and social work based content phase. The topics covered included reviewing the history of immigration in each country, current laws and policies, current issues driving national discourse and policy changes, current social work services provided to immigrants and refugees and a discussion of similarities and differences between countries in the social work profession. These postings required the use of outside materials and current media sources. The pattern of posting responses and reacting to at least two other postings was followed throughout the course. The final posting asked students to evaluate the course and offer suggestions and recommendations for a next offering. Table 1 provides an overview of the course assignments and goals.

Face-to-face meetings of students and faculty within each cohort were built into the course to address any challenges, questions or integration of the material as necessary. This component emphasized the human nature of the course and allowed for learning and discussion about cultural nuances.

Administratively, the authors view this course as jointly developed and simultaneously offered yet managed by each institution consistent

TABLE 1. Assignments and Goals

Course assignment	Percentage of course work	Goal of assignment
Growing up in my group exercise	20%	To create a sense of connectedness among the Dutch & U.S. students through postings & responses. Respond to 2 postings.
National identity essay & discussion	10%	To post an essay stating what makes one Dutch or American & respond to 2 essay postings.
National history & values on immigration paper and discussion	25%	To develop & post a brief paper on the history of immigration in your country & the current societal & legal issues. 1 response.
Current issues driving immigration policy & services essay & discussion	15%	To post an essay on the topic from a SW perspective & respond to 1 posting.
SW values & services in immigration arena discussion	15%	To provide a description of 2 types of services & the role of SW in the services. Respond to 1 posting.
Similarities & differences discussion	10%	To review postings & discuss in essay format the topic. What can we learn from each other? Respond to 1 posting.
Evaluation & next steps discussion	5%	To provide an overall evaluation of the course w/suggestions for next offering.

with their policies. Registration was handled by each institution, as was recruitment for the course. The course was offered as an elective within the social work curriculum at each university.

Since this is a course with a jointly developed and delivered syllabus, credit assignment was a consideration. Each institution awarded academic credit to their students; however, some consistency was desired. The reality of the translation of credit systems between the European Community and the United States can be quite complex (U.S. Department of Education, 2003). Both credit systems in the final analysis are based on the number of contact and course work related hours. This elective course was offered at JMU for 2 U.S. credits and at INHOLLAND for 3 ECTS or the equivalent of 3 U.S credits because of the language difference for the Dutch students.

From an educational delivery perspective the instructors viewed this course as one course with 14 students and two instructors. All online course assignments were done in English allowing both instructors to be fully involved. Since the course was a pilot, having a first offering was the key consideration. Future offerings anticipate 20 to 25 students divided fairly evenly between Dutch and American students.

Addressing the administrative concerns by having registration, credits and any payments handled by each university the final consideration was the technology platform for the delivery of the class (Loring, 2002). Each university is a licensee of Blackboard. That fact freed each administration to allow the instructors to choose which version and university licensee to use. Language accessibility for the American students in particular dictated that the JMU Blackboard be used for the course delivery. The familiarity with Blackboard in Dutch assisted the Dutch students with the transition to the format in English. Each instructor had Blackboard access as a course administrator allowing each to post and edit assignments before making them available to the students. This feature of the course platform fostered the ability for true collaboration and equality in the delivery of the course. The instructors viewed this aspect as vital in presenting a true joint effort to the students.

The asynchronous capabilities of Blackboard allowed the Dutch and U.S. students to read carefully what was written and respond at their own pace. About 10 days were scheduled for each topic and posting cycle. For the Dutch students responding exclusively in English for the first time in a social work course Blackboard allowed them time to carefully craft their replies.

LESSONS LEARNED:
STUDENTS' AND FACULTY EXPERIENCES

Lessons learned are discussed from what the student's work revealed about the topic, the technology, and their learning as well as from the perspective of the faculty developing the course. Student responses to evaluation questions from Blackboard as well as in a face-to-face meeting in the Netherlands are presented. Student permission was received to use class postings anonymously in this work.

Student Responses and Perspectives

Fourteen students enrolled in the pilot course, eleven JMU students and three INHOLLAND students. One INHOLLAND student withdrew before completing the course for a total of thirteen students completing the course. There were six females and five males from JMU and a female and male from INHOLLAND completing the offering. Tracking the postings indicates that all students participated in each of the seven assignments (see Table 1) as required.

In the traditional classroom setting, faculty-student and student-to-student interaction promotes a sense of connectedness among class members setting the stage for learning and sharing (Randolph & Krause, 2002). The first two postings attempted to create this setting. The students did an excellent job responding to the Growing Up in My Group exercise if just measured by the quantity of output. The quality of the responses was notable as well. The level of personal disclosure was remarkable from the co-developers' perspective. Both sets of students talked candidly about positive, negative, and conflicting messages received growing up. Several U.S. students were frank about types of racial and class prejudice they were exposed to and the impact it has had on them as they have created their own values. Several factors may account for this apparent openness and trust. One is that the JMU students for the most part knew each other as well as the instructor. The INHOLLAND students also had a personal relationship with their instructor. A second factor is that all but two of the U.S. students were social work students. The assumption inherent in this statement is that social work students may be more accustomed to introspection and analysis regarding themselves and others although the non-social work students' work was not noticeably different. Available research lends credence to these observations stating that trust is a key element developing online communication as well as rules that create a need to engage in discussion. Trust is also built online as participants provide, interpret and share knowledge, on immigration in this case (Ridings, Gefen, & Arinze, 2002; Chou, 2001). Warf, Vincent, and Purcell (1999) reported that several students in their course felt freer to express themselves online than in a traditional classroom.

Through this exercise the students found similarities in several areas including the influence of parents versus friends, the value of work and education, the important role of religion and perceptions of poverty. Students commented on each other's postings as well as posed questions to each other. The Dutch students commented on the JMU students' awareness of their backgrounds and the impact and perhaps awareness this created about immigration in general. Both sets of students commented on stereotypes that were dispelled as well as stereotypes they had not considered particularly as relating to Asian Americans.

As the response postings went back and forth based on the Growing Up in My Group exercise the instructors noted that greetings and personal comments increased in the body of the postings. The number of response postings required for this exercise was two and over fifty percent of the students responded three times. This seeming comfort and personal interaction level stayed fairly stable for the remainder of the course. In examining the assignments it appeared that the bulk of the more personalized communications occurred after the initial response posting for each assignment.

The students universally liked the Growing Up in My Group exercise stating that it provided them with a means of discussing who they are and providing some insights into the influences of the many groups that impact them. Some cultural divergence surfaced with the Dutch students stating that the U.S. students seemed more "trained in analyzing and writing about themselves and thinking about their roots." The U.S. students tended to see the Dutch students as more independent and individualistic with one stating "that is very cool and respectable because I have never been one to be original or verve away from the norm." Both the Dutch and U.S. students stated numerous times and in various ways that just because people are different on several levels they can still share the same values and ideas. This exercise provided a context for the immigration specific discussions that made up the bulk of the course.

Focusing on the specific content of the course, immigration, students stated in general that finding information relating to immigration history and current immigration laws and policies pushed all of them to look beyond their usual sources of information. All the students indicated in a variety of ways that they "were amazed about what I didn't know about my own country and system." Many of the U.S. students were struck by the length of history in the Netherlands as compared to the U.S. as well as the role and impact that colonization has played and is playing in the Netherlands. Another new concept to U.S. students was guest workers and the impact this has had in Dutch society. Dutch students on the other hand generally felt that the U.S. has had strict immigration laws for quite awhile and is not as tolerant of asylum seekers. The Dutch students were very aware of the impact of September 11, 2001 both for the United States but also for Holland. One Dutch student stated "Kinda funny that something that happens to your country (U.S.) reflects on ours that much. . . Talk about mass hysteria." The Dutch students saw the rise and assassination of Pim Fortuyn, a charismatic Dutch politician with an ethno-nationalistic ideology, as connected to post 9/11 feelings toward immigrants particularly those of Arab descent.

Concomitantly, U.S. students also commented extensively on the impact of 9/11 on both immigration policy and how many American citizens view those members of U.S. society who do not reflect the White Anglo Saxon ideal. "As a social work student, these circumstances and changing views on immigration are very unsettling. I am upset at how our country has reacted to the 9/11 attacks in some regards, not regarding the war on terror but more specifically immigration and racial stigmas that have arisen in the wake of the attacks."

Asking students to comment on the delivery of services from a social work perspective allowed students to draw on class and outside experiences. The students clearly identified with the social work profession in looking to possible solutions that focus on integration and early language acquisition by immigrants and their children. Both sets of students saw the elementary school as a focal point for service delivery and connecting to immigrant families. A unifying theme for both sets of students was their solution focused thinking and their realization of social and political realities. "Being able to see through a country's unfounded fears is a quality that good social workers should possess and I've seen a great many examples of this in reading all the postings" said a U.S. student. In a closing post one of the Dutch students commented "I think there is more to learn from each other than can be done in one course . . . " From the authors perspective this indicates that important connections were made, and that students brought their own life experiences into the course postings as well, previous knowledge that go well beyond what we as instructors can offer alone, demonstrating that instructors are not the only source of information.

Some of the JMU students who participated in this pilot course also participated in the travel study course that has been offered for the past six years and were able to meet the Dutch participants after the course ended. JMU and INHOLLAND students provided the following feedback in a meeting at INHOLLAND University after the completion of the course:

- provide a site for translation of certain Dutch/English phrases or words
- have the opportunity for several real time chats
- include pictures of students and add the names toward the end
- work in partners on a small project
- have more equal numbers of Dutch and U.S. students
- enable students to delete or edit their work before the final posting
- have the assignment dates posted from the very beginning
- do this again using the same or another current issue
- continue to use Blackboard for the platform

The comments of the first student cohort indicate an investment in this type of course programming and an interest in improving the delivery for the future participants. The students were able to create a community online demonstrating the interest, capacity and opportunity to communicate and interact with each other sharing information, resources and experiences. The fact that the students unanimously indicated that the course should be offered again demonstrates the personalized value possible in this type of course offering. Students were also able to suggest future topics that have currency with social work in both countries, again demonstrating their interest as well as the value of the course concept for a variety of topics.

Faculty Perspectives

Faculty workload was an ongoing factor in the construction of the course once the decision to go ahead was made. Neither of the co-developers received release time to work on course development slowing down progress in the initial phases. Lack of dedicated time for the course by the co-faculty after loading and beginning the course lead to some confusion among students relating to course details such as posting dates initially. Collis (1999) notes in her work the importance of being realistic about what faculty can and will do and designing the course to reflect these realities. Having delivered the course once the co-instructors will divide monitoring assignment postings. In a course of this nature having co-developers and instructors was a benefit and a necessity. The team approach allowed the workload to be shared as well as providing a sounding board for ideas and solving challenges related to students and the course in general. The team approach also provided immediate access to players impacting the course development and delivery at each institution insuring meeting the timelines developed. Having access to Blackboard support at each university was critical too, allowing technical and pedagogical questions to be answered in real time for each instructor. The course platform was user friendly for faculty and students alike and was flexible enough to handle all course demands. Student evaluations indicated the course platform was easy to navigate. Blackboard will be the platform of choice for the next offering of the course based on both student and faculty input.

Confronting the instructors at the outset were three issues: the language differences, course recruitment, and lack of a template. The language difference impacted course recruitment in the Netherlands. The Dutch students fear of having to write in English was a major factor in the small numbers (3) signing up for the course. Students at INHOLLAND indicated that they were more comfortable speaking rather than writing English. One student completing the course indicated that it took twice as much time for each assignment because of translation time. Additional credit was indeed warranted for the Dutch students. In spite of the language difficulties confronting the Dutch students they were not precluded from participating fully or effectively based on their actual postings. Their posts were always responsive to the themes and they participated fully in the give and take of the discussions.

Since this was a new and pilot course for both universities the faculty recruited students and used their relationships with students to create a pool of interested students. At JMU students going on the May study trip to INHOLLAND were a natural source with all but one taking the course even though it was a pilot and a new format. Three additional JMU students took the course for a total of eleven U.S. students and two Dutch students completing the course. Starting the course after each university's semester began complicated recruitment. The next offering of the course is on the books and it is hoped that enrollment numbers will improve particularly for Dutch students. This course could be linked with the study trip for both universities; however, the developers view the course as a stand alone course intended to expand the number of students able to have an international experience. Students interested in the travel course will likely continue to be a core of the students taking the course but the course is broader than an adjunct to the travel course.

The lack of a course template was more of consideration for the faculty members although students had questions relating to time commitments and workload considerations. Individual face-to-face meetings and an initial required group session allayed many student concerns, as did the opportunity to assist in creating and critiquing a new style course offering at both schools. The meetings were time consuming and will likely be required until the course is mainstay in each curriculum. An additional group meeting was held after enrollment to and one toward the end of the course to answer any questions. These two meetings were not required with about a quarter of the U.S. students attending.

The instructors relied on prior course development skills as well as experiences in creating an atmosphere for class discussion. Translating those skills to an online setting required reworking some existing exercises and carefully crafting assignments such as the similarities and differences posting. Simplicity was deemed important, since faculty were not present to interpret during individual student posting sessions. Postings tended to be done quite late based on the times noted electronically on the postings. For the next offering the instructors will revisit each assignment editing them into shorter more concise sentences for the ease of translation. Also close attention will be given to removing any jargon, metaphors or slang (Loring, 2002). After the initial offering the instructors are comfortable and confident in the course approach used and will use it again. It is felt that the template with the two initial posting focusing on creating a rich qualitative base of personal and cultural musings provide a strong segue into other current event or social policy topics. Asking all students to develop a paper on immigration history and current immigration issues was effective in insuring all students had the information base to engage in the more applied assignments leading to well-versed postings. All of the students' comments were relevant and thoughtful. The faculty developers intend to address each of the suggestions for the next offering.

Evaluation

Course assessment and evaluation takes place in various ways both individually and collectively. From a collective standpoint the course was judged to be a success and worth replication by both students and faculty. Evaluation criteria for individual students were presented in the course syllabus on Blackboard. Evaluation criterion centered first on the posting of all assignments and discussion reactions by the times noted in the syllabus and indicated by the posting time automatically generated. Content driven postings for each assignment were judged for the depth of content presented and evidence of the use of linked and suggested materials. Required responses were evaluated as to whether the noted number was submitted by the time deadline and on the quality of the response content and the direct connection to the content being discussed.

The quantitative evaluation was an important tool for faculty and fostered time management for students. The subjective grading of the content was time intensive. Content evaluation improved for both faculty members over the course of the semester as each faculty member became more comfortable with evaluating and commenting on the work of students not in their program. Evaluating comments of the "other" program required each faculty member read beyond their differing biases. The US professor could not be overly impressed, given her lack of proficiency in written Dutch, at the ability of the Dutch students to write professionally in English. The Dutch professor could not be swayed at the surface quality of the US students' writing. Both faculty members had to develop the ability to look for content related to the learning objectives and critical thinking in a different manner, not always focused on language usage. The content, flow and logic of statements had to be evaluated. The faculty members gained new insights into the concepts of grading in a cross-cultural context and into their own biases regarding students not physically in their program.

CONCLUDING THOUGHTS

Research has consistently confirmed that distance education and online courses are comparable to traditional classroom courses when it comes to student learning and satisfaction (Menon & Coe, 2000; Schoech & Helton, 2002). Increasing the number of descriptive and research based articles focused on internationally collaborative social work education using technology based teaching methods can promote another means of internationalizing social work education.

Drawing from the reflections of the students both written and oral, the participants established common bonds, recognized cultural diversity as well as similar professional values and see this type of course offering as valuable and worth repeating. This pilot course demonstrates that international collaboration, teaching and evaluation is possible. Furthermore, a course of this nature can be quite productive and even fun. The novelty and independence of this course along with the currency of the topic appealed to the students.

REFERENCES

Anders, J.R. (1975). Internationalism in social work education. *Journal of Social Work Education*, 11, 16-21.

Bateson, M.C. (1994). *Peripheral Visions: Learning along the way*. New York: Harper Collins.

Boehm, W.W. (1980). Teaching and learning international social welfare. *International Social Work*, 23, 17-24.

Boyle, D., & Cervantes, B. (2000). The implementation of a sustainable social work exchange program: The University of Georgia and the University of Veracruz. *Professional Development*, 3(2): 11-23.

Chou, C. (2001). Formative evaluation of synchronous CMC systems for a learner-centered Online course. *Journal of Interactive Learning Research*, Summer-Fall, 173-191.

Collis, B. (1999). Designing for differences: Cultural differences in the design of WWW-based course-support sites. *British Journal of Educational Technology*, 30 (3), 201-215.

Desruisseaux, P. (2000). As exchanges lose a political rationale, their role is debated. *The Chronicle of Higher Education*, 23 (46), 52-53.

European Communities. (2002). *Socrates: Gateway to education*. [Brochure]. Brussels, Belgium: Author.

Ford, K., & Ericson, C. (2003). An international exchange: What, so what, and now what? *The Journal of Baccalaureate Social Work*, 8(2), 97-108.

Healy, L.M. (1986). The international dimension in social work education: Current efforts, future challenges. *International Social Work*, 29, 135-147.

Healy, L.M. (1988). Curriculum building in international social work: Toward preparing professionals for the global age. *Journal of Social Work Education*, 24, 221-228.

Hokenstad, M.C. (1984). Curriculum directions for the 1980's: Implications of the new curriculum policy statement. *Journal of Education for Social Work*, 20, 15-22.

Holmes, T., & Mathews, G. (1993). Innovations in international cross-cultural social work education. *Arete*, 18(1), 43-47.

INHOLLAND University, 2003, *Instellingplan 2003-2006*. Retrieved January 26, 2004, from http://www.inholland.nl/documents/Instellingplan_versie4.1_hmrversie.pdf.

James Madison University, University Planning and Analysis, 2002, *JMU Mission Statement*. Retrieved January 26, 2004 from http://www.jmu.edu/ie/JMUmission.htm.

Johnson, A.K. (1999). Globalization from below: Using the Internet to internationalize social work education. *Journal of Social Work Education*, 35(3), 377-393.

Link, R.J. (1999). Internationalizing your classroom and field practica: Why and how. *Bachelor Program Update*, 21.

Lorenzetti, J.P. (2003). Tony Bates' twelve lessons for distance education administrators. *Distance Education Report*, 7(8), 1-3.

Loring, L. (2002). Six steps to preparing instruction for a worldwide audience. *Journal of Interactive Instruction*, 14(3), 24-29.

Menon, G., & Coe, J. (2000). Technology and social work education: Recent empirical studies. *Research on Social Work Practice*. 10(4), 397-399.

NRC Webpagina (2000, mei 20). De multiculturele samenleving. Retrieved January 28, 2004 from http://www.nrc.nl/W2/Lab/Multicultureel/inhoud.html.

Nuffic (2003, February 27). *Theme Internationalization*. Retrieved January 28, 2004 from http://nuffic.net/common.asp?id=443&instantie=0.

Randolph, K., & Krause, D. (2002). Mutual Aid in the Classroom: An instructional technology application. *Journal of Social Education*, 38(2), 259-271.

Ridings, C., Gefen, D., & Arinze, A. (2002). Some antecedents and effects of trust in virtual communities. *Journal of Strategic Information Systems*, 11, 271-295.

Sanders, D.S. (1977). Developing a graduate social work curriculum with an international-crosscultural perspective. *Journal of Education for Social Work*, 13, 76-83.

Schoech, D., & Helton, D. (2002). Qualitative and quantitative analysis of a course taught via classroom and internet chatroom. *Qualitative Social Work 1(1)*, 111-124.

Shedletshy, L., & Aitken, J. (2004). *Human Communication on the Internet*. Boston, MA: Pearson Education, Inc.

Smith, A., & Rose, R. (2003). Build and teach a successful online course. *Technology & Learning*, 23(9), 16-18.

U.S. Department of Education. (2003). *European Community-United States of America Cooperation Program 2004 Guidelines and Application Materials*. Retrieved January 28, 2004 from http://www.ed.gov/programs/fipseec/ec-us2004guidelinescov.pdf.

v. Ryssen, S. (2001). De Hoop van Pandorra, ICT in het onderwijs, hfst.6.

Warf, B., Vincent, P., & Purcell, D. (1999). International collaborative learning on the World Wide Web. *Journal of Geography*, 98(3), 141-148.

Wu, A. (2003). Supporting electronic discourse: Principles of design from a social constructivist perspective. *Journal of Interactive Learning Research*, 14 (2), 167-185.

Yoder, M. (2003). Seven steps to successful online learning communities. *Learning & Leading with Technology*, 30(6), 15-21.

A Child Welfare Course for Aboriginal and Non-Aboriginal Students: Pedagogical and Technical Challenges

Jacquie Rice-Green
Gary C. Dumbrill

SUMMARY. This chapter describes the development of a Web-based undergraduate child welfare course for Aboriginal and non-Aboriginal learners. Rather than simply incorporate an Aboriginal perspective into Eurocentric pedagogies and course structures, the authors disrupt the dominance of Western ways of knowing in education by designing the course to situate Western knowledge as *a* way of knowing rather than *the* way of knowing and the frame from which all other perspectives are understood. In this research the authors describe the differences between Aboriginal and

Jacquie Rice-Green, MSW, is Assistant Professor, School of Social Work, University of Victoria, P.O. Box 1700 STN CSC, Victoria BC V8W 2Y2, Canada (E-mail: jlgreen@uvic.ca).

Gary C. Dumbrill, PhD, is Assistant Professor, School of Social Work, McMaster University, Kenneth Taylor Hall, Room 319, 1280 Main Street West, Hamilton, Ontario, L8S 4M4, Canada (E-mail: dumbrill@mcmaster.ca) Home Page: http://socserv. mcmaster.ca/dumbrill/.

This project was supported by a University of Victoria Dean of Human and Social Development Innovation Fund Award and a University of Victoria Innovation in Teaching Award.

[Haworth co-indexing entry note]: "A Child Welfare Course for Aboriginal and Non-Aboriginal Students: Pedagogical and Technical Challenges." Rice-Green, Jacquie, and Gary C. Dumbrill. Co-published simultaneously in *Journal of Technology in Human Services* (The Haworth Press, Inc.) Vol. 23, No. 3/4, 2005, pp. 167-181; and: *Web-Based Education in the Human Services: Models, Methods, and Best Practices* (eds: MacFadden et al.) The Haworth Press, Inc., 2005, pp. 167-181. Single or multiple copies of this article are available for a fee from The Haworth Document Delivery Service [1-800-HAWORTH, 9:00 a.m. - 5:00 p.m. (EST). E-mail address: docdelivery@haworthpress.com].

European thought and reveal how Web-based courses can be designed in ways that do not perpetuate Eurocentrism. *[Article copies available for a fee from The Haworth Document Delivery Service: 1-800-HAWORTH. E-mail address: <docdelivery@haworthpress.com> Website: <http://www.HaworthPress.com> © 2005 by The Haworth Press, Inc. All rights reserved.]*

KEYWORDS. Web-based learning, indigenous knowledge, child welfare, pedagogy, social work education

INTRODUCTION

This chapter describes the development of a Web-based undergraduate child welfare course at the School of Social Work, University of Victoria, Canada. The course presented two design challenges. Firstly, because the school delivers education to on-campus and also distance students, parallel versions of the course were needed–one in a Web-based format and the other in a classroom format. Both versions of the course were required to have the same learning content and outcomes. A second challenge was that course pedagogy needed to meet the learning needs of both Aboriginal and non-Aboriginal students as well as prepare students for child welfare work in both Aboriginal and non-Aboriginal communities.

The authors were uniquely placed to respond to these challenges. Jacquie Rice-Green is an Aboriginal professor from the Haisla Nation with experience in child welfare practice and also teaching in Aboriginal and non-Aboriginal contexts. Gary C. Dumbrill is a White professor originating from London, England, who has experience in child welfare practice, teaching, and also in designing and delivering Web-based courses. Working as a team, and both believing it important to deconstruct and disrupt the dominance of Western knowledge in education, the authors identified the differences between European and Aboriginal ways of knowing and considered the implications for both classroom and Web-based courses. Supported by a grant from the University of Victoria, Faculty of Human Development "Dean's Fund for Innovations in Computer Mediated Material" as well as an "Innovation in Teaching Research Award," the authors developed a model for building parallel classroom and Web-based courses that are suitable for both Aboriginal and non-Aboriginal learners.

The results of the project are described below. First, the course history and context is described. The course pedagogy is explained and an overview of the course content is presented. The course architecture and structure, which utilized modified "learning objects," is discussed. Issues that arose in constructing the course are debated and finally the course outcomes are detailed and conclusions are drawn.

COURSE HISTORY CONTEXT

Since being founded in 1978, the School of Social Work at the University of Victoria, Canada, has placed emphasis on delivering distance education (DE) as well as classroom education. The emphasis on DE was driven by a desire to make social work education accessible to those in remote parts of Canada. The viability of this venture was inspired by the Open University in Britain, which opened in 1969, and by 1978 was meeting with unprecedented success making higher education available through DE to those who would not usually attend university. The University of Victoria's DE efforts met with similar success and were bolstered by research that showed that the school's classroom and DE courses were equally effective in conveying social work education (Callahan & Rachue, 1988; Callahan & Wharf, 1989; Callahan & Whitaker, 1988; Cossom, 1988).

By the late 1990s, almost the entire school curriculum was available in both classroom and DE formats enabling students to take almost any course at a distance or on campus. DE content was delivered through a "correspondence" model that involved a traditional "course pack" and e-mail support. Currently, seventy-five percent of the school's students elect to take their courses by DE and it is now possible to complete almost all the required course work for an undergraduate social work degree in this manner. The school maintains the equivalency of DE and classroom education by insisting that the DE and classroom version of each course have the same content and learning outcomes.

In the late 1990s the school began migrating its DE courses into a Web-based model using WebCT as the delivery platform. Migration occurs when existing course material is due for renewal and involves an instructor updating the classroom content and corresponding DE manual followed by a faculty DE coordinator and technician moving the updated DE content into a WebCT format. This mode of migration caused the schools initial WebCT courses to be based on a similar pedagogy to a correspondence method of DE.

Although the school's DE program began increasing the accessibility of higher education in the 1970s, post secondary education at that time remained almost non-existent among Canada's Aboriginal peoples, who are also referred to in Canada as "First Nation's" peoples in recognition of them being the original Indigenous people of the nation now known as Canada. This lack of post-secondary education among First Nation's people needs to be understood historically. Beginning in the late 1800s, attempts were made through Canada's residential school systems, to strip Aboriginal peoples of their culture and identity. Children were separated from their families and communities, prohibited from speaking their native language or practicing traditions, and forced to learn European traditions–a practice that is now recognized as a form of cultural genocide (Downey, 1999). Formal "education," therefore, was not offered to First Nations people as a form of enlightenment, but was used as a political tool of subjugation. Even when forced attendance in residential schools began to dwindle in the 1950s and 1960s, the system continued to subjugate because prior to the 1970s, Aboriginal students were required to relinquish their identities (status) as First Nation's people to obtain post secondary education. Even when this requirement was removed, Aboriginal students needed to be strong minded and spirited to leave their communities (reserves) and cope with transition to new towns, cities, and colleges/universities which were often hostile to their presence.

Despite these difficulties, First Nation's students pursued higher education. Graduates returned to their communities and found ways to bring higher education to these communities in a manner that was relevant to Aboriginal peoples. Additionally, First Nation's graduates who began working in universities and colleges, began to challenge these institutions to meet the needs of Aboriginal learners and they also challenged the dominance of Western notions of knowledge and teaching.

Through the work of these graduates, it became evident that the vision of increasing the accessibility of education through DE did not hinge simply on delivering courses across geographic distances. Making education assessable also depended on understanding and bridging the gap between the Eurocentric notions of knowledge held by the academy and the ways of knowing of learning held by those not from European traditions. Bridging this gap requires deconstructing European dominance. From the Victoria school's beginning, efforts had been made to deconstruct dominant societal discourses, but as the school increased its focus on First Nations social work, it began to learn important lessons about the ways European dominance occurred through social work education process itself. It was important, therefore, in the migration of DE courses into a WebCT format, to articulate, consolidate, and incorporate these lessons into the pedagogy of the new Web-based courses. The authors decided to undertake this articulation, consolidation, and incorporation when asked to update and migrate the school's child welfare practice course into WebCT. We decided to not only use this migration as an opportunity to explore the pedagogical issues of WebCT delivery to Aboriginal and non-Aboriginal students but to also address the pedagogical and design issues of parallel course construction in WebCT and classroom formats. Our pedagogy was developed through our experience of co-teaching courses together and is effective and appropriate for both Aboriginal and non-Aboriginal learners.

PEDAGOGY

Pedagogy is political. As mentioned above, "education" has been used as a pretext for removing Aboriginal children from their communities and indoctrinating them in Western/European knowledge systems. Although residential schools no longer exist, educational systems remain steeped in Eurocentric knowledge. This bias in education is often invisible to those from the dominant Western culture because society is so steeped in this culture that Western ways can appear to be the "normal" or natural way of being (Dumbrill & Maiter, 1996; Yee & Dumbrill, 2003, Dumbrill, 2003). Yet far from neutral, an educational system that uncritically adopts a Eurocentric stance is covertly perpetuating the residential school project because it continues to indoctrinate students into Western ways of knowing (Rice-Green & Dumbrill, 2003). There is, of course, nothing wrong with Western ways of knowing, as long as they are identified as "a" way of knowing rather than "the" way of knowing. Instructors, therefore, must make the nature and origins of the knowledge they impart evident to the learner. Additionally, in social work education with its focus on social inequalities, the relationship between Western knowledge and the dominant power systems that marginalize people within society must also be made known.

The Victoria school makes the nature and origins of knowledge known by not only teaching students to recognize and identify the dominance of Western/European knowledge but also by de-centering that knowledge and emphasizing "other" ways of knowing–particularly Aboriginal ways of knowing. Almost all the school's courses now contain

Aboriginal content. The school recently began to offer Aboriginal students the opportunity to obtain a social work degree that specializes in First Nations social work. This option is exercised by students choosing core and elective courses that focus specifically on issues from a First Nations perspective. In these specialized courses students focus on teachings from community elders and community healers, and they learn protocols when approaching these First Nation's experts. Such teaching is also included in the school's other courses to ensure that all those who may work with First Nation's individuals, families or communities understand the importance of protocol, history and relationships to Aboriginal peoples.

In adopting the above pedagogy, we take what we refer to as a radical, structural, feminist, anti-racist, and First Nations stance. Our radical and structural stance is similar to that articulated by Paulo Freire who, in "The Pedagogy of the Oppressed," provides students with the opportunity to effect social change by learning about the class mechanisms that drive oppression and shape their lives (Freire, 2001). Our feminist and anti-racist stance is similar to that of bell hooks (1994) who expands Freire's class analysis to challenge societal, racial, sexual, and class boundaries in pursuit of social justice. Our First Nations stance understands and deconstructs colonialism in the context of a historical analysis similar to the work of Emma La Rocque (2001), who asserts that "'voice is a textual resistance technique' and must be used as an attempt to begin to balance the legacy of dehumanization and bias entrenched in Canadian studies about native peoples" (p. 13).

Our stance is appropriate for both Aboriginal and non-Aboriginal social work students because a part of social work education for all students is to understand the links between the personal issues families face and broader societal inequalities. This approach also fits particularly well for Aboriginal students because it validates the historical trauma experienced by Aboriginal peoples as a result of colonization and begins a process of resisting ongoing colonization.

We apply the above pedagogy through a constructivistic approach. In both classroom and Web-based settings, we see ourselves as being "guides on the side" rather than "sages on the stage" (Reeves & Reeves, 1997). A constructivist educator does not see knowledge as "facts" or "truth" in which the student needs to be instructed, but considers that which we regard as knowledge and truth to be the result of perspective. Indeed, constructivists contend that "knowledge and truth are created, not discovered by the mind" (Schwandt, 1994, p. 125). Our educational role as guides fits well with our radical position because like Freire we conceptualize education as a dialogue between the educator and students–a process in which both learn and are changed. There is, however, a caveat to constructivism within a radical pedagogy. Constructivist thought has postmodern leanings which can cause the educator to slide into a position that considers all views to be "true" and "valid." We avoid this slippage by holding the position that all "truths" are not equal or "valid." For instance, we would not accept overtly racist arguments or sentiments as viable, and we resolve the tensions this causes in our postmodern leanings in a similar manner to Leonard (1994, 1997) who embraces deconstruction as a means of dismantling the "truths" that support existing class and power relationships.

Our role as educational guides and a focus on process and dealing with racism and other forms of oppression fits well with Aboriginal teaching traditions. Learners and teachers within Aboriginal settings have inherent respect for collective learning, which is emphasized by a statement within most Aboriginal communities that, "it takes a community to raise children." So, by incorporating a constructivistic and radical position, students have an opportunity to explore Aboriginal philosophies (theories) without contention.

COURSE CONTENT

Because we were designing a "child welfare practice" course that prepares fourth-year undergraduate students for work in a child protection or other mandated child welfare setting, our content focused primarily on the micro practice of helping families and communities keep children safe and healthy. Content is also needed to connect micro practice to social issues on a mezzo and macro level. It would serve little purpose for social workers to help families cope with their individual problems without helping them connect these problems to broader societal issues that compound and in some cases cause these ills. This is particularly so in Aboriginal communities where it is not possible to grasp the dynamics of individual or family problems outside an understanding of colonialism.

In this course, we approached practice believing that social workers need to know what they are doing and why they are doing it. Consequently, we adopted as a text the book, "Child Abuse: Toward a Knowledge Base" (Corby, 2000). This book does not focus on the "how to" of practice but on a critical exploration of the theories and knowledge on which child welfare practice is based. We supplemented this European text with a collection of readings that added knowledge from a broad range of other perspectives–particularly Aboriginal perspectives. We then applied these texts by emphasizing praxis and provided opportunities for students to connect course material to their own experience and to the experience of others in the course. In keeping with our pedagogy, we ensured that connections were made between these experiences and broader political and societal issues. From this mix of theory, praxis and critical analysis, we worked through the implications for child welfare social work practice. This process is compatible with Freire's emphasis on students connecting personal issues to political realities and is also compatible with working in Aboriginal contexts where an understanding of the ways history and colonization have impacted families and communities is crucial. We anticipated that this approach would teach students to engage in micro practice while and also recognizing, identifying and addressing the social inequalities that compound and sometimes cause the problems these families face. The course content was compiled as shown in Table 1.

COURSE ARCHITECTURE

We used "learning objects" to construct the course. Learning objects are virtual "granular" instructional units built around specific teaching objectives that are portable and can be reused in several courses (Recker, Walker & Wiley, 2000; Wiley, 2000). A learning object may be a RealAudio lecture, an online PowerPoint presentation, a series of HTML pages, a group exercise in a virtual seminar room, or any similar online activity.

The potential of learning objects lies in their granularity and portability. Once a pool of objects is established, they can be used like a collection of LEGO blocks to build a variety of courses. Learning objects are quickly becoming a central part of the pedagogy of Web-based instruction (Hodgins, 2000). Learning objects are particularly viable in dual course development because an object can be constructed in a Web-based and classroom format. For instance, an online child welfare quiz can also be constructed as a classroom quiz. An online RealAudio PowerPoint presentation can also be a classroom PowerPoint presentation. A classroom small group discussion can also be a WebCT small group discussion. Utilizing this architecture, we built the content for each week of the course with learning objects. By constructing each ob-

TABLE 1. Course Content

Wk	Topic	Description	Broad Learning Outcome
1	Opening Circle	Introduce course and each other. Establish a focus on "healing" which is taking care of one's own and others' wellness when engaging in course material. Provide overview of course.	Dialogue between students and instructors established. Expectations clarified. A focus on self-care and the care of each other in the course established.
2	History	Examine and critique the dominant Western discourse of child welfare and the ways this has impacted each of us and our histories. Review and un-suppress the history of child care in Aboriginal communities.	Awareness of political dimensions to the way child welfare work is established. Students learn Aboriginal child welfare and the historical child care practices of First Nation's people are affirmed.
3	Values, legislation & case examples	Review child welfare legislation, social work values and also Aboriginal values in relation to child care and communities. Operationalize these concepts by having students apply them to case examples.	Students understand and can apply child welfare legislation as well as understand and apply social work and First Nation's values when engaging in this work.
4	Dealing with abuse & neglect	Examine theories that attempt to explain physical child abuse and consider interventions.	Students understand the nature, causes and prevalence of physical abuse, as well as ways to intervene in such cases.
5	Dealing with abuse & neglect cont. . . .	Examine theories that attempt to explain child neglect and consider interventions.	Students understand the nature, causes and prevalence of child neglect, as well as ways to intervene in such cases.
6	Dealing with abuse & neglect cont. . . .	Examine theories that attempt to explain child sexual abuse and also theories that attempt to explain emotional maltreatment and consider interventions.	Students understand the nature, causes and prevalence of sexual abuse and emotional maltreatment, as well as ways to intervene in such cases.
7	Anti-oppressive skills in child welfare	Examine anti-oppressive practice (AOP). Although AOP is considered in every class, in this session AOP is considered in its own right.	Students' understanding of AOP is reinforced.
8	Risk reduction	Examine risk measurement and risk reduction.	Students understand the strengths and limitations of risk assessment.
9	Ongoing work with families	Consider ongoing casework.	Students consolidate learning by applying course content to real case examples.
10	Looking after children	Examine working with children in care, issues of permanency planning and adoption.	Issues in working with children in care are understood.
11	Cases that go wrong	Undertake an in-depth analysis of a case that "went wrong." In this class students utilize course learning to conduct an in-class analysis of a child who died as a result of physical abuse at home with his parents.	Applying course content in the analysis of a child homicide case reinforces the depth of students' learning.
12	Cases that go wrong cont. . . .	Undertake an additional in-depth analysis of a case that "went wrong." Students utilize course learning to conduct an in-class analysis of a child who died while in care.	Applying course content in the analysis of an additional child homicide case further reinforces the depth of students' learning.
13	Closing Circle	Consolidation of learning and ending ceremonies.	Formal course learning is concluded.

ject in a classroom and also a Web-based form, we ensured the equivalency of the Web-based and classroom versions of the course.

Although learning objects solved our design problems, they created pedagogical conflicts. Indeed, learning objects are usually constructed as "metadata," which is the notion that each object is self-contained, complete in itself, self-describing and able to achieve a specific learning objective (Oakes, 2002). This conflicts with a pedagogy that emphasizes the way knowledge interconnects and the ways power mechanisms shape what we regard as "knowledge." As well, the notion of knowledge being complete in itself de-emphasizes the process and praxis, which are central to our pedagogy. To overcome these limitations, instead of constructing learning objects as discrete items of knowledge, we constructed them as "way-points" on a learning journey. These way-points remained portable and reusable, but rather than being comprised of consumable knowledge items, they were constituted as points at which students could engage and consider bodies of knowledge. Way-points, therefore, are unlike learning objects because they are not simply independent structures that contain knowledge for students to absorb, but are interconnected structures that enable students to absorb information while they critically evaluate that information and connect it to other items of knowledge. In other words, unlike learning objects that are independent of each other and are self-contained, way-points are designed to be interconnected and interdependent.

Because way-points are interconnected, their sequencing is crucial. For instance, early in the course we constructed an "object" in the form of a child welfare quiz (which has been made publicly available online http://web2.uvcs.uvic.ca/courses/sw475/). Although the quiz communicates factual information, it was also designed to disrupt dominant discourses that situate current Eurocentric notions of child welfare as epitomizing civilized behaviour toward children. The construction of this way-point uses exactly the same educational strategy employed by MacFadden, Herie, Maiter and Dumbrill in their "constructivist, emotionally-oriented model of web-based instruction" (in press). The purpose of this model is to disrupt taken for granted social constructions and open students to alternative ways of conceptualizing issues–particularly alternatives that fall outside the established "truth" of dominant societal discourse. By introducing, through a quiz, historical information about advanced child welfare systems that pre-date European civilization, this way-point brings students to a place where they are ready to challenge the assumption that modern child welfare practice is the most advanced way of helping families. It is important that this point be reached early in the course because it establishes a questioning about taken for granted practices that are important when engaging with the rest of the course material. With the modifications described above, learning objects provide the ideal course architecture. Objects, modified as way-points, provide students with a learning journey in which they do not simply consume information, but rather question and construct their own sense of the subject being taught.

COURSE CONSTRUCTION

Once we had designed the course, a school DE coordinator and technician undertook construction. The separation of design and construction relieves instructors from learning the mechanics of WebCT assembly. Yet separating design and construction can create problems. In our project, the boundary between pedagogy and construction became blurred because we had neglected to explain our model to the technician and DE coordinator. Not understanding our stance, they began to challenge the course design and also its content. In a traditional classroom, an administrator or technician would never question a professor's course content, but when work is spread across a team such questioning easily occurs.

To make progress, the team had to refocus and be reminded of who was responsible for which aspect of the project. This clarification, however, created further problems because, although it gave us control of content, it placed the mechanics of the course structure firmly outside our control. Our suggestions of replicating the course structure innovation shown by MacFadden, Dumbrill, and Maiter (2000) in creating a Web-based virtual campus in their work at the University of Toronto, School of Social Work, was rejected by those responsible for construction. The MacFadden team, using the "First Class" Web-based platform, eased students' transition to online learning by creating a virtual campus. Rather than encountering a collection of online files, students moved among virtual seminar rooms where they met for discussions, attended a virtual lecture theater to view RealAudio presentations, and visited a virtual library to collect course readings. The rationale for rejecting this model was that all the Victoria school's Web-based courses were being built in the same manner to enable students to move easily from one course to another. Additionally, the technician was unsure if she could reproduce, in a WebCT environment, the level of sophistication MacFadden and colleagues achieved in a First Class environment.

These rationales made sense: students need consistency in course design. Also, although WebCT is capable of simulating a campus like environment, it is less user-friendly than the First Class system. As a result of these constraints, we were prevented from using the full potential of WebCT as a course platform.

OUTCOMES

The classroom course was co-taught by a male and a female First Nation's professor from September-December 2002. Ten students registered with one drop out, resulting in nine students completing the course. Of these, eight were female and one was male. One student was Metis, one was of Chinese origin, and seven were white with European origins. The WebCT course was taught by a female First Nations professor from May-August, 2003. Thirty-five students registered with one dropping out resulting in 34 students completing the course. There were thirty females and four males. Diversity statistics were not collected in this course but there was at least one Aboriginal participant.

Outcomes were determined by a qualitative analysis of course assignments, examining course evaluation data, and collecting in-depth qualitative feedback from three students (two who took the course in a WebCT format and two who took it in a classroom format). The outcomes of each course were similar. The dropout rates were very low. The average grade for each course was A− and a qualitative examination of the course assignments (case studies) found no noticeable differences in the learning outcomes. Students in both the WebCT and the classroom course rated the course highly in their end-of-course evaluations, although there were some negative comments from WebCT students.

Positive comments from both cohorts indicated that both groups learned the importance of critically analyzing child welfare situations and the importance of understanding historical and colonial contexts in child welfare practice. This critical analysis not only enabled students in both cohorts to recognize the ways child protection work can be punitive toward marginalized communities, particularly Aboriginal communities; but also enabled students to recognize how they could work in a mandated child protection setting and still work in respectful ways with Aboriginal as well as other communities in the interests of children and families. Students from both courses agreed that the relationship and communication with professors was adequate with the DE students being particularly appreciative of the opportunities Web-Based learning brought to communicate with the instructor to debrief readings and assignments. Students in both cohorts believed that the course helped prepare them for working with families in a child welfare setting and that they appreciated the challenge they encountered in person and in online discussions.

Importantly, students in both cohorts appreciated the ability to ask questions of the professor that they felt were difficult questions. For example, students in both cohorts wanted to meet and learn from elders in local Aboriginal communities but began, as a result of the course, to wonder how they could do this without imposing on these communities. Students showing this concern indicate a respect for Aboriginal communities and suggests our goal of teaching about dominance, colonialism, First Nation's history, and the importance of respectful relationship building and partnership with communities was achieved. The only negative evaluation comments came from one WebCT student who believed that she would have obtained a richer experience from the classroom course. Given the lower numbers in the classroom course and the fact that two instructors were available, these comments are probably valid.

CONCLUSIONS

The similarity in the Web-based and classroom course outcomes, the positive student evaluations, and the low dropout rates indicate that our model for course development was effective. In addition, we believe that our radical, structural, feminist, anti-racist and First Nations stance did justice in this course to the breadth of issues that social work students must address when engaging in child welfare practice. The approach we adopted also allowed us to be respectful of students from Aboriginal and non-Aboriginal learning traditions. The modification of "learning objects" to "way-points" as our course architecture allowed us to gain the benefits of learning objects while also incorporating holistic ways of knowing as well as connecting micro issues and social work practice to broader societal issues.

Further exploration and development of our model is needed. The key to this ongoing development is partnership and relationship. Aboriginal, and non-Aboriginal educators must work together to disrupt colonization by ensuring that European ways of knowing are not represented in education as "the" way of knowing. European thought needs to be identified in teaching and courses as simply "a" way of knowing and instructors must learn to respect and offer alternative ways of understanding and knowing. This is particularly so in Web-based education where design architecture such as learning objects, which views education as to the consumption of information, can further marginalize holistic Aboriginal ways of knowing. Without paying attention to both decolonization and holistic knowledge systems, Web-based education may bridge geographic divides, but will reinforce the divides between different peoples and differing ways of knowing.

REFERENCES

Callahan, M., & Rachue, A. (1988). *A comparison of drop outs and graduates from a BSW distance education program.* Paper presented at the Canadian Association of Schools of Social Work, Learned Societies Conference, University of Windsor, Ontario.

Callahan, M., & Wharf, B. (1989). Distance education in social work in Canada. *Journal of Distance Education, 4*(2), 63-80.

Callahan, M., & Whitaker, W. (1988). *Off-campus practicum in social work education in Canada.* Paper presented at the Canadian Association of Schools of Social Work, Learned Societies Conference, University of Windsor, Ontario.

Corby, B. (2000). *Child abuse: Towards a knowledge base* (2 ed.). Buckingham, England: Open University Press.

Cossom, J. (1988). Generalist social work practice: Views from BSW graduates. *Canadian Social Work Review, 5,* 297-315.

Downey, M. (1999, April 26, 1999). Canada's 'genocide.' *Maclean's, 112,* 56-58.

Dumbrill, G. C. (2003). Child welfare: AOP's nemesis? In W. Shera (Ed.), *Emerging perspectives on anti-oppressive practice.* (pp. 101-119). Toronto: Canadian Scholars' Press.

Dumbrill, G. C., & Maiter, S. (1996). Developing racial and cultural equity in social work practice. *The Social Worker, 64*(3), 89-94.

Freire, P. (2001). *Pedagogy of the Oppressed* (M. B. Ramos, Trans.) (30 ed.). New York: Continuum.

Hodgins, H. W. (2000). The future of learning objects. In D. A. Wiley (Ed.), *The Instructional Use of Learning Objects: Online Version.* Retrieved October 14, 2001 from: http://reusability.org/read/chapters/hodgins.doc.

hooks, b. (1994). *Teaching to transgress.* New York: Routledge.

LaRocque, E. (2001). *The Colonization of a Native Woman Scholar.* In C. Miller, P. Churchryk, M. Smallface, Marule, B. Manyfingers, and B. Deering (Eds.), *Women of the First Nations: Power, Wisdom, and Strength* (pp. 11-18). Winnipeg, Manitoba: University of Manitoba Press.

Leonard, P. (1994). Knowledge/power and postmodernism: Implications for the practice of a critical social work education. *Canadian Social Work Review, 11*(1), 11-26.

Leonard, P. (1997). *Postmodern welfare: Reconstructing an emancipatory project.* London, England: Sage.

MacFadden, R. J., Dumbrill, G. C., & Maiter, S. (2000). Web-based education in a graduate faculty of social work: Crossing the new frontier. *Journal of New Technology in the Human Services, 13*(1&2), 27-38.

MacFadden, R. J., Herie, M., Maiter, S., & Dumbrill, G. C. (in press). Achieving high touch in high tech: A constructivist, emotionally-oriented model of web-based instruction. *Journal of Teaching in Social Work.*

Oakes, K. (2002). An objective view of learning objects. *Training and Development, 56*(5), 103-105.

Recker, M. M., Walker, A., & Wiley, D. A. (2000). Collaboratively filtering learning objects. In D. A. Wiley (Ed.), *The Instructional Use of Learning Objects: Online Version.* Retrieved October 14, 2001 from: http://reusability.org/read/chapters/recker.doc.

Reeves, T., & Reeves, P. (1997). Effective dimensions of interactive learning on the World Wide Web. In B. Khan (Ed.), *Web-based instruction* (pp. 59-66). Englewood Cliffs, NJ: Educational Technology Publications.

Rice-Green, J., & Dumbrill, G. C. (2003). *Developing diverse and inclusive social work knowledge systems.* Paper presented at the Canadian Association of Schools of Social Work Annual Conference: Diversity and inclusion, putting the principles to work, Halifax, Nova Scotia.

Schwandt, T. A. (1994). Constructivist, interpretivist approaches to human inquiry. In N. K. Denzin & Y. S. Lincoln (Eds.), *Handbook of qualitative research* (pp. 118-137). Thousand Oaks, CA: Sage.

Wiley, D. A. (2000). Connecting learning objects to instructional design theory: A definition, a metaphor, and a taxonomy. In D. A. Wiley (Ed.), *The Instructional Use of Learning Objects: Online Version.* Retrieved October 14, 2001 from: http://reusability.org/read/chapters/wiley.doc.

Yee, J. Y., & Dumbrill, G. C. (2003). Whiteout: Looking for Race in Canadian Social Work Practice. In A. Al-Krenawi & J. R. Graham (Eds.), *Multicultural Social Work in Canada–Working with Diverse Ethno-Racial Communities* (pp. 98-121). Toronto, Ontario: Oxford University Press.

Web-Based Education in the Human Services: Use of Web-Based Video Clips in Counselling Skills Training

Paul Jerry, PhD
Sandra Collins, PhD

SUMMARY. This use of web-based video clips for counsellor skills training is used in the Campus Alberta Applied Psychology Counselling Initiative which provides Master's-level counsellor education at a distance. The core counselling skills course is delivered through the Web using digital video clips of counselling skills demonstrations, chat room skills practice and weekly discussion forums. A follow-up face-to-face Summer Institute allows learners to receive live feedback on their skill development. Course content is grounded in the construct of the *working alliance* (Bordin, 1979). Course activities use Bloom's taxonomies of learning objectives. Program evaluation suggests that learners are meeting competencies as they move from this course to practicum placements. *[Article copies available for a fee from The Haworth Document Delivery Service: 1-800-HAWORTH. E-mail address: <docdelivery@haworthpress.com> Website: <http://www.HaworthPress.com> © 2005 by The Haworth Press, Inc. All rights reserved.]*

Paul Jerry and Sandra Collins are affiliated with the Centre for Graduate Education in Applied Psychology, Athabasca University, 1 University Drive, Athabasca, Alberta T9S 3A3 Canada.

[Haworth co-indexing entry note]: "Web-Based Education in the Human Services: Use of Web-Based Video Clips in Counselling Skills Training." Jerry, Paul, and Sandra Collins. Co-published simultaneously in *Journal of Technology in Human Services* (The Haworth Press, Inc.) Vol. 23, No. 3/4, 2005, pp. 183-199; and: *Web-Based Education in the Human Services: Models, Methods, and Best Practices* (eds: MacFadden et al.) The Haworth Press, Inc., 2005, pp. 183-199. Single or multiple copies of this article are available for a fee from The Haworth Document Delivery Service [1-800-HAWORTH, 9:00 a.m. - 5:00 p.m. (EST). E-mail address: docdelivery@haworthpress.com].

Available online at http://www.haworthpress.com/web/JTHS
© 2005 by The Haworth Press, Inc. All rights reserved.
Digital Object Identifier: 10.1300/J017v023n03_02

KEYWORDS. Counsellor education, web-based learning, video, counselling psychology

This discussion of the use of web-based video clips for counsellor skills training takes place in the context of the Campus Alberta Applied Psychology: Counselling Initiative (CAAP). CAAP is a partnership between Athabasca University, the University of Calgary, and the University of Lethbridge. This graduate counsellor education initiative was developed to address the need for an accessible and flexible distance-based Master's degree in counselling psychology. The program adheres to an adult learning orientation, is competency-based, and offers courses through alternative delivery methods, using web-based delivery, summer institutes and weekend seminars, and, where numbers permit, off-campus course instruction. The goal of the program was designed to meet the needs of learners who wanted to be able to take courses at a distance, continue working, and complete a degree on their own timelines. These learners had personal, family, and job-related responsibilities to balance with their desire to continue their professional training and many are not able to attend traditional on-campus programs. Many were in positions where they were already providing some form of counselling services and wished to increase their knowledge and skills, as well as their employability and autonomy.

Geographically, CAAP learners are split between urban (60%) and rural (40%) settings. The need for professional and graduate education in rural settings has been noted, if only to address equity issues in terms of access and quality (Barbopoulos & Clark, 2003). CAAP developed its programs with this issue in mind. At current registration (winter 2004) 17% of CAAP learners are male, 83% female. Academic background at entrance is a minimum of a four-year bachelor's degree in areas such as psychology, social work, nursing and child/youth care.

CAAP 605: Developing a Working Alliance is a course in the Campus Alberta program that serves as the core counselling skills development experience. Learners are enrolled in this course in their second semester after completing a counselling theories course. The counselling theories course is delivered entirely online, using web-based courseware. Is this course offered online also? In the language of distance education CAAP 605 would be classified as a "blended delivery" course (Palloff & Pratt, 1999). The course runs for a five-week online session normally scheduled in the spring (May-June) and a three-week face-to-face summer institute session normally scheduled in the summer (July.) The course weighting is a three-credit half-course typical of graduate courses in the Canadian university context. In the context of the university semester system, CAAP 605 bridges spring and summer semesters, May to July. The main intent of this scheduling is to allow employed learners to use summer break as an opportunity to attend the (mandatory) summer institute classes.

SIZE OF CLASS

Class size is typically set at 20 learners per section, with a maximum of 22 learners for pedagogical and pragmatic reasons. Fahy, Crawford, and Ally (2001) discuss the issues of network *density* and network *intensity*. Network density is calculated as a ratio between the actual number and the total potential number of connections in the network. A standard formula for calculating network density proposes that there is a limit to the number of interactions that can be reasonably expected to occur in a time-limited computer mediated conferencing session. Network intensity refers to the depth and intensity of interactions in the network. Various formulae have been proposed to measure intensity including a sent-received ratio for conference postings and a frequency count above minimum participation requirements. The variables of time and number of individuals in a network need to be balanced for all members to participate in a computer-mediated conference at a level of integration of the material consistent with educational aims (e.g., Bloom 1956.) At maximum capacity, one course may have as many as six sections of 20 learners, each taught by a different instructor. CAAP 605 uses both instructors and teaching assistants (TAs) (one instructor and one TA per section) that manage instructional and skills practice activities.

TYPE OF CONTENT

The pre-Institute component of CAAP 605 consists of five units which cover the theory and skills related to the working alliance as well as basic information necessary for success in the Summer Institute. The Summer Institute consists of three weekly units that emphasize skills acquisition and development of counselling competency. It is expected that learners pass the content portion of the pre-Summer Institute before participating in the Summer Institute. The course focuses on the understanding and acquisition of skills for use in interpersonal and counselling contexts. Emphasis is placed on learning a microskills approach to counselling practice within the context of developing a working alliance. The theoretical framework for the application of these skills draws heavily from the construct of the working alliance as originally articulated by Bordin (1979) and extrapolated by Horvath and Symonds (1991) and Geslo and Carter (1994). Currently, the working alliance model is conceptualized visually in Figure 1.

Jerry, Demish, and Collins (2003) describe the essence of this model.

> A client seeks help from a counsellor and describes his/her current state, ostensibly a life situation or problem that encapsulates where he/she "is now." The process of gaining agreement on goals involves an exploration of where the client is now in contrast to where the client "wants to be." The counsellor and client then seek agreement on the tasks that will be required in order to reach where the client wants to be, bridging the now–then discrepancy. The trusting relationship develops as goals are met and tasks are successfully completed. (p. 4)

PEDAGOGY

Conceptual Underpinnings

This intentional grounding in the working alliance construct serves two purposes. The first is to train future counsellors in a model that has strong empirical support. The second is to propose the application of the collaborative and relational principles of the working alliance as a model for online learning in human services. The working alliance is described as an ongoing condition of the relationship between a counsellor and a client where both individuals are in agreement about the goals of the relationship, the tasks that will be used to reach those goals, and that these goals and tasks will continue to occur within the context of a trusting relationship. The CAAP program has consciously adopted the philosophical stand that the core features of the working alliance are applicable to any successful relationship and the knowledge and skills acquired in CAAP 605 form the meta-context in which all interaction occurs (educational, programmatic, clinical), providing both learners

FIGURE 1. The Working Alliance Model

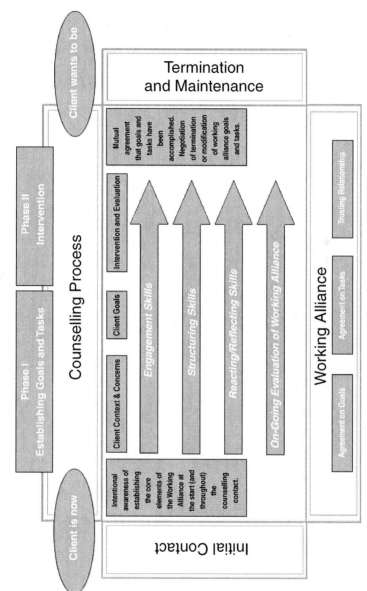

These three elements of the working alliance continue throughout the counselling process and are intentionally managed by the counsellor using the specific skills described in the Skills Taxonomy.

and faculty an opportunity to be purposeful and collaborative about their participation in the program.

Conceptually, the program works from a constructivist notion of knowledge development (Kanuka & Anderson, 1998). Learning in the online environment is generated through social interaction. The CAAP program applies the research (Gunawardena, Lowe, & Anderson, 1997) that proposes an active pattern of knowledge construction through a series of phases including sharing/comparing of information; discovery and exploration of dissonance or inconsistency among the ideas; testing of the proposed syntheses of the evolving knowledge; negotiation of meaning and/or co-construction of knowledge that culminates with an active phrasing of agreement statements; and applications of the newly constructed meaning. These phases are informally monitored during a course.

CAAP also maintains an awareness of, and deliberately addresses, generally accepted principles of online community development (Rovai, 2002; Pallof & Pratt, 1999). This includes the active process of learners and faculty maintaining an online presence (Jerry, Demish, & Collins, 2003; Jerry, Collins, & Demish, 2003). Rourke, Anderson, Garrison and Archer (1999) describe this as the ability of participants to project themselves socially and affectively into the virtual community. Specific techniques have included focusing on the emotional needs of the online community as a whole (e.g., taking account of the "felt" tone of communications in a section as a whole, and actively responding with questions for clarification of the intent of a learner's postings); checking in at key points in the term with questions about how people are doing with the workload; participating in "coffee room" chat discussions about the happenings in learners' and professors' lives (not unlike the casual conversation that happens at seminar breaks in the face-to-face context); and using symbols (emoticons) and parenthesized comments to integrate affect into the text dialogue. Other active methods of creating presence have included quick turn-around time for e-mail responses (within the hour, within the day), ongoing activity on the discussion boards (so that learner responses are attended to on a regular basis, not once a week), and availability by phone for those times when a purely online discourse is not sufficient to meet the needs of the learner. These skills have their parallel in clinical work in the form of being emotionally available and present to clients (e.g., Winnicott, 1971).

Finally, CAAP 605 (as with all CAAP courses) designates the type of learning targeted through various learning activities, based on Bloom's taxonomy of learning objectives (Bloom, 1956; Krathwohl, Masia, &

Bloom, 1965). Current critics of adult distance and web-based learning express a frustration that much of what is offered online has been cobbled together from face-to-face courses with little reference to sound educational theory and pedagogical practice (Garcia Del Dujo, 2003). Where applicable, each CAAP course maps its objectives onto Bloom's *knowledge, affective,* and skills (*psycho-motor*) domains. Since this is an applied practice professional program, emphasis is placed in all courses on the application of knowledge to practice. The focus on the development of professionally-relevant attitudes and beliefs is sometimes ignored in university programs. By continually linking course objectives to professional practice competencies and the including experiential and reflective activities, learners are challenged to address personal biases and attitudinal barriers. Figure 2 shows the Bloom mapping for CAAP 605.

Learners are assessed based on their participation in online activities (both qualitative and quantitative measures), the quality of the academic work submitted (e.g., term papers graded in a manner consistent with graduate education), counselling skills development through the use of live and videotaped practice during the Summer Institute, and comprehensive integration of learning through the completion of a final reflective paper. For example, the qualitative and quantitative criteria for weekly postings to discussion forums for CAAP 605 are listed in Table 1.

Synchronous and Asynchronous Activities

All CAAP courses make use of both synchronous and asynchronous activities. During the five-week on-line portion of the course, learners interact in weekly asynchronous bulletin board-style lessons to discuss core readings (available through a digital reading room) on the history, theory, and practice of the working alliance. Learners read the assigned readings and log into the discussion boards to respond to questions posted by the instructor. The instructor's role is to facilitate the discussion, provide clarification regarding the readings, and to guide the interaction from the level of recalling the facts in the readings to a level of synthesis of knowledge and understanding of the concepts being covered. At the end of atypical week, a section of 20 learners will have posted approximately 300 responses that include interactions with the instructor and other learners. CAAP 605 is a paced group delivery course meaning that all learners complete each week of the course together as a cohort. During the middle three weeks of this session, learners also make use of web-based video clips of counselling skills

FIGURE 2. CAAP 605 Assignment Mapping to Bloom's Taxonomies

Level of Learning	Criteria for Demonstration of Learning	Course Evaluation Component				
		Online Discussion	Skills Coding Assignments	Chat-Room Transcript Assignment	Summer Institute Videotape Practice	Integrative Paper
Cognitive Domain						
Knowledge	• observe and recall information • know major ideas • master subject matter					
Comprehension	• understand content and grasp meaning • interpret facts, compare, contrast • provide examples					
Application	• use information, methods, concepts, theories in new situations • solve problems using required skills or knowledge					
Analysis	• identify patterns and organization of parts • recognize hidden meanings or implications					
Synthesis	• use old ideas to create new ones or generalize to new situations • integrate knowledge from several areas • predict, draw conclusions					
Evaluation	• compare and discriminate between ideas or models • assess value of theories and concepts • make choices based on reasoned argument • recognize subjectivity					
Affective Domain						
Awareness	• demonstrate self-awareness, sensitivity towards others, personal responsibility • identify areas for personal change					
Commitment	• adopt a self-reflective attitude toward personal and professional activities • exhibit values and attitudes appropriate to the context and professional role • seek personal and professional development					
Skills Domain						
Simulated demonstration	• demonstrate purpose, structure, and application of skill, procedure, or strategy • implement skill, procedure, or procedure in practice contexts according to prescribed step-by-step criteria					
Generalization	• attend to the intrapersonal, interpersonal, and contextual factors in choice of skill, procedure, or strategy • generalize use of skill, procedure, or strategy to applied contexts					
Responsive implementation	• demonstrate skill, procedure, or strategy fluently, flexibly, and creatively • introduce new combinations of skills • adapt and integrate components of procedures and strategies to address emergent needs					

demonstrations. Each week's learning activities are tied to one aspect of the working alliance and specific counselling microskills. Learners view a series of video clips in their web browser that are tied to coding grids for tracking the demonstrated skills (see Figure 3.) The intent is that learners have an opportunity to view and become competent at identifying skills "in action." Each video clip demonstrates greater and greater complexity of skill use. Finally, weekly assignments have learners view a "quiz" video where the coding grid is submitted as a web form to the instructor for grading. Figure 3 shows a screen shot of Dr. Jerry in a video clip demonstration page.

The final week of this session makes innovative use of a logged chat room activity that allows learners to engage in skills practice with their

TABLE 1. Discussion Board Grading Criteria for CAAP 605.

Evaluation Component	Grading Criteria	Weighing (10 marks)
Extent of Participation	Participation in each weekly forum, according to the specific requirements of the week. Two comments minimum per week in response to the postings of other students.	4 marks
	Every week of the spring session, students will be expected to participate in an online discussion forum, containing a set of questions for discussion or issues for reflection. In addition, students will be expected to contribute to an on-going "Personal Journey" forum. Responses to questions or issues posted in the forums must be no longer than 100-150 words. The discussion forums can be accessed directly from the Study Units or from the Discussion Forums link provided under Communication Tools on the menu bar. Please be careful to select the appropriate forum for each week.	
	You should look at your participation in the discussion forums as roughly equivalent to the three hours you would traditionally spend in an on-campus graduate seminar. Your reading, preparation, and assignment time takes place in addition to those three hours.	
Quality of Comments	• Core constructs accurately identified and described • Material from previous units integrated to formulate ideas and generate dialogue • Original thoughts or ideas contributed • Consistent evidence of accurate analysis of concepts • New and related perceptions of an issue raised • Ability to synthesize, compare or contrast concepts with concepts from other theoretical approaches • Relevant readings and research cited to support points	6 marks
	The quality of your comments is evaluated on the basis of criteria similar to those used in evaluating written assignments. Comments should demonstrate that students have read the background material and have given thought to the issues raised. Note that marks are awarded for a pattern of responses; individual responses are not graded.	

peers. In this assignment, learners are assigned a peer to interact with in a chat room. While the instructor has no specific role in the chat rooms (other than grading the resulting assignment), the weekly discussion forums continue with the participation requirements the same as in previous weeks. While online chat is not as instantaneous as a live conversation (and misses nonverbal cues), we have found that learners who engage in this activity have an "almost-there" live practice experience before immersing themselves in the summer face-to-face practice sessions. An added advantage of using the chat room is that learners can download their "instantly transcribed" counselling session for skills coding and analysis. This assignment is submitted in a transcript-style format with a requirement that learners correctly identify the skills used (as in the coding grid assignments of the previous weeks) and also provide commentary about the apparent effect of their skill usage on the conversation. For example, the learner might identify an open question

FIGURE 3. Screenshot of CAAP 605 Video Clip Demonstration Page

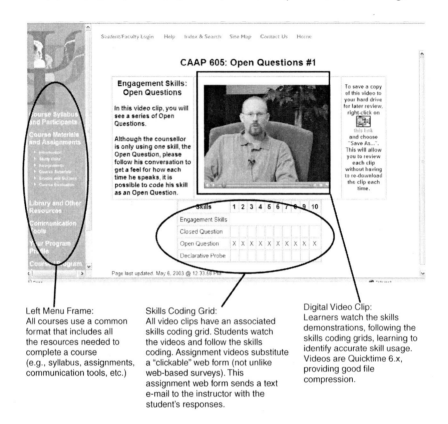

Left Menu Frame: All courses use a common format that includes all the resources needed to complete a course (e.g., syllabus, assignments, communication tools, etc.)

Skills Coding Grid: All video clips have an associated skills coding grid. Students watch the videos and follow the skills coding. Assignment videos substitute a "clickable" web form (not unlike web-based surveys). This assignment web form sends a text e-mail to the instructor with the student's responses.

Digital Video Clip: Learners watch the skills demonstrations, following the skills coding grids, learning to identify accurate skill usage. Videos are Quicktime 6.x, providing good file compression.

as the skill used. In a second column, he or she would also add whether or not the skill was appropriate to the conversational context and whether or not it produced the desired result (e.g., an open-ended response as opposed to a yes/no response).

Platform Used

The platform that delivers all CAAP courses is a custom developed courseware package developed by Athabasca University called *Bazaar*, currently in its seventh version. It contains many of the typical features of a courseware package including conferencing boards, chat, audio, video, internal e-mail, a white board, the ability to attach files, upload presentations, etc. This platform was embedded in a comprehensive program web site (available: http://www.abcounsellored.net) following generally accepted guidelines for large-scale web architecture (Rosenfield & Morville, 2002). Courses have used nearly every variation of online collaborative and teaching tools with the exception of live real-time audio or video (technologies which we are currently exploring).

In the context of educational theory, each course follows a similar design with common elements in each lesson: an overview, learning objectives, key terms and concepts, digital and print-based readings, step-by-step study process, and online discussion questions or activities. Each course is connected to a digital reading room that contains links to electronic resources to support learner learning. The standardization of content initially raised concerns among faculty about academic freedom. However, the feedback from formal course evaluation and informal student feedback sessions evaluation measures has been overwhelmingly positive about the quality of the content and learning processes, the transparency of the connection between course content and overall competency outcomes for the program, and the depth of interaction and learning possible in the online environment.

Issues Involved in Design, Delivery, and Learning

The main issues involved in the design and delivery of CAAP 605 and the use of counselling skills video clips are educational, logistical, and technological. CAAP 605 constitutes the first skills-based course in a program geared towards applied professional practice. As such, we wanted learners to be able to see and correctly identify the skills they would eventually be putting into practice during the Summer Institute. Secondly, we wanted learners, many of whom will have had undergraduate, workshop, or on-the-job skills training to become comfortable with our theoretical (working alliance) and practical (microskills) approach to counselling. Finally, the skills coding assignments, the chat-room transcription assignment, and the Summer Institute live practice are designed to lead learners to a strong level of competency in the mechanics of counselling. This intention follows the rough dictum of Bloom's see/know, accept/value, and do/practice process (educational activity in each of the knowledge, affect and psycho-motor domains).

Technologically, the programs involved in the delivery of CAAP 605 had traditionally used a VHS videotape of counselling skills which was mailed to learners. With the advent of Web-based courseware and increasing bandwidth availability, the program chose to explore digital video as a medium. The result is an on-demand curriculum that is flexible in its delivery. The use of Quicktime 6.x and its default .mov format allows for high-quality video with file sizes ranging from 3 megabytes to 14 megabytes depending on the length of the clip. in a format common to most computer users regardless of platform. In addressing "last mile" issues (Macneil, 2003), learners in rural settings (e.g., the far North in Canada) with connections unable to deal with the video file size were sent a CD-ROM of all video clips, assignments and supporting course documentation.

Logistically, any skills-based program will grapple with the non-local nature of Web-based learners (Jerry & Bryson, 2003; Wood, 1998). Within CAAP 605, any learner can review and revisit any video clip at any time. The minor convenience of not endlessly rewinding video tape is apparent. More importantly, each video clip and its related educational content becomes a learning object that can be linked to other courses (e.g., the first practicum course where a review of skills may be appropriate), or reviewed during the Summer Institute as additional demonstrations or points of clarification during skill acquisition.

Related to logistics is the issue of faculty time and motivation related to the online learning paradigm. The level of planning and preparation for an online course delivery is by necessity greater than for a classroom delivery. Whereas the lecturer can approach a classroom time with notes and an outline, potentially drawing on knowledge and experience with the subject matter, an on-line course in the Campus Alberta program requires a greater level of pre-prepared detail (subject matter/content, directions for completing learning activities) to be available in the courseware for when students log on and begin to work. This results in a potentially inordinate amount of time being spent in course development vis-à-vis other university demands such as research and publication, teaching time, and service commitments. In the Campus Alberta experience, two of the three partner institutions have face-to-face as well as online expectations of their professors. These expectations range from four to five courses per academic year, of which the online courses may be included. These professors have articulated concerns about balancing the tensions of their commitments between virtual and non-virtual workload assignments. To date, these challenges have been met with support from each department's administration, with the expectation of inclusion of online courses in annual faculty workloads. The opportunity to include this work as part of one's research portfolio is also there. Issues that remain in a state of tension include the respective universities' tenure and performance criteria (what weight is placed on course development and alternative delivery formats) and what time/weight might be assigned to on-line course development and delivery versus that assigned to on-campus development and delivery.

In regard to intellectual property rights, the Campus Alberta program works with a policy that the program owns the courses (as a whole package). The program seeks out experts in their fields (including faculty) to write the courses and it is expected that they will incorporate their own material to a large degree. The program's copyright agreement allows course authors continued ownership of their own material, gives the program shared copyright to use the materials for the purposes of the course, and prohibits them from using the course as a whole in any other venue, since the program has paid for that specific product of their work. Faculty that move to other institutions are able to make use of their own developed content but cannot port a CAAP course in its entirety.

OUTCOME

Related Outcome Data Such as Course Evaluations, Grades, and Research

Based on initial evaluation (2 program years), the following observations were made:

Changes from Previous Versions of the Course

Nearly all the courses in CAAP have been developed "from scratch" for the mounting of this program. Those that were not developed from scratch were derived from templates of current parallel courses in the partner universities. Each course has been assigned to a course coordinator who implements changes each semester, based on evaluations from learners and instructors. A regular three-year revision cycle is in process with minor course changes implemented each year. In the case of CAAP 605, this re-development is both technological (i.e., exploring the use of Flash© embedded video clips) and pedagogical (i.e., re-organizing video clips for better demonstrating skills progression; capturing new literature on the counselling process.)

Lessons Learned and Pitfalls to Avoid

As innovators, we were stepping out into new territory on two fronts, online delivery of applied professional practice training and joint inter-university delivery of graduate training. There have been a number of lessons along the way. Primary among them is the tendency to underestimate the time and energy involved in developing online learning processes. Non-distance education faculty are stretched beyond their comfort zones into areas of curriculum design not normally required of them. A year and a half lead time appears to be ideal for development of a graduate course in this format.

Faculty expectations are also varied. Issues include developing an understanding of the nature of on-line teaching including time demands and the mastery of technology.

Research Needed and In Progress

A brief list of key issues currently under exploration as a result of the CAAP experience include:

- managing and moderating affect in the online environment. Following Thomerson and Smith's (1996) notion that positive affective experiences are correlated to cognitive achievement, we are exploring specific techniques in online communication that address the perceived emotional tone of an online posting. (Jerry, Demish, & Collins, 2003)
- integration of the counselling construct of the working alliance in the delivery practices of the program. Our aim is to extend the working alliance model to online communication and evaluate the effectiveness of its use as a means of managing relationships in an online community. Some areas of exploration will include the effect of the deliberate use of the working alliance in online participation, learner satisfaction, and learning outcomes. (Jerry, Collins, & Demish, 2003)
- the similarity and differences in learning outcomes between learners trained in this environment and those in traditional on-campus programs. (assessed at course objective and program objective levels)
- Further evaluation is also required of the grade distributions for distance and on-campus learners taken courses deemed as equivalent. Our initial data show no consistent patterns, so current data suggests the potential for parity. (Russell, 1999)

CONCLUSION

Web-based education has come into its own. Research exists that suggests that on-line and distance delivery modes have comparable outcomes to classroom-based experiences (Russell, 1999). The human services sector will always require new, competent professionals with a variety of skill sets, serving rural and urban locations. The Campus Alberta Applied Psychology: Counselling Initiative is active in the delivery of competency-based professional education for counsellors at the master's level.

Each course of the Counselling Initiative is grounded in Bloom's taxonomy as a means of addressing the criticism that on-line adult learning is often an afterthought to face-to-face course delivery, with little reference to educational theory. CAAP 605 presents a counselling model based on the current and empirically-supported construct of the *working alliance* which suggests that the counsellor and client need to have agreement on the goals of the counselling relationship, agreement on the tasks that will help to reach those goals, and that these activities will occur in the context of a trusting relationship.

The use of Web-based technology has provided for a number of challenges including delivery format, bandwidth issues, and faculty development and teaching time. Overall, the Campus Alberta program is currently delivering nine mainly Web-based blended delivery courses to approximately 260 graduate students. The program remains optimistic that the Web is a viable and rich context for graduate education in the human services.

REFERENCES

Barbopoulos, A., & Clark, J. M. (2003). Practising psychology in rural settings: Issues and guidelines. *Canadian Psychology, (44)*4, 410-424.

Bloom, B. S. (Ed.) (1956) *Taxonomy of educational objectives: The classification of educational goals: Handbook I, cognitive domain.* Toronto: Longmans, Green.

Bordin, E. S. (1979). The generalizability of the psychoanalytic concept of the working alliance. *Psychotherapy: Theory, Research & Practice, 16*(3), 252-260.

Fahy, P. J., Crawford, G., & Ally, M. (2001). Patterns of interaction in a computer conference transcript. International Review of Research in Open and Distance Learning, (2)1. Retrieved March 2004: http://www.irrodl.org/content/v2.1/fahy.html.

Garcia Del Dujo, A. (2003). Pedagogy in virtual learning environments. In A. M. Vilas, J. A. Gonzalez, & J. M. Gonzalez, *Advances in Technology-Based Education: To-*

wards a Knowledge-Based Society, Proceedings of the Second International Conference on Multimedia and ICTs in Education, Volume I, 201-210.

Garrison, D. R., Anderson, T., & Archer, W. (2000). Critical inquiry in a text-based environment: Computer conferencing in higher education. *The Internet and Higher Education, 2*(2-3), 1-19.

Geslo, C. J., & Carter, J. A. (1994). Components of the psychotherapy relationship: Their interaction and unfolding during treatment. *Journal of Counselling & Development, 41*(3), 296-306.

Gunawardena, C. N., Lowe, C. A., & Anderson, T. (1997). Analysis of a global online debate and the development of an interaction analysis model for examining a social construction of knowledge in computer conferencing. *Journal of Educational Computing Research, 17*(4), 397-431.

Horvath, A. O., & Symonds, B. D. (1991). Relation between working alliance and outcome in psychotherapy: A meta-analysis. *Journal of Counselling Psychology, 38*(2), 139-149.

Jerry, P., & Bryson, B. (2003). Developing a Professional Identity in an Online Learning Environment. In L. J. Cleland (Ed.), *Consultation Proceedings: 9th Annual Building Tomorrow Today: Alberta Regional Consultation for Career Development*, 49-54.

Jerry, P., Collins, S., & Demish, H. (2003). Defining the challenges: The juxtaposition of technology and humanity in distributed learning environments. *Proceedings of the 20th Annual Conference of the Canadian Association for Distance Education.*

Jerry, P., Demish, H., & Collins, H. (2003). Managing affect and attitude in distance education. *Proceedings of the 9th Annual North American Web-based Learning Conference,* 41-49.

Kanuka, H., & Anderson, T. (1998). Online social interchange, discord, and knowledge construction. *Journal of Distance Education 13*(1), 57-74.

Krathwohl, D. R., Masia, B. B., & Bloom, B. S. (1965). *Affective domain: The classification of educational goals (Taxonomy of educational objectives.)* Longman Schools Division: Pearson Education Co.

Macneil, D. (2003). *High speed bandwidth and higher education.* Keynote Presentation, Ninth Annual North American Web-based Learning Conference, Oct. 18-21, 2003, St. John, NB.

Palloff, R. M., & Pratt, K. (1999). *Building learning communities in cyberspace: Effective strategies for the online classroom.* San Francisco: Jossey-Bass.

Rosenfield, L., & Morville, P. (2002). *Information architecture for the World Wide Web* (2nd edition). Sebastopol, CA: O'Reilly & Associates, Inc.

Rourke, L., Anderson, T., Garrison, D., & Archer, W. (1999). Assessing social presence in asynchronous text-based computer conferencing. *Journal of Distance Education, 14*(2), 50-71.

Rovai, A. P. (2002). Building sense of community at a distance. *International Review of Research in Open and Distance Learning, 3*(1), 1-10.

Russell, T. (1999). *No significant difference phenomenon (NSDP).* Raleigh, NC: North Carolina State University.

Thomerson, J. D., & Smithe, C.L. (1996). Student perceptions of the affective experiences encountered in distance learning courses. *The American Journal of Distance Education, 10*(3), 37-48.

Winnicott, D. W. (1971). *Therapeutic consultations in child psychiatry.* New York: Norton.

Wood, J. (Ed.) (1998). *The virtual embodied: Presence/Practice/Technology.* New York: Routledge.

Building a Predominantly
Web-Based Course from Face-to-Face
and Interactive Video Pilots:
Administrative Skills
for Social Work Practice

Paul P. Freddolino
David G. Knaggs

SUMMARY. This paper describes the design, development, pilot, and revision of a predominantly web-based macro social work practice course on administrative skills required for all MSW students at Michigan State University, a Research I, land grant university. The course was intentionally developed in stages, first in a face-to-face (F2F) and interactive video (ITV) setting and then predominantly online after content revision and update. The course uses streamed videotaped lectures as a central teaching format, with extensive use of discussion boards and other interactive tools. The contributions made by the F2F and ITV iteration will be highlighted, along with lessons learned from multiple online replications.

Paul P. Freddolino, PhD, is Professor and Coordinator of Distance Education and Off-Campus Programs, School of Social Work, Michigan State University, 254 Baker Hall, East Lansing, MI 48824.

David G. Knaggs, MSW, is Partnerships Coordinator, and Clinical Instructor, School of Social Work, Michigan State University Outreach and Engagement, Garden Level, Room 16, East Lansing, MI 48824.

[Haworth co-indexing entry note]: "Building a Predominantly Web-Based Course from Face-to-Face and Interactive Video Pilots: Administrative Skills for Social Work Practice." Freddolino, Paul P., and David G. Knaggs. Co-published simultaneously in *Journal of Technology in Human Services* (The Haworth Press, Inc.) Vol. 23, No. 3/4, 2005, pp. 201-213; and: *Web-Based Education in the Human Services: Models, Methods, and Best Practices* (eds: MacFadden et al.) The Haworth Press, Inc., 2005, pp. 201-213. Single or multiple copies of this article are available for a fee from The Haworth Document Delivery Service [1-800-HAWORTH, 9:00 a.m. - 5:00 p.m. (EST). E-mail address: docdelivery@haworthpress.com].

Digital Object Identifier: 10.1300/J017v023n03_03

KEYWORDS. Internet-based instruction, videoconferencing, online learning, social work macro practice

BACKGROUND

When asked what types of skills were 'missing' in recently hired MSW employees at direct practice agencies, a group of experienced practitioners identified three key areas: grant-writing skills; familiarity with the budgeting process; and knowledge of human resources, including staff relations, team building, and supervision. These conversations–which generated similar results in an off-campus MSW program site–led to the development of an innovative survey course covering administrative skills. This course is now required of all MSW students at Michigan State University regardless of their clinical or organization/community practice concentration.

Piloted as a face-to-face (F2F) course linked with a fully interactive second classroom through high-speed interactive video (ITV), the course is now offered in totally face-to-face, web-assisted and almost-entirely-online formats. The online version, which uses technology tools to enhance the learning of substantive content, is the focus of this report.

SW845-Administrative Skills for Social Work Practice: **This course is designed to provide the student with an understanding of how social work agencies function as organizational entities, and to introduce a number of skills required for effective social work practice within organizations.** The primary objective of this course is the enhancement of student understanding and skills in negotiating the organizational context of social work practice. Specifically, this course is intended to expand students' knowledge of and skill in critical elements of effective administrative practice in recognition of the fact that many graduate students will perform administrative functions at some point in their careers.

COURSE CONTENT

Course content evolved through a series of discussions between the authors during the summer and fall of 2000. It was agreed that the course would assist students to:

1. Understand mission statements, strategic directions, goals, and organizational planning;
2. Clarify ethical issues, such as clients' rights and social justice, and examine ethical dilemmas involved in carrying out organizational mandates that may conflict with professional ethics;
3. Appreciate the impact of gender, race, ethnicity, sexual orientation, religion, and economic class on the functioning of organizations;
4. Acquire beginning skills in administrative functions including leadership, team building, program planning, grant writing, and supervision.

Although the specific details of assignments and the content of lectures and readings have changed somewhat over the past three years, the essential modular structure of the course remains as originally developed for the first iteration. Specifically, the course is divided into sixteen modules, corresponding to the sixteen weeks in the typical semester. These modules are:

Module	Topic
1	Introduction to the course; review of assignments
2	Mission statements, needs, goals, and outcomes
3	Program logic models
4	Program designs
5	Evaluation plans
6	Budgeting and Gantt charts
7	Recruitment and selection
8	Team building
9	Leadership
10	Supervision; stress management
11	Public relations; collaborations
12	Management information systems and IT
13	Strategic planning
14	Students finish assignments
15	Students finish assignments
16	Final evaluation; students present best proposals

During the first six weeks of the course (through Module 6) the focus is on thoughtfully creating a design and plan for an effective human service program. The primary assignment for this half of the course is a 20-page grant proposal, including a mission statement, needs and goals, a program logic model, program design (the actual program activities), an evaluation plan, a timeline for the project, and a budget with justification. The remainder of the course content turns to the implementation of an effective human service program. The primary assignment for this half of the course is a twelve-page Implementation Plan covering various aspects of financial management, personnel management, information management, and strategic planning.

COURSE DEVELOPMENT

To understand how the online version of the course has evolved we must go back to MSU's eleven-year-old ITV-based distance education MSW program (Freddolino, 1998). This successful program offers all required MSW courses to students in several fixed ITV sites around the state (Freddolino and Sutherland, 2000). Field education requirements are completed at affiliated agencies close to where students live or work (McFall and Freddolino, 2000). The entire program is based on implementing two core concepts essential for adult learners: the primacy of relationships, and the value of interaction (Freddolino, 1996). These two concepts established the foundation upon which the first iteration of this course (in a F2F and ITV setting) was developed, with the faculty creators knowing that the second iteration would be predominantly online.

The first phase focused on content design and module development. Beginning in January, 2001, the class was first delivered in a standard face-to-face classroom-based design, with an additional distance education section participating through a live interactive video connection using high-speed compressed video technology. This initial phase allowed the testing of the content design and the assignments in a "live" environment, and it permitted piloting of the module approach to the content. From a course production standpoint, as the live feeds of the lectures for each module were transmitted to the distance education site the lectures were also videotaped so they could later be converted into streamed video files. This provided a very valuable set of resources that could be utilized in producing the online course.

One of the two faculty members working on the design had extensive experience with the use of interactive video technology in education, as well as some knowledge of web based instruction and design. This knowledge and prior experience helped the faculty team begin the task with an informed idea of how the detail of the design steps would eventually meld into the online course. This prior knowledge also facilitated the early commitment of web designers and technical consultants from the university's online instruction design team and provided the faculty with much clearer advance knowledge of what help to request from technical support personnel.

Creating an online course requires the active involvement of each of several very distinct skill areas. Each of these areas has a characteristic perspective and a unique contribution to make to the overall effort. Building the development team involved a conscious effort to harness the energy and commitment of the various disciplines into a unified whole.

The team members represented major skills sets that included: substantive content expertise (the faculty), content design, learning theory, visual design, site mapping, module layout, and streaming video lecture support. Bringing this group together early in the design process meant that the online course could be developed from the beginning with a shared view of its component parts. Having two faculty members as part of the design team made it possible to continually reflect on the process and the resulting products, refining the material en vivo.

The second phase occurred during the summer of 2001, when the two faculty developers and the technical support staff collectively reviewed the course content; the videotapes of class lectures; assignments and grading experiences; and student feedback. Decisions on what to add, delete, and revise were made on a module-by-module basis, and then implemented during that summer. The instructors learned that it takes a significant amount of time to translate course content from a classroom environment to a web environment. On average it took two-to-three times as long to prepare each week's course work as a face-to-face class would take.

It was at this point that the advantages and limitations of the F2F and ITV pilot experience became apparent. One very practical advantage as noted above is that the videotaped lectures provided content that could be easily converted to digital format for the online version of the course. Although some relatively minor editing and about two hours of new taping were required, the major substantive content of the course was done.

A major disadvantage of this, however, was the strong disincentive–i.e., a lot more work–to do any additional fine-tuning.

A second major advantage of the F2F and ITV experience is that the instructors obtained first-hand live feedback concerning how well the assignments worked (from the instructors' perception) and how they were perceived by students. This feedback influenced the revision process as the course was prepared for online. Nevertheless, the instructors still did not have an experience base for how the assignments would work online and what would be needed to enhance the content for the online environment.

The development team recommended adding an online exercise that required the students to complete the minimum tasks needed to participate in an on-line environment, including downloading all of the free required software applications. This required "Technology Walk-Through" assignment asked students to practice all of the skills needed to navigate the course successfully including: downloading lectures; submitting assignments to the course web site; posting comments and questions to the asynchronous discussion boards; and participating in a synchronous chat-room environment. By the Fall 2001 semester, the predominantly online course was ready for delivery.

The goals of the third phase were to integrate the course content into an on-line format and to test and debug the delivery through student feedback at key points in the semester. During this phase the class met face-to-face four times during the sixteen weeks of the semester at the following points:

1. Week 1: Introductions of faculty and students and review of course content and expectations.
2. Week 3: Meet with technical support staff, to obtain student feedback on their experiences with the on-line environment and course content, and to resolve any remaining technology issues. Student experiences with, and evaluation of, the "Technology Walk-Through" formed a major part of the session's work.
3. Week 8 (mid-semester): Complete a group decision-making/team building simulation and generate mid-semester feedback about the course to date.
4. Last day of class, during exam week: Presentations by the authors of the best grant proposals in a simulated funding agency board meeting environment, and completing the final course evaluation.

The next phase required another major editing, revision and redesign of the class based on the evaluation results from two semesters' experience with the first online version. The key issues going into the next version are presented in the form of "lessons learned" from this online experience.

1. *There was a significant range of skill and knowledge possessed by the students* (Ashery, 2001). Furthermore, the beginning familiarity of students with a Web-based environment had a great impact on their learning curve. It took considerable effort to bring students unfamiliar with online work up to the minimal level of skill needed to successfully complete the class (Reid, n.d.). This experience reinforced the development team's commitment to the Technology Walk-Through at the beginning of the course.

2. *The stress level of students was considerable.* There were two major sources of student stress in this course. Both were anticipated and planned for, but the combined effect of the two sources of stress created the need for corrective action. The first source of stress stemmed from the learning curve required of students who were relatively unfamiliar with an online, web-based environment. The technical expectations, even when approached one at a time, had a cumulative effect on the students that quickly mounted (Eastmond, 1998).

   The second stress came from the content of the course itself. The course was designed to establish a basic understanding of the major technical functions of a human services organization. For many students, particularly those interested in clinical practice, these functional content areas were also unfamiliar. This unfamiliarity resulted in considerable self-doubt, which also was a significant source of stress. It was doubly stressful to deal with entirely new content such as budgets as well as a new online environment.

   Adjustments were made at several points to allow students a longer learning curve in both of these areas. Assignments were reduced or eliminated and deadlines extended to allow increased time for the participants to become confident that they could, in fact, meet course expectations (Butler, 2004).

   While the course was redesigned to reduce the stress level, the instructors believed that some stress created a natural and helpful pressure to push reluctant students to dive into unknown areas. At the end of the course, many students felt a sense of accomplishment from having successfully overcome the stress, as well as pride in having developed competence in unfamiliar areas (Wernet, Olliges, and Delicath, 2000).

3. *There was a high level of recognition by the students that they needed to develop competency in the online environment if they were to succeed as professionals.* Even as they complained about the stress of working in unfamiliar areas, most students acknowledged that competence in online work would be essential to their marketability and their ultimate success as professionals (Vernon and Lynch, 1999).

4. *Providing a wide range of options and choices is not always a good thing.* While good online pedagogy suggests that different students learn in different ways and should have choice, having too many choices available sometimes generated different problems. For example, in an effort to "personalize" the course, the instructors created multiple ways for students to connect with one another and with the faculty: chat-rooms, online office hours, e-mail, and module-specific question and comment areas. During the mid-year review, many students commented that there were so many ways to connect they could not decide which to use. With a more focused and managed communication process this reaction might have been avoided.

5. *The transfer of knowledge, approaches and content from a face-to-face environment to a web-based environment is both maddening and enlightening.* It is natural to approach a new effort using the same set of assumptions and practices that have served well in another context. But it is clear that creating an effective web-based experience is substantively different than creating an effective classroom learning experience. Competence and skill sets helpful in one context may not transfer well to the other (Collins, 1999). The first online version of the course clearly needed revision!

THE CURRENT VERSION

Based on this experience and the lessons learned, the next (third) predominantly online version of the course has been offered for three semesters by the first author. It was offered in fall and spring semesters as a three-credit course required for all MSW students regardless of concentration. For the three semesters, the total class sizes have been 17, 32, and 39; the latter two were taught with a Teaching Assistant in keeping with the school's policy of providing a TA for any labor-intensive web course when enrollment exceeds twenty.

The University has its own online instructional design team that has developed a "homegrown" platform with considerable functionality for delivering online courses. Special course features included streamed video lectures; online office hours in a chat-room format; online assignments in a chat-room format; weekly asynchronous discussion topics; and peer-review of one major electronically submitted assignment. The specific course content was described above. While some modules have been fine-tuned, the essential administrative skills content is the same.

Student learning objectives from the first version were specified above. These have not changed. Learners demonstrated a wide range of readiness for online learning. Students range in age from 22 to the late 50s. All have been admitted to the MSW program. Approximately 90% are female. More than 60% work full-time or part-time in human service agencies.

The course contains both teacher-centered (e.g., lectures) and learner centered (e.g., discussion boards, peer-reviews) resources in keeping with recent instructional theory and learner-centered principles (Miller and Miller, 1999; Wagner and McCombs, 1995). In addition to traditional written assignments submitted electronically, there is one online synchronous chat-room assignment related to sexual harassment in the workplace; a required online peer-review assignment requiring evaluation of three grant proposals submitted by other students; and a minimum of five required substantively-relevant postings to asynchronous bulletin board topics in the course.

The level of involvement by the instructor and TA is high, with a minimum of one visit to the site required daily, and two or more per day commonplace. Instructors must provide feedback and encouragement on a daily basis, with an expectation of a reply to a web posting within 24 hours. Instructors must grade two large assignments, the Grant Proposal (20 pages) and the Implementation Plan (twelve pages). The authors (instructors) have prepared:

- core lectures, available on the course web site in streamed video and audio-only formats; these were mostly edited from the original ITV lectures;
- reading assignments from a text, a course pack of readings, and various online sources;
- required, fixed date written and online assignments;
- asynchronous student discussion board topics; instructors try to encourage maximum student participation by adding comments

when appropriate (e.g., when a question is asked and no one else
has provided a direct answer);
- online synchronous office hours

The course is still divided into weekly modules. Each module contains assigned readings from the text, course pack and web sources; relevant online documents in PDF format; a set of lectures available in
video and audio-only formats; a list of assignments due; links to relevant discussion boards for the module; and a link to provide anonymous
feedback.

Activities and credit-earning assignments are predominantly at the
individual level with the exception of two group projects, and the majority of the course is asynchronous. Assignments include:

- initial technology orientation–the "Technology Walk-Through" (5%)
- 20-page grant proposal (40%)
- peer reviews of three randomly-assigned student proposals (10%)
- online supervisory role-play group exercise (2.5%)
- in-class team-building group exercise (2.5%)
- 12-page implementation paper (40%)
- five required substantive discussion board postings; up to 2.5% of
  the grade can be lost for failure to post the minimum five.

In general drop-out rates are low because this is a required course.
Typically, two or three students will drop out in the first week of the
course, and perhaps one or two may drop later in the semester. These
students transfer to a face-to-face section of the course, or take it in a
later semester. Outcome and process evaluation data reveal:

- Students consistently report that the grant proposal assignment is
  incredibly time-consuming, difficult, and worth it. Surprisingly, a
  majority report they would rather do the entire project individually
  (to gain mastery of the component pieces) than to work on group
  proposals. They also value the peer review of other proposals.
- The online supervisory role play done in the chat room is highly rated.
- The discussion boards are generally viewed positively, but students would like to see additional credit for this type of participation, or have it count positively in the total course grade.
- The Implementation Plan assignment is seen as necessary, but not
  as highly rated as the grant proposal project. Several students
  noted that because they had several courses with end-of-semester

projects, the Implementation Plan was generally considered "busy work" rather than a good learning experience.
- Students would like to see more text-based resources on the site, such as transcripts of the lectures or presentation slides to accompany the lectures.

One additional observation is that having one online course in a program where most other courses are face-to-face presents unique challenges in creating an online interactive environment. We have found that most graduate social work students (and probably other students as well) would prefer to communicate in person rather than online, so if three students happen to be in this online course and also in a traditional face-to-face class, they are more likely to use their F2F time to talk about the online course than they are to use the online resources to talk about the other course. This puts an upper limit on how far the virtual community in the SW845 course can go.

NEXT STEPS

The first author has begun the task of transferring course content from the homegrown courseware platform to the ANGEL platform recently licensed by the university (http://cyberlearninglabs.com/). The exact advantages and disadvantages of this transition are not known at this time. What is known is that the transition will be used as an opportunity to add more options for students to access the substantive course content, consistent with recent research showing students will utilize a wide range of online content options when they are available (Brown and Liedholm, 2003). The changes will be responsive to student feedback in several respects:

- Transcripts of the lectures will be added as pdf documents.
- Presentation slides will be added to most lectures, together with instructions on how to download a free presentation viewer if students do not have the software.
- Lectures will be 'fine-tuned' or replaced as necessary to keep them current.
- Additional online resources will be identified and linked to reduce the size of the required course pack of materials students must purchase.

While these changes reflect our commitment to continuous quality improvement the process is never ending, so these changes simply lead to the next set of questions. Specifically it will be important to determine whether providing these additional resources actually is seen by students as helpful, or if they report that the additional "tools" are seen as "more work."

One final comment appears to be in order. In addition to all of the (mostly positive) comments about the value of the course content, students are almost universally reporting great progress in their comfort with and capacity in using online technologies. Each semester has produced several students who came with almost nothing, struggled through the process, but reported profound positive change at the end. For these students, and for many others as well, the course accomplished both important content learning and significant technology skill-building goals.

CONCLUSION

The course is a continuing work in progress, with changes expected each year and major revisions anticipated every two to three years. From our experiences thus far, we would highlight three "guiding principles" for developing online and hybrid courses:

- Offering content first in a face-to-face environment provides valuable opportunities to examine course content, assignments, and process in a teaching/learning context familiar to most instructors.
- Where available, an interactive video environment provides an opportunity to "capture" digital products (e.g., videotapes of lectures and guest speakers) that can be used in the online environment. Furthermore, the special challenges of encouraging interaction and supporting achievement of learning goals "at a distance" force instructors to tackle some of the instructional process issues they will confront online. (Cyrs, 1997)
- Quality in online and blended courses ultimately results from the same processes of piloting and revising and fine-tuning that quality face-to-face courses require. There are no shortcuts.

REFERENCES

Ashery, R. S. (2001). The utilization of technology in graduate schools of social work. *Journal of Technology in Human Services, 18*(1/2), 5-18.
Brown, B. W., & Liedholm, C. (2003). How students use online materials in a virtual principles of microeconomics class. Paper presented at the Eastern Economic Association, New York, NY, February.

Butler, D. W. (2004). Online survival skills: Ten proven distance learning study techniques. Available at http://distancelearn.about.com/cs/onlinestudyskill/a/survival_skills.htm?once=true& (retrieved 5/20/04).

Collins, M. (1999). I know my instructional technologies: It's these learners that perplex me. *The American Journal of Distance Education, 13*(1), 8-23.

Cyrs, T. E. (1997). Teaching at a distance with the merging technologies: An instructional systems approach. Las Cruces, NM: New Mexico State University.

Eastmond, D.V. (1998). Adult learners and Internet-based distance education. *New Directions for Adult & Continuing Education, 78* (summer), 33-41.

Freddolino, P. P. (1998). Building on experience: Lessons from a distance education M.S.W. program. *Computers in Human Services*, 15 (2/3), 39-50; co-published simultaneously in Raymond, F. B. III, Ginsberg, L., & Gohagan, D. (Eds.), *Information Technologies: Teaching to Use, Using to Teach*. Binghamton, NY: The Haworth Press, Inc.

Freddolino, P. P., & Sutherland, C. (2000). Assessing the comparability of classroom environments in graduate social work education delivered via interactive instructional television (IITV). *Journal of Social Work Education, 36*(1),115-129.

Freddolino, P. P. (1996). The importance of relationships in creating a quality learning environment in an interactive TV classroom. *Journal of Education for Business*, 71, 205-208.

McFall, J. P., & Freddolino, P. P. (2000). Quality and comparability in distance field education: Student reports comparing three program sites. *Journal of Social Work Education*, 36(2), 293-307.

Miller, S. M., & Miller, K. L. (1999). Using instructional theory to facilitate communication in Web-based courses. *Educational Technology and Society, 2*(3). Available at http://ifets.iece.org/periodical/vol_3_99/miller.html (retrieved 5/20/04).

Reid, J. (n.d.). What every student should know about online learning. Available at http://illinois.online.uillinois.edu/IONresources/onlineLearning/reid.html (retrieved 5/20/04).

Vernon, R., & Lynch, D. (1999). Social Work and the Web. Pacific Grove, CA: Wadsworth.

Wagner, E. D., & McCombs, B. L. (1995). Learner-centered psychological principles in practice: Designs for distance education. *Educational Technology, 35*(6), 32-35.

Wernet, S., Olliges, R., & Delicath, T. (2000). Postcourse evaluations of WebCT classes by social work students. *Research on Social Work Practice, 10*(4), 487-505.

Field Clusters Online

Suzanne Bushfield

SUMMARY. Social Work education relies heavily on agency-based field instruction to assist students in developing skills, and in integrating theory, practice, and research. Web-based components of field instruction may offer advantages in the integrative process, which relies on reflection, responsive communication, and feedback. Using an online format for the integrative field seminar, a new MSW advanced generalist program in a large metropolitan area implemented an experimental model for delivery of field seminars. Results indicate high student satisfaction, greater depth of discussion, improved student involvement, and integration of learning in field. *[Article copies available for a fee from The Haworth Document Delivery Service: 1-800-HAWORTH. E-mail address: <docdelivery@haworthpress.com> Website: <http://www.HaworthPress.com> © 2005 by The Haworth Press, Inc. All rights reserved.]*

KEYWORDS. Field instruction, online courses, integrative learning, discussion boards

The integration of education, practice and research has been called "the essence of social work, both as a profession, and as a field of study

Suzanne Bushfield, PhD, MSW, is Assistant Professor of Social Work, Arizona State University West, P.O. Box 37100, Phoenix, AZ 85069-7100 (E-mail: suzanne.bushfield@asu.edu).

[Haworth co-indexing entry note]: "Field Clusters Online." Bushfield, Suzanne. Co-published simultaneously in *Journal of Technology in Human Services* (The Haworth Press, Inc.) Vol. 23, No. 3/4, 2005, pp. 215-227; and: *Web-Based Education in the Human Services: Models, Methods, and Best Practices* (eds: MacFadden et al.) The Haworth Press, Inc., 2005, pp. 215-227. Single or multiple copies of this article are available for a fee from The Haworth Document Delivery Service [1-800-HAWORTH, 9:00 a.m. - 5:00 p.m. (EST). E-mail address: docdelivery@haworthpress.com].

(Sherraden & Sherraden, 2000). Field education is designed to assist students in this critical integrative process. Effective integration may be dependent on collaboration, reciprocity, resources, and relationships shared by field agencies and social work programs (Bogo & Globerman, 1999). Despite some concerns about social work being more "high teach" than "high tech" (Gingerich & Green, 1996, p. 26), technology is a critical tool to assist in this integration. Technology, or the "cyber community" has become another dimension of the person's environment (Gonchar & Adams, 2000). Technologically-based practice may offer new opportunities to encourage dialogue and engagement (Van Soest, Canon, & Grant, 2000).

There is evidence that a "good field placement" is one which contains quality supervision, relevant learning, careful communication and monitoring, as well as accessibility and responsiveness (McFall & Freddolino, 2000). Field instructors are essential both in gate-keeping for the profession, and in assisting the student's development of professional skills, values, and knowledge. Increasingly, agencies require students who can fill a need for them, as well–through delivery of services. Yet, social work educators are ultimately responsible for ensuring the delivery of effective learning in field. Greater reliance on technology to accomplish field education objectives may present challenges, but it also provides opportunities for improved communication and integration of learning objectives.

Despite concerns about technology expressed by faculty, a web-based course delivery format for field integrative seminars was thought to be a valuable laboratory to promote linkages between technology, theory, and practice. Effective teaching in the field should include a context for linking "doing" and "thinking" (Fortune, McCarthy, & Abramson, 2001). The goal of web-based clusters was thought to be clearly consistent with "augmenting the sense of community" within and between the classroom and field agencies (Potts & Hagan, 2000, p. 144), one of the features missing from the larger, live classroom-based integrative field clusters. In addition, the web cluster was created to capitalize on "teachable moments" from the field (Havighurst, 1972; Knowles, 1980), and to promote reflective practice (Schon, 1983). A web-based format was thought to be a legitimate approach to addressing a number of problems encountered in field education: the need for a less fragmented, more consistent control of the integrative process; the need for improved "fit" between classroom and field learning; the need to ensure the quality of field education (Raskin, 1994).

BACKGROUND

A new MSW program was developed in a large metropolitan area. The program offers an Advanced Generalist program concentration, and contains both a 2-year MSW program and a 1-year Advanced Standing MSW program, limited to select candidates who have obtained a BSW and met additional admissions criteria.

The MSW program's mission is to prepare its students for advanced generalist practice with a strong emphasis on cultural proficiency within the changing and emerging specialized fields of practice that characterize growing, dynamic metropolitan areas. Specific goals of the program include providing students with the knowledge, skills, and values to practice as advanced generalists in a culturally grounded and ethical manner across systems of all sizes and enhancing the development and dissemination of knowledge through faculty and student contribution to social work scholarship and research.

FIELD CLUSTER DESIGN

Clusters were originally conceived as integrative field seminars. All faculty participated as field liaisons, making periodic visits to students in field. The program assigned students to small cluster sections, with each faculty member assigned a single cluster. Assignments were made based primarily on geographic location of field placements. The focus and content of clusters was left to individual faculty. Continuous program evaluation, based in part on exit surveys each year, revealed low faculty and student satisfaction with field clusters. The concerns expressed included inconsistent and irregular cluster meetings, unclear objectives, the student's sense that it was an "add on," and lack of faculty investment in the course delivery. Faculty were not in agreement as to the purpose of the course; some focused on processing of field experiences, and others on using guest speakers to enhance community networking.

Following the first year of the MSW program operation, adjustments were made. Students were assigned to large cluster sections, with a few designated faculty assigned. Clusters focused on community networking, relying heavily on scheduled guest speakers. At the end of the second year, feedback from evaluations was very negative. Concerns included continued lack of satisfaction, now for additional reasons of the large group being inhospitable to discussion of individual field experiences and dilemmas. In addition, due to irregular scheduling and re-scheduling of cluster meetings, due to guest lecturer availability, students complained that they did not receive sufficient notice of cluster meetings. A faculty retreat focused on field issues resulted in a new plan for field clusters. The consensus of faculty was to return clusters to small groups, assign faculty who requested to teach clusters, and create a common syllabus with specific course assignments for field clusters.

As one of the faculty interested in teaching the field cluster, I applied for and received an internal university instructional development support grant to develop an online version for the field cluster. My goals for the course were to: (1) address any problems or issues that arise in the field setting, and foster the integration of the classroom and internship learning; (2) enhance the professional use of self; and (3) foster professional development and socialization.

The online cluster was developed during the summer, and implemented in Fall, 2003. Students were unaware that they had been assigned to an online section for cluster until the first day of classes, as they were again assigned based on geographic location of their field agencies. Students were informed that they had been assigned to an "experimental" version of field cluster, and that following the first face to face meeting, all clusters would be held online, using the student's access to Blackboard for the course. Students were oriented to the layout of the Blackboard course, were given hard copies of the course syllabus, and assignments and expectations were reviewed. Since students did not know in advance that this would be an online course, they were offered the option of changing to another live section. No one chose this option. The students were aware that this online cluster would be evaluated and compared to live cluster meetings, to determine if it was a viable option. Initial student feedback was very positive. Students all introduced themselves, and described their field placements, as this initial meeting was intended to help students get to know the members of their online cluster.

COURSE DETAILS

The platform used was BlackBoard (version 6.0). MSW level courses are taken concurrently with field internship. Students enrolled in the 2-year MSW program take the course for four consecutive semesters and students in the 1-year advanced standing MSW program take the course for two consecutive semesters (15 weeks/1 hour per week). The course, combined with faculty duties as field liaison, counts on faculty load as one course per semester.

There were no additional direct costs associated with web-based delivery; the course was offered live for other sections. The web-based course was developed and implemented as a pilot project, and funded by a one-time faculty development grant. It should be noted that there is significant technological support on campus for faculty, including workshops and seminars on use of Blackboard, technical support staff assigned to each college on campus, and standardization of formats (templates) for creation of web-supported courses. Also, this was not the author's first experience in developing online courses. The internal grant obtained provided a stipend during the summer to prepare the course. Clusters are offered in the Fall and Spring, with class size limited to 20. The web cluster attempted to adapt a shared, standardized course syllabus for field with asynchronous, online participation in regular discussion topics and specific assignments.

Integrative field seminars (known as "clusters") were problematic, according to assessment data, for reasons of scheduling, consistency of course content and expectations, and student perception of clusters being an "add on" without clear course credit and expectations. A web-based cluster was designed in order to test a different approach to the cluster, and evaluate student outcomes. It was thought that the web-based course would eliminate the primary student concern about scheduling.

Credit for the course is associated with field credits; this is not a stand alone, credit bearing, course; rather, it is a required component of field, with its associated 5 credits per course, and is intended to supplement learning in field.

CONTENT

The integrative seminar is intended to assist students in: (1) addressing any problems or issues that arise in the field setting; (2) fostering the integration of classroom and internship learning; (3) enhancing the professional use of self; and 4) fostering professional development and socialization. Course content is somewhat dependent on students' field experiences.

LEARNER

Student Learning Objectives: There are both Foundation year and Concentration year objectives; clusters contain a mix of students from

Foundation and Concentration years, as well as Advanced Standing students, who have both Foundation and Concentration year objectives.

Foundation year objectives are to help students: (1) apply critical thinking skills; (2) practice within the values and ethics of social work, especially the respect for diversity; (3) demonstrate professional use of self; (4) understand forms and mechanisms of oppression and discrimination, and strategies that advance social and economic justice; (5) understand and interpret history of social work profession, its structures and issues; (6) apply knowledge and skills of generalist social work perspective to practice with systems of all sizes; (7) critically analyze and apply knowledge of biopsychosocial and spiritual variables and use theoretical frameworks to understand the interactions among and between individuals, families, groups, organizations, and communities; (8) analyze the impact of social policies; (9) evaluate relevant research and apply findings to practice; (10) use communication skills differently with a variety of populations; and (11) understand and use information technology to facilitate practice and promote social work goals.

Concentration year objectives build on the foundation year, through application of knowledge and skills of more autonomous advanced practice in the area of concentration. Students are expected to demonstrate leadership in influencing policy formulation and change, in applying advance practice theories, and in designing, conducting, and disseminating evolutions of their own practice and those of other relevant systems.

This wide range of objectives is intended to include objectives which may be introduced in other components of the curriculum, in addition to field. Attempts were made to address these objectives by integrating weekly, focused online discussion topics, intended to coincide with the developmental stages of field: anticipation, disillusionment, confrontation, competence, and culmination (Sweitzer & King, 1999).

Web-based instruction may be particularly well-suited to integrative learning, because it allows for more time, review, and reflection on topics. Students engage in dialogue with each other, and are better able to draw on their shared experiences from the classroom, combined with their unique experiences in field. The characteristics of the learners include: older than average students, 12% were male and 88% female; 37% are non-white, 63% white; two thirds attend school full-time, and many students are working at jobs in addition to fulfilling internship requirements in a community-based agency (72% employed); many also are balancing work and family within a diverse and sprawling metropolitan area.

The clusters require a high degree of learner involvement and inter-activity. Since many instructors use Blackboard as a supplement to live courses (for digital readings on reserve, communication, discussion topics), the technology was readily accessible to students who had gained familiarity with the formats in other courses. Technology is very well supported on this campus through technopolis, a student comput-ing center, the informational technology staff, and through the technol-ogy consultant assigned to the College of Human Services, where the social work department resides.

INSTRUCTOR

The instructor serves primarily as a facilitator, providing early and frequent "intrusive" involvement in the discussion board. Directed, fo-cused discussion topics early in the course are gradually replaced by more student-driven discussions.

STRUCTURE

The cluster course is structured around focused discussion topics, de-signed to support the following themes: (1) assist students in ethical and culturally relevant decision making; (2) help students operationalize their learning objectives in field; (3) promote understanding of their professional use of self; (4) recognize the interconnectedness of prac-tice, policy, and research; (5) support one another in the transition from social work student to social work professional, with autonomous prac-tice across multiple systems; and (6) promote the identification of gaps and resources regarding marginalized groups or unexplored areas of practice.

The focus is balanced between individual and group levels. All topics require students to provide their own input, as well as to respond and in-teract with other students. Giving and receiving feedback is expected, and is designed to meet the goal of developing a cohesive interactive group to meet student needs for support, integration, and development of the professional use of self. In addition to group discussion, students must complete an individual assignment of a case presentation. Stu-dents are then assigned to critique specific cases as presented.

The content of the course is driven equally by the discussion topics created by the instructor and by the responses and case presentations contributed by the students. By posing questions to students from the outset, the instructor has modeled an approach to learning which engages the student in reflection on practice. By requiring students to respond/react to other students' discussion postings, the level of discourse is deepened and shaped to address not only individual concerns, but larger issues of policy and macro practice.

For purposes of the discussion board topics, the instructor reads all postings, at least weekly. Data is collected regarding both the quantity and quality of student participation on the blackboard. For the larger assignment connected to the course, including the Case Presentation, Process Recording, Professional Development Plan, Description of Agency, and Community Resource List, students are provided with additional guidelines in the course syllabus/assignment sheet. The Case Presentation and Process Recording assignments include a scoring rubric. Students then critique each other's case presentations and process recording, using the scoring rubrics. They then are allowed to provide general feedback on the case and interview as well. This somewhat asymmetrical process predisposed the discussion board to longer and more complex entries toward the end of the semester when case presentations were due. However, some students accomplished their entries earlier on in the semester and were the recipients of more thorough and thoughtful feedback.

The course is not essentially designed for modularity. However, the planned sequencing of focused discussion topics is designed to mirror the "stages of an internship" as described by Sweitzer and King (1999): anticipation, disillusionment, confrontation, competence, and culmination. The class is designed to be asynchronous, allowing students to participate weekly according to their own schedules. Live meeting times are posted, during which time the instructor is online for real time responses, and targeted assignments have weekly deadlines.

PEDAGOGY

The cluster is primarily learner-centered, encouraging students to bring to the group any issues or concerns encountered in the field placement. It is designed to promote reflective practice, based in part on John Dewey's notion of reflection: "Active, persistent, and careful consideration of any belief or supposed form of knowledge in the light of the grounds that support it, and the further conclusions to which it tends" (Dewey, 1991, p. 6). The active engagement of the learner in using language to describe both verbal and non-verbal transactions assists the student in attending to both objective and subjective evidence. The field cluster is clearly founded on the concepts of co-construction of meaning, the interdependence of systems, and the interlocking, interconnectedness of theories, practice, and research. Agencies, communities, groups, families, and individuals benefit from the constant infusion of students into the realm of practice for field instruction, just as students could not become effective practitioners without the critical component of field instruction. Technology is seen as a critical tool to assist in the collaboration between schools of social work and social agencies.

Early engagement of students in the cluster groups is essential to its success. An initial, face to face meeting was facilitated by the instructor. In addition, very active involvement on the part of the instructor is critical in the early weeks I chose to respond to every student entry in the first two weeks, making sure that my responses always request feedback from someone else and invite further discussion. Gradually, I waited longer to respond, so that other students will respond more readily to their colleague's postings. The field cluster emphasizes the process of experiencing and integrating theory and practice ethically in the context of diversity. Web-based clusters attempted to address the affective dimension of diversity, through exchanges of different world views. This is thought to be a significant component for developing cultural competence (Gutierrez, Fredricksen, & Soifer, 1999). Specific discussion topics asked students to address their encounters with people of difference, and to address or challenge their sensitivity to difference at a personal level.

RESOURCES

Blackboard tools incorporated in the course include: announcements; course information (syllabus and readings on digital reserve); instructor information; assignments; communication tools (e-mail); discussion board; links to web sites, field manual, field forms, important departmental and university information, NASW, student social work organization activities, job opportunities, licensure information, other relevant agency and community networking information, etc.; course management tools, including the gradebook and tracking of student participation/responses; digital drop box, for student submission of assignments and ability of other students to access these for group collaboration; and live talks, for office hours and occasional important announcements, mini-lectures, etc.

OUTCOME

No one dropped out of the experimental cluster but a number of students requested transfer into the online cluster. (This was not granted.) Since the web cluster was designed as a pilot project, evaluation was an important component. Information was gathered from student evaluations of the course, student evaluations in field, and comparisons with student evaluations in live clusters. In addition, faculty were asked to review the discussion board to compare the quantity and quality of discussion online with what occurred in the live clusters. Evaluation was very positive; every student expressed strong support of the web-based cluster (see Table 1). Positive aspects specifically mentioned in the evaluations included the flexibility for scheduling, the opportunity to take time to think through important discussion topics, and the opportunity to have more in depth discussion of a variety of topics, which might not have taken place in the time-limited live cluster. A number of students acknowledged that in a live class, they would rarely participate in discussions; yet, online, they were very comfortable expressing themselves. Overall satisfaction with the web cluster was higher than the live clusters.

Faculty teaching the live clusters were asked to review the web cluster comments. The following reflects the feedback from faculty teaching the live clusters:

> I was impressed with the students' willingness to share information, make suggestions, and ask questions.

> I especially liked the way you got students to dissect the placement; to look at the cultural context, working with difficult

TABLE 1. Course Evaluations: Web Cluster and Live Cluster Mean Scores (1-4)

Questions	Web	Live
Were the discussion topics helpful in integrating classroom theoretical learning with field practice experience?	3.6	3.0
Did the cluster allow you to network effectively with your classmates?	3.6	3.6
Did the cluster provide timely feedback to your questions about field?	3.8	2.8
Did the cluster assist you in the development of your "professional use of self"?	3.6	3.4
Would you recommend the cluster to other students?	3.9	2.9

clients, and the stages in the process. It was as though you had them thinking on both levels: the environment, and their role as social workers in that setting.

I believe you were very effective in helping the focus on context, their place in that context, and the practice related issues, including: their strengths and weaknesses, ethical issues, practice issues in terms of assessment and management, and how the role of the worker and the agency fit into the larger policy picture.

Your model created a much more focused process. You did a nice job of getting students to relate the discussions to their field experiences. The level of exchange was about the same amount as I had in the classroom, but your content was much richer and focused.

Overall program outcome data was available, in aggregate form, to address student self-rating of their mastery of specific learning objectives. This data is gathered as an exit survey of all graduating MSW students. Learning objectives specific to field and the integration of theory and practice are included, but students are not asked about individual courses or instructors. It is significant to note that, while there was no specific question in the overall program outcome evaluation related to field clusters, a number of students inserted specific comments about the positive aspects of the online field cluster. These include:

The on-line cluster was awesome, and I recommend it.

Due to the demands on our time during the second year, with the applied projects, one thing that helped was the online cluster. Friends of mine wanted to know how they could get into my section, because our time was helpful, and their time was wasted.

Having the opportunity to be in the online cluster was positive. I was able to get questions answered quickly, and received good ideas from other students as well as Dr. __. I hope the online clusters will continue.

I loved my field placement, and learned so much there. I especially appreciated the online cluster, where I had a chance to think through some difficult issues, and ultimately do a better job in field.

The online cluster shared a syllabus with live clusters. The primary difference was using online delivery while the live clusters met bi-weekly. During the course of the semester, other faculty teaching the live clusters began to incorporate my discussion topics into their live discussions. Many faculty were interested in a hybrid model: combining the live clusters with online discussion formats. Periodically, the department used the clusters as a way of communicating timely information to all students in field. This included distribution of packets for field evaluation and a number of other important matters. Since the web-based cluster had no scheduled live meetings, it was necessary to "track students down" in other ways to distribute the materials and information. Currently the social work program assigns students to clusters by location of field placement; liaison duties did not necessarily correspond to the students assigned to a faculty's cluster. In other words, I might have in my cluster some students for whom I am the faculty field liaison, and some who have other faculty serving as liaison; the students assigned to me as liaison may or may not be assigned to my cluster. Faculty expressed strong sentiments that cluster groups and liaison assignments should coincide, so that clusters could function more efficiently and effectively.

The missing link in the web clusters is the agency-based field instructor. While field instructors of students involved in the web clusters expressed no concerns, a few had been apprised of the web clusters by their students in field, and reinforced the students' positive reaction. Future endeavors will attempt to engage the field instructors in online discussion as well, to better improve the school-field linkages. There is a need for continued research in the outcomes of various models related to field. For social work programs, the heavy reliance on field based learning is often not accompanied by evaluation of best practices. There is limited data to support the impression that the web-based clusters provided an opportunity for earlier attention to problems that arise in the field, and this needs further exploration, since it may be a critical key to successful field education.

REFERENCES

Bogo, M., & Globerman, J. (1999). Interorganizational relationships between schools of social work and field agencies: Testing a framework for analysis. *Journal of Social Work Education, 35/2,* 265-274.

Dewey, J. (1991). *How we think.* Buffalo, NY: Prometheus Books.

Fortune, A., McCarthy, M., & Abramson, J. (2001). Student learning processes in field education: Relationship of learning activities to quality of field instruction, satisfaction, and performance among MSW students. *Journal of Social Work Education,* 37/1, 111-126.

Gingerich, W.J., & Green, R.K. (1996). Information technology: How social work is going digital. In P. Raffoul & C.A. McNeece (Eds.), *Future issues for social work practice,* 19-28. Boston, MA: Allyn & Bacon.

Gonchar, N., & Adams, J.R. (Fall, 2000). Living in cyberspace: Recognizing the importance of the virtual world. *Journal of Social Work Education,* 36/3, 587-600.

Gutierrez, L., Fredricksen, K., & Soifer, S. (1999). Perspectives of social work faculty on diversity and societal oppression content: Results from a national survey. *Journal of Social Work Education,* 35/3, 409-420.

Havighurst, R.J. (1972). *Developmental tasks and education* (3rd ed.) New York: McKay.

Knowles, M.S. (1980). *The modern practice of adult education: From pedagogy to andragogy* (2nd ed.). New York: Cambridge Books.

McFall, J., & Freddolino, P. (Spring-Summer, 2000). Quality and comparability in distance field education: Lessons learned from comparing three program sites. *Journal of Social Work Education,* 36/2, 293-307.

Panos, P. (2003). TechNotes–The internet archive: An end to the digital dark age. *Journal of Social Work Education,* 39/2, 343-348.

Potts, M., & Hagan, C. (Winter, 2000). Going the distance: Using systems theory to design, implement, and evaluate a distance education program. *Journal of Social Work Education,* 36/1, 131-145.

Raskin, M. (1994). The Delphi study in field instruction revisited: Expert consensus on issues and research priorities. *Journal of Social Work Education,* 30/1, 75-89.

Reisch, M., & Jarman-Rohde, L. (Spring/Summer, 2000). The future of social work in the US: Implications for field education. *Journal of Social Work Education,* 36/2, 201-214.

Schon, D.A. (1983). *The reflective practitioner: How professionals think in action.* New York: Basic Books.

Sherraden, M., & Sherraden, M. (Spring, 2000). Asset building: Integrating research, education, and practice. *Advances in Social Work,* 1/1, 61-78.

Sweitzer, H.F., & King, M. (1999). *The successful internship: Transformation and empowerment.* Pacific Grove, CA: Brooks-Cole.

Van Soest, D., Canon, R., & Grant, D. (Fall, 2000). Using an interactive website to educate about cultural diversity. *Journal of Web Education,* 36/3, 463-482.

Student Perspectives of Online Discussions: Strengths and Weaknesses

Timothy Barnett-Queen
Robert Blair
Melissa Merrick

SUMMARY. Limited research exists that examines student perceptions of online discussions in fully online classes. This is a report of initial investigation into undergraduate distance education majors' perspectives of the pedagogical value of online discussions. Over a two semester period (Spring and Fall, 2003), students taking the same online course delivered using Web Course Tools (WebCT) were surveyed regarding opinions of online discussions. The students surveyed were undergraduate students enrolled in a fully online degree program at New Mexico State University (NMSU). Although limitations exist due to small sample size and a non-standardized data collection instrument, findings from this exploratory study offer insight into undergraduate distance education student opinions of the strengths and weaknesses of online discussions as a pedagogical tool.

Timothy Barnett-Queen, PhD, is Assistant Professor (E-mail: trbqueen@nmsu. edu), and Robert Blair, PhD, is Assistant Professor, School of Social Work, New Mexico State University, MSC, 3SW, P.O. Box 30001, Las Cruces, NM 88003-8001.

Melissa Merrick, MSW, is Clinical Services Case Manager, St. Mary's Home for Boys, 16535 SW TV Highway, Beaverton, OR 97006-5143 (E-mail: reception@ stmaryshomeforboys.org) (send to Ms. Merrick's attention).

[Haworth co-indexing entry note]: "Student Perspectives of Online Discussions: Strengths and Weaknesses." Barnett-Queen, Timothy, Robert Blair, and Melissa Merrick. Co-published simultaneously in *Journal of Technology in Human Services* (The Haworth Press, Inc.) Vol. 23, No. 3/4, 2005, pp. 229-244; and: *Web-Based Education in the Human Services: Models, Methods, and Best Practices* (eds: MacFadden et al.) The Haworth Press, Inc., 2005, pp. 229-244. Single or multiple copies of this article are available for a fee from The Haworth Document Delivery Service [1-800-HAWORTH, 9:00 a.m. - 5:00 p.m. (EST). E-mail address: docdelivery@haworthpress.com].

Digital Object Identifier: 10.1300/J017v023n03_05   *229*

KEYWORDS. Asynchronous discussions, online discussions, online pedagogy

Online discussions are often used in distance education to engage students in dialogue about curricular topics. According to Swan et al. (2000), incorporating and valuing dynamic online discussions significantly increase the probability of success in online courses. Involving students in interactive dialogue increases their learning as well as their satisfaction with the web-based instruction (Sanders, 2001). As class topics are discussed online, students increase their understanding of the materials and build rapport with their classmates (Clawson, Deen, & Oxley, 2002; Tiene, 2000). Further, Coulter, Konold, and Feldman (2000) note that giving students frequent opportunities to debate, ponder, and hypothesize the impact of various course concepts, increased their involvement in online discussions.

A caution is raised in a companion to this study reported elsewhere by Barnett-Queen, Blair, and Merrick (in press). Instructors planning to use online discussions for the first time should consider using these discussions sparingly as students and instructors can quickly become overwhelmed with the volume of text in online discussions. Students new to online discussions are also often anxious about what is required and how they will be graded, therefore, instructors should provide useful information in a way that is understandable, easily accessible, and engaging (Sanders, 2001). According to Land and Dornisch (2000), "by providing guidelines for reflection and revision, students progressively deepened their understanding, as they clarified ideas, asked questions, and refined their initial conceptions" (p. 375). According to Smith, Ferguson, and Caris (2002), in addition to challenging students, instructors must be readily available to provide support and constructive feedback, guiding students toward higher quality online discussions.

In spite of these suggestions, there is little empirical guidance as to what methods and practices facilitate effective online discussions (Wells, 2000; Holt, Kleiber, & Swenson, 1998). According to Althaus (1977), "the structure of online discussions undoubtedly contributes to student outcomes and assessments, but it is unclear which kinds of structures help students achieve the most desirable benefits" (p. 173). Clearly, the current understanding of how to facilitate effective online discussions is incomplete. An area of research that is especially sparse is that of student reactions to online discussions (Tiene, 2000).

Despite limited knowledge, this study has incorporated current knowledge of best practices for online student discussions. Online discussions were a primary component of the online courses being studied and were held throughout the semester. At the end of the semester, students' perceptions of these discussions were surveyed. Results of this research may expand our current empirical knowledge-base of what methods and practices facilitate effective online discussions.

ONLINE COURSE DESIGN

The undergraduate human behavior course discussed in this report was a four-semester-hour course delivered using WebCT (2003) exclusively. The course was offered three times, with data collected during the second and third offerings. With few exceptions, the course was delivered in the same manner each semester. No face-to-face class sessions were held either semester. However, during both semesters, three "real time chats" were required for all students enrolled. All materials and weekly assignments were posted to the course's WebCT site prior to the beginning of each semester. Materials needed throughout the course, such as the syllabus and routine assignment instructions, were always available to students at various content pages within the course's WebCT site. However, no more than three weeks' assignments were available at any given time to attempt to prevent students from becoming overwhelmed with the required course work. Discussion areas were activated approximately five days in advance of their start-up date and were locked (so no additional postings could be made) within one day of the deadline for each discussion. The discussion area would remain accessible but locked for student reference for approximately one week following the discussion's termination and then archived to keep the discussion area from becoming cluttered with a high volume of discussion topics.

The major constructivist pedagogical tool used to deliver this human behavior course during each semester was the online discussion tool in the WebCT software package. Coursework included required textbook readings from a traditional social work undergraduate human behavior textbook and its student manual (Zastrow & Kirst-Ashman, 2004), a human growth and development reader (Sattler, Kramer, Shabatay & Bernstein, 2004), instructor "lecture notes" in narrative format and online articles selected by the instructor, teaching assistant and students. Eight films available at video rental outlets were also used to supplement and highlight text readings and to augment online discussions.

Each week of the semester one or more asynchronous discussions were held, facilitated initially by the instructor or teaching assistant and then by student dyads. Each week's primary discussion focused on its required readings. Additional discussions, which occurred somewhat less frequently, were taken from student workbook assignments and required videos. After the first three weeks of each semester, all discussions were facilitated by student dyads. Additional assignments included an individual term paper, a mid-term and final exam.

Early in each semester, students were required to self-select into two groups. The first was a discussion dyad which would be required to facilitate two routine weekly class discussions. The second was a video discussion group which consisted of three or four students. At least one of the required videos was assigned to each video group for a group discussion project each semester. Each video discussion took the form of a WebQuest (Dodge & March, 2004). Webquest is a flexible online resource that allows instructors or students to set up a problem or task for others to accomplish and then guides their work with web-based resources (Peterson, Caverly, & MacDonald, 2003). It was developed in 1995 by Dodge and March (2004).

The discussion facilitation dyads were required to develop, in consultation with the course's teaching assistant, discussion questions drawn from the dyad's assigned week's readings. Prior to the start-up date, discussion instructions and the discussion questions were posted to the designated WebCT discussion area. After review by the teaching assistant and instructor and prior to the start-up date of the discussion, the discussion area was opened to the class with the instruction that no postings be made to it prior to the discussion start-up date and time.

Participants were given 96 hours to answer the assigned number of discussion questions. Each answer was required to be approximately two typed single-spaced pages in length. Participants were required to use textbook readings and other assignment materials to support and defend their answers. Critical thinking as well as appropriate personal opinion was expected in each answer. Examples of acceptable answers to discussion questions were provided to the class at the beginning of the semester. An evaluation rubric was developed by the instructor and teaching assistant with which to assess student answers and the contents of the rubric was shared with each student. Students were given an additional 48 hours to reply (2-3 paragraphs required for acceptable reply) to one other student's answer of each of the questions the student did not answer herself. As a result, each participant was working with each of the four discussion questions: answering two and responding to two other student answers of the remaining two questions.

Discussion dyad facilitators were responsible to monitor the discussion during the answer and response period and post responses in a timely manner to each student's answers to discussion questions. The facilitator responses were to briefly summarize the facilitator's understanding of the participant's posting, comment on it and then pose an additional question to the participant to extend and deepen the discussion, much as a face-to-face discussion leader would do. Participants were encouraged but not required to reply to these facilitator probes. In addition, facilitators were required to read and comment on student replies to each other's discussion question answers. Depending on the topic under consideration (some were quite controversial), what other pressures students were facing, and other such intervening variables, some discussions became quite robust and lengthy. Others, particularly around the times that other assignments were due, met only the minimum requirement of the assignment. At the conclusion of each week's routine discussion, the facilitators were given 24 hours to post a 2-3 paragraph summary and synthesis of the week's discussion activity.

During the course's initial two semesters, discussion facilitators were required to develop four discussion questions that were posed to the class in the designated week's discussion area. Students not facilitating were responsible for answering two of the four questions. In addition, participants were required to respond to two other students who had answered questions different from what they had answered. These assignment specifications required students to grapple with each of the four discussion questions.

The second semester data was collected for the present study (the third semester the course was taught) an adjustment was made to the routine weekly discussion assignment based on information gathered during the first course's data collection. It became clear that along with the other assignments of this course, students thought that being required to answer two discussion questions each week was excessive. As a result, during the third semester, each student was required to answer one of three discussion questions and reply to two students who answered the remaining two questions.

METHODS

Design

This research report, along with a similar study described elsewhere (Barnett-Queen, Blair & Merrick, in press), was conducted in conjunction with similar studies in the College of Business at New Mexico State University. Each of the three faculty has collected data in classes taught which have used online discussions either to support the traditional classroom (blended format) or as a pedagogical tool for courses delivered exclusively online.

Sample

Undergraduate distance education student opinions and perceptions about the use of asynchronous discussions were solicited over two semesters from students enrolled in a social work course designed and delivered for a new fully online major at NMSU named Bachelors of Human and Community Services (BHCS). The one-semester course is similar to a single-semester social work HBSE course. The course, named Human Behavior and Social Systems (HBSS), is one of the core courses of the new online major.

Drop-out rates were similar in each semester's offering of HBSS; approximately three students dropped the course during the first three weeks. Data was collected during semesters two and three of the new BHCS major. During the last two weeks of each semester, students enrolled in the course were asked to voluntarily complete an online survey inquiring into opinions and perceptions about how online discussions were used in the course.

During the first semester in which students were surveyed, every student (n = 10) enrolled in the course completed the survey and all completed surveys were usable for this study. During the second semester of data collection, the same data collection instrument was used and 4 of 5 of the students enrolled in the course completed the survey; however, one of the participant's data was not usable (n = 3).

Instrument

The instrument used in this research was a modified version of an unpublished survey developed by E. Sautter (2002). Modifications were made to the survey with permission (E. Sautter, personal communication, July 23, 2002). The survey consisted of four sections. The first section asked a short series of open-ended questions soliciting perceptions of the usefulness of the online discussions to enhance learning the content of the course. The next section inquired through Likert-like scales, opinions of how the online discussions helped or hindered personal reflection on course topics, interaction in the class between instructor with student and student to student, critical thinking, self-expression, and the quality of online discussions compared to traditional face-to-face discussions. The third section inquired about how much time participants spent reading fellow-student discussion postings and on how many occasions students visited the online discussions. The final section was dedicated to demographic information.

Procedure

Data was collected through the use of an online survey. Students in both classes were invited to participate by personal e-mail from the instructor. The survey was made available on each class's WebCT home page approximately two weeks before the end of the semester. The WebCT software prevents multiple submissions and protects the privacy of the participants.

RESULTS

Sample

Demographic details of all respondents are reported in Table 1. In addition to the relatively small sample size, it is important to note that all participants but one were female (n = 12). There were only four European-American participants and with respect to age most were non-traditional undergraduate students.

Qualitative Findings

The survey posed a brief series of open ended questions. Content analysis was used to discover patterns of participant responses. In the first open-ended question, respondents were asked to think about a face-to-face class discussion and how the discussion experience aided in the learning of assigned material. Most respondents (n = 11) reported

TABLE 1. Sample Demographics

		BHCS (N = 13)
Gender		
	Female	12 (92%)
	Male	1 (8%)
Ethnicity		
	European-American	4 (31%)
	Hispanic	7 (54%)
	Native-American	2 (15%)
Age Range		
	22 - 25 Years	1 (8%)
	26 - 30 Years	4 (31%)
	31 or older	8 (61%)

face-to-face classes were useful when group discussions, hands on exercises, and presentations were used. One individual reported that face-to-face class settings actually isolate students.

Next participants were asked to use the characteristics they described in the first qualitative question to determine if online discussions could be as effective as face-to-face discussions. Student responses indicated that online discussions could be as effective when the discussions included power point style presentations and students actively participated. Respondents who did not believe online discussions were as effective conveyed how lack of immediate clarification leaves room for error. The third and fourth qualitative questions focused on how online discussions enhanced or hindered learning (see Table 2). Student active participation and required preparation were highlighted as enhancing learning, while excessive workload and personal discussions hindered learning.

The final qualitative question asked respondents what changes they would suggest to improve the effectiveness of online discussions. While some reported no changes were needed, about one-third reported that changes to the amount or required work and flexibility in discussion format would be beneficial. Additional suggested changes included increased participation from the instructor, greater structure for the discussions, and reminders to students on the possibility for misinterpreting student responses.

TABLE 2. Qualitative Findings

Qualitative Question #3

Now think specifically about the discussions conducted online in this course. How did the online discussion(s) enhance your learning of the course content?

LEARNING WAS ENHANCED BECAUSE THE DISCUSSIONS:

92.3% (12) reported discussions encouraged student interaction and required participation

61.5% (8) also reported discussions required students to prepare answers and think deeper about subjects

7.7% (1) reported discussions supplemented other assignment

Qualitative Question #4

How did the online discussion(s) hinder your learning of the course content?

ONLINE DISCUSSIONS HINDERED LEARNING BECAUSE:

38.5% (5) Discussion work load was excessive and discussions had too many rules

23.0% (3) Discussions became too personal vs. professional and were misinterpreted which turned focus away from assigned discussion materials

ONLINE DISCUSSIONS DID NOT HINDER LEARNING:

38.5% (5) noted discussion did not hinder learning

N = 13

Quantitative Findings

Participants were asked to indicate both the hours spent each week working on discussions (Table 3) and on average, on how many separate occasions each week they visited their online discussions (Table 4). As indicated, all of subjects reported spending three or more hours weekly in online discussions, and 77% reported spending six or more hours.

Table 5 summarizes the ten modified Likert-scale inquiries made from participant responses. A first look at the data reveals substantial agreement among the participants. A sizeable majority of all respondents agreed that online discussions, regardless of who was facilitating, tended to foster more interaction between instructor and students as well as student with student than did traditional in-class discussions (items 1 through 4). Three strong areas of agreement were item 4 (stu-

TABLE 3. Hours Spent Each Week

	(N = 13)
Less than 3 hours weekly	0 (0%)
3 - 5 hours weekly	3 (23%)
6 - 8 hours weekly	5 (38%)
More than 8 hours weekly	5 (38%)

TABLE 4. Separate Visits Each Week

	(N = 13)
Fewer than 3 per week	0 (0%)
3 - 6 per week	0 (0%)
7 - 10 per week	1 (8%)
More than 10 per week	12 (92%)

dent-led discussions encouraged more student-to-student interaction), item 5 (online discussions led to more critical thinking than traditional discussions) and item 9 (quantity of student input greater than traditional discussions).

Ambivalence was reported about online discussions encouraging more student-instructor interaction (items 1 and 2). While the majority agreed that such encouragement took place, it seems clear that for some students the manner in which the instructor participated and interacted with students during online discussions seemed to garner a lower opinion than did inquiries about student-to-student interaction. One possible reason for this ambivalence might be that the instructor for these courses has intentionally "stepped aside" to foster greater student-to-student and student-to-teaching-assistant interaction. It is possible that the instructor's lack of participation may have been interpreted as instructor absence when in reality the instructor was consistently monitoring the weekly discussions whether posting responses or not. It is also not clear if the disagreement about instructor-to-student interaction is perceived negatively by participants or rather reflects the reality that the instructor was in fact stepping aside. Clarification to the ambivalence is desirable for future data collection.

It appears that participants felt that online discussions promoted better understanding of course concepts than is typical of in-class dis-

TABLE 5. Student Opinions of Online Discussions

	Strongly Agree	Agree	Neutral	Disagree	Strongly Disagree
1. Instructor-led online discussions encouraged more instructor-to-student interaction than in a typical in-class discussion.					
BHCS	8 (62%)	2 (15%)	1 (8%)	2 (15%)	
2. Student-led online discussions encouraged more instructor-to-student interaction than in a typical in-class discussion.					
BHCS	6 (46%)	2 (15%)	2 (15%)	3 (23%)	
3. Instructor-led online discussions encouraged more student-to-student interaction than in a typical in-class discussion.					
BHCS	7 (54%)	5 (38%)	1 (8%)		
4. Student-led online discussions encouraged more student-to-student interaction than in a typical in-class discussion.					
BHCS	8 (62%)	5 (38%)			
5. Online discussions encouraged more critical thinking about course content than in typical in-class discussions.					
BHCS	7 (54%)	6 (46%)			
6. Online discussions promoted better understanding of basic course concepts than in typical in-class discussions.					
BHCS	5 (38%)	5 (38%)	1 (8%)	2 (15%)	
7. Online discussions caused me more self-consciousness about viewpoint expression than in typical in-class discussions.					
BHCS	3 (23%)	2 (15%)	3 (23%)	2 (15%)	3 (23%)
8. I considered others' opinions and arguments more carefully in the online discussions than I would have in a traditional in-class discussion.					
BHCS	5 (38%)	3 (23%)	4 (31%)	1 (8%)	
9. The quantity of student input was greater in online discussions than is typically the case in traditional in-class discussions.					
BHCS	12 (92%)	1 (8%)			
10. The quality of student input was greater in online discussions than is typically the case in traditional in-class discussions.					
BHCS	7 (54%)	2 (15%)	3 (23%)	1 (8%)	

BHCS N = 13

cussions (item 6). As mentioned previously, it was interesting to find that participants were somewhat ambivalent about the level of self-consciousness caused by online discussions *versus* in-class discussions (item 7).

Item 8 results are striking from an instructor's perspective. Approximately two-thirds of all respondents indicated they considered others' opinions and arguments more carefully in the online environment than in face-to-face settings. Despite the heavy workload reported in the qualitative inquiry, students perceived themselves as taking seriously what others posted to the discussions, more so than was likely to happen in a face-to-face setting. Equally strident were the findings in Items 9 and 10 in which all but one of the respondents strongly agreed that the quantity of student input was greater online and approximately two-thirds thought the quality of student input was greater than in traditional face-to-face discussions.

Age and Experience of Participants

Contrary to what one might expect, older students did not appear to be disproportionately inexperienced with online discussions. Approximately one-third (n = 4) of respondents who reported being 30 years of age or older had no previous experience with online discussions. This finding can partially be explained by the typical demographics of the participants. These students were primarily returning non-traditional part-time students who were pursuing the second half of their undergraduate degree in an exclusively online format.

Experience with Online Discussions

One participant who reported instructor-led online discussions did not encourage more instructor-to-student interaction than traditional classroom discussions had previous experience with online discussions. However, when asked if student-led online discussions encouraged more instructor-to-student interaction, two participants who disagreed had some previous experience with online discussions. It would seem that previous experience with online discussions might have something to do with participant expectations of instructor-to-student interaction during online discussions.

The result that less than one-third of all participants thought that online discussions made them more self-conscious about expression of personal opinion seemed to be in contrast with findings reported in other literature. One might reasonably speculate that some of the self-consciousness could easily have derived from lack of experience with the technology.

DISCUSSION

The purpose of this exploratory study was to assess undergraduate distance education student opinions regarding the use of online discussions as a teaching tool. Results indicate that the majority of students reported a positive experience with online discussions in BHSS. For example, all participants indicated that online discussions enhanced learning. The majority of participants also rated both the quantity (n = 12; 92%) and quality (n = 9; 69%) of online discussions as greater than was typically the case in traditional face-to-face discussions.

Moreover, the manner in which discussions were used in this course seemed to create an interactive learning environment that facilitated increased understanding of course materials as indicated by the finding that 77% (n = 10) of all subjects either agreed or strongly agreed that online discussions promoted better understanding of basic course concepts than was typical during traditional discussions. Further, the use of online discussions seemed to facilitate critical thinking, one of the course's objectives, more than typical in-class discussions as indicated by a 100% agreement rating in Item 5 (Table 5).

Requiring students to lead most of the course's discussions seemed to create an interactive learning environment in which students appeared more willing to voice controversial opinions and to disagree with each other, the teaching assistant, and the instructor. An important question left unanswered by this study is that it may be possible that the level of instructor involvement in the discussions also helped facilitate the interactive environment which led to the positive perceptions of online discussions. While a minority of students voiced the desire for more instructor involvement it is possible that higher levels of such involvement could negatively affect the interactive learning environment thus lowering student opinions about the utility of the discussions in this course.

Student discussion facilitation assignments also reduced the time and effort that would have been required for the instructor or teaching assistant to lead all discussions. Nonetheless, a significant amount of time was needed by the instructor to provide initial guidelines for the discussions, review student-proposed discussion questions, to be actively involved in the discussions and provide on-going progress feedback to each student. Despite this time, a minority of participants indicated that they would have preferred more structure for the discussions, and greater participation from the instructor. This intense level of interaction and its consequent demands on time seems to suggest the need for small numbers of students in online courses and the availability of a teaching assistant. As noted by Smith et al. (2002), Hislop (1997), and Chabon et al. (2001), online courses tend to be significantly more demanding for both the instructor and the students than traditional face to face courses.

As previously noted, two students during the first semester indicated that a decrease in the workload was needed. From this information, student requirements were reduced for the second semester of data collection. No participants reported an excessive workload during their matriculation through the course during the second semester of data collection. In providing online courses, the authors have struggled to maintain a balanced workload for the students that is both challenging and demanding, yet not overwhelming. One way of monitoring the workload, as was done in this study, is to solicit student perceptions, and from that feedback, to make modifications in the workload and course design.

Limitations of the Study and Need for Future Research

The primary limitations of this study were the small convenience samples and the non-standardized data collection instrument. In future studies, larger samples will be needed to increase the generalizability of the findings. As noted previously, the data collection instrument needs to be updated and standardized. Additional instruments will also need to be developed and used that effectively tap the various dimensions of student perceptions of online discussions.

Findings also indicate that previous experience with online discussions may have impacted student perceptions surveyed for this study. Therefore, future researchers may need to consider conducting longitudinal studies that examine how student perceptions of online discussions might change over time. Further, to expand our knowledge of the components of effective online discussions, various discussion models may need to be developed, evaluated and compared to other discussion models to determine which are most effective in which circumstances.

For example, this study identified one model of online discussions that used student-led dyads to propose and post questions that could be discussed by the entire class. In future research this model could be evaluated against other models to determine which is most effective.

REFERENCES

Althaus, S. (1997). Computer-mediated communication in the university classroom: An experiment with online discussions. *Communication Education, 46*, 158-174.

Barnett-Queen, T. R., Blair, R. G., & Merrick, M. (in press). Undergraduate and graduate student perceptions of asynchronous discussions in distance and distributed learning environments. [Special Issue] *Journal of Technology in Human Services.*

Chabon, S., Cain, R., & Lee-Wilkerson, D. (2001). Facilitating those dreaded discussions on diversity, through threaded discussions: An inter-institutional, internet-based model. *Distance Education, 22*(1), 137-143.

Clawson, R., Deen, R., & Oxley, M. (2002). Online discussions across three universities: Student participation and pedagogy. *Political Science & Politics, 35*(4), 713-718.

Coulter, B., Konold, C., & Feldman, A. (2000). Promoting reflective discussions: Making the most of online resources in your classroom. *Learning and Leading with Technology, 28*(2), 44-49.

Dodge, B., & March, T. (2004). *The Webquest page.* San Diego: San Diego State University. Retrieved April 16, 2004, from http://webquest.sdsu.edu.

Hislop, G. W. (1997, November). "Evaluating an Asynchronous Graduate Degree Program." *Proceedings, Frontiers in Education,* Los Alamitos, CA: IEEE CS Press.

Holt, M., Kleiber, P., & Swenson, J. (1998). Facilitating group learning on the internet. *New Directions for Adult and Continuing Education, 78*, 43-51.

Land, S., & Dornisch, M. (2002). A case study of student use of asynchronous bulletin board systems (BBS) to support reflection and evaluation. *Journal of Educational Technology Systems, 30*(4), 365-377.

Peterson, C., Caverly, D., & MacDonald, L. (2003). Techtalk: Developing academic literacy through WebQuests. *Journal of Developmental Education, 26*(3), 38-39.

Sanders, D. (2001, Spring). Student attitudes toward Web-enhanced instruction in an introductory biology course. *Journal of Research on Computing in Education, 33*(3), 251-262.

Sattler, D. N., Kramer, G. P., Shabatay, V., & Bernstein, D. A. (2000). *Lifespan development in context: Voices and perspectives.* Boston: Houghton-Mifflin.

Smith, G., Ferguson, D., & Caris, M. (2002). Teaching over the web versus in the classroom: Differences in the instructor experience. *International Journal of Instructional Media, 29*(1), 61-67.

Swan, K., Shea, P., Fredericksen, E., Pickett, A., Pelz, W., & Maher, G. (2000). Building knowledge building communities: Consistency, contact, and communication in the virtual classroom. *Journal of Educational Computing Research, 23*(4), 359-383.

Tiene, D. (2000). Online discussions: A survey of advantages and disadvantages compared to face-to-face discussions. *Journal of Educational Multimedia & Hypermedia, 9*(4), 371-384.

WebCT (2003). Web Course Tools (Version 3.8 Campus Edition) [Computer software]. Lynnfield, MA: WebCT, Inc.

Wells, J. (2000). Effects of an online mediated communication course, prior computer experience and internet knowledge, and learning styles on students' internet attitudes, computer-mediated technologies, and new educational challenges. *Journal of Industrial Teacher Education, 37*(3), 22-53.

Zastrow, C., & Kirst-Ashman, K. K. (2004). *Understanding human behavior and the social environment* (6th ed.). Belmont, CA: Wadsworth/Thompson.

Social Work Ethics Online: Reflective Learning

Marilyn A. Biggerstaff

SUMMARY. Using e-learning (Blackboard™), a course in ethics promotes reflective learning and critical thinking skills for graduate social work students as participants in an on-learning experience. Reflective learning, based on Schön's (1983) "reflective inquiry," is facilitated with participants' engagement in weekly case-based discussion of ethical and legal concepts. The internet course exemplifies the principle of "say-writing" (Wegerif, 1998) as an effective strategy for promoting reflective learning. *[Article copies available for a fee from The Haworth Document Delivery Service: 1-800-HAWORTH. E-mail address: <docdelivery@haworthpress.com> Website: <http://www.HaworthPress.com> © 2005 by The Haworth Press, Inc. All rights reserved.]*

KEYWORDS. Online learning, reflective learning, social work ethics

The roles of the professions create special moral rights and duties (Callahan, 1988). Ethics is the study of morality with special attention to laws, morality and codes of conduct (Feldman, 1978). The challenge

Marilyn A. Biggerstaff, DSW, LCSW, is Professor, School of Social Work, Virginia Commonwealth University, 1001 West Franklin Street, Richmond, VA 23284-2027.

[Haworth co-indexing entry note]: "Social Work Ethics Online: Reflective Learning." Biggerstaff, Marilyn A. Co-published simultaneously in *Journal of Technology in Human Services* (The Haworth Press, Inc.) Vol. 23, No. 3/4, 2005, pp. 245-257; and: *Web-Based Education in the Human Services: Models, Methods, and Best Practices* (eds: MacFadden et al.) The Haworth Press, Inc., 2005, pp. 245-257. Single or multiple copies of this article are available for a fee from The Haworth Document Delivery Service [1-800-HAWORTH, 9:00 a.m. - 5:00 p.m. (EST). E-mail address: docdelivery@haworthpress.com].

Available online at http://www.haworthpress.com/web/JTHS
© 2005 by The Haworth Press, Inc. All rights reserved.
Digital Object Identifier: 10.1300/J017v023n03_06

for the developing professional is to distinguish between values (personal, societal, and professional), morals (societal, familial, personal, and faith-based) and ethics in professional practice. Social work ethics are typically introduced early in the professional curriculum and most often learning about professional ethical principles is taught as part of the practice sequence. Social workers most often understand the ethical principles underpinning social work practice but may not necessarily be able to translate these principles into practice. Further, use of a code of ethics framework as the center of professional ethics content does not expose the learner to laws and court interpretations guiding practice in the states and jurisdictions.

As a result of the interface between personal, societal, and professional values in the ethical practice of social work, teaching ethics involves individuals in questioning and contemplating their personal values and the relationship of these with professional ethics. The traditional classroom setting rooted in presentation, discussion and summarizing may not facilitate the important role of reflection in the individual learning processes. Reflective learning, based on "reflective inquiry" (Schön, 1983, p. 69), is a process of research-in-practice whereby the learner is confronted by uncertainty in a situation, constructs a set of responses, defines professional actions, and experiments with a problematic situation discovering the consequences and limitations of each possible action (Schön). Reflective learning is part of critical thinking, "the careful examination and evaluation of beliefs and actions" (Gibbs & Gambrill, 1996, p. 3).

Reflective learning and inquiry appear on the surface as antithetical to models of web-based education in the human services. In social work the World Wide Web (WWW) is most often associated with courses involving the dissemination of facts, for example research methods (Stocks & Freddolino, 2000) and social work history (Faux & Black-Hughes, 2000) rather than practice and ethics. However, a number of reports in the professional literature support the use of online education in the teaching and learning of diversity issues. Bertera and Littlefield (2003), MacFadden, Maiter and Dumbrill (2002) as well as Van Soest, Canon and Grant (2000) report that social work students engaged in online discussion forums on sensitive issues including cultural diversity and societal oppression can experience positive impacts as a result of participation in web-based forum discussions. Underlying the development of this graduate level course in professional ethics is the assumption that course participants can engage in reflective or critical thinking using the electronically delivered course design.

This paper describes the use of on-line learning of social work ethics from a reflective thinking perspective. First, a model for use of the internet in teaching social work ethics is described including the course content and the principles underlying the course. The assumptions underlying the discussion method used to engage participants in critical thinking about social work ethics are detailed. A discussion follows describing the advantages and challenges of an online course for the teaching and learning of social work ethics.

COURSE CONTENT: LEARNING OBJECTIVES

The graduate level course, Social Work Ethics, is based on the principle of the Council on Social Work Education's statement that

> Social work education programs integrate content about values and principles of ethical decision making as presented in the National Association of Social Workers Code of Ethics. The educational experience provides students with the opportunity to be aware of personal values; develop, demonstrate, and promote the values of the profession; and analyze ethical dilemmas and the ways in which these affect practice, services, and clients. (CSWE, 2002)

The purposes of the course as stated in the university bulletin are to

> Examine the history and development of the value base and ethical principles of the social work profession. Investigate codes of ethics for professional practice, with special attention to the principles of human relationships, integrity, social justice, and competence. Analyze ethical dilemmas in clinical social work practice. Consider mechanisms for the enforcement of ethical codes.

Upon completion of the course, students who meet the specific learning objectives of the course will demonstrate knowledge and skills in

1. analyzing the origins of values and ethical principles in social work practice and the application of these principles to their own social work practice;
2. demonstrating knowledge of the ethical principles of service, social justice, dignity and worth of persons, importance of human relationships, integrity and competence through

the application of these principles to social work practice situations;

3. demonstrating skill in the application of ethical principles of the social work profession to a practice situation of the student's choice; and

4. applying the principles of enforcement of social work ethics in the practice of social work as well as the responsibilities of social work practitioners in upholding principles of ethical practice.

COURSE FORMAT

Social Work Ethics is a stand alone course offered to specialization year MSW students with the addition of interested doctoral level students. The ethics course was developed as an online learning offering and has not been offered in a face-to-face format. The course uses the Blackboard™ platform accessible to students after they complete the university's enrollment process. The 3-credit hour graduate course is offered one semester each academic year, lasting 15 weeks. To date, the course has been offered 4 times with enrollment ranging from 14 to 24 participants per semester offering.

Using Blackboard's™ features, the internet delivered learning experience uses asynchronous processes. Instructional design emphasizes the students and instructor as course participants. The instructor interacts with other participants using e-mail and discussion threads. Social work graduate students from the school's two campuses can enroll in the course. This is the only course offered across campuses as well as the only totally online course offered by the school of social work.

The content of each of the 15 sessions includes lecture materials written by the instructor presented online in Blackboard™. These materials include interactive links to important documents and supplemental materials available on the WWW. Supplemental reading materials are provided for each course session in addition to a bibliography for participants' use in gaining a greater depth of understanding of each course topic. The university's internet-based journals provide an additional time-saving capability allowing the participants to access required readings through e-journals. Unfortunately, older materials are not often available with electronic publication access. Access to legal documents and statutes relevant to ethics topics are easily integrated into each applicable course session.

The social work ethics course is case-based, a widely accepted approach for examining professional ethics. Each course session presents a case challenging participants to apply the knowledge and principles from the online lecture and supplemental readings to address the dilemmas posed by the case situation. Each session focuses on a principle of social work ethics (e.g., confidentiality and privacy, integrity and professional competence, truthfulness and full disclosure, etc.). Legal aspects of social work practice are included (e.g., duty to warn, reporting suspected child abuse and neglect, etc.) as well as practical aspects of managing unethical professional practices (e.g., impaired professionals, violations of practice codes developed by states' legal regulations for professional practice).

Participants' responses to the case material are a core aspect of the internet-enabled learning experience. Emphasis is placed on the participants reading, applying, and understanding the course content, and considering and thinking about colleagues' responses to the cases and challenging each other. During each session each participant is required to post his or her responses to the case material and to questions designed by the instructor to guide case decision-making. The course format requires that posting of responses using the Discussion Board section of Blackboard™ must be completed on or before a set deadline for each weekly course session. Participants are encouraged to access the Discussion Board, review and comment on other participants' responses to the case; however, participants are not required to post comments using threaded discussions. Each participant is identified by his or her own name in postings on the Discussion Board.

EVALUATION AND GRADING OF PARTICIPANTS

In addition to use of asynchronous discussion of the case materials, course assignments include a graded individual or group on-line presentation on an ethics topic of the participants' choice. Depending on the size of course enrollment, 3 to 4 online sessions are devoted to participants' presentations of an ethical issue of interest, either individually or in small groups (2-3 participants). Participants are encouraged to pursue individual interests in social work practice ethics that go beyond the instructor-designed course content. A posted example of a quality online presentation is provided as a guide for development of participants' presentations. The individual or group presentations include a participant-developed case accompanied by questions developed by the presenters to guide the responses of other participants using the threaded discussion format.

A final written assignment requires each course participant's individual analysis of his or her presentation topic and case. Participants are encouraged to use feedback and discussion from the case discussion resulting from their online presentations in developing the final graded paper.

Final course grades are assigned based on the following criteria:

> Participation in each on-line course session, evidence of completion of all readings and assignments, and preparation to participate fully in seminar discussions and exercises (20%);
>
> Development of a written Personal Framework for Ethical Social Work Practice (10%);
>
> Preparation of a course seminar during part of one course session based on the ethical issue of the participant's choice and a case (40%), and
>
> Analysis of an ethical principle in social work practice–a final paper on the ethical issue of the participant's choice presented in the course seminar including the participant's analysis of his or her case (30%).

The grading criteria for participation in the online course carries the expectation that participants will craft individual responses to the case taking into account the application of the course content, demonstrating the ability to apply the content to the dilemmas posed by the case, and integrating knowledge from other social work content areas (e.g., social work practice and social policy).

All written assignments are submitted electronically. This allows the instructor to comment on the paper and return these electronically to participants resulting in a friendlier and speedier turn around of instructor feedback. Criteria for evaluating assignments (personal framework, course seminar and analysis of an ethical principle) and the reflective learning and critical thinking skills demonstrated by participants include the personal processes of applying material and critical thinking about the case; synthesis of the participant's responses to the case, not merely repeating what others have stated; and, constructing an understanding of self as the social worker in the case situation. This last criterion is the application of "say-writing" (Wegerif, 1998, p. 40) by taking a stand, defending a position, and listening and responding to the say-writing of other participants. The interactive nature of the course renders different criteria than those used in face-to-face courses where the evaluative criteria are largely based on individual work and do not include the interactive components of the online course.

COURSE ASSUMPTIONS AND PRINCIPLES

Teaching and learning of professional ethics require reflective or critical thinking. An important assumption underlying the design and delivery of the online course on social work ethics is that participants will be more willing to express themselves openly in text versus face-to-face communication. This is what Wegerif (1998) calls "say-writing, a cross between writing and speech" (p. 40). Say-writing is more than the expression of fact in response to the questions posed for case analyses.

The expression of fact is sought to ensure that participants can identify the principles exemplified in each case. However, the goal is for participants to explain the case events, recognize the ethical dilemma(s), and demonstrate their abilities to derive solutions. An example of the expression of fact is found in one participant's posted summary of her response to a case (participants granted permission to use anonymized examples of their work).

> *Any time there is a conflict between confidentiality and the duty to warn is a difficult situation in this field. That being said, the best protection a social worker can use to cover her/himself is the appropriate use of supervision. The supervisor's job is to guide their supervisee's actions and ensure they are in accordance with agency policy, ethical responsibility, and practice standards to ensure clients are being treated properly and workers are acting accordingly. It is also the supervisor's job to oversee any situations in which the worker or agency could be in jeopardy either ethically or legally.*

An example of say-writing is found in the comments of one participant to another in a Discussion Board during a session.

It truly is amazing that a practitioner can completely be unable to see the forest for the trees, isn't it? How could Althea have had any reason to believe Mary was "improving" and in the first stages of recovery from any intervention when she was clearly stating that she was barely functioning at every session for three weeks. Sounds more like the poor woman was rapidly "losing power" instead of gaining it, doesn't it?

The first respondent replies,

It certainly does! Lack of energy to do very much of anything is most definitely a loss of power, in my opinion.

Another example of a say-writing interchange among participants is found in the following participant's comments about the case and the response from a colleague.

[1st participant] *Apparently it is common for domestic violence victims to neglect their children. They are often still trying to deal with their abuse or to get over the effects of their abuse and do not have much emotional resources to care for their children (which is completely understandable). If Althea probed into Mary's most recent background and not on her childhood problems initially, she might have been able to pick up on what is "currently" happening in Mary's life.*

[2nd participant] *You're so right. I wonder what Althea actually put in her notes for the initial assessment. How could she have ignored the critical issues that this single mother was so depressed and not seen the need for immediate intervention to ameliorate that condition as it related to safety for her and her small children? A psychoanalyst might be expected to concentrate on issues from her past more than on her present, but social workers are supposed to think and assess more globally.*

Say-writing is encouraged for course participants. However, this process is a social dimension of asynchronous learning networks and must be encouraged and facilitated by the tone set for the course in the instructional design and course organization and the messages given by the instructor. This is referred to as facilitation discourse by Shea, Pickett, and Pelz (2003). While the instructor can interject prompts to participants in comments posted during the weekly discussion inter-changes, it is important for the say-writing process to emerge among participants, developing group norms for the social network with re-sponses evolving, being accepted and encouraged through active colle-gial participation. The instructor assumes the role of facilitator as the course progresses. The instructor's presence in the course design in-volves the "facilitation and direction of cognitive and social processes" (Shea, Pickett, & Pelz, p. 65).This is a challenge to some participants who have excessive need for approval from the instructor and seek out endorsement for their specific discussion comments. As the course ex-perience progresses, participants begin responding to each other and not directly to the instructor. During the first three sessions, the instructor provides direct comments on the participants' entries on the Discussion Board. After this period, the instructor's comments are limited to cor-rections of misperceptions in the application of content. After three ses-sions participants are usually more comfortable with the content as well as the course medium. The instructor can make more general comments and refer specific questions to the participants as a whole. The forma-tion of a participant group emerges to handle questions and deal with specific issues about the content and the online course experience.

OUTCOMES:
ADVANTAGES AND CHALLENGES
OF THE ONLINE ETHICS COURSE

Reflective learning can be prompted and achieved in an online course. This occurs by promoting a learning community among partici-pants that defines and encourages a peer consultation experience in the learning process. Rather than the comments among participants being instructor prompted and guided, participants develop their abilities and skills to respond to the differences in their comments on cases in the Discussion Board. The instructor takes a back seat, observing the pro-cess of peer consultation while interjecting comments and prompts as necessary to move the process toward a peer consultation network de-veloped among all participants. Participants read, apply, and understand the course content while considering and thinking about their personal responses to the case material. Both the format as well as the instructor of this e-learning experience promote consideration of the course mate-rial and reflection on personal, social, and professional values in response to the case stimuli. Often in the traditional classroom experience, students do not have the time to consider their responses from a reflective perspective and reflect facts in their discussions of course material or try to get their share of "air time" (Meyer, 2003, p. 56). Thinking-in-action (Schön, 1983) is limited by the time that can be devoted to participant interaction and discussion. This time is constrained in the classroom while the process can be expanded in the internet-enabled learning experience. Say-writing encourages careful consideration of the opinions of others.

The e-course format does not allow participants to hide behind the contributions of others, described as "self-censorship among students, including shyness, being unprepared and large class size" (Bertera & Littlefield, 2003, p. 56). The e-learning format developed for the online ethics course strives to promote active, reflective participation and learning. The approach used by the instructor sets the stage for participant rather than student status among all enrolled in the course. The e-learning format encourages peer consultation, a process of using other participants for feedback in resolving the ethical dilemmas posed by the case. This peer consultation process is an essential element for professional use in resolving ethical dilemmas as these arise in social work practice.

The flexibility of the round-the-clock technology promotes opportunities for reflection in participation. In this course, the electronic format promotes learner autonomy. Participants are not prompted by the instructor to respond to each other's posting. Rather, the learning environment creates and encourages the opportunity for engagement with colleagues and reflection-in-action with peer feedback. The processes of participant engagement are what Bransford and colleagues (2000) refer to as community centered learning. This is particularly important in exploring professional ethical dilemmas, as peer feedback is an essential element in the social worker's resolution of ethical challenges as these arise in the real world of professional practice.

Feedback and requests for clarification promote reflection-in-action. E-learning provides the opportunity to read, comprehend, analyze and interpret the reactions, questions, and input from colleagues in written rather than verbal communication. Meyer (2003) notes "time for reflection is the key to the learning of many students, and a few seconds in class may not be sufficient time to reflect and think about a course topic" (p. 63).

A course in professional ethics delivered and experienced using asynchronous internet processes is not without challenges for the participants and instructor. Participants must manage their personal computers, assuring that virus protection software is enabled, and maintain easy and fast access through an internet service provider. Online course participation can be frustrating for participants who lack basic skill and comfort in managing the internet.

Although the weekly course schedule provides a time line for each course session, participation requires self-direction and the ability to actively manage the learning processes. The time required for reading the online materials and posting responses to the case for each online session is equivalent to the 2 1/2 hour per week standard graduate class. Reflection and interaction with colleagues beyond the initial posting of case responses requires additional time.

INSTRUCTOR CHALLENGES

Instructor involvement in the course is time intensive. The case discussion format requires that the instructor read the discussion board entries, and in the beginning phase of the course, prepare feedback for participants for posting on the threaded discussion. A challenge for the instructor is providing feedback in the reflection-in-action model rather than relying on summaries of comments that emphasize an external definition of what is right or acceptable. This type of response discourages reflection-in-action and the development of critical thinking skills that serve as the foundation of the ethics learning and exploration processes. Instructor time is also spent responding to participants' technical issues, integrating additional sources to increase participants' understanding of specific topics or correct misunderstandings, and responding to questions about course assignments.

EVALUATION OF THE ONLINE ETHICS COURSE

Over the past four years, few participants ($n = 3$) have dropped the course within the university's withdrawal period. Of these, only one participant withdrew from the course stating a need for in-person contact with the instructor. The other two participants opted to enroll in another graduate elective offering. Qualitative outcome data from almost all course participants reflect that the course content was challenging, the e-learning format encouraged critical thinking, and reflective learning was facilitated by having the time to reflect on the ethics issue and respond in writing to the dilemma presented in the case. Participants with little computer experience and no e-learning experience were able to master the technology and did not report that this hampered their learning experiences. The course content remains appealing across cohorts of graduate social work students as this course will be offered with full course enrollment for the fifth consecutive year in the fall 2004.

CONCLUSION

The use of online learning to promote reflective learning and critical thinking skills in social work ethics is challenging. The case-based ethics course requires participants to post identified reactions to the case material with a critical analysis of the ethical dilemmas represented in the case for each course session. Over time, participants engage in "say-writing" (Wegerif, 1998) reflecting critical thinking rather than merely responding to the facts posed for each case analysis. The process of "say-writing" emerges during the course. Initially discussion board entries are fact based responses to the cases; gradually these move to lively discussions of the ethical principles and alternatives presented by the online lecture materials and multiple postings of reactions to other participants' ideas and conclusions about the specific case material. Course participants are encouraged by the instructor and colleagues to develop and demonstrate their personal values as these interact with social work ethical principles. The e-learning format is successful in exposing participants to community centered learning (Bransford et al., 2000) by encouraging the use of peer feedback in the process of resolving ethical dilemmas. The skills in using peer consultation and feedback are essential elements in the resolution of ethical dilemmas in social work practice.

REFERENCES

Bertera, E. M., & Littlefield, M. B. (2003). Evaluation of electronic discussion forums in social work diversity education: A comparison of anonymous and identified participation. *Journal of Technology in Human Services, 21,* 53-71.

Bransford, J., Brown, A., Cocking, R., Donovan, M., & Pellegrino, J. W. (Eds.). (2000). *How people learn: Brain, mind, experience, and school.* Washington, DC: National Academy Press.

Callahan, J. C. (Ed.) (1988). *Ethical issues in professional life.* New York: Oxford University Press.

Council on Social Work Education. (2002) Educational Policy and Accreditation Standards. Alexandria, VA: Author. Retrieved December 14, 2004 from http://www.cswe.org/.

Faux, T. L., & Black-Hughes, C. (2000). A comparison of using the internet versus lectures to teach social work history. *Research on Social Work Practice, 10*, 454-466.

Feldman, F. (1978). *Introductory ethics*. Englewood Cliffs, NJ: Prentice-Hall, Inc.

Gibbs, L. & Gambrill, E. (1996). *Critical thinking for social workers*. Thousand Oaks, CA: Pine Forge Press.

MacFadden, R. J., Maiter, S., & Dumbrill, G. C. (2002). High tech and high touch: The human face of online education. *Journal of Technology in Human Services, 20*, 283-300.

Meyer, K. A. (2003). Face-to-face versus threaded discussions: The role of time and higher-order thinking. *Journal of Asynchronous Learning Networks, 7*, 55-65.

Schön, D. A. (1983). *The reflective practitioner: How professionals think in action*. NY: Basic Books.

Shea, P. J., Pickett, A. M., & Pelz, W. E. (2003). A follow-up investigation of "Teaching Presence" in the SUNY learning network. *Journal of Asynchronous Learning Networks, 7*, 61-80.

Stocks, J. T., & Freddolino, P. P. (2000). Enhancing computer-mediated teaching through interactivity: The second iteration of a World Wide Web-based graduate social work course. *Research on Social Work Practice, 10*, 505-518.

Van Soest, D., Canon, R., & Grant, D. (2000). Using an interactive website to educate about cultural diversity and societal oppression. *Journal of Social Work Education, 36*, 463-480.

Wegerif, R. (1998). The social dimension of asynchronous learning networks. *Journal of Asynchronous Learning Networks, 2*(1), 34-49. Retrieved January 14, 2004 from http://www.aln.org/publications/jaln/v2n1/v2n1_wegerif.asp.

Translating Research into Practice: The Role of Web-Based Education

Kenneth R. Weingardt
Steven W. Villafranca

SUMMARY. Clinical Practice Guidelines (CPGs) constitute a major focus of recent efforts to narrow the gap between research and practice. However, CBGs cannot effectively change clinical practice unless they are effectively disseminated. The present article describes a web-based course designed to teach nurses about a CPG for the management of alcohol withdrawal. In it, we outline the details of our web-based course, including its technical characteristics, organization, structure, and clinical content. Next, we outline several adjunctive strategies that may improve the effectiveness of such web-based educational interventions. Finally,

---

Kenneth R. Weingardt, PhD, and Steven W. Villafranca, MA, are affiliated with the Center for Health Care Evaluation, VA Palo Alto Health Care System, Stanford University School of Medicine.

Address correspondence to: Kenneth R. Weingardt, PhD, VAPAHCS, 795 Willow Road (152), Menlo Park, CA 94025 (E-mail: ken.weingardt@med.va.gov).

Support for this project was provided by the Department of Veterans Affairs (VA) Health Services Research and Development Service, and the VA Program Evaluation and Resource Center.

[Haworth co-indexing entry note]: "Translating Research into Practice: The Role of Web-Based Education." Weingardt, Kenneth R., and Steven W. Villafranca. Co-published simultaneously in *Journal of Technology in Human Services* (The Haworth Press, Inc.) Vol. 23, No. 3/4, 2005, pp. 259-273; and: *Web-Based Education in the Human Services: Models, Methods, and Best Practices* (eds: MacFadden et al.) The Haworth Press, Inc., 2005, pp. 259-273. Single or multiple copies of this article are available for a fee from The Haworth Document Delivery Service [1-800-HAWORTH, 9:00 a.m. - 5:00 p.m. (EST). E-mail address: docdelivery@haworthpress.com].

we discuss other ways that web-based education may prove useful in disseminating evidence-based practices in human service delivery settings. *[Article copies available for a fee from The Haworth Document Delivery Service: 1-800-HAWORTH. E-mail address: <docdelivery@haworthpress.com> Website: <http://www.HaworthPress.com> © 2005 by The Haworth Press, Inc. All rights reserved.]*

KEYWORDS. Clinical practice guideline, web-based intervention, e-learning

NARROWING THE RESEARCH-PRACTICE GAP

Like most scientists, researchers working in human services presumably want their findings to influence practitioner behavior. However, successful researchers must focus their resources on getting grants, conducting studies and publishing articles in peer reviewed journals. Conversely, line staff responsible for the day-to-day provision of human services often want to be kept informed of the latest research, but rarely have the time or the training necessary to search, review, evaluate, and synthesize the scientific literature within the context of their daily work. The result of this disjunction has come to be known as the "research-practice gap" (Lamb & Greenlick, 1998).

Despite the availability of empirically-supported treatments for patients with psychiatric and substance use disorders, established research-based interventions have generally not been widely adopted in clinical practice (Lamb et al., 1998). Federal agencies including the Substance Abuse and Mental Health Services Administration, the National Institute on Drug Abuse, the National Institute on Alcohol Abuse and Alcoholism, and the National Institute on Mental Health are all well aware of this gap and have been actively soliciting grant applications to address this problem for the past several years (Minkoff & Cline, 2003) (NIDA, 2003) (NIAAA, 2001) (NIMH, 2003).

Clinical Practice Guidelines (CPGs) constitute a major focus of recent initiatives to bridge the gap between research and practice. CPGs attempt to translate research into practice by systematically reviewing the literature and then deriving evidence-based recommendations, tools and/or strategies for the treatment of a particular disease or disorder in the form of an algorithm that guides the practicing clinician through a series of decisions and actions (Institute of Medicine, 1990; 1992). Examples of CPGs include the American Psychiatric Association's Clinical Practice Guideline for the treatment of psychiatric disorders (APA, 2002), the New York State Department of Education Social Work Practice Guideline (NYS Education Department, 2002), and the Department of Veterans Affairs/Department of Defense Clinical Practice Guideline for the treatment of patients with substance use disorders (VHA/DoD, 2001) (see Figure 1).

CPGs bring the research literature one step closer to the practitioner by synthesizing the evidence and providing recommendations for changing clinical practice. However, a CPG can only influence clinical practice if it is actually *implemented*, meaning that the guideline is successfully moved out of the abstract phase of development and into the actual world of health care decision making and action (Institute of Medicine, 1992). And for a guideline to be implemented, it must first be *effectively disseminated* (Van Arminge & Shannon, 1992)– meaning that a practitioner must first become aware of a guideline and be-

FIGURE 1. Course Map

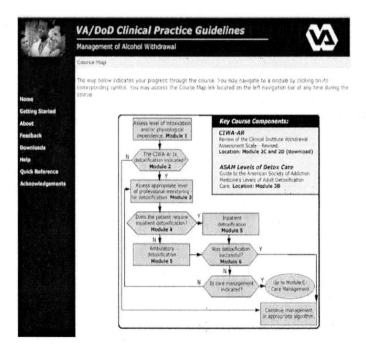

come familiar with its content before he or she can decide whether or not to follow its recommendations.

Web-based educational interventions are particularly well suited for this dissemination role. A well designed web-based training application can be quite effective at delivering what Rogers (1995) refers to as "how-to knowledge," which consists of information that is necessary to use an innovation (such as a CPG) properly. According to researchers who study the diffusion of innovations (Rogers, 1995), this knowledge stage is particularly crucial, for when an adequate level of knowledge is not obtained prior to the trial and adoption of an innovation, rejection and discontinuance are likely to result.

In the present article, we describe a web-based course (www. detoxguideline.org) that we have developed to disseminate a set of recommendations from the "VHA/DoD Clinical Practice Guideline for the Assessment and Management of Substance Use Disorders in Primary and Specialty Care" (VHA/DoD, 2001). The purpose of this project is to facilitate implementation of evidence-based practices to objectively screen medical and surgical patients for risk of Alcohol Withdrawal Syndrome (AWS).

We chose this recommendation as the initial focus of our dissemination efforts because AWS represents a serious threat to the well-being of a substantial portion of surgical, trauma, and acutely ill patients, and results in unnecessary, costly medical care expenditures. Severe AWS has been associated with mortality rates ranging up to 40% (Wartenberg et al., 1990). Even in less severe cases, failure to provide prophylactic treatment for alcohol withdrawal can change a normal postoperative course into a life-threatening situation in which the alcohol dependent patient requires intensive care (Spies & Rommelspacher, 1999). Training medical and nursing staff to objectively monitor the severity of AWS risk has been found to significantly improve patient outcomes (Sullivan, Sykora, Schneiderman, Naranjo, & Sellers, 1989).

In the sections that follow, we outline the details of our web-based course, including its technical characteristics, organization, structure, clinical content, and the various measures and methods that we are using to evaluate its efficacy. Next, we outline several adjunctive strategies that can accompany the web-based educational intervention and may be necessary to address the intrapersonal, interpersonal, organizational and systematic barriers that can prevent changes in actual clinical practice. Finally, we discuss future directions and other ways that web-based education may prove useful in disseminating evidence-based practices in human service delivery settings.

COURSE DESCRIPTION

Overview

The authors have developed a self-paced, interactive course which closely follows the step-by-step decision tree outlined by the authors of the Department of Veterans Affairs/Department of Defense Clinical Practice Guideline for the Management of Substance Use Disorders (VHA/DoD, 2001). Although the entire CPG is quite voluminous, our course focuses exclusively on several key recommendations made in the guideline regarding the detection, assessment and prevention of Alcohol Withdrawal in medical and surgical patients. Learners follow a case study depicting a nurse and patient going through the series of decisions and actions that are recommended in the guideline. The course begins with the patient's initial admission to the hospital, through an assessment of intoxication using a breathalyzer, and includes step-by-step instruction in the administration and coding of the Clinical Institute for Withdrawal Assessment–Alcohol, Revised [CIWA-Ar, c.f. (Sullivan et al., 1989)], which is a 10-item objective measure of patient's risk of developing Alcohol Withdrawal Syndrome. The interface was designed around a "course map" that closely resembles the CPG algorithm. Clicking on any of the symbols in this map takes the user to the corresponding module. See Figure 1 to view the course map or access it online at www.detoxguideline.org.

Design and Development

This course was built in collaboration with graduate students from the San Jose State University Department of Instructional Technology. Four masters-level practicum students worked with the CourseBuilder extension to Macromedia's Dreamweaver 4.0 development platform to generate basic HTML pages for the course. The photographic case study sequences were produced with the help of a professional producer, a photographer and actors at a location provided with the assistance of the Greater Los Angeles VA Health Care System. Photographic sequences with subtitles, as well as several other animated sequences, were optimized in Adobe Photoshop 6.0 and Macromedia Fireworks 4.0, with the final version presented using Macromedia Flash 5.0.

Design and development of the web-based course began in January, 2002, and was completed in August, 2002. The course has been subjected to periodic technical testing and content review throughout its development. Informal beta testing was conducted internally, with approximately 15 individuals providing detailed feedback. Beta testing and feedback was also provided by the practicum students and their classmates, who reviewed the course as part of their internship requirement. Content level review was provided by subject matter experts to ensure that the course adhered to both the word and spirit of the original guideline document. Finally, and perhaps most importantly, the course was reviewed by a group of 16 medical and surgical nurses at the VA Puget Sound Health Care System who provided initial, formative feedback on the content design, usability and practical relevance of the course.

An innovative aspect of our web-based course is that it incorporates a "Quick Reference" feature that was always available to the learner through a link on the left bar. Our Quick Reference feature was designed to serve as an Electronic Performance Support System [(c.f. (Gery, 1991)]. Whereas traditional web-based courses are designed to teach the learner a particular set of facts or skills that must be memorized and later recalled, an Electronic Performance Support System is designed to provide just enough information to get the job done. The Electronic Performance Support System was geared towards health care providers who are naïve about the guidelines for the management of AWS. This support system was designed to exist independent of the web-based course. Consequently, the learner can quickly find answers to frequently asked questions about AWS without having to find the content in the course itself. As a result of its relative ease of use, the course has been approved to provide Continuing Medical Education credit within the VA system.

Pedagogical Approach

While an asynchronous Web-Based Training course is largely considered to be an instructivist strategy, the present course also contains several constructivist elements. For instance, the integration of a realistic case study throughout the course is consistent with many constructivist design principles. Jonassen (1994), a well known proponent of constructivist theory, highlights many of the advantages that may accrue from this approach. For example, the case study presentation provides learners with authentic tasks embedded within a real-world case-based learning environment. Honebein (1996) also highlights the importance of embedding learning in a realistic and relevant context. In our course, features such as the Electronic Performance Support System and the course map serve to maximize learner control, a concept that is central to the constructivist approach (Wilson & Cole, 1991).

We believe that the use of both instructivist and constructivist elements has advantages over the use of a single model. An instructivist approach allows for individuals with small amounts of time (such as busy medical staff) to identify and access relevant material in a relatively short time, while simultaneously addressing the needs of individuals who have time to engage with the material in more detail. A constructivist approach contributes to the transfer of training through the use of realistic and job relevant tasks. The instructivist approach stresses the problem solving aspects of instructional design and allows for an accurate assessment of learning objectives (knowledge transfer), while the constructivist approach is learner centered and emphasizes the process, rather than the product of learning. We contend that a blending of these models will result in maximum learner benefit.

Student Learning Objectives

Each step on the decision tree represents a module of the course, and each module is designed around a single student performance objective. Participants proceed step-by-step to determine a patient's level of intoxication and/or physiological dependence at the time of admission, assessment of the signs and symptoms of AWS, categorization of patient into inpatient or outpatient detoxification, and, finally, assessment of the success of detoxification.

Target Audience

Our target audience are members of hospital nursing staff who work on inpatient general medicine and surgery units. Staff members who work in settings that provide specialized treatment services for detoxification or substance use disorders will not be included in the sample. The rationale for focusing on general practitioners is that they typically have less training in the detection and management of AWS than staff of acute psychiatry and detoxification units, hence deriving more benefit than participants recruited from practice settings where staff are more likely to have received such training.

OUTCOME MEASURES

Our measures fall into four general categories (1) Measures of exposure to the intervention, (2) Measures of learning, (3) Measures of knowledge and skill transfer, and (4) Measures of patient-level and systems-level outcomes (see Figure 2). These categories roughly correspond to the four-level model of training evaluation developed by Donald Kirkpatrick during the late 1950s (Kirkpatrick, 1959a; 1959b; 1960a; 1960b).

1. Measures of Exposure to the Intervention

Measures in this category indicate whether participants actually received the intervention as intended. Because participants are assigned a unique password and subject identifier, we can track how much time they spend viewing the course material overall, as well as how much time they spend on specific presentations and interactive activities within the course. Using web tracking software, we will also track which part of the Electronic Performance Support System features they access, and for how long. Participants will also be required to take a pre-test when they first access the online materials, and a post-test once they complete the course.

2. Measures of Learning

A Level II evaluation assesses the extent to which students have learned new skills, knowledge, or abilities as the result of an intervention. The difference between scores on a test administered before and after the online intervention (pre- and post-test) serves as our measure of learning. Ten multiple choice items on this pre- and post-test will as-

FIGURE 2

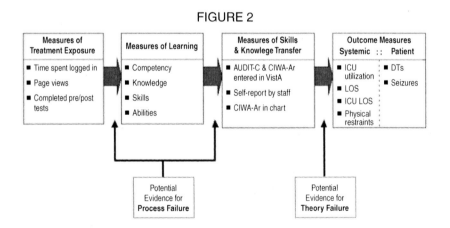

sess participants. Assessment questions cover such topics as knowledge of the signs and symptoms of alcohol withdrawal, the CIWA-Ar scales and scoring conventions, and the American Society for Addiction Medicine patient placement criteria for detoxification.

3. Measures of Knowledge and Skill Transfer

Measures in this category indicate the degree to which participants who were exposed to the intervention actually change their clinical practice behavior in accordance with the recommendations of the CPG. On the Kirkpatrick scale, this would constitute a Level III Evaluation, which measures the knowledge and skills transfers into changes in behavior (i.e., the extent to which the learner's behaviors changed due to the training program). It attempts to answer the question–Are the newly acquired skills, knowledge, or aptitudes being used in the everyday environment of the learner?

The primary measure of knowledge or skills transfer is the incidence of screening for AWS risk using the CIWA-Ar. The CIWA-Ar is a valid and reliable 10 item scale for clinical quantification of the severity of AWS which has successfully been incorporated into the usual clinical care of patients undergoing alcohol withdrawal (Schumacher, Pruit, & Phillips, 2000). An increase in the rate of CIWA-Ar administration following training would indicate that practitioners are changing their behavior in response to our web-based educational intervention. We are currently collaborating closely with our Information Technology staff to implement a template for the CIWA-Ar in the VA's Computerized Patient Record System. By so doing, we hope to facilitate both the collection of this data by nursing staff, and the periodic reporting of this data as a measure of guideline concordance.

4. Measures of Patient-Level and Systems-Level Outcomes

Because our course is being evaluated in the context of a health services research project within the Department of Veterans Affairs, we have the good fortune of having access to administrative databases that automatically track a wide variety of patient-level variables. These are patient outcomes that we expect to be affected by our intervention, and include (1) Intensive Care Unit admission and readmission, (2) Intensive Care Unit Length of Stay, and (3) Overall in-hospital length of stay. Measures 1-3 will be obtained from national VA administrative databases, and will be compared for patients treated by nurses who received the intervention versus those who did not. We expect patients who are treated by nurses who receive the intervention will experience Alcohol Withdrawal Syndrome less frequently, and consequently will require fewer trips to the Intensive Care Unit, and shorter time spent in the hospital.

PILOT STUDY RESULTS

Our web-based course was recently used as an integral part of training nursing staff to administer the CIWA-Ar at the VA Puget Sound Health Care System. Participants met together in a conference room and KRW spent approximately one hour showing nurses the online course, which focused predominately on use of the CIWA-Ar to assess the signs and symptoms of withdrawal. Sixteen attended the training and evaluation session over the course of two days.

All participants filled out a pre- and post-test, and a course evaluation form. Initial reactions to the online intervention were overwhelmingly positive. Using a 5 point rating scale (where 1 is "poor" and 5 is "excellent"), respondents were asked to rate the usefulness and appropriateness of course content, the reality and presentation of the case study information, and design features such as, logical presentation of content and use of graphics and color. Mean ratings for all ten evaluation items ranged from 4.25 to 4.63, with no items rated below a 4. The 100% of pilot study participants agreed strongly with the statement, "I like that I can review the material contained in this online program at my own pace at any time," and 100% of participants expressed a strong interest in taking such an online course for Continuing Medical Education credit. In fact, the course is now offered for Continuing Medical Education credit within the VA system. When given the opportunity to provide open-ended feedback, one nurse indicated that she thought the course was "very comprehensive," and another wrote "Realistic case study, easy to navigate, I love the online ease and availability." Finally, a comparison of pre- and post-test scores indicated that exposure to the course may result in significant improvements in knowledge about the standardized assessment of the signs and symptoms of AWS. Among those who have already completed the course, post-test scores tend to be higher than pre-test scores. Although this trend is not yet statistically significant, it may well reach that level once more learners have completed the course and more data is available for analysis.

DISCUSSION

Web-Based Education Alone Is not Enough
to Narrow the Research Practice Gap

While successful knowledge transfer such as that achieved with our Web-Based course is a necessary precondition for translating research into practice, such a narrow educational approach when used alone is unlikely to effect enduring changes in clinical practice. In fact, the empirical literature on guideline implementation in medicine has clearly demonstrated that interventions designed to change clinical practice are much more likely to be successful when they combine multiple approaches (Grol, 2001; Shaneyfelt, 2001).

Approaches to changing clinical practice can be classified within one of two general categories: approaches that focus on factors *internal* to the clinician, and those that focus on factors *external* to the clinician (c.f. (Weingardt, in press), (Grol, 1997, 2001; Grol & Grimshaw, 1999). Strategies belonging to the first category attempt to change clinical practice by influencing the *internal* cognitive and affective processes of the individual practitioner. This would include marketing strategies that focus on developing an attractive product adapted to the needs of the target audience, for example disseminating brochures or other promotional materials designed to raise practitioners' awareness of a change initiative. Educational approaches themselves fall into this category as well, as they focus on changing the internal cognitive processes of the learner by providing instruction regarding new knowledge and skills.

The second category of strategies that focuses on factors *external* to the clinician can serve as powerful complements to internally-focused approaches such as web-based education. To be maximally effective, a web-based educational intervention could be embedded in a larger intervention focused on external, systemic influences. For example, we plan to embed our Preventing Alcohol Withdrawal web-based course within a larger organizational intervention that we refer to as a Guideline Implementation Group. The structure and process of this group is roughly analogous to what the Organizational Development literature refers to as a Process Action Team (French & Bell, 1999; Kinlaw, 1992). These groups will consist of key facility stakeholders, including representatives of the Chief of Staff's office, medical and surgical nurses and nurse managers, and Information Technology staff. This group will meet regularly in order to (a) document existing processes of care with regard to the prevention and management of AWS, (b) identify the barriers (interpersonal, social, and organizational) that might prevent nurses from routinely screening patients for risk of withdrawal, and (c) developing a concrete plan to overcome these barriers and to ensure that the web-based educational intervention is successfully completed by all nursing staff.

Another externally-oriented approach in our effort to increase rates of screening for AWS, is to work closely with Information Technology staff to complete the development of an electronic clinical reminder for the CIWA-Ar screening measure using the VA's Computerized Patient Record System. If a patient screens positive for recent and/or excessive alcohol consumption, a template will automatically pop up on the nurse's desktop reminding him or her to conduct the screening, and providing a convenient way to easily enter the resulting data. This type of approach to practice change could be considered *organizational*, in that the focus is on creating structural and organizational conditions to improve care, as well as *behavioral* in that it focuses on reinforcing the desired performance.

FUTURE DIRECTIONS

Although this article focuses predominately on the role of asynchronous web-based training in the dissemination and implementation of clinical practice guidelines, there are many other innovative, and as yet unexplored, roles that web-based education might play in the process of translating human services research into practice. Such potential roles may include the use of asynchronous web-based training in the dissemination of empirically-supported, manual-based therapies and the use of synchronous e-Learning platforms for a variety of clinical training applications.

Synchronous Web-Based Education for Clinical Training

"Synchronous e-Learning" is a term describing a real-time, instructor-led learning event in which the instructor and all learners are logged on at the same time and communicate directly with each other, but are not physically present at the same location (Weingardt, in press). Synchronous e-Learning platforms are often referred to as virtual classrooms or web-conferences, and commercial versions are currently being offered by companies such as Placeware, WebEx, Interwise and Hewlett Packard.

One way in which these synchronous platforms could be leveraged for clinical training is to use them to facilitate case observation and real-time clinical supervision. For example, a web-cam in the therapy room could be used to transmit a live audio and video stream of the interaction between a trainee who is learning an empirically-supported treatment and his or her client, to a clinical supervisor down the hall or anywhere else she or he has broadband internet access. Another potential application is for group supervision or training workshops. In this scenario, a clinical expert would be able to meet virtually with a group of geographically dispersed trainees to provide supervision and feedback regarding the implementation of an empirically supported treatment in their practice setting. Immediately following the implementation of the WBT, participants will be invited to attend a follow-up Virtual Classroom presentation where they can ask questions of clinical experts and the guidelines working group, interact in real time with their fellow physician-participants, and discuss the challenges of implementing the guidelines in their own practice settings.

CONCLUSION

The potential role of web-based education in narrowing the gap between research and clinical practice may be quite substantial (Weingardt, in press). Powerful authoring tools make it increasingly feasible and cost-effective to transform the content of Clinical Practice Guidelines and Manual Based Therapies into interactive and engaging web-based training applications. Such applications may increase the accessibility of empirically-supported treatments to clinicians, which may in turn increase the rate at which clinicians choose to adopt research-based recommendations into their daily practice. Although it is important to acknowledge the interpersonal, intrapersonal and organizational barriers that may prevent rapid changes in clinical practice, it seems likely that web-education, both asynchronous and synchronous, will play an increasingly important role in the future.

REFERENCES

APA. (2002). American Psychiatric Association Practice guideline for the treatment of patients with substance use disorders: Alcohol, cocaine, opioids. In J. S. C. McIntyre (Ed.), *American Psychiatric Association Practice Guidelines for the Treatment of Psychiatric Disorders, Compendium 2002.* Washington, DC: American Psychiatric Association.

French, W. L., & Bell, C. H. (1999). *Organizational Development: Behavioral Science Interventions for Organization Improvement, Sixth Edition.* Upper Saddle River, NJ: Prentice Hall.

Gery, G. (1991). *Electronic Performance Support Systems*. Tolland, MA: Gery Associates.

Grol, R. (1997). Beliefs and evidence in changing clinical practice. *British Medical Journal, 315*, 418-421.

Grol, R. (2001). Improving the quality of medical care: Building bridges among professional pride, payer profit and patient satisfaction. *Journal of the American Medical Association, 286*(2), 2578-2601.

Grol, R., & Grimshaw, J. (1999). Evidence-based implementation of evidence-based medicine. *The Joint Commission Journal on Quality Improvement, 25*(10), 503-513.

Honebein, P. (1996). Seven goals of the design of Constructivist learning environments. In Wilson, B. (Ed.), *Constructivist Learning Environments*, 17-24, New Jersey: Educational Technology Publications.

Institute of Medicine (1990). *Clinical Practice Guidelines: Directions for a New Program*. Washington, DC: National Academy Press.

Institute of Medicine (1992). *Guidelines for Clinical Practice: From Development to Use*. Washington, DC: National Academy Press.

Jonassen, D. H. (1994). Thinking technology: Towards a constructivist design model. *Educational Technology*, 34(4), 34-37.

Kinlaw, D. C. (1992). *Continuous improvement and measurement for total quality: A team-based approach*. San Diego: Pfeiffer & Co.

Lamb, S., & Greenlick, M. R. (Eds.). (1998). *Bridging the gap between practice and research: Forging partnerships with community-based drug and alcohol treatment*. Washington, DC: National Academy Press.

Minkoff, K., & Cline, C. A. (2003). The missing link between science and service. *Psychiatric Services, 54*(3), 275.

NIAAA. (2001). *Adoption of Alcohol Research Findings in Clinical Practice* (Program Announcement PA-01-058). Bethesda, MD: National Institute on Alcohol Abuse and Alcoholism.

NIDA. (2003). *Behavioral Therapies Development Program* (Program Announcement PA-03-066). Bethesda, MD: National Institute of Drug Abuse.

NIMH. (2003). Dissemination and Implementation Research in Mental Health. PA-02-131.

NYS Education Department (2002, 10/29/03). *Social Work Practice Guideline* [Web Site]. Office of Professions. Retrieved 01-21-04, 2004, from the World Wide Web: http://www.op.nysed.gov/cswguides.htm.

Rogers, E. M. (1995). *Diffusion of Innovations* (4th ed.). New York: Free Press.

Shaneyfelt, T. M. (2001). Building bridges to quality, Editorial. *Journal of the American Medical Association, 286*(20), 2600-2601.

Spies, C. D., & Rommelspacher, H. (1999). Alcohol withdrawal in the surgical patient: Prevention and treatment. *Anesthesia and Analgesia, 88*, 946-954.

Sullivan, J. T., Sykora, K., Schneiderman, J., Naranjo, C. A., & Sellers, E. M. (1989). Assessment of Alcohol Withdrawal: The revised clinical institute withdrawal assessment for alcohol scale (CIWA-Ar). *British Journal of Addiction, 84*, 1353-1357.

Van Arminge, M., & Shannon, T. E. (1992). Awareness, assimilation and adoption: The challenge of effective dissemination and the first AHCPR-Sponsored Guidelines. *Quality Review Bulletin, Dec. 1992*, 397-404.

VHA/DoD. (2001, April 2001). *VHA/DoD Clinical Practice Guideline for the Assessment and Management of Substance Use Disorders in Primary and Specialty Care* [Download from website]. The Management of Substance Use Disorders Working Group. Retrieved September 12, 2002, 2002, from the World Wide Web: http://www.oqp.med.va.gov/cpg/SUD/SUD_CPG/frameset.htm.

Wartenberg, A. A., Nirenberg, T. D., Liepman, M. R., Silvia, L. Y., Begin, A. M., & Monti, P. M. (1990). Detoxification of alcoholics: Improving care by symptom-triggered sedation. *Alcoholism: Clinical and Experimental Research.*

Weingardt, K. R. (in press). The role of instructional design and technology in the dissemination of empirically-supported, manual-based therapies. *Clinical Psychology: Science and Practice.*

Wilson, B., & Cole, P. (1991). A review of cognitive teaching models. *Educational Technology Research and Development, 39*(4), 47-64.

Working Across
the Disciplines/Shifting Perspectives:
Student Experiences with an Online Course
Focused on Interdisciplinary Practice
with Children and Families

Patricia A. MacKenzie, PhD
Dora Leigh Bjornson

SUMMARY. As more universities and other places of higher learning respond to the changing needs of the community-bound learner, new technologies are being harnessed to shift the delivery of historically "classroom-bound" programs to alternate and more universally accessible formats. This article describes how an online course uses interactive exercises to engage students in mutual exploration of cross and/or interdisciplinary work. The course serves students from various professional schools, including social work, child and youth care, nursing, and education. Through the use of online discussion and case-study role-plays, it fa-

Patricia A. MacKenzie, PhD, is Associate Professor and Dora Leigh Bjornson is Program Director of Distance Education at the University of Victoria School of Social Work.

Address correspondence to: Patricia A. MacKenzie, PhD, University of Victoria, School of Social Work, P.O. Box 1700, STN CSC, Victoria, B.C. V8W 2Y2.

[Haworth co-indexing entry note]: "Working Across the Disciplines/Shifting Perspectives: Student Experiences with an Online Course Focused on Interdisciplinary Practice with Children and Families." MacKenzie, Patricia A., and Dora Leigh Bjornson. Co-published simultaneously in *Journal of Technology in Human Services* (The Haworth Press, Inc.) Vol. 23, No. 3/4, 2005, pp. 275-298; and: *Web-Based Education in the Human Services: Models, Methods, and Best Practices* (eds: MacFadden et al.) The Haworth Press, Inc., 2005, pp. 275-298. Single or multiple copies of this article are available for a fee from The Haworth Document Delivery Service [1-800-HAWORTH, 9:00 a.m. - 5:00 p.m. (EST). E-mail address: docdelivery@ haworthpress.com].

Available online at http://www.haworthpress.com/web/JTHS
Digital Object Identifier: 10.1300/J017v023n03_08

cilitates an experiential learning environment that is reflective of the student's own practice in a learning setting. *[Article copies available for a fee from The Haworth Document Delivery Service: 1-800-HAWORTH. E-mail address: <docdelivery@haworthpress.com> Website: <http://www.HaworthPress.com> © 2005 by The Haworth Press, Inc. All rights reserved.]*

KEYWORDS. Distance learning, social work education, online courses, web-based education, instructional technology

INTRODUCTION

This article will describe how an online course used interactive exercises to engage students in mutual exploration of cross and/or interdisciplinary work. The Faculty of Human and Social Development at the University of Victoria has a large distance education program to accommodate a geographically distributed student body. More than 65% of students enrolled in the Faculty's Schools of Social Work, Child and Youth Care, and Nursing select distance education as their method of baccalaureate degree completion. Faculty from these three professional schools within the Faculty of Human and Social Development, in consultation with several BSW and Human Service programs across the province of British Columbia, worked together to develop a thirteen week, 1.5 unit credit course Human and Social Development 465: Interdisciplinary Practice with Children and Families (HSD 465). The course was written by one of the authors (MacKenzie) and designed for distance education delivery using a fully integrated WebCT format. The course is delivered using WebCT with the course website providing the sole teaching/learning platform. In addition to the course website, print-based materials (a collection of readings and a student study guide) are produced and delivered via WebCt to support student learning.

LITERATURE REVIEW

As more universities and other places of higher learning respond to the changing needs of the community-bound learner, new technologies are being harnessed to shift the delivery of historically "classroombound" programs to alternate and more universally accessible formats. Most human service practitioners believe that students should be exposed to education programs with a technological delivery (Abell and Galinsky, 2002). There is a groundswell of support for the potential of communication technologies to provide online learning environments that enhance the teamwork skills of learners and respond to the shifting realities of professional human service practice (McLoughlin and Luca, 2002). Increasingly, the literature on computer-mediated learning promises that these new technologies offer improved capacity to create courses designed to facilitate a collaborative approach to learning where individuals from varied backgrounds and disciplines come together to pool collective knowledge and develop a new kind of teamwork practice (McLoughlin, 2000). This is not to say that computer-mediated courses do not have potential pitfalls. Making an assessment of exactly what is occurring "in the moment" in a classroom that operates a "virtual community" is very difficult. There are emerging methodological approaches that may hold the promise of how such virtual classrooms can be analyzed and better understood (Kinnevy and Enosh, 2002).

Human service education in the field of social work, nursing, child and youth care, and education has experienced a profound transformation over the past decade. A significant body of literature demonstrates that delivery of these professional programs via distance education modalities is being demanded by community-bound learners, and that student-student and student-instructor interaction is essential to student satisfaction and overall program success (Randolph and Krause, 2002). The interactivity and connection with others that is built into online courses is valued by human service practitioners who expect more dialogue between students and between students and instructors (Khan, 1997). Online courses need to be well designed with clear guidelines for learners to follow and with the understanding that the teacher shifts a role from "sage on the stage" to "guide on the side" (Reeves and Reeves, 1997). Other research has shown that embedding theoretical material into a practice-based and problem-oriented learning strategy increases the accessibility of human service education programs and are likely to bring about substantially greater learning success than those who do not (Ouellette, 2000). Many disciplines within the human service field frequently conduct important work in a group setting with other disciplines. Yet, there is little opportunity in many human service educational programs to learn alongside other disciplines while a student (Lewis, Garcia, and Hallock, 2002).

This paper will describe the development of an online course on interdisciplinary practice that is designed to provide such learning opportunities. Interdisciplinary practice relies on multiple perspectives and is based on professionals drawing on the experiences and knowledge of one another. To work in an interdisciplinary setting the practitioner must have a clear understanding of their own discipline and an appreciation of the contribution of others, including the perspective of the client. The interdisciplinary practitioner requires effective communication skills, the ability to think critically and to be continuously reflective on one's own practice. Since this course was developed to prepare students for such professional practice roles, the course is structured to assist students to apply theoretical course material to practice. As such, the course attempts to simulate interdisciplinary practice settings. When students engage in the case based role plays, they are expected to be familiar and articulate about their own disciplinary perspective. The role plays allow students to demonstrate effective communication skills by engaging in interactive online discussions with fellow students in the online groups.

TARGET AUDIENCE:
THE LEARNERS

Most of the students who enroll in this course reside outside of the University of Victoria's main campus region. However, students who live within the greater Victoria area also register since this particular course in not offered in a traditional classroom setting. There is no face-to-face interaction in this course although traditional telephone consultation between instructor and students does occur. All online activities that are moderated are asynchronous. Efforts to have students access the chat room function of WebCT in the initial offering of the course led to frustration due to the insufficient capabilities of the computer systems used by many students. As a result, the chat room function of WebCT has not been used for more recent offerings of the course. However, it has been our experience that while it is not a requirement of the course, students often prefer to talk with each other "in the moment" and will independently pursue opportunities for "synchronous conversation." They do this by either arranging to speak with each other by telephone or by coordinating face-to-face meetings. A unique aspect of the course is the intentional design of "mixing" students from various programs and academic disciplines within the same section of the course. Students are divided into small study groups that intentionally place them with students from other disciplines as well as from different geographical locations. The small groups work together throughout the course to develop interdisciplinary responses to practice-based scenarios and inter-professional practice questions. Students from various disciplines register for this course as no similar course exists within each discipline. As a result, students from various professional schools and programs come together to share the same "virtual classroom" space. In this space, students from various disciplines work together to:

- define and develop an understanding of their own discipline
- explore the concepts of interdisciplinary practice
- gain a common understanding of factors that contribute to effective interdisciplinary practice with children and families
- become familiar with child welfare legislation, the child protection process, and the organizational context of working with children and families.

Delivery, Support, Resources, and Administrative Infrastructures

Human and Social Development 465: Interdisciplinary Perspectives on Working with Children and Families (HSD 465) is delivered over a single thirteen-week semester, and is offered twice a year. It carries 1.5 units of credit and would constitute 20 percent of a typical full-time single-semester course load for a student at the University of Victoria. The median class size has been 29 students for the sections of the course offered to date. The average drop rate of 8.5% is comparable to the 10% average drop rate for other courses offered within the Faculty (see Table 1). The median grade for students completing HSD 465 is 77% or a "B" grade. This grade is considered to be the average grade achieved by students in the program.

Extraordinary delivery costs for this course are minimal, as the budget for the instructor stipend, technical support staff and WebCT platform are part of the University of Victoria's infrastructure for distance education. The University of Victoria has a dedicated server for WebCT courses, with WebCT Version 3.8 (campus edition) as the course management software currently supported. Its Computing User Services offer tutorials, workshops, instructional web pages, and individual consultation to assist faculty and staff members in becoming proficient with computers and various instructional technologies. The University of Victoria also provides key support for distance education course development and delivery through its Online/Distance Education Services Group. This department offers technical and learning support to web-based students via the Online Help Website, e-mail,

TABLE 1. Drop Rates for HSD 465 2001 to 2003

2001 Winter		
	Section 50	32 students completed of the 35 registered
	Section 51	11 students completed of the 15 registered
	Section 52	21 students completed of the 25 registered
2002 Winter		
	Section 50	18 students completed of the 19 registered
	Section 51	34 students completed of the 38 registered
	Section 52	26 students completed of the 28 registered
2003 Winter		
	Section 50	32 students completed of the 33 registered
	Section 51	29 students completed of the 30 registered

Total of 259 registrations, with 237 students (91.5%) completing course

and telephone service, which is staffed for extended hours, six days a week. In addition, each program within the Faculty of Human and Social Development assigns responsibility for the delivery and overseeing of the WebCT courses to their respective Distance Education Program Directors. Ongoing administrative support is provided to both students and instructors by the distance education Office and Technical staff in each respective School.

COURSE CONTENT AND LEARNING ENVIRONMENT

This course was specifically designed to help students in three professional schools within the Faculty of Human and Social Development acquire the theoretical and practical foundations that are required to meet the core practice competencies for Child Welfare Workers as identified by British Columbia's Ministry of Children and Family Development. These competencies can be found on the Ministry website.[1] The course is a requirement for those pursuing the University of Victoria's Child Welfare specialization designation on their BSW or BA (Child and Youth Care) degrees. Students from other disciplines are also interested in the course due to growing awareness of the importance of being prepared for the interdisciplinary nature of most human service practice settings. As a result, the course has been well subscribed by students who are not necessarily pursuing a child welfare career path. Students from within the Faculty of Human and Social Development as well as those from other related programs (e.g., Education, Dispute Resolution, Psychology and Sociology) may also take the course as an elective credit.

The course takes places in the "virtual classroom" of an online environment and was designed for distance delivery using a Web Course Tools (WebCT) interface. WebCT is a course management system that provides a set of functions and tools for creating and facilitating web-based learning environments. There was no face-to-face involvement between the instructor and students or between students in this course design. The interdisciplinary nature of the course influences the content, the delivery methods, and learning process experienced by students. The web-based learning activities in this course are designed to be interactive and to illustrate how practice with children and families benefits from an interdisciplinary perspective and collaborative practice strategies. Students are expected to use previous knowledge in their own specific discipline to explore core issues related to child and family life such as early intervention, family relationships, child welfare, child development, social policy and education. However, as the overall goal of the course is to prepare students to understand the interdisciplinary nature of human service practice, students experience working across disciplinary boundaries by engaging with students from other disciplines in online interactive exercises. A list of the course objectives are provided in Appendix 1.

The course website contains links to websites of interest, detailed notes covering core themes and explicit directions on how to participate in the online course and online discussion groups. The content on the course website is supplemented by of a selection of readings available in a print package, This print package further exposes students to a range of disciplinary perspectives on working with children and families, the history of various disciplines, and key concepts in collaborative practice. Each unit explores a particular aspect of the theoretical foundations of interdisciplinary practice and links each interactive online exercise back to the guiding principles of collaborative practice strategies.

As a fully integrated WebCT course, the only learning/teaching platforms available to students and the instructor were the tools available on the WebCT course site. The primary tools utilized in this course centred around facilitation of asynchronous online discussion and activities. The emphasis on an asynchronous virtual classroom served a number of purposes: (1) with students participating from across Canada, an asynchronous environment removed barriers that a time difference of up to 4.5 hours would bring if the course was delivered in real-time. (2) most students of the University of Victoria Faculty of Human and Social Development professional schools are employed and/or carrying family responsibilities, therefore the opportunity to participate within a more flexible timeframe allows the coursework to fit within most student schedules. (3) it does not apply the pressure of real-time response as would be the case in a "chat room" type of environment. Instead, students have time and opportunity to reflect on the subject at hand and consider their response before posting to the class. Responses posted by students to the course site are most often well-written, and of a high academic quality. The four discussion tools featured in HSD 465 include:

1. asynchronous discussion on "Main Discussion Board" used for online asynchronous communication between the instructor and all students.
2. several asynchronous "Small Group Discussion Topics" used for online communication between 5 to 7 students assigned to each small group and between instructor and these small groups. Only the instructor and the students within each small group have access to their own "Small Group Discussion Topics." Two example topics are: "examine the relationship of gender and ethnicity to the group's understanding of the problems faced by this family" and "discuss how your group came to consensus around which discipline would take the lead in initiating requests for additional information from the family."
3. course-specific private e-mail messaging used for online communication either between the instructor and an individual student, or between students.
4. the "Social Café" is an unstructured discussion topics tool that provides a more casual space for student to student communication. The Social Café is used primarily for informal social exchanges between students and differs from a regular discussion forum in that it is optional, has little structure and is not a moderated space. On occasion, students use the Social Café to share ideas for assignments, compare notes about their respective role plays and to have general unstructured discussion about the course format. While the instructor has access to the Social Café, discussion is intended to be entirely student-driven and is not moderated by the instructor.

COURSE ASSIGNMENTS

There are three main assignments in the course:

1. *Reflective Journal.* The reflective journal is submitted by students after completion of the fifth unit and again following completion of the final unit. It is worth 40% of the overall course grade. The goal of the journal was to prompt integration of the student's views of the readings and web material/activities with their own experiences, biases, and knowledge of interdisciplinary practice. The instructor assesses the journal to determine if the student's understanding of course readings and their ability to make their own critical inquiry of the course material is comprehensive.

2. *Online Participation in Interactive Role-Plays.* The overall goals of the role play component are to (a) assist students in the development of skills required to participate and lead discussion around the values, tensions, questions, and strategies embedded in interdisciplinary theory and practice, (b) build on students' understanding of working to consensus, and (c) reflect on how discipline specific goals and objectives influence teamwork. Interactive role plays comprises 30% of the overall course grade and is constructed around the students' participation in and subsequent discussion of these interactive exercises. The timing of the online discussion/interactive role-plays is woven throughout twelve weeks of the course and is based primarily on the content of 6 of the 13 course units. These particular units placed emphasis on increasing students' understanding of the characteristics and complexities of interdisciplinary practice by actually engaging in the structured role-plays and later debriefing them with other members of their small group and the instructor. The debriefing is facilitated by the instructor posing a series of questions after reviewing each small group's final summary. These questions are structured around the process elements of the group work and asks the students to again use the Small Group Discussion Topics to post and respond to questions that focus on process (e.g., "how" decisions were taken) rather than content (e.g., "what" the decisions were).

3. *Summary Paper–The Personal Practice Framework.* In this 5000 word summary essay, students are asked to reflect on their experiences of the course. The assignment is worth 40% of the overall course grade and is designed to provide a means for students to:

(a) demonstrate their understanding of interdisciplinary practice, (b) make deeper integrative connections between the influences of their disciplinary knowledge and interdisciplinary practice, and (c) reflect on what they learned about themselves and others during the interactive role-plays and other group work. In addition, students must define and describe their own personal practice framework for interdisciplinary practice and reflect on how this framework will contribute to their current or future work with children and families. Students are also expected to summarize what they learned about organizational practices, values, ethics, child welfare legislation, and the child protection process. From this reflection, they are invited to generate a list of what they felt were key characteristics, supports, and barriers of interdisciplinary practice and to make a statement of what they will contribute in the future to support interdisciplinary and collaborative practice.

The Learning Process

The WebCT based course presents materials in such a way as to facilitate an experiential learning process. This experiential learning begins at the start of the course when students are divided into small discussion groups of 5 to 7 students. Students stay in the same small group for the duration of the course and the majority of the interactive exercises are conducted within this small group setting. The first online interactive activities are designed to gently introduce the students to the course and to each other. The first online exercise asks students to post information about themselves under the "Introductions" Discussion topic on the course website. The second online exercise poses a preliminary set of questions about interdisciplinary practice and asks students to post a few lines to their classmates about their previous experience with interdisciplinary practice. These online conversations occur during the first two weeks of the course and serve the following functions:

- provide an opportunity for students to become familiar with the WebCT environment and help to lessen any preliminary anxieties they might have about working online,
- encourage students to share information with each other about their personal and professional backgrounds. Students find this exchange of information to be interesting and introducing the backgrounds that students bring to the course acknowledges their wisdom

- ask students to reflect on their current or previous experiences with interdisciplinary and/or uni-disciplinary work and to share these perspectives with other members of their small group.

In the required posting of an introductory message, students provide information that assists the instructor in the formation of small groups of five or six students that reflect a balance of experience, background, and discipline. Students are also prompted to engage in discussion within their small group informally via WebCT e-mail, as a means of preparing for upcoming task-based group activities.

Two types of WebCT Discussion Tools are used by students to engage with each other in the two different sets of online interactive exercises. One set of interactive exercise requires students to post written text in response to sets of questions based on the course readings and material that outline the principles of interdisciplinary practice. The online interaction within small groups begins when a student first posts a written response to the set of questions that are on the course site on the Small Group Discussions Topic page. Other students then join in and either post their own views on the questions or respond/add to postings of other students. After the exchange of several postings, one student from the group assumes the role of synthesizer and summarizes the collective work of the small group, posting that summary to the Main Discussion Topics page for all students in the course to view online.

Students also use the Small Group Discussion Topics to engage in the another set of interactive exercises. The second set involves students in participating in online role-plays. The role-plays were written by the instructor to simulate a case-based interdisciplinary team meeting. For these online exercises, the small groups that have been discussing specific questions on course material within the Small Group Discussions Topic are re-configured into an interdisciplinary "team." The task for each "team" is to design a team response to particular practice (clinical) situations involving children and families. Students are sent a private e-mail by the instructor that provides them with a written description of a particular team role (for example, as a discipline specific practitioner or "client"). From this e-mail, students are expected to gather information about the scope of the practitioner's practice, determine what the relationship of that particular practitioner would be to the case situation and prepare to engage in the role-play online. The online role-play within small groups begins when a student first posts a response to the Small Group Discussion Topics which "opens" the interdisciplinary team meeting. Other students then join in with their own discipline-specific (or "client" view) information and objectives by posting their own views on the questions or responding/adding to postings of other students. After the exchange of several postings, one student from the group assumes the role of synthesizer and summarizes the interdisciplinary team work plan and/or recommendations for action. That summary is posted to the Main Discussion Topics page for all students in the course to view online. Throughout the course, students take turns in assuming responsibility for synthesizing, summarizing and posting the small group work. Along with details pertaining to each of the case-based scenarios, the instructor e-mails a series of questions related to the role-play, suggests supplementary readings, and provides discussion prompts for students to use in their reflective journaling (see Appendix for an example). These are assigned either immediately, prior to, or within the timeframe of each asynchronous group discussion and serve to focus connection of specific core concepts to the case study.

Students also work on their own during the term. They are expected to explore the theoretical course material by doing the readings, examining website material, and reflecting on this content by responding via e-mail to a set of questions that are posted periodically on the website by the instructor. Students are also invited to add their own thoughts on both course content and group process by keeping an electronic version of a reflective journal. The reflective journal is essentially a word-processing document that students maintain on their own computer system. Students submit this document to the instructor at the end of Week 5 and Week 13 of the course by sending it as an attachment to a private e-mail to the instructor. The instructor reviews the journal entries and returns the journal with comments via the same electronic route.

The Instructor Role

During this course, students work online with classmates to discuss themes and concepts about interdisciplinary practice and to take part in practice-based scenarios. The role of the instructor is similar to that described by MacFadden et al. (2002) as a "guide on the side" rather than as a "sage on the stage." The instructor is an observer/participant of each group's interaction. The instructor occupies two distinct roles in this particular course. Firstly, the instructor engages with the role-plays by simulating the role of "case manager" who receives all of the interdisciplinary team reports. In this way, the instructor/manager may post further questions to the specific Small Group Discussion Topic, add important information about practice realities, comment on the work plans that are developed, and to generally "ground" the group discussion in both theory and practice. Secondly, the instructor acts as both a content consultant and quality assurance monitor of the group processes that can be seen by viewing the text messages in all online Small Group Discussion Topics. The instructor also monitors the course website to ensure that there is full participation by all students, that the small groups are attending to task, that groups are not getting "stuck" in negative group dynamics, and that everyone understands the specifics of the interactive exercise. While each group is encouraged to be self-directed, members can contact the instructor privately via e-mail or telephone should there be a problem within the group (i.e., someone not fully participating, someone being overbearing or disrespectful).

In addition to acting as a catalyst to stimulate discussion, we found that the instructor must also attend to what MacFadden et al. (2002) refers to as the "emotional topography" of the course and to help students to pay attention to courtesy. It was occasionally important to remind students that mutual respect and support for group members are essential to success. In the interaction with students as individuals and as collectives within a group, instructors have a responsibility to model how a good team member considers others' points of view and focuses on ideas, not people. As well, instructors find that students need to be encouraged and taught how to give adequate feedback to comments and suggestions made by other group members. The instructor often has to intervene using one or more of the online tools to encourage students to go beyond simply agreeing or disagreeing with another group member's perspective. This is done by either sending individual students a private e-mail or by posting a more general comment to the entire small group on the Small Group Discussion Topic suggesting that they try to add substantive comments to each others' work each time they make a contribution. Rather than criticizing the students, however, it is important that the instructor gives more gentle guidance by "modeling." This means posting or e-mailing sample responses to a question, or suggesting specific ways the group could delve a little deeper into the discussion. In the HSD 465 course, such interventions have certainly been necessary, although not always successful. At times posting suggestions that "model" can end up "silencing" students or ending the dialogue. Students have made comments about feeling under undue scrutiny by the instructor in these situations and criticized for making "errors of omission." Unless the instructor approaches these intervention tasks with a great deal of sensitivity, students may feel apprehensive about e-mailing or posting comments that "are not right" or "are not thorough enough." Failing to be sensitive to students as learners on a journey of exploration rather than experts at a destination, may lead students to feel unsupported and unfairly criticized.

The Interactive Role-Plays–Examples and Lessons Learned

Participating in the online role-plays means that students are required to take on a role, consider how they would respond or contribute in this case situation, post their views to the group discussion forum and respond to others' contributions. The roles are "played out" via the online discussion exercise. An example of an online role play is provided in Appendix 2. This enactment allows them to "play" with the theory. In this "play," students are invited to be both actor and observer to see how various factors and differing ideas about the scope and responsibility of disciplinary roles influence how concepts of interdisciplinary and collaborative practice models may or may not work. Once the role-play has concluded and students step out of the role they played, further learning occurs as students post their responses to "process questions" raised by either the instructor or other students and debrief each role-play using the Small Group Discussion Topic. This allows students to post messages to each other concerning their views on the outcome of the role-play, and to reflect individually and collectively on how the theoretical material influenced their emerging understanding. At this point the instructor also enters the discussion venue (Small Group Discussion Topic) of each group by posting questions that ask them to think about how the online interaction helps to promote a collaborative practice model. We have found that students value the online case-based role-plays. Students suggest that these exercises provide an opportunity to become aware of the interdependence among the various disciplines and the value of collaboration among disciplines. The examples below are comments made by students in their Reflective Journals about the value of the role-play for integrating theory with practice.

Example One

What became apparent to me was how easy it is to disempower group members in practice. This became clear following the completion of the role-play. In the role of "Marty" the medical social worker, I attempted to play my role by operating in a "silo" as we talked about in the online discussion group. . . As I worked through the activity and advocated for my client and his needs, I did so un-

knowing that Joe (the "client" role) was present in the meeting as well. What transpired from the discussion was Joe expressing his frustrations surrounding everyone's decision-making that was external to him. As the activity continued, I believe this was an excellent simulation of how group members can become disempowered operating in "silos" independent from one another. But in placing this learning experience in relation to interdisciplinary practice, it outlines the importance of each group member having the liberty to voice their input into the planning and decision-making. Instead of Joe being a passive member in the group, an atmosphere could have been created where he was an active player in the discussion and viewed as an expert in his own experience. I believe that Joe would have felt more empowered by the group if this approach would have been more actively pursued. In terms of my own practice, this activity was an excellent simulation of what to avoid in interdisciplinary practice. (John, 2002)

Example Two

I have been reading other student's comments, and perhaps frustrations expressed over the online component to this course. There seems to be a strong opinion that it cannot accurately capture the group experience as we are not physically together within a group. But while this may be true, working on an interdisciplinary team may require collaboration over great distances, and this is something I have experienced personally living in the North. It would be ideal if team members could come together in one room, but this is often a luxury we don't get. I have been present in teleconferences where group members are in different places in the N.W.T. or Alberta and this is often common practice. So, while the on-line component may not be ideal, we as students and social workers need to be open to other modes of communication and methods of learning. For myself, I have enjoyed the on-line component to the course, I have been using many of the ideas presented both in the readings and from other students' contributions in my work in child welfare. Interdisciplinary practice needs to capitalize on the "overlapping" of disciplines and sharing of ideas. For example, I was involved more recently in a case conference concerning a young boy named "Sam." He presented some behavioural and academic difficulties that were assessed by a speech-language pathologist and a psychologist. The purpose of the meeting was to share the results of the assessments with the foster parent, his teacher, the special needs coordinator and myself as the CPW. The information disclosed suggested that "Sam" was very much a visual learner. Both the psychologist and speech-language pathologist confirmed this. During the meeting the foster parent shared that "Sam" has difficulty remembering morning routines and the sequence in which they need to be performed. The information overlapped to a large degree–I suggested that "Sam" try using some visual aides in the home to assist him with his morning routines. Pictures of making the bed, brushing one's teeth, remembering his lunch and so forth could easily be depicted in his room as a learning tool to teach him independence in this area. This is how I believe interdisciplinary practice can work when information is being shared and connections are being drawn. (Louise, 2002)

Example Three

Our group's experience with the last role-play highlighted for me the need for group members to listen to each other in interdisciplinary practice. While the Child Protection Worker may hold the power to make decisions, the CPW may not have all of the knowledge or information to make informed decisions. There needs to be an effort made to value opinions and view advocates as allies instead of rivalries. From my perspective, this appears to be a major barrier during case conferences with different agencies. (Etta, 2002)

Reflecting on Outcomes–A Qualitative Evaluation of Learner Experience

In this course we begin with fairly lofty goals and objectives for the learner experience. The learning plan for the course is based on the belief that opportunities for making personal meaning and building relationships across disciplines are integral to interdisciplinary practice. Yet, how do we know that the simulated interactive exercises give students this opportunity? The objectives stated in the course outline (see Appendix 1) are quite ambitious. What we failed to do when preparing the course and delivering it for the first few times was to determine how we would assess whether students achieved the course objectives. A traditional end-of-course evaluation form is available online on the course website and most students took the time to complete the evaluation asked of them. Unfortunately, the course evaluation does not specifically ask students to give their own assessment of how well the course helped them to meet the course objectives. As a result, finding answers to the questions about: how well the course content and format met the course objectives, how students benefited from the opportunities of the interactive exercises and how they developed an appreciation of collaborative practice among various disciplines remains elusive. There were no pre-test/post-test instruments used to measure students' understandings of interdisciplinary practice. The formal course evaluation documents do not provide adequate data to answer these questions. It is only by reviewing the students' responses to course assignments that we are able to get a glimpse of what the course has meant to individual student learning. We engaged in a qualitative evaluation of how students used the course to explore the conceptual material and then to practice the skills that support interdisciplinary relationships and teamwork. This was done by reviewing the dialogue in the interactive exercises, examining the entries made in individual student reflective journals and assessing the final assignment for the integration of the theoretical concepts into a practice framework. The grading criteria are included in Appendix 3. The analysis of these written tests suggests that it is the interaction with each other via the virtual "written-text conversations" that takes place during the role plays via the Small Group Discussions Topic that provides the most profound learning experience. In this way, our experience with this course echoes the findings of MacFadden et al. (2002). Like these researchers we find that strategies that build upon peer helping, cooperative learning tasks and play-like activities contribute to a good emotional climate between students and this leads them to report a positive experience that aided their learning. Excerpts from the reflective journal entries and narrative comments on the course evaluation speak to the student's positive experience with the course. Some comments include:

> *This course has given me important knowledge for myself as I try to work collaboratively in the helping profession of social work, especially in the field of child protection where often other community partners look to government to provide solutions when the issues should be collectively addressed. I have found that often people tend to misconstrue my role and what I can and cannot do.*

The expectations given are too high, and frustration occurs. It is my hope that I can take the learning from this course to help create alternative ways and means to alleviate this process, and approach problem-solving from a collective basis I think the online activities contributed to my understanding of the nature of interdisciplinary practice in that I am actively studying this process, instead of just "doing it blind." The wide range of individuals within this course with the diversity and differing self-locations of my classmates contributed vastly to my existing knowledge base. (Monica, 2002)

I admit that I was extremely intimidated by the format of this course as I have never learned through WebCT before and I do not like computers in general. I spend all day working on a computer screen and I do not have a personal computer at home mainly for that very reason. I did not like the time limit format given for the online assignments and that the grades of others were contingent upon my response. I have an issue with the timing thing in that I am taking this course via distance education because I simply cannot structure the academic part of my life right now, and distance education is supposed to provide me with flexibility. I am just a tad perturbed that others' grades are dependent on me when I know I cannot always fulfill that responsibility to others' satisfaction. However, I also know that this mutual dependence on others is a reality of the real practice world. (John, 2002)

I think I have come to appreciate that the limited emphasis on interdisciplinary education and practice may well be due to lack of understanding of what interdisciplinary is and what promotes or hinders its functioning. I think that often teams get together to plan without having a formal background or understanding of interdisciplinary practice. It is an expectation in many workplace environments, but that does not mean that everyone understands the goals or values of this model of practice. Knowing that conflicting values are a source of conflict in group situations, I think that it could be helpful as well as educational for teams to discuss the values of interdisciplinary practice and what it means for the group to have this perspective. In the future, I can see how this course will help me contribute to the development of interdisciplinary practice in the field. (Etta, 2002)

Conclusion and Recommendations for Future Research

This course provided the opportunity for students who are "community bound" and unable to access traditional on campus courses to access a course that was new to the curriculum. Structuring the course to use interactive role plays to teach interdisciplinary practice worked quite well. Due to the use of the web-based tools to guide and structure small group work, students were able to "act out" the integration of theoretical material by engaging in interactive role plays with each other. The most valuable resource that the course provided to the student was regular, structured and easy access to each other, despite the separation of geography. Our experience with HSD 465 has convinced us that using a web-based course provided an excellent venue for helping students from various disciplines and across geographic distance to expand their understanding of their own disciplinary perspectives and to develop an appreciation for the perspectives of others. Students enjoyed engaging with each other using the web-based discussion tools and were able to have contact with students in other geographic locations that they would not normally have. Good team building experiences occurred in these virtual classrooms and students seemed to readily develop what Randolph and Krause (2002) describe as "mutual aid discourses" while participating in the interactive online exercises.

More research is needed on how we measure learning outcomes in all human service educational programs. This course, like many others, needs better evaluation tools to determine how well students were able to meet specific course objectives and whether the content and process of a web-based course facilitated meeting such objectives. While the reports from students who have taken this course have been relatively complimentary about both the course content and the use of web-based discussion tools to guide and structure interactive groupwork, it remains to be seen whether the exposure to a web-based course in interdisciplinary practice actually leads students to behave differently in their subsequent practice worlds. However, we also do not have information as to whether this curriculum taught in a traditional classroom environment makes a difference to subsequent practice either. One major piece of research that would inform human service education would be comparative studies of the same interdisciplinary practice curriculum offered in different formats (web-based environment versus a traditional classroom setting). It would be valuable to have followed up contact with students once they have finished the course and are in their respective practice worlds. It is at this point that they may be able to best describe the utility of the web-based delivery and relevance of the course material for the "real world" experience of the field.

Lastly, more research on how students experience the virtual classroom environment of platforms such as WebCT will make valuable contributions to those who are interested and committed to innovative curriculum and delivery models that are designed to serve the community-bound learner.

NOTE

1. http://www.mcf.gov.bc.ca/sted/overview/htm

REFERENCES

Abell, M., and M. Galinsky (2002). Introducing Students to Computer-Based Group Work. *Journal of Social Work Education,* Vol. 38, No. 1 (Winter, 2002) pp. 39-54.

Kahn, B. (Ed.) (1997). *Web-Based Instruction.* Englewood Cliffs, NJ: Educational Technology Publications

Kinnevy, S., and Enosh, G. (2002). Problems and Promises in the Study of Virtual Communities. *Journal of Technology in the Human Services,* Vol. 19, No. 2/3, 2002 pp. 119-134.

Lewis, L. F., Garcia, J., and Hallock, A. (2002). Applying Group Support Systems in Social Work Education and Practice. *Journal of Technology in the Human Services* Vol. 20, No. 1/2, 2002, pp. 201-225.

MacFadden, R., Maiter, S., and Dumbrill, G. (2002). High Tech and High Touch: The Human Face of Online Education. *Journal of Technology in the Human Services,* Vol. 20, No. 3/4, 2002, pp. 283-300.

McLoughlin, C., and Luca, J. (2002). A learner-centred approach to developing team skills through web-based learning and assessment. *British Journal of Educational Technology,* Vol 33. No. 5, 2002, pp. 571-582.

McLoughlin, C. (2000). *Cognitive engagement and higher order thinking through computer conferencing: We know why but do we know how?* Teaching and Learning Forum 2000 http://lsn.curtin.edu.au/tlf/tlf2000/mcloughlin.html.

Ouellette, P. (2000). Moving Toward Technology Supported Instruction in Human Service Practice. *Journal of Technology in the Human Services,* Vol. 16, No. 2/3, 2000, pp. 97-111.

Randolph, K. and Krause, D. (2002). " Mutual Aid in the Classroom: An Instructional Technology Application" *Journal of Social Work Education,* Vol. 38, No. 2 (Spring/ Summer, 2002) pp. 259-271.

Reeves, T. and Reeves, P. (1997). Effective Dimensions of Interactive Learning on the World Wide Web. In B. Kahn (Ed.), *Web-Based Instruction.* Englewood Cliffs, NJ: Educational Technology Publications, pp. 59-66.

APPENDIX 1

Course Objectives for HSD 465:
Interdisciplinary Practice with Children and Families

By the end of the course, students will be able to:

- demonstrate their understanding of the core concepts of interdisciplinary practice and to make a case for their own personal/professional framework for this form of practice.
- anticipate and develop a plan for accessing the supports and addressing the barriers to interdisciplinary practice in their future work with children and families.
- be familiar with the dynamics of interdisciplinary teamwork.
- influence each other's professional approaches to practice with children and families.
- develop communications skills to work effectively in an online environment and reach consensus on an issue.
- develop a critical perspective on interdisciplinary practice.
- develop an awareness and appreciation of the interdependence amongst disciplines.

APPENDIX 2

Sample Online Interactive Exercise: Case-Based Scenario:
Interdisciplinary Team Meeting 3

HSD 465: Interdisciplinary Practice with Children and Families

Instructions to Students (posted on course website)

This exercise will simulate an interdisciplinary team meeting. The overall goal is to develop a plan of action for the family described in the case below.

You will need to nominate a coordinator who will be responsible for synthesizing the group's efforts to develop a plan of action for the family and to post that plan to the instructor.

Time Frame: Week Four: Tuesday 12:01 am to 11:59 pm Thursday

There are 3 parts to this exercise.

Part 1: Discussion

In your group, discuss values, tensions and questions inherent in interdisciplinary practice. Begin your discussion about planning by trying to generate a list of characteristics of a helping relationship that integrates the perspectives of the child, youth, family and community. Some examples (there are lots of others!) of what might be included in the list are:

- Respectful
- Honest
- Open
- Clear understanding of roles
- Sharing of knowledge/information (both client's and the professional's)
- Sharing of decision-making
- Clear understanding of responsibilities
- Equitable
- Client included in planning

APPENDIX 2 (continued)

Part 2: Role-Play #1

As a learning activity for the last unit, you were asked to review the practice-based scenario below and to gather information about the scope of practice of the role that was assigned to you by the instructor. In your online discussion group (and keeping in the role assigned to you), participate in a multidisciplinary team meeting to develop a plan for this family.

All group members must post their responses (and counter responses) within the 72 hour period. The coordinator should plan to summarize the group discussion at the end of this period, send the group a draft of the summary for review and then submit the final draft to the instructor. Group members should review the plan and offer suggestions for revisions within 24 hours after receiving the draft.

Note: Relax, there is no pre-determined right or wrong way of working with the family, rather the focus is on providing you with an experience from which you can analyze how you (and others) work within the multi-disciplinary team.

THE SCENARIO
The Family

Joe, grandfather, age 52
Kim, mother, aged 26
Josh, son, aged 3

The family lives together in a basement suite close to town. Joe is the primary caregiver of both Kim and Josh. He has recently suffered a severe and incapacitating heart attack. Kim has a severe mental illness that is stabilized with medication but she is not able to take responsibility for Josh's care. Josh is an active 3 year old who is not yet toilet trained.

The child protection worker has initiated the multidisciplinary team meeting after a recent visit to the home. The visit was in response to a complaint from a neighbour about the smell in the apartment–"there is a three year old kid living in the apartment–I don't know how he can survive that stench." When the child protection worker visited, there was indeed an overpowering smell of stale air and urine. Joe told the child protection worker that he was trying to care for his daughter and grandchild and Josh regularly wets the bed, which accounts for the smell.

Team Roles–(assigned by the instructor to individual students in each group via private e-mail)

1. Child protection worker (social work, child and youth care, ed. psych, psychology): You have visited the home in response to a complaint from the neighbour.
2. Mental health worker (social work, nursing, medicine, psychology): You have been working with Kim for some time and have made several attempts to help her.
3. Community health worker (medicine, nursing, occupation therapy, social work, psychology, recreation, child and youth care, education): You have recently become involved with this family after receiving a request from the family physician who is concerned about Josh's delayed development.
4. Social worker: You have been working with Joe in the outpatient cardiac rehabilitation program. You are concerned about the negative effect of this family stress on Joe's health.
5. Joe: You are still feeling unwell and are somewhat embarrassed and angry that neighbours have snitched on you and your family. You want help but on your own terms.
6. Day care worker: You have been working with Josh since he began attending your private home day care three months ago. You are concerned that this little boy is often disheveled and hungry when he arrives at day care. He speaks very little and often fights with other children. You would prefer that Josh no longer attend your daycare and feel he needs a more specialized environment.

Part 3: Debrief and Discussion

Time Frame: Week Four: Thursday 12:01 am to 11:59 pm Sunday

Use the following questions to debrief your individual and collective experiences of participating in the role-play from last week by discussing the questions provided below.

All group members must post their responses (and counter responses) to your "Small Group Discussion Topic" within the 72 hour period.

- How did you decide who would be the case manager?
- What were the power dynamics in your meeting? Did the family have any power? Was there a hierarchy amongst disciplines?
- How do power differences impact information sharing? Was some people's information valued more highly?
- What kind of information did you share as you developed the plan?
- How did you make decisions in your team? Did someone guide the discussion? Who had the power or was it shared?
- Did anyone perceive they had an ethical dilemma related to information sharing? If so, how did you handle this in the meeting?
- Did anyone feel that confidentiality was breached?
- Did anyone withhold information?
- What role did the family play in deciding what information was shared?
- How did your awareness of the legislation and your professional code of ethics impact your information sharing?

APPENDIX 3

Grading Criteria for Assignments

ASSIGNMENT ONE: REFLECTIVE JOURNAL EVALUATION (30%)

Grading Criteria:

1. Ability to demonstrate integration of course readings and web material with your own experience and knowledge. (10%)
2. Ability to use critical thinking and self-reflection in discussing your thoughts and feelings about the group work and the course in general. (10%)
3. Ability to communicate your ideas and organize your paper clearly, thoroughly and concisely. (10%)

ASSIGNMENT TWO: ONLINE PARTICIPATION (40%)

Participating in the "virtual classroom" discussions and the role-plays will develop and strengthen your understanding of the theoretical foundations of interdisciplinary practice. These activities will also provide you with insights into how others identify the issues and challenges and give you some idea of how you would reach consensus around varying approaches to working with children and families in an interdisciplinary practice setting.

During the course, you will be able to demonstrate your developing ability to make effective contributions to online discussion and problem-solving. You will also coordinate discussion in a small-group and prepare a written summary of that discussion for your group and the instructor. Guidelines for participating in and coordinating online discussion are provided later in this unit.

SPECIFIC GRADING CRITERIA

- Timeliness–assessment of the promptness of your submissions and responses to the on-line activities. (10%)

APPENDIX 3 (continued)

- Frequency–an assessment of the thoroughness and regularity of your online participation. (10%)
- Preparation–an assessment of how well you prepared for the online activities and related the online activities to the course material. (10%)
- Leadership–an assessment of the way in which you took advantage of opportunities to lead discussions, problem solve, assume the role of Group Coordinator and address the learning needs of your group. (10%)

ASSIGNMENT THREE: PERSONAL PRACTICE FRAMEWORK (30%)

GRADING CRITERIA

1. Demonstration of an understanding of the core concepts of interdisciplinary practice. (9%)
2. Demonstrated ability to articulate an emerging personal/professional framework for interdisciplinary practice. (9%)
3. Thoroughness of the documentation and synthesizing of your learning from the instructional materials, on-line discussions, small-group experiences, the course readings and website exploration. (7%)
4. Clarity of writing, grammar and use of a proper form of academic citations (APA or similar). (5%)

Evaluating the Efficacy of Traditional and Web-Assisted Instruction in an Undergraduate Social Work Practice Class

Helen Petracchi
Gayle Mallinger
Rafael Engel
Carrie W. Rishel
Carol Washburn

SUMMARY. This article addresses the dearth of research utilizing a quasi-experimental design and student performance measures in assessing web-assisted instruction in social work undergraduate practice courses. Social work students were randomly placed into two sections of a practice course. The experimental section (n = 18) students received 50% of course lectures with web-assisted instruction while the compari-

---

Helen Petracchi, PhD, Gayle Mallinger, MSW, and Rafael Engel, PhD, are affiliated with the School of Social Work, University of Pittsburgh.

Carrie W. Rishel, PhD, is affiliated with the Division of Social Work, West Virginia University.

Carol Washburn, EdD, is affiliated with the Center for Instructional Design and Distance Education, University of Pittsburgh.

Address correspondence to: Helen Petracchi, PhD, University of Pittsburgh, School of Social Work, 2010 C.L. 4200 5th Avenue, Pittsburgh, PA 15260.

[Haworth co-indexing entry note]: "Evaluating the Efficacy of Traditional and Web-Assisted Instruction in an Undergraduate Social Work Practice Class." Petracchi et al. Co-published simultaneously in *Journal of Technology in Human Services* (The Haworth Press, Inc.) Vol. 23, No. 3/4, 2005, pp. 299-310; and: *Web-Based Education in the Human Services: Models, Methods, and Best Practices* (eds: MacFadden et al.) The Haworth Press, Inc., 2005, pp. 299-310. Single or multiple copies of this article are available for a fee from The Haworth Document Delivery Service [1-800-HAWORTH, 9:00 a.m. - 5:00 p.m. (EST). E-mail address: docdelivery@haworthpress.com].

son class (n = 18) received identical lectures delivered in traditional face-to-face format. There were no statistically significant differences on assignments, the midterm exam and a final videotaped exam project between the two sections. These results suggest students in an undergraduate social work practice course learn similarly regardless of course format. *[Article copies available for a fee from The Haworth Document Delivery Service: 1-800-HAWORTH. E-mail address: <docdelivery@haworthpress.com> Website: <http://www.HaworthPress.com> © 2005 by The Haworth Press, Inc. All rights reserved.]*

KEYWORDS. Web-assisted instruction, practice, teaching, technology

LITERATURE REVIEW

Distance education has become an increasingly acceptable mode of delivering social work instruction (Siegel, Jennings, Conklin, & Flynn, 1998). Benefits to students include the provision of increased technological competence and access to educational opportunities otherwise unavailable to those students unable to attend traditional social work programs (Petracchi & Patchner, 2000). The most frequently offered courses via distance education are human behavior in the social environment, social welfare policy, and social work research (Siegel et al., 1998). Many recent studies have assessed and are supportive of the use of web-assisted course delivery in the aforementioned courses (Patterson & Yaffe, 1994; Stocks & Freddolino, 2000; Van Soest, Canon, & Grant, 2000; Wernet, Olliges, & Delicath, 2000).

Social work educators have historically had reservations about providing social work practice content in a web-assisted format. The development of communication skills, the mentoring relationship between professor and student, and the expansion of critical thinking ability are believed to be among the essential aspects of the social work student's professional socialization, a key goal of introductory practice classes (Kemp, 1998; Siegel et al., 1998). Traditionally, social work educators have believed fostering interaction between the professor and student and among peers could be accomplished solely through the conventional classroom formats, with face-to-face interactions. Critics of web-assisted social work education express concern about isolating students and faculty from one another. They forecast increased contact by e-mail (an often used communication tool in distance education) will result in the promotion of social distance, fundamentally eliminating the essence of personal communication which is necessary for professional social work practice (Kreuger & Stretch, 2000).

However, recent studies suggest web-assisted delivery actually provides increased interface with peers and faculty (Patterson & Yaffe, 1994; Stocks & Freddolino, 2000; Van Soest, Canon, & Grant, 2000). Computer-mediated interaction has enhanced student satisfaction by creating enthusiasm for assignments, increasing participation, and facilitating relationships (Frey, Yankelov, & Faul, 2003; McCombs, 1994; Mowrer, 1996). Communication tools available in web-assisted course management systems can actually serve to promote relationships between student and instructor (Wernet et al., 2000) with students perceiving e-mail interactions with faculty as highly valuable (Frey et al., 2003). In fact, Van Soest and colleagues (2000) reported web-assisted instruction offered a useful device for students to discuss sensitive issues they might otherwise have been reluctant to discuss in class.

Independent learning is a quality of distance education that may be especially adaptable to social work undergraduate students. Effective systems for independent learning are characterized by student responsibility, student choice, widely available instruction, and a variety of methods and media (Wedemeyer 1977, 1981). Control is an important concept associated with independent learning. Learner control over the time and place to receive instruction is often perceived as a primary advantage. In fact, Garrison and Baynton (1987) have extended this concept to a model where effective control of the learning process results from a balance of three optimal conditions: the learner's opportunity to make choices, the learner's skills, and the support available to the learner. But much of the recent literature addressing distance learning in social work education has focused on student satisfaction (Frey et al., 2003; Petracchi & Patchner, 2000; Rudolph & Krause, 2002; Stocks & Freddolino, 2000; Van Soest et al., 2000) though many have expressed concern about the *effectiveness* of distance learning (Thyer, Artelt, Markward, & Dozier, 1998). Research on the efficacy of this method of instruction, specifically web-based technology, is equivocal. Faux and Black-Hughes (2000) found that students participating in a traditional face-to-face classroom did better on a post-test measure examining mastery of course material than did those taught through the Internet. However, Thurston and Cauble (1999) examined the efficacy of a multimedia approach to teaching child welfare content to undergraduates and found a significant, positive difference on pre- and post-test measures of general knowledge for the viewed modules, supporting the use of multimedia.

The current study extends Thurston and Cauble's (1999) research by assessing the efficacy of web-assisted learning with undergraduate social work students enrolled in a beginning social work practice class. This practice course introduces students to social work generalist practice, defined as the application of knowledge, values, and skills of the general method of problem solving. Students in the course develop beginning skills in utilizing effective techniques of client worker communication, structuring helping interviews, and establishing, maintaining and terminating relationships. Focus in the course is given to the application of these skills to client/consumer groups of various sizes and in various multi-cultural contexts. This paper describes an evaluation of the course when one section was offered with web-assistance. An experimental design was utilized to evaluate the following hypotheses:

1. Students receiving web-assisted instruction in an undergraduate social work practice course would not differ significantly from their peers receiving traditionally delivered instruction as measured by performance on exams and assignments.
2. Students enrolled in the web-assisted class section would significantly improve their technological expertise compared to those in the comparison class receiving traditional instruction.

METHOD

Design. This study used a comparison group design to evaluate the two hypotheses. In the experimental class section, students received their instruction with a combination of web-assistance and face-to-face instruction while students in the comparison class section received exclusively face-to-face instruction.

Students were placed into one of the two class sections during registration. During the summer prior to their junior year, students registered for their fall social work courses with the Student Services Specialist who was unaware that an experimental teaching method was going to be used in the first practice course, *Interventive Methods I: Generalist Practice.* Since both sections of the course met at the same time, the Student Services Specialist put the first student to register into section one, the next student into section two, etc. Therefore, there was no systematic bias to student assignment to either the experimental web-assisted section or the comparison group face-to-face section of the course. On the first day of classes, the experimental web-assisted class met in an assigned room with their instructor. At this meeting, students were told the class would be offered with web-assistance. Any student who wished to change sections of the class was given the opportunity to do so. None chose to switch from the class to which they were assigned.

Sample. The study sample consisted of first semester social work majors at a large, urban university in the Midwest. In this program, BSW students matriculate as social work majors in their first semester, junior year. There were 36 students in the sample, with 18 assigned to each section of the class. The median age of the sample was 21 years. Fifty-three percent were traditional-aged students (21 years or younger); 88 percent (n = 32) were female. Only 39 percent of the sample students had any paid work experience while 50 percent had some volunteer experience.

Intervention. The instructors for each section of this undergraduate social work practice course were matched for years of professional social work practice experience and a shared learner-centered approach and constructivist perspective to education. The instructors prepared their weekly lesson plans and lectures together with each of the classes utilizing the same texts, syllabus, midterm exam, written assignments, and final evaluation project. The instructors also developed and used common role plays, simulations, and group exercises.

Both the experimental web-assisted class and the comparison class of students received their weekly instruction for two hours and fifty minutes, covering the same lecture material and participating in the same role plays and group exercises (see Table 1). However, the experimental web-assisted class received 100 percent of their weekly lecture material online using Blackboard technology. These web-based lectures were designed utilizing discussion boards, e-mail features, and links to additional websites. The experimental web-based students then met for the other half of their allotted weekly class time face-to-face with their experimental course instructor and peers. During these face-to-face meetings, students in the web-based class participated in role plays and group exercises led by the instructor.

Unlike the experimental web-assisted class, the comparison class met face-to-face with their instructor and peers for the entire weekly class period. The instructor did not use e-mail to communicate with the comparison class of students and there were no web-assigned readings.

Three guest speakers met with both the experimental and comparison sections of this course combined into one large lecture room. The experimental web-assisted section discussed the lecturer's content using the course-management system's online discussion board during the subse-

TABLE 1. Course Delivery Differences Between the Experimental and Comparison Classes

Classroom Activity	Experimental Classroom (Web-Assisted Section) (N = 18)	Comparison Classroom (Traditional Face-to-Face Instruction) (N = 18)
Class Lecture (approximately 50% of course content)	100% online	100% face-to-face
Discussion of Lecture Content (approximately 10% of course content)	100% online	100% face-to-face
Role Play, Group Exercises, & Guest Speakers (approximately 40% of course content)	100% face-to-face	100% face-to-face

quent week; the comparison section discussed the content of the guest's lecture in person.

Measures. In both sections of this course, assignments were individually completed by students (there were no group assignments or projects), with the exception of the class participation requirement which was partially based on classroom group activities. A subjective paper required students to apply the general method learned in the course to an assessment of a family characterized in a popular movie. Rubrics (a set of evaluative criteria) were developed and used to grade subjective assignments with each student submitting an assignment identified only their social security number. No other identifying information was included in assignments that could have influenced grading. The midterm examination for both classes was an objective, multiple choice exam scored by the University's Office of Measurement and Evaluation.

The final assignment in this course involved a videotaped role play exam. Both the experimental web-assisted students and the comparison students were required to implement the same role play simulation and were given identical written assessment outlines. Because the instructors would be unable to evaluate the videotaped role play simulations anonymously, a third instructor who had taught a similar foundation social work practice course in the graduate program was employed to evaluate the final videotaped assignments. This instructor possessed no information regarding whether a student she was evaluating on the videotaped role play was a member of the web-assisted experimental class or the comparison class.

In addition, both groups of students completed a questionnaire adapted from the Technology Assessment Survey Student Competency Inventory developed by the University of Indiana School of Social Work (May 2003). This survey queried students about their comfort with Blackboard technology, library and computer access, and their ability to utilize the web. Students were asked to respond to survey questions on a five-point Likert scale ranging from one (1) "I do not know how to do this task" to five (5) "I can perform this task without any help." Eleven items assessed students' perceived competence using Blackboard course management technology to access course syllabus, retrieve e-mail, and access assignments. Nine items assessed students' perceived computer availability and ability to access and use library resources online. In this section, questions included such things as "I can access *Social Work Abstracts* online" and "I can use a browser to access PittCat (the University's online catalog system)." Five questions addressed the student's perceived ability to utilize internet browsers. An example of an item examining perceived expertise in this area would include, I can use a search engine (such as Google or Yahoo) to find specific information. Variables were created from the average score in each of the three categories of questions, by summing the responses and dividing by the number of questions with responses, thereby controlling for missing responses. Three variables reflect these measures: one for comfort with Blackboard technology, one for library and computer access, and one for ability to utilize the web.

Data Collection. The Technology Assessment Survey Student Competency Inventory was administered to both course sections at the beginning and end of the semester. The objective midterm was completed in the seventh week of the semester, the subjective assessment assignment was due in the eleventh week of the term, and the final videotaped examination was submitted at the last class period.

RESULTS

Group Differences. There were no statistically significant differences in the composition of the two class sections in work experience, volunteer experience, traditional versus nontraditional student status or age. The comparison class section included all four males in the study but given the small number of males, there was no reason to believe gender differences impacted hypothesis tests.

Hypotheses. Independent sample t-tests were used to test the first hypothesis that students receiving web-assisted instruction would demonstrate the same mastery of course content as comparison students receiving traditionally delivered instruction. As displayed in Table 2, each class had 18 students. As hypothesized, there were no statistically significant differences in scores between the two classes on the written assignment, midterm examination, or final videotaped assignment. The mean scores for the two groups on each assignment are nearly identical.

Since significance is difficult to obtain with small samples, the effect size, or the impact of the experimental web-assisted instruction on the scores of each of the assignments was calculated. The reported effect size for each assignment was quite low: the effect size on the midterm was .09, while the effect size on the written assignment was .17 and the effect size on the final video assignment was $-.09$. These findings suggest the method of teaching had little impact on the class assignments' scores.

The second hypothesis predicted that given greater exposure to various forms of technology, the experimental web-assisted class would significantly improve their technological expertise when compared with those students in the traditional face-to-face class. All students were asked to rate their ability to perform a variety of technological tasks associated with using Blackboard, library resources, and web browsing at the start of the semester and again at the end of the semester. As seen in Table 3, the students in both classes began the semester with

TABLE 2. Group Differences on Class Assignments

Assignment	N	Mean	Standard Deviation	t-value	Effect Size
Midterm:					
Web-Assisted	18	9.72	1.87	.291	.09
Traditional	18	9.55	1.54		
Written Paper:					
Web-Assisted	18	9.94	1.83	.521	.17
Traditional	18	9.67	1.32		
Final Video:					
Web-Assisted	18	9.33	1.37	$-.272$	$-.09$
Traditional	18	9.50	2.20		

TABLE 3. Average Pretest and Posttest Scores on the Technology Assessment Survey Student Competency Inventory

Class:	Blackboard			Library Related			Browser		
	Pretest	Post-test	Mean Differ-ence	Pretest	Post-test	Mean Differ-ence	Pretest	Post-test	Mean Differ-ence
Web-Assisted	3.39	3.69	.30	2.99	3.41	.42	3.66	3.67	.01
Traditional	3.38	3.67	.29	3.38	3.56	.18	3.81	3.89	.08

high self-ratings with different technological applications. Regardless of class, their ratings were even higher at the end of the semester.

Analysis of covariance was used to test the hypothesis that the web-assisted class would report greater technological comfort. The results of these analyses, however, indicated there were no statistically significant differences between the experimental web-assisted class and comparison class in each of the three competency areas.

DISCUSSION

The purpose of this study was to evaluate the effectiveness of web-assisted instruction as compared to a traditional face-to-face classroom format in an undergraduate social work introductory practice course. It was expected that students in the experimental web-assisted course section would not significantly differ from students in the comparison group receiving traditional face-to-face instruction as measured by performance on assignments and exams. It was also expected that students in the web-assisted course section would demonstrate significantly greater improvement in their technological expertise than students receiving traditional instruction.

The results of this study support the first hypothesis but not the second. Students in the experimental web-assisted course section demonstrated a similar degree of learning when compared with students in the traditional section of the course. However, students in the experimental web-assisted section of the course did not demonstrate greater improvement in their technological expertise when compared with the students in the class receiving traditional face-to-face instruction.

While the prevalence of web-assisted course delivery has increased in social work education over recent years (Siegel et al., 1998), research focusing on the efficacy of web-assisted instruction has had mixed results. On the one hand, Faux and Black-Hughes (2000) found that students in a traditional face-to-face classroom demonstrated mastery of course material better than those taught via the Internet. On the other hand, some work suggests web-assisted instruction benefits students by promoting relationships between students and instructor, increasing participation and enthusiasm for assignments, and providing a medium to discuss sensitive issues (Frey et al., 2003; McCombs, 1994; Mowrer, 1996; Van Soest et al., 2000; Wernet et al., 2000). And, Thurston and Cauble (1999) found that students in a multimedia enhanced undergraduate social work practice course mastered content better than their traditionally taught peers. The current study supports the results reported by Thurston and Cauble (1999) in that students in the web-assisted class section scored at similar or higher levels on all three course assignments when compared with their peers in the traditional classroom. But the current study results extends that which preceded it by utilizing random assignment, multiple methods of evaluation, and blind raters to produce a more rigorous design.

From a practical standpoint, the current study should also provide reassurance to social work educators interested in utilizing web assistance in their practice course delivery. The effective teaching of important social work knowledge and skills was not lost when the students in the current study were taught with web-assistance.

The results of the current study relative to the second hypothesis were disappointing but there may be several reasons that explain the lack of significant improvement in the technological expertise of students in the experimental web-assisted course when they were compared with their peers in the traditionally delivered classroom. The University where this study was conducted has made a tremendous financial commitment to technology development and utilization over the past few years. Since social work students at this University do not matriculate until their junior year, it is possible the University's efforts to train technologically-proficient students is reflected in the high level of comfort students report in the pretest survey relative to the Blackboard technology used in the course, library access, and their ability to utilize the web. This possibility is also supported by the fact that, when given an opportunity to change from the experimental web-assisted course section to the other traditional comparison section of the course, no students availed themselves of this opportunity (perhaps because they felt a high degree of comfort with the web). Moreover, with pretest scores as high as they were, it was not surprising that no statistically significant improvements were found, though it is possible the instrument used to assess technological competence was not sensitive enough to detect differences in improvement between the two groups. Obviously these findings are not generalizable to other universities and colleges. The results of the current study call for replication in other social work programs. Again, these results should be comforting to social work educators interested in utilizing web-assistance in their classrooms given the matriculating students' level of technological competence. Since this course was web-assisted with approximately 50% of the content delivered using the web, future research is needed to determine whether similar courses that are 100% web delivered would achieve similar results.

CONCLUSION

As much of the contemporary research in social work distance learning has focused on student satisfaction, most of these studies conclude with calls for research to address effectiveness of distance education (Frey et al., 2003; Petracchi & Patchner, 2000; Rudolph & Krause, 2002; Stocks & Freddolino, 2000; Thyer, Artelt, Markward, & Dozier, 1998; Van Soest et al., 2000). Results of the current study found the web-assisted course was just as effective as the traditional course in transferring knowledge and beginning social work practice skills to students. Therefore, we, as social work educators, should not fear utilizing the web in assisting, and delivering a social work practice course to undergraduates as this does not appear to compromise their learning. Moreover, given the comfort level with technology suggested by the students in this study, we should feel free to incorporate technology into our traditional courses, as well as into our curriculum in general, developing program outcome measures reflecting our expectation that social work students will leave their academic careers able to participate in the global technological community.

REFERENCES

Faux, T.L., & Black-Hughes, C. (2000). A comparison of using the internet versus lectures to teach social work history. *Research on Social Work Practice, 10,* 454-557.

Frey, A., Yankelov, P., & Faul, A. (2003). Student perceptions of web-assisted teaching strategies. *Journal of Social Work Education, 39,* 443-457.

Garrison D.R., & Baynton, M. (1987). Beyond independence in distance education: The concept of control. *The American Journal of Distance Education, 1*(1), 3-15.

Hiltz, S.R. (1986). The virtual classroom: Using computer mediated communication for university teaching. *Journal of Communication*, 36, 94-105.

Indiana University (May 2003). Technology Assessment Survey Student Competency Inventory. Retrieved from BPD_L@LISTSERV.IUPUI.EDU.

Kemp, S. (1998). Should two years of practice experience be essential to teach required practice courses: Yes. *Journal of Social Work Education, 34,* 329-335.

Krueger, L.W., & Stretch, J.J. (2000). How hypermodern technology in social work education bites back. *Journal of Social Work Education, 36,* 103-114.

McCombs, M. (1994). Benefits of computer-mediated communication in college courses. *Communication in Education, 43,* 171-183.

Mowrer, D.E. (1996). A content analysis of student/instructor communication via computer conferencing. *Higher Education, 32,* 217-241.

Patterson, D.A., & Yaffe, J. (1994). Hypermedia computer-based education in social work education. *Journal of Social Work Education, 30,* 267-278.

Petracchi, H., & Patchner, M.E. (2000). Social work students and their learning environment: A comparison of interactive television, face-to-face instruction and the traditional classroom. *Journal of Social Work Education, 2,* 335-346.

Rudolph, K.A., & Krause, D.J. (2002). Mutual aid in the classroom: An instructional technology application. *Journal of Social Work Education, 38,* 259-271.

Siegel, E., Jennings, J., Conklin, J., & Flynn, S.A.N. (1998). Distance learning in social work education: Results and implications of a national survey. *Journal of Social Work Education, 34,* 71-81.

Stocks, J.T., & Freddolino, P.P. (2000). Enhancing computer-mediated teaching through interactivity: The second iteration of a world wide web-based graduate social work course. *Research on Social Work Practice, 10,* 505-519.

Thurston, L.P., & Cauble, E. (1999). Using interactive multimedia to build child welfare competencies in social workers. *Journal of Research on Computing in Education, 32,* 298-307.

Thyer, B., Artelt, T., Markward, M., & Dozier, C. (1998). Evaluating distance learning in social work education: A replication study. *Journal of Social Work Education, 34,* 291-295.

Van Soest, D., Coanon, R., & Grant, D. (2000). Using an interactive website to educate about cultural diversity and societal oppression. *Journal of Social Work Education, 36,* 463-480.

Wedemeyer, C. A. (1977). Independent study. In A.S. Knowles (Ed.), *The International Encyclopedia of Higher Education.* Boston: Northeastern University.

Wedemeyer, C. (1981). *Learning at the back door: Reflections on nontraditional learning in the lifespan.* Madison, WI: University of Wisconsin.

Wernet, S.P., Olliges, R.H., & Delicath, T.A. (2000). Postcourse evaluations of Web CT (Web Course Tools) classes by social work students. *Research on Social Work Practice, 10,* 487-505.

COMPENDIUM

This final section contains a brief compendium of web-based courses that contains summary information including course information, instructor, course goals, requirements and lessons learned. Additional information is available from the compendium contributors at:

<compendium\compendiumintroduction.doc>

[Haworth co-indexing entry note]: "Compendium." Acker et al. Co-published simultaneously in *Journal of Technology in Human Services* (The Haworth Press, Inc.) Vol. 23, No. 3/4, 2005, pp. 311-319; and: *Web-Based Education in the Human Services: Models, Methods, and Best Practices* (eds: MacFadden et al.) The Haworth Press, Inc., 2005, pp. 311-319. Single or multiple copies of this article are available for a fee from The Haworth Document Delivery Service [1-800-HAWORTH, 9:00 a.m. - 5:00 p.m. (EST). E-mail address: docdelivery@haworthpress.com].

Available online at http://www.haworthpress.com/web/JTHS
Digital Object Identifier: 10.1300/J017v023n03_10

COURSE INFORMATION

- Title: The Legal Environment of Social Work Practice
- URL: http://www.uregina.ca/cce/offcampus/distance_courses/sw420.htm
- Level: BSW level
- Area: Policy
- Number face-to-face sessions: 0
- Tools used: All tools within WebCT, E-mail, Discussion forum, Tests and quizzes administered online, Exercises (interactive), Phone calls via traditional phone lines

INSTRUCTOR

Mona Acker, Associate Professor and Assistant Dean, Faculty of Social Work, University of Regina, 3737 Wascana Parkway, Regina, Saskatchewan, S4S 0A2, Canada <mona.acker@uregina.ca>

COURSE GOAL

To provide an understanding of legislation an expression of social policy and their impact on professional social work practice, policy and ethics.

COURSE REQUIREMENTS

1. Group visit to a Correctional Centre or Courtroom in session with paper describing the experience and referring to the literature. Requires use of organization and leadership skills (20%)
2. Term Paper on one of a provided list of topics relevant to course content (35%)
3. Weekly Bulletin Board group discussion assignments (15%)
4. Midterm and final exams (15%)
5. Participation (15%)

LESSONS LEARNED

Keeping up with the evolving technology as well as the development and delivery of an online course is a heavy time commitment not recognized as research for promotion and tenure purposes.

COURSE INFORMATION

- Title: Human Behavior and Social Systems
- URL: http://vrc.nmsu.edu:592/de_schedule/FMPro
- Level: BSW level
- Area: HBSE
- Number face-to-face sessions: 0
- Tools used: _WebCT, Web site, e-mail, discussion forum, chat, FAQ, guest speakers, PowerPoint, exercises, webquests

INSTRUCTOR

Timothy Barnett-Queen, PhD, Assistant Professor, New Mexico State University, School of Social Work, MSC 3SW, P.O. Box 30001, Contact_City, Las Cruces, NM 88003-8001, United States <trbqueen@nmsu.edu>

COURSE GOAL

Human growth and development over the life cycle, from conception through death. Study of individual's interrelationship with the major systems will be emphasized. Web-based course and part of CHSS major in Human and Community Services.

COURSE REQUIREMENTS

1. Class attendance and participation. (In an online course this refers to completion of major and weekly assignments on time and participating in all online activities: discussions, e-mail, chats, etc.)
2. Mid-term and Final Exam
3. Individual Project Assignment
4. Participation in class WebCT e-mail, web-discussions, chats and Internet assignments
5. Small group viewing of selected videos and preparation for in-class discussion of videos
6. Small group WebCT discussion leadership on selected readings.
7. Completion of weekly assignments found in the weekly assignments content page on WebCT

LESSONS LEARNED

Importance of quick turn around time on student postings to discussions and e-mails. Course design is critical. Online courses are time consuming.

COURSE INFORMATION

- Title: Interdisciplinary Practice with Children and Families
- URL: Available mid January 2004 (contact instructor)
- Level: BSW level
- Area: Micro/Macro Elective
- Number face-to-face sessions: 0
- Tools used: WebCT with Web site, e-mail, interactive simulations, and interactive exercises

INSTRUCTOR

Patricia MacKenzie, Associate Professor, University of Victoria, P.O. Box 1700, STN C, Victoria, BC, V8W 2Y2, Canada <patmack@uvic.ca>

COURSE GOAL

To expose students to principles and theories of interdisciplinary practice with children and families and to have time explore the operationalization of these principles through structured role plays and simulated case conferencing.

COURSE REQUIREMENTS

1. Group work–interactive online exercises of simulated role plays and case studies (40%)
2. Reflective Journal (30%)
3. Personal Practice Framework paper (30%)

LESSONS LEARNED

Students learn the application of principles and theories when they are able to have interaction with other students. The "virtual" classroom provides great opportunities for students to engage with each other.

COURSE INFORMATION

- Title: Human Behavior in the Social Environment
- URL: http://webct.uta.edu/webct
- Level: BSW
- Area: HBSE
- Number face-to-face sessions: 0
- Tools used: Website, listserv, e-mail, tests, & quizzes, discussion forum, chat

INSTRUCTOR

Peggy Quinn, PhD, Associate Professor, University of Texas at Arlington, School of Social Work, Box 19129, Arlington, TX 76019-0129 USA <quinn@uta.edu>

COURSE GOAL

HBSE I explores, within the context of strengths and empowerment based perspective, the behavioral and social science knowledge of the bio-psycho-social development of individuals from birth through adolescence and young adulthood.

COURSE REQUIREMENTS

1. Descriptions of four observations of children and teens
2. Four discussion exercises
3. Two projects: a brochure and a list of useful resources
4. One group project and one individual presentation

LESSONS LEARNED

Instructions must be very clear. Placing information in more than one location can be more confusing than helpful. It takes a ton of work to even get started.

COURSE INFORMATION

- Title: Survey of Research Methodology
- URL: www.capella.edu
- Level: MSSW level
- Area: Research
- Number face-to-face sessions: 0
- Tools used: _Web site, e-mail, LearningSpace course management software; discussion forum, PowerPoint, interactive exercises, WebQuests, telephone

INSTRUCTOR

William Ross, Assistant Professor, Capella University, 15111 Possumwood Drive, P.O. Box 4349, Houston, TX 77084-6494, USA <william _ ross@pvamu.edu>

COURSE GOAL

To examine how research relates to/influences the professional practice; apply the research process to problems, issues, or program evaluation; explore the major research methodologies and research designs used in scientific research; examine the role of ethics in research.

COURSE REQUIREMENTS

1. Postings require students to answer a particular question, do a self-assessment, or demonstrate completion of a particular homework assignment.
2. Discussions are more involved and students are required to post their first participation of 250 words (minimum). Then students respond to at least one other learner for each discussion question. These responses should be thoughtful, insightful, helpful, and critical, if necessary. If a learner or Instructor responds to your posting, please follow through with the thread of discussion to make sure you respond to all comments made and insight gained.
3. The third activity is participation in a research support team group, Team Discussions. Assignments will be made to teams in the first unit. Please select a team name. Students post certain assignments to their

team group for help and insight. Team members comment on research problems or concerns as an aid to understanding and application of the research process. Team members respond to each other with insightful comments on each other's application of research knowledge to the problems or concerns and selection of research publications and websites. Finally, two members of research support teams are assigned by the course facilitator to review your final course project during unit 9 of the course.

LESSONS LEARNED

Communicate with learners on a regular basis; create a virtual campus through the Web where the needs of the learners can be met; develop creative approaches to identifying and solving problems/resolving issues. If possible, make the answer "yes." Understand how people learn and provide programs responsive to differing learning styles.

COURSE INFORMATION

- Title: Advanced Use of IT in Human Services
- URL: http://www2.uta.edu/cussn/courses/6355/
- Level: MSSW, PhD
- Area: Micro and Macro
- Number face-to-face sessions: 4
- Tools used: _Chat, Webpage, online debates, online guest speakers, listserv, e-mail, telephone, FAQ, WebCam, PowerPoint, quizzes

INSTRUCTOR

Dick Schoech, PhD, University of Texas at Arlington School of Social Work, Box 19129, Arlington, TX 76019-0129 <schoech@uta.edu>

COURSE GOAL

To view human services as a data/information/knowledge based profession and to investigate the computer and telecommunication tools available to work with the data/information/knowledge necessary to support clients and human service practice.

COURSE REQUIREMENTS

1. Personal/professional web page
2. Weekly posting on discussion forum or quiz over readings
3. Online debates
4. Application reviews of significant human service applications
5. Technology Application Paper containing a systems analysis and solution options
6. PowerPoint presentation

LESSONS LEARNED

Present lecture content using website, text, readings, and exercises. Chat functions as class discussion. Structure is required. Online course consistently scores as personal and as effective as face-to-face courses. Poor technical support will result in decreased satisfaction and learning.

REFERENCES

Schoech, D., & Helton, D. (2002). Qualitative and quantitative analysis of a course taught via classroom and internet chatroom *Qualitative Social Work*, 1(1), 111-124.

Schoech, D. (2000). Teaching over the Internet: Results of one doctoral course. *Research on Social Work Practice*, 10(4), 467-486.

Index

BOOK ORDER FORM!

Order a copy of this book with this form or online at:
http://www.HaworthPress.com/store/product.asp?sku=5631

Web-Based Education in the Human Services
Models, Methods, and Best Practices

___ in softbound at $34.95 ISBN-13: 978-0-7890-2630-9 / ISBN-10: 0-7890-2630-9.
___ in hardbound at $69.95 ISBN-13: 978-0-7890-2629-3 / ISBN-10: 0-7890-2629-5.

COST OF BOOKS _____

POSTAGE & HANDLING _____
US: $4.00 for first book & $1.50
for each additional book
Outside US: $5.00 for first book
& $2.00 for each additional book.

SUBTOTAL _____

In Canada: add 7% GST. _____

STATE TAX _____
CA, IL, IN, MN, NJ, NY, OH, PA & SD residents
please add appropriate local sales tax.

FINAL TOTAL _____
If paying in Canadian funds, convert
using the current exchange rate,
UNESCO coupons welcome.

❑BILL ME LATER:
Bill-me option is good on US/Canada/
Mexico orders only; not good to jobbers,
wholesalers, or subscription agencies.

❑ Signature _____

❑ Payment Enclosed: $ _____

❑ PLEASE CHARGE TO MY CREDIT CARD:
❑ Visa ❑ MasterCard ❑ AmEx ❑ Discover
❑ Diner's Club ❑ Eurocard ❑ JCB

Account # _____

Exp Date _____

Signature _____
(Prices in US dollars and subject to change without notice.)

PLEASE PRINT ALL INFORMATION OR ATTACH YOUR BUSINESS CARD

Name

Address

City   State/Province   Zip/Postal Code

Country

Tel   Fax

E-Mail

May we use your e-mail address for confirmations and other types of information? ❑Yes ❑No We appreciate receiving
your e-mail address. Haworth would like to e-mail special discount offers to you, as a preferred customer.
We will never share, rent, or exchange your e-mail address. We regard such actions as an invasion of your privacy.

Order from your **local bookstore** or directly from
The Haworth Press, Inc. 10 Alice Street, Binghamton, New York 13904-1580 • USA
Call our toll-free number (1-800-429-6784) / Outside US/Canada: (607) 722-5857
Fax: 1-800-895-0582 / Outside US/Canada: (607) 771-0012
E-mail your order to us: orders@HaworthPress.com

For orders outside US and Canada, you may wish to order through your local
sales representative, distributor, or bookseller.
For information, see http://HaworthPress.com/distributors

(Discounts are available for individual orders in US and Canada only, not booksellers/distributors.)

Please photocopy this form for your personal use.
www.HaworthPress.com

BOF05